Dear Sir:

As y

your son has

assure you th

safe. You nee

provided you

lowing instru

you will rece

Should you ho

structions ev

be the penalt

1. F

MR JACOB FRANKS
5052 ELLIS AVE
CITY

SPECIAL

CHICAGO.
MAY
31
1 AM
1924
ILL.

w out

can

fely

our

# THE
# LEOPOLD AND LOEB
# FILES

# THE
# LEOPOLD AND LOEB
# FILES

AN INTIMATE LOOK
AT ONE OF AMERICA'S
MOST INFAMOUS CRIMES

## NINA BARRETT

MIDWAY

AN AGATE IMPRINT

CHICAGO

Typographical errors in primary source materials have been silently corrected for reader convenience. Authorial additions and elisions are marked with brackets. Original punctuation, style, and formatting have been retained and corrected only for consistency.

Printed by Hing Yip Printing Co. Ltd., China

The author would like to acknowledge the contributions to this book made by Northwestern University, its Library, its academic community, and the materials maintained in the University's Leopold and Loeb collection.

All letters and photos in Part V were reproduced with permission by the family and estate of Elmer Gertz.

*The Leopold and Loeb Files*
ISBN-10: 1-57284-240-7
ISBN-13: 978-1-57284-240-3
eISBN-10: 1-57284-819-7
eISBN-13: 978-1-57284-819-1

First printing: July 2018

10 9 8 7 6 5 4 3 2 1          18 19 20 21 22

Midway Books is an imprint of Agate Publishing. Agate books are available in bulk at discount prices. Learn more at agatepublishing.com.

# Contents

Introduction | 1

## Part I: The Ransom Note

1   May 21, 1924 | 6
Bobby Franks walks home

2   A man of more than ordinary education | 8
The ransom note

3   Nathan Leopold | 12

4   Richard Loeb | 16

## Part II: Confessions and Other Statements of Leopold and Loeb

5   What can one say in such a case? | 20
Transcripts of the interrogations

6   He looked rather worried | 22
Leopold in denial

7   Keener mentally than the average | 25
Leopold as "prodigy"

8   Fake tortoiseshell spectacles, rather weak | 27
Leopold fails to drop his glasses

9   A student of sexual perversion | 31
Leopold's interest in Aretino

10  He wasn't sober enough to go home | 36
Leopold's alibi

11  Ashes to ashes, and dust to dust | 38
Leopold as atheist

12  A falling out of cocksuckers | 39
The incriminating letter

13  This has got me pretty worried | 46
The link to the Underwood portable typewriter

14  He is a liar or mistaken | 55
Loeb in denial

15  We intended to murder him | 59
Leopold's account of the murder

16  That is all I have to tell about the murder of Robert Franks | 65
Loeb's account of the murder

17  It was he who did the act | 73
Leopold's corrections of Loeb

18  I have been made a fish | 76
Loeb's corrections of Leopold

19  I told Mrs. Franks her son had been kidnaped | 79
Leopold reenacts the phone call

20  It is the duty of a parent to stand by his child | 81
A visit from Leopold's father

21  Pure love of excitement, or the imaginary love of thrills | 85
Why they did it

22  I never read that | 89
Loeb denies plagiarizing the ransom note

23  No man could feel happy | 91
Ettelson confronts Leopold

## Part III: The Hulbert-Bowman Report

24 **A perfect case for the death penalty | 94**
Clarence Darrow calls in the alienists

25 **IN RE: NATHAN LEOPOLD, JUNIOR | 97**
The scope of the psychiatric reports

26 **I am small, my heart is pure | 98**
The brilliant baby Leopold

27 **The governess | 100**
A woman of very peculiar mentality

28 **Happiness is a perfume | 103**
Leopold's mother

29 **Never been attracted to the opposite sex | 106**
Leopold's love life

30 **King and slave | 108**
Leopold's fantasy life

31 **Partners in crime | 113**
Deeds Leopold and Loeb had previously committed together

32 **For Robert's sake | 114**
The fatal pact, part I

33 **Rope | 119**
Sharing the guilt of the crime

34 **No question of remorse or guilt | 121**
Leopold declares himself legally sane

35 **Her absurd taste in dress | 123**
Blaming the governess

36 **The father is fair and just | 127**
Loeb's family background

37 **Her word was law | 129**
Loeb's governess

38 **Forensically inadvisable to question him | 133**
The mystery of the "A, B, C, D" crimes

39 **Criminal "Master Mind" | 135**
Loeb's fantasy life

40 **In dramatic whispers | 136**
Loeb recounts the murder again

41 **This tickled my sense of humor | 138**
Loeb takes stock of his feelings

42 **I have always been sort of afraid of him | 143**
Loeb contemplated killing Leopold

43 **A pathological minimum of self-criticism | 144**
Blaming the governess, again

## Part IV: The Court Transcript

44 **We throw ourselves upon the mercy of this court | 149**
Darrow's surprise tactic

45 **I object, if your Honor please | 152**
Crowe and Darrow square off

46 **That is what comes from reading detective stories | 155**
Loeb pretends to give his friends a scoop

47 **I wouldn't put it past that man, Mitchell | 158**
Leopold casts aspersions

48 **I will plead guilty before a friendly Judge | 162**
Leopold, cornered

49 **What is the defense trying to do here? | 165**
The legal question of insanity

50 **What is a mitigating circumstance? | 169**
Darrow urges open-mindedness

51 **Do not spank these naughty boys | 174**
Crowe demands the extreme penalty

52 **An underdeveloped emotional attitude toward life | 178**
The psychological diagnosis

53 **I don't recall asking the boys that question | 183**
The doctor dodges Crowe

54 **Unfit for publication | 190**
The fatal pact, part II

55 **No remorse, no regret, no compassion | 194**
Loeb struck the blow

56 **I did not have time | 197**
Why it was forensically inadvisable to question Loeb
about his past crimes

57 **Just from the waist down | 201**
Why was the corpse undressed in two stages?

58 **Responsibility, mitigation, turpitude | 207**
The prosecution defines its terms

59 **What mercy did they give that little tot? | 210**
The prosecution's case for the extreme penalty

60 **You stand in a relationship of father to these
defendants | 212**
The defense urges wisdom and understanding

61 **If these boys hang, you must do it | 214**
Caverly's lonely decision

62 **Giving the people blood is like giving them their
dinner | 221**
Darrow's appeal for judicial progressiveness

63 **The death of poor little Bobby Franks should not be
in vain | 228**
Darrow concludes his argument

64 **How do you undress a child? | 236**
Crowe drops his bombshell

65 **This court will not be intimidated by anybody | 243**
Caverly rebukes Crowe

66 **Grief, worry, broken heart | 246**
The wait

67 **The dictates of enlightened humanity | 248**
Caverly's verdict

68 **What have they to look forward to? | 252**
Reactions to the decision

69 **Lifers | 254**
Collateral damage

## Part V: The Gertz Papers: Leopold's Later Years

70 **Elmer Gertz | 258**

71 **How bitterly I regret the past | 260**
The 1953 parole bid

72 **Nothing monstrous in his current bearing | 264**
Gertz meets Leopold

73 **The correction of the century | 268**
The 1957 clemency hearing

74 **I have gotten over being nineteen | 275**
The 1958 parole bid

75 **Say what you damn please | 280**
The parole years in Puerto Rico, 1958–1963

76 **Happiness is a perfume (reprise) | 287**
The final years, 1963–1971

Epilogue | 290
Acknowledgments | 291
Resources | 292
Index | 293

PEOPLE 3
v.
LEOPOLD and LOEB

CONFESSIONS AND OTHER 3
STATEMENTS OF LEOPOLD
AND LOEB

# Introduction

LIKE ARCHAEOLOGISTS, who spend the bulk of their time sifting through sand and dirt for fragments of artifacts they hope will help reconstruct history, archivists perform a lot of manual and, on the whole, rather routine labor. They empty home attics and institutional basements of boxes of old folders, notebooks, and correspondence, most of which would bore a general audience to tears unless mined someday by an inspired researcher who can spin documentary evidence into a compelling story. But every once in a while, just as an archaeologist happens upon the remains of a lost city or the unidentified tomb of a pharaoh, an archivist makes a sensational find: the documentary evidence for a famous story that has already entered the realm of myth.

In June of 1988, Kevin Leonard, then assistant university archivist at Northwestern University Library, made such a discovery. He'd been sent down from Evanston to Northwestern University's Law School on the university's Chicago campus to pick up the school's administrative records from the late nineteenth and early twentieth centuries. They were stored in a vault in the Law School's basement, in walls of boxes that Leonard and a colleague spent all day lugging out to a van and shuttling back to Evanston every time the van filled up. It was dirty, physically demanding work, and toward the end of the day Leonard was tired and starting to worry about getting the last load packed up and making it back to Evanston in time to return the van. By then, sorting the boxes he wanted from those with no foreseeable archival value, he had cleared a path to the back wall of the vault—also a path backwards in time, to where the vault's earliest deposits had been placed. There in a back corner on the floor was a brown paper bag, its top rolled closed. Leonard wasn't sure he wanted to open it; he was in a hurry now, and he also suffers from arachnophobia, the morbid fear of spiders, and he could just imagine what might be crawling around in there after the many years the bag must have been lying on the basement floor. But then his archival instinct got the better of him—surely no one had looked inside the bag in decades—and he stooped down, unrolled the top, and gingerly reached inside.

The first item he pulled out was a neatly typed note on a yellowed sheet of paper that read like something from a piece of early twentieth-century detective fiction. "Dear Sir," it began. "As you no doubt know by this time your son has been kidnapped. Allow us to assure you that he is at present well and safe." The words did not immediately ring a bell with Leonard, but the next item he pulled from the bag caused an instant shock of comprehension. It was the note's envelope, also yellowed, marked special delivery, and hand addressed in block letters to MR. JACOB FRANKS, 5052 ELLIS AVE, CITY. It was postmarked May 21, 1924.

Born in Chicago and well steeped in its lore, Leonard knew exactly who Mr. Jacob Franks was, and he knew as well that by the time Franks's trembling hands had opened this very envelope on the morning of May 22, his son Bobby was already dead, and what was to become the most famous murder case in Chicago—and possibly U.S.—history had already been set in motion. The brutal and senseless murder of 14-year-old Bobby Franks, the hunt for his killers, their identification as two

The envelope that held Leopold and Loeb's ransom note.

wealthy, privileged, brilliant University of Chicago law students named Nathan Leopold and Richard Loeb, and the subsequent legal drama in which celebrity attorney Clarence Darrow stepped in to rescue the killers from the gallows—all of this had been an international news sensation in that summer of 1924.

Quickly dubbed the "Crime of the Century," the case has indeed continued to haunt the American psyche throughout subsequent decades, even as other sensational murders have competed for its dubious tagline. Since that summer's orgy of newspaper coverage, the story has been revived again and again in book, film, and theatrical narratives and interpretations, including Alfred Hitchcock's 1948 psychological thriller *Rope*, Meyer Levin's best-selling 1956 novel *Compulsion* (also made into a play and a film), Stephen Dolginoff's dark 2003 musical *Thrill Me*, and nonfiction accounts like Hal Higdon's *Leopold and Loeb: The Crime of the Century* and Simon Baatz's *For the Thrill of It*.

From the moment of their remarkable and remarkably detailed twin confessions in police custody 10 days after the murder, the guilt of Leopold and Loeb has never been in question. In that sense, the crime was only very briefly a mystery. Yet its persistent fascination lies in its essentially inscrutable nature, which both demands and somehow ultimately evades all attempts at satisfactory explanation. With each retelling the story has become even more—rather than less—mythological. As historian Paula Fass has written, "Because the case and the protagonists were rapidly engulfed in the evolving public discourse and the stories were vivid, the public portrayals overwhelmed the identity of the individual characters. When Leopold eventually wrote his own memoirs he had difficulty distinguishing the fact from the fiction of his own identity, so completely had he and the story in which he had participated been enveloped and defined in the public spaces of the culture."

This makes Leonard's discovery in the basement of the Law School even more extraordinary. For the ransom note—a chilling and creepy artifact of the case, but not an especially illuminating one—was not the only contents of the paper bag. Also inside were three bulkier and even more astounding documents. There was a black cardboard binder enclosing a 517-page document labeled "Confessions and Other Statements of Leopold and Loeb." This proved to be an original carbon copy of the transcript of the statements made by the killers in police custody beginning the night before they actually confessed. It includes the interrogation period during which they were still trying to outwit their questioners and documents the steps by which they were cornered into telling the truth. Then, in addition to the actual confessions, it covers a session in which Leopold's and Loeb's confessions, given in isolation, were read aloud before one another, giving each a chance to address the other's discrepancies. It also includes transcriptions from much of the subsequent day on which detectives took Leopold and Loeb, along with a convoy of enthralled newspaper reporters, on a bizarre field trip to several of the key locations mentioned in their accounts to confirm the details of their stories.

Heavily leaked to reporters almost instantaneously, these statements formed the basis for the characterizations of Leopold and Loeb that sprang to life in the papers and have endured ever since, especially Leopold's cold intellectual brilliance, his supposed mastery of 15 languages, his interest in pornographic literature, and the implication of a sexual relationship between him and Loeb. And they preserve verbatim each boy's first-person account of the murder of Bobby Franks, including the only major point on which they vehemently contradicted one another: who had physically committed the murder.

The other two documents Leonard found in the bag were twin bound copies of the reports submitted by the team of psychiatrists summoned by defense attorney Clarence Darrow to assess the sanity of the boys. Darrow was hoping for one of two outcomes that might help his case: either evidence that might support an insanity defense, or evidence of some mental disease or medical abnormality that might mitigate the sentencing. Therefore these reports contain a wealth of information about the killers' physical health and history as well as the results of exhaustive inquiries into their psychological and especially their fantasy lives. They also contain details about the murder not included in the confessions, and intimate portraits of the boys' families, education, and upbringing.

When he later connected the contents of this mysterious bag with the contents of a box he had found nearby in the vault, Leonard realized that all these materials had been in the possession of Harold Hulbert, a member of the team of psychiatrists hired by Darrow. The box contained materials related to another murder case in which Hulbert had been a consulting psychiatrist, as well as correspondence from Hulbert stating his intention to bequeath the evidence from several of his most interesting cases to Northwestern.

Now cataloged in the Northwestern University Archives, the papers complement another remarkable collection of materials related to Leopold and Loeb that had also been bequeathed to Northwestern and are housed in the library's Charles Deering McCormick Library of Special Collections. These are the papers of Elmer Gertz, the Chicago attorney who secured Leopold's eventual parole in 1958, despite his "life plus 99 years" sentence. Gertz had acquired a wealth of documents relating to the original crime—including, most spectacularly, a 4,411-page transcript of the court case in which Darrow faced off against State's Attorney Robert Crowe to try to persuade Judge John Caverly that Leopold and Loeb should not receive the death penalty. In addition to preserving a raw portrait of the rhetorically brilliant Darrow at work, the transcript includes the testimony of nearly 100 witnesses and constitutes a record of one of the earliest court cases in which psychiatric evidence was extensively used to influence sentencing.

Gertz's papers also contain revealing drafts of Leopold's statements made during various parole appeals that assessed his role in the murder from an adult perspective, and scores of fan letters sent to Leopold in prison following the publication of his memoir, *Life Plus 99 Years*. The voluminous Gertz-Leopold correspondence, which grew more intimate as the years went by, also provides a revealing glimpse of Leopold's postprison years, which he spent as privately as he could manage in Puerto Rico—sometimes seeming to struggle with his newfound fame as the United States's most rehabilitated criminal.

In the spring of 2009, I curated an exhibit called *The Murder That Wouldn't Die: Leopold & Loeb in Artifact, Fact, and Fiction* at Northwestern University Library. Items from both the Hulbert and Gertz collections were displayed—including the ransom note, the Confessions, the psychiatric reports, and the court transcripts—along with books, DVDs, CDs, theatrical programs and posters, and other memorabilia relating to works based on the case.

The response to the exhibit was immediate and extraordinary: instant confirmation that this murder really hasn't ever died, either in the local or national consciousness. There was television, radio, newspaper, and magazine coverage, including a *Harper's Magazine* excerpt from the Confessions in which both Leopold and Loeb are confronted by a psychiatrist about whether they understood that the murder was morally wrong. Two theatrical companies that happened to be in the rehearsal stages for Leopold and Loeb–related productions brought their casts and crews to do background research. (One of the productions was of *Rope*, the other of *Never the Sinner*, the debut work by Academy Award–winning screenwriter John Logan, which was based on research he did in the Gertz collection as a Northwestern undergraduate.)

But the most remarkable response came from people still claiming—more than eight decades later—some personal connection to the case. There was a visitor in his 90s who told me he'd been a classmate of Bobby's at the Harvard School and still remembered seeing both Leopold and Loeb around the neighborhood in the week between the murder and their arrests; several contacts by people claiming to own artifacts from the Loeb mansion, which had stood vacant but still furnished for many years before being demolished; and, toward the end of the exhibit's run, several descendants from one of the families, who came hoping there might be something in one of these documents that finally made sense of what their infamous ancestor had done.

But an exhibit can only display the documents as artifacts, not as texts. This book invites the reader inside their pages. Each one of the book's five sections dissects a different document or group of documents, dividing it into short chapters to examine its most important, interesting, or revealing elements. Each chapter also includes a short taste of coverage of the story as it was unfolding in the daily newspapers, to give readers a sense of how the media not only amplified but also very colorfully shaped the public narrative about the case.

*The Leopold and Loeb Files* can be read as an introduction to the case, but my hope is also that readers who have encountered the story in its many other forms might gain additional perspective by seeing it unfold in the words of the original participants—and through the eyes of the world that was watching.

# PART I
# The Ransom Note

# 1
# May 21, 1924

## BOBBY FRANKS WALKS HOME

IT WAS WEDNESDAY. In Washington, D.C., President Calvin Coolidge took a chlorine-gas cure for a throat ailment and resolved to take more walks in the fresh air. In the Williamsburg section of Brooklyn, New York, a teenaged robber alternately referred to as the "2-gun girl" and the "bob-haired bandit" held up the owner of a picture-framing store at gunpoint, taking $60 in cash, but returning $5 of it to him after he told her he was supporting a wife and two children in Russia. In Chicago, Illinois, fearing a law-enforcement raid, the operators of a bootleg brewery dumped thousands of gallons of beer into a sewer, causing a geyser of beer to spurt up five feet into the air from a manhole for more than an hour, attracting the attention of the police.

Also in Chicago, State's Attorney Robert Crowe was addressing the twin scourges of gun violence and rampant bribery of judges by launching a new crusade to stop judges from issuing gun permits to anyone other than sworn police officers. John R. Caverly, chief judge of the criminal court, promised to give his full cooperation.

But Caverly and Crowe were about to be diverted by another development. That afternoon, in the wealthy Kenwood neighborhood of Hyde Park, 14-year-old Bobby Franks stopped on his way home from school to umpire a baseball game his friends were playing. A little after 5 p.m., he waved goodbye and continued toward home, three blocks away. A car pulled up alongside him as he walked, and his neighbor and second cousin, 18-year-old Richard ("Dick") Loeb, called out to him. He introduced the pal who was with him, 19-year-old Nathan ("Babe") Leopold. Bobby and Loeb had played tennis a few days ago at the Loebs' mansion, just down the block from Bobby's home, and Loeb asked Bobby to get into the car so they could talk about the tennis racket he'd been using. So Bobby got in.

Within minutes, Bobby was dead, bashed in the head with a chisel, a rag stuffed into his mouth to muffle his cries, suffocating him. Then Leopold and Loeb drove down to a field in northern Indiana, stopping on the way to eat a snack of hotdogs and root beer in the car, with the dead boy's body in the back seat wrapped in a blanket. Then they made a second stop so Leopold could call his sweetheart to confirm an upcoming date. In a marshy field where Leopold often went bird-watching, they poured acid over the naked body, hoping to disfigure it beyond recognition, and then stuffed it into a drainage pipe where they were sure it would never be discovered. On the way home, they stopped so Leopold could phone his aunt and uncle just to let them know he might be a little late giving them a lift home that evening.

Late that night the phone rang at the Franks home. Bobby's parents, Jacob and Flora, were frantic with worry about their son, who had failed to come home for dinner. Jacob had called his close friend and attorney Sam Ettelson, and together they'd gone over to Bobby's school to look for him or someone who had seen him.

So it was Flora who picked up the phone and was informed by a male voice identifying himself as "Mr. Johnson" that her son had been kidnapped and was being held for ransom. "We will let you know tomorrow what we want," Mr. Johnson informed her ominously. "We are kidnappers and we mean business. If you refuse us what we want or try to report us to the police, we will kill the boy." Then Mr. Johnson abruptly hung up, and Flora fainted.

Right: The iconic surviving photo of Bobby Franks, said to have been taken shortly before his murder.

Chicago History Museum, DN-0077041

# 2
# A man of more than ordinary education

## THE RANSOM NOTE

### The Note Arrives

Family friend and attorney Sam Ettelson spent a sleepless night with Jacob Franks after helping him search the neighborhood and the Harvard School for clues about Bobby Franks's disappearance. After hearing about "Mr. Johnson's" sinister conversation with Flora Franks—who took the kidnapper's call while they were out, and had not yet recovered from her faint when they returned—they paid a quiet 2 a.m. visit to the detective bureau to ask for advice. But they refused any practical help from police because they were afraid that any visible detective activity, or publicity that might come from an item on the police blotter, could trigger a fatal reaction from the kidnapper. Ettelson also called the phone company and requested that any further calls to the Franks home be traced. But in the morning he was told by a friend of the family that the friend "had called the home and had heard telephone operators gossiping about the tracing of the calls"—a bit of gossip which any calling kidnapper might similarly happen to hear—and so Ettelson immediately called off the tracing of the line.

He was still present to witness the arrival of the ransom note by special-delivery courier at 9 a.m. the next morning. "Its deliberate tone struck terror into our hearts," he told reporters. For the second time in 24 hours, Bobby's mother fainted, and a doctor had to be called.

T HE RANSOM NOTE that arrived at the Franks home the next morning assured Jacob Franks that his son was still "well and safe" but threatened that, should he fail to obey instructions for delivering a $10,000 ransom payment, "his death will be the penalty." Franks spent much of that day preparing the money in accordance with the demands. Around 3 p.m., "Mr. Johnson" phoned again with detailed instructions about getting into a Yellow cab that would be sent to the house shortly to take Franks to a drugstore where he would wait for yet another set of instructions to be phoned to him there. But Franks could hardly focus on what Mr. Johnson was saying, because he had just gotten another call, from his brother-in-law Ed Gresham, who'd gone down to a morgue in northern Indiana to look at the corpse of a boy found in a culvert that morning on the unlikely chance that it might be Bobby's. Gresham was calling from the morgue to confirm that it was.

From the moment the case hit the city papers, it was front-page news. The *Chicago Daily Tribune* called it "one of the most baffling in the city's annals," not just because the coroner who examined the body could not immediately determine the cause of death, but because the kidnapper's motivation was completely mystifying. If the boy had really been kidnapped for money, why had the kidnapper killed him without waiting to see if the ransom would be paid?

Speculation immediately focused on the two obvious clues: a pair of horn-rimmed spectacles found near Bobby's body, and the ransom note itself, whose text, the newspapers—as well as detectives—quickly concluded, had been written by "a man of more than ordinary education." But why would such a man need to obtain such a large sum of money by such unsavory means? Was he a drug addict with an expensive habit? A teacher at Bobby's school who knew his rich father would pay any price to get him back? A sexual predator who had killed Bobby in order not to be identified after molesting him, then concocted the ransom note as a smoke screen?

H.P. Sutton, an expert employed by the Royal Typewriter Company, identified the type on the note as belonging to "an Underwood portable typewriter purchased less than three years ago," with a defective lowercase *t* and *f* (see page 9). In addition, he asserted, the writer was a novice typist. "A person using the touch system strikes the keys pretty evenly," he said. "The man who wrote this was either a novice at typing or else used two fingers. Some of the letters were punched so hard they were almost driven through the paper, while others were struck lightly or uncertainly."

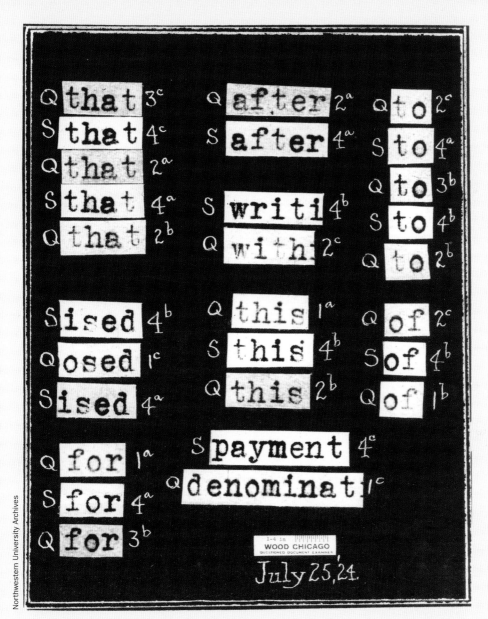

Forensic typewriting sample from the ransom note, introduced as evidence in the case.

Detectives also quickly noticed a peculiar resemblance the note bore to a fictional ransom note that had recently appeared in a short story by Christopher B. Booth called "The Kidnaping Syndicate" in *Detective Story Magazine*. The *Chicago Daily Tribune* published the notes side by side to highlight the similarities—the businesslike introduction, followed by four numbered instructions along the same lines—and concluded that the letter to Franks, "though couched in even more faultless rhetoric than the letter of the fiction writer, seems simply, paragraph by paragraph, paraphrased from that author's work."

"Look for the suspect with that magazine in his possession," detectives concluded, "and you'll pretty nearly have the man who killed Robert Franks."

**DEAR SIR:** The note was generically addressed to "Sir" because Leopold and Loeb typed it up the evening before the murder, before deciding for certain whom the victim would be.

**DETECTIVE STORY MAGAZINE:** The newspapers somewhat exaggerated the similarity between the note and a fictional ransom note published in a story in the May 3, 1924, issue of *Detective Story Magazine*, assigning four numbered paragraphs to the fictional letter so it would more exactly match the format of the note to the Franks family. In the fictional story, "The Kidnaping Syndicate," as in the real-life case, a detective notes the language and tactics of a superior breed of kidnapper: "I think . . . you're up against a most unusual criminal," he tells the victim's husband. "An educated man, I should say; a man whose mind has been trained to think along very logical lines. It's certainly something new in kidnaping."

**FOUR-BAR CANCEL:** When asked for a possible explanation of why the postmark would have been wrong, Chicago postal historian Leonard Piszkiewicz noticed the use of four lines, or bars, across the faces of the stamps to cancel them, and replied that the four-bar was a brand new cancellation stamp at the time. In fact, before this discovery its first documented use had been 10 days later than this, on May 31. Piszkiewicz speculated that the special delivery clerk hadn't yet got the hang of this newfangled rubber stamp, which worked differently from the old steel ones—and that's why the date setting hadn't been changed to May 22. In addition to its significance to the Leopold and Loeb case, the envelope is now the earliest known use of the four-bar cancel in Chicago postal history.

**INCORRECT POSTMARK:** The murder was committed around 5 p.m. on May 21 and the letter was mailed late that evening, so clearly it could not have actually been stamped at 1 a.m. on the morning of May 21. The postmarks on the reverse side of the envelope confirm that it was actually being processed in the early morning of May 22, arriving at the Main Post Office at 2 a.m. and in the Hyde Park office at 6 a.m.—before being delivered to the Franks home around 9 a.m.

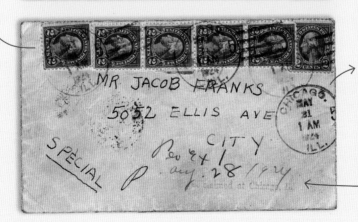

Dear Sir:

As you no doubt know by this time your son has been kidnapped. Allow us to assure you that he is at present well and safe. You need fear no physical harm for him provided you live up carefully to the following instructions, and such others as you will receive by future communications. Should you however, disobey any of our instructions even slightly, his death will be the penalty.

1. For obvious reasons make absolutely no attempt to communicate with either the police authorities, or any private agency. Should you already have communicated with the police, allow them to continue their investigations, but do not mention this letter.

2. Secure before noon today ten thousand dollars, ($10,000.00). This money must be composed entirely of OLD BILLS of the following denominations:
$2,000.00 in twenty dollar bills
$8,000.00 in fifty dollar bills
The money must be old. Any attempt to include new or marked bills will render the entire venture futile.

MR JACOB FRANKS
5052 ELLIS AVE
CITY
SPECIAL

**CLUES IN THE TYPEFACE:** Brilliant as they were, Leopold and Loeb failed to foresee what an expert would be able to deduce from analyzing the note: that it had been written on an Underwood portable typewriter with a defective lowercase *t* and *f*—and that the typist was a novice or someone using two fingers, since "some of the letters were punched so hard they were almost driven through the paper, while others were struck lightly or uncertainly."

**HANDWRITTEN ADDRESS:** The envelope was handwritten after the killing, rather than typed up in advance, again so that Leopold and Loeb could wait till the last minute to select a victim. It was mailed on the way home from hiding Bobby's body—after Leopold had already telephoned the Franks home, calling himself "George Johnson," and told Mrs. Franks that her son had been kidnapped but was safe.

(2)

3. The money should be placed in a large cigar box, or if this is impossible in a heavy cardboard box, SECURELY closed and wrapped in white paper. The wrapping paper should be sealed at all openings with sealing wax.

4. Have the money with you prepared as directed above, and remain at home after one o'clock P.M. See that the telephone is not in use.

You will receive a future communication instructing you as to your future course.

As a final word of warning - this is a strictly commercial proposition, and we are prepared to put our threat into execution should we have reasonable grounds to believe that you have committed an infraction of the above instructions. However, should you carefully follow out our instructions to the letter, we can assure you that your son will be safely returned to you within six hours of our receipt of the money.

Yours truly,
GEORGE JOHNSON
GKR

**GKR:** One of the myths that grew up around the note, sometimes reported as fact, was that the three initials appearing below the GEORGE JOHNSON signature belonged to Germaine K. ("Patches") Reinhard, one of Loeb's occasional girlfriends. A few days after the confessions, when someone apparently told police that her initials had been added to suggest that the very professional-sounding note had been typed by a secretary, Reinhard was called in for questioning. Described by the *Chicago Daily Tribune* as a "chic shocker nicknamed 'Patches,'" she told the paper she had worked her way up as Loeb's girlfriend from only getting what she described as "the bad nights of the week, the Tuesdays and the Thursdays, you know," to getting "the big nights, Saturdays and Sundays," and had last been out with him two days after the murder. Detectives released her after examining the letters under a microscope and seeing that they actually said GEOR, as if the paper had slipped out of the typewriter before the first attempt at a signature was completed.

# 3
# Nathan Leopold

The Leopold mansion, where it then stood at 4754 Greenwood Avenue.

Chicago History Museum, DN-0077059

## THE MYSTERIOUS GLASSES

Once detectives learned from the Franks family that the pair of spectacles found near Bobby Franks's body had not belonged to him, those glasses became one of the most intriguing potential clues in the case. Opticians initially called in to examine the glasses felt sure—based on the "extraordinarily small" lenses and the short length of the ear supports—that they must have belonged to a woman. When a detective assured them they must be mistaken, since there was no suspicion of any woman being associated with the case, one of the opticians insisted that "It would be a strange kind of a man, a little bit of a wizened face fellow, who could wear these." Then, to illustrate his point, he attempted to fit the spectacles on one of the detectives. "The effect was grotesque," a reporter commented in the May 24 *Chicago Daily Tribune*. "The supports scarcely reached the officer's ears."

NINETEEN-YEAR-OLD Nathan F. Leopold Jr. was the precociously smart son of a wealthy and well-respected Hyde Park businessman, Nathan F. Leopold Sr. He lived in a mansion about a block and a half away from the Harvard School, where Bobby Franks was a student; Leopold himself was an alumnus. After skipping his senior year there, Leopold had entered the University of Chicago at the age of 16 and graduated with a brilliant academic record. Now he was taking law classes at the University of Chicago and planning to transfer to Harvard Law School in the fall.

In his free time he was an avid bird-watcher with a private collection of more than 2,000 specimens, and he had published two scientific papers on his findings in *The Auk*, the most prestigious U.S. journal for professional ornithologists.

It was the bird-watching that first led detectives to question Leopold on Sunday, May 25. They had heard that he sometimes led groups of bird-watchers to the area around Wolf Lake near the Illinois-Indiana border, where Bobby's body had been found. He was not, at this point, by any means a suspect. The detectives treated him deferentially, assuring him that they just wanted to find out what other ornithologists or hunters or people he knew frequented that area—and whether any of them wore glasses.

He told them that he had been visiting the area for years, most recently the weekend before the murder on Saturday, May 17, and Sunday, May 18, and he furnished them with a handwritten, signed statement about these two visits.

Leopold told them that he himself did not wear glasses—which was true to the extent that he had only worn his new reading glasses for a few months before the headaches they had been prescribed to address disappeared and he stopped wearing them. He had already realized from reading newspaper accounts that the glasses found near the body must have fallen out of his

A photographic copy of Leopold's initial handwritten statement to detectives.

Nathan Leopold, 1924.

pocket, where he had forgotten he had left them; he had already ransacked his room in the hopes that he was wrong, to no avail. His best strategy now, he was betting, was to hope that the glasses couldn't conclusively be traced to him—but if they were, he would claim that he must have lost them during one of these recent birding trips.

He told the detectives about a "heavy date" he had to get to that afternoon with his sweetheart, implying that he'd appreciate their not inconveniencing him any further. They were happy to send him on his way. They were looking for suspects with plausible, logical motives: teachers from the Harvard School who might have been in need of ready cash, which Leopold clearly wasn't; known "perverts," "morons," and "degenerates" who might have been interested in molesting a young boy; and "dope fiends" who might have been desperate for ransom money.

But they were also working on tracking down the manufacturer of the pair of spectacles. The hinges on the frames turned out to be quite unusual, and it seemed that only three pairs of spectacles with these distinctive hinges had been sold in the Chicago area, all by the Almer Coe optical company. A few days later, a massive search of the company's prescription records connected one of these pairs to an attorney who was currently traveling in Europe, a second to a lady who was currently wearing them, and the third to Leopold.

On the evening of Thursday, May 29, police returned to Leopold's house. They were still deferential, parking down the block in front of an apartment building to avoid embarrassing the Leopold household. Rather than taking him to the state's attorney's office, where they might be seen by reporters, they brought him to the LaSalle Hotel, where State's Attorney Robert Crowe politely questioned him about the glasses. This time, Leopold admitted that the suspicious pair resembled a pair he owned, but he insisted he wasn't aware of having lost his. They must be somewhere in his room at home. Crowe sent him back to the house to hunt for the glasses, escorted by detectives, but Leopold could find only his empty eyeglass case.

At this point his oldest brother Foreman ("Mike") became concerned. It might be a good idea, he thought, to make a call to Sam Ettelson, the prominent attorney and former state senator who lived next door. He had known the family for years and would certainly be happy to tell the detectives that Leopold couldn't possibly be mixed up in this sordid case. Ettelson, of course, also happened to be the close friend and attorney of Jacob Franks, and had spent the night of Bobby's disappearance at the Franks home, sharing every agonizing moment of the wait to hear back from "Mr. Johnson." He was there in the morning when the ransom note arrived, and later when the call came from the Indiana morgue. And it turned out that he was over at the Franks house right then, as they discovered when they tried to phone him at home.

So Nathan and Foreman Leopold, escorted by the detectives, drove over to the Franks house four blocks away, where they explained to Ettelson about the little mix-up with Leopold's glasses. Ettelson did, in fact, tell the detectives that he'd known Leopold all of the young man's life and that really they shouldn't be wasting their time on him. But then one of the detectives took him aside and said something to him that caused him to tell Nathan and Foreman that probably the best course here was for Nathan to continue cooperating with the state's attorney and let justice take its course. As they left, he told the detectives to make sure that Crowe kept him up to date about any developments.

This time, rather than returning to the LaSalle Hotel, they took Leopold to the state's attorney's office for further questioning, and then the detectives returned to the Leopold house and conducted their own search.

They found nothing there that would directly connect him with the murder, but they did find two items they regarded as highly suspicious: a handgun, for which Leopold had no permit, and a peculiar letter from Leopold to his friend and fellow University of Chicago student Richard Loeb.

# 4
# Richard Loeb

Chicago History Museum, DN-0077054

The Loeb mansion at 5017 Ellis Avenue, just down the block and across the street from the Franks home.

T HE LOEB FAMILY lived in a mansion just down the block from the Franks mansion, and the two families were related: Bobby Franks's maternal grandmother and Richard Loeb's paternal grandmother were sisters. Loeb's youngest brother, Tommy Loeb, was a year behind Bobby at the Harvard School. Like both the Frankses and the Leopolds, the Loebs were a German Jewish family that had gone from rags to spectacular riches in the United States, and of the three, the Loebs were the most socially prominent. Loeb's father, Albert Loeb, was an attorney who was also the close personal confidant of Sears, Roebuck co-owner and chairman Julius Rosenwald; Albert himself had become the company's vice president. Jacob Loeb, Albert's younger brother, was also a high-profile Chicago attorney who had served as president of the city's board of education.

Anna Loeb, Loeb's mother, was a member of the Chicago Woman's Club, which supported charitable and social causes.

Like Leopold, Loeb was precocious. He finished high school two years early, entered the University of Chicago at age 14, and had already done his freshman year when he first made friends with Leopold, who was just matriculating. Junior year, he transferred to the University of Michigan to finish his undergraduate degree, but by the spring of 1924 he was back at the University of Chicago doing graduate work in constitutional history and resuming his friendship with Leopold.

Richard Loeb, 1924.

Whereas Leopold prided himself on his superior intellect, Loeb had the social gifts he lacked: he was good-looking, popular, and charming. He was also a voracious reader of mysteries and crime stories—an avid subscriber to *Detective Story Magazine*, as a matter of fact.

Because of his well-known obsession with crime and detective fiction, none of his friends were terribly surprised that Loeb seemed especially fascinated by the mystery of Bobby's murder. When he insisted that several of his fraternity friends, who also happened to be reporters covering the case for the Chicago papers, take a drive along 63rd Street to try to identify which drugstore the kidnapper had intended to send Jacob Franks to for the next installment of his ransom instructions, they just thought it was Loeb playing detective. They didn't think it was odd, either, that he tagged along with them to the inquest, where Jacob Franks and Sam Ettelson were among those listening to the graphic details of the coroner's report. When his mother remarked at the family dinner table that whoever could do such a thing ought to be tarred and feathered, she didn't think it was strange that Loeb chuckled. And no one took the slightest note of him standing on the sidewalk outside his own home four days after the murder, watching six of Bobby's Harvard School classmates carry his coffin out of the Franks house down the block to the hearse that would drive him to his final resting place at Rosehill Cemetery.

Under questioning, Leopold at first told police that he couldn't remember what he had done on the afternoon of May 21. Finally, after hours of interrogation, he slowly began feeding them the details of the alibi he and Loeb had agreed to use if one of them were to be arrested within a week of the crime. He said he had spent the afternoon and evening of May 21 in Loeb's company, lunching, drinking too much, and trying to pick up girls.

But detectives wondered about that. The letter written to Loeb that they had meanwhile found in Leopold's room sounded suspiciously like an angry lover's letter. There had been some sort of disagreement between the boys, in which Leopold refused to admit that he had acted wrongly. "Now it is up to you to inflict the penalty for this refusal," he wrote to Loeb, "at your discretion, to break friendship, inflict physical punishment or anything else you like, or on the other hand to continue as before." If Loeb should choose to end the friendship, though, Leopold cautioned him, "extreme care must be used. The motif of a falling out of cocksuckers would be sure to be popular, which is patently undesirable, and forms an unknown but unavoidable bond between us."

# PART II
# Confessions and Other Statements of Leopold and Loeb

# 5
# What can one say in such a case?

## TRANSCRIPTS OF THE INTERROGATIONS

P REPARED AS EVIDENCE for the proceeding *People of the State of Illinois v. Nathan F. Leopold, Jr. and Richard Loeb,* the Confessions and Other Statements of Leopold and Loeb constitutes perhaps the most extraordinary historical artifact of the case: 571 neatly typed pages of actual dialogue, beginning at 1:35 a.m. on Friday, May 30, in the office of State's Attorney Robert Crowe, as he questions Leopold about how he might have come to lose his spectacles so close to the place where Bobby's body was found.

These were pre-*Miranda* days; the suspects had no attorneys present and certainly weren't warned about the dangers of self-incrimination. Initially both the Leopold and Loeb families were so convinced of the outrageousness of the idea that either boy could have been associated with the murder that they encouraged their sons to cooperate fully with the investigation. "While it is a terrible ordeal both to my boy and myself to have him under even a possibility of suspicion," Nathan Leopold Sr. told reporters, "yet our attitude will be one of helping the investigation rather than retarding it. . . . And even though my son is subjected to the hardships and embarrassment of being kept from his family until the authorities are thoroughly satisfied that this supposed clew [sic] is groundless, yet my son should be willing to make the sacrifice, and I am also willing for the sake of justice and truth."

Loeb's mother, Anna Loeb, could barely spare a thought for such nonsense. "There really is nothing to say. What can one say in such a case?" the *Tribune* quoted her as saying. "I wish I knew what to say. The affair will so easily straighten itself out."

Crowe took full advantage of the chance to interrogate the boys with no interference, and also of Leopold's arrogant assumption—shared by some in the press—that he was brilliant enough to match wits with the detectives on his own.

Although we know in retrospect that the suspects are lying or prevaricating on particular subjects, the dialogue still has an astonishingly frank quality that projects the personalities of the protagonists clearly. These dialogues preserve, so many years later, the raw elements of the sensational stories about Leopold and Loeb that instantly sprang up in the press and were immortalized by dramatizations such as *Rope* and *Compulsion.*

THE CONFESSIONS AND OTHER STATEMENTS OF LEOPOLD AND LOEB are a series of transcripts, neatly indexed and bound between sturdy black covers. They record statements that unfolded over the course of roughly 72 hours, like a series of one-act dramas, each introduced with the time of questioning and a list of dramatis personae present, including the name of the shorthand reporter who took the original notes. We see characters enter and exit the stage as the plot unravels, including Franks family friend and attorney Sam Ettelson, who was indeed called in once it became clear that the Leopold boy from next door was looking less and less innocent; guest witnesses called in with bits of new and damning testimony; and, poignantly, a cameo appearance by Nathan Leopold Sr. at the point where he has finally realized just how much trouble his son is in.

I N D E X

| Statement of | Page | |
|---|---|---|
| Nathan F. Leopold, JR. | 1 | Confession |
| Richard Albert Loeb | 44 | " |
| "        "        " | 76 | Confession read to defts. |
| Nathan F. Leopold, Jr. | 111 | "      "      "      " |
| Loeb, Leopold | 154 ) | Identifying drug stores & stationery store |
| H. C. Stranberg | 156 ) | Sold stationery to Leopold |
| Leopold & Loeb | 166 | Examination as to Sanity |
| "        " | 287 | Identifying automobile |
| "        " | 290 | Identifying exhibits |
| Leopold, Loeb & others | 309 ) | Re phone call from Rent-a-Car to Louis Mason |
| Sam Barish | ) | |
| Max Tockerman | 314 ) | "                    " |
| Mrs. Lucile Smith and Jeanette Smith | 322 ) | Re meeting Willys-Knight near 108th St., May 21st. |
| Nathan F. Leopold, JR. | 327 | Re phone call to Jacob Franks |
| Aaron B. Adler | 332 | Re selling hydrochloric acid |

------------------------------------------

Prior to Confession

| Nathan F. Leopold, Jr. | 352 | Alibi statement |
|---|---|---|
| "    "    "    " | 438 | In re typewriter |
| "    "    "    " | 442 | "    "    " |
| "    "    "    " | 446 | "    "    "    and alibi |
| Morris Shanberg | 449 | "    "    " |
| Arnold Maremont | 454 | "    "    " |
| Lester Abelson | 462 | "    "    " |
| Howard Oberndorf | 469 | "    "    " |
| Nathan Kaplan | 478 | "    "    " |
| Nathan F. Leopold, Jr. | 493 | "    "    " |
| Richard A. Loeb | 512 | |

# 6
# He looked rather worried

## LEOPOLD IN DENIAL

Few reporters blurred the lines between fact and fiction with as much flair and abandon as Maurine Watkins, the same reporter who had managed to crash Bobby Franks's funeral and who would later create the enduring fictional character Roxie Hart in her play *Chicago* (also based on a historical 1924 Chicago murder trial). Sketching in some imaginative context to the interrogation of Nathan Leopold, her reporting in the May 31 edition of the *Chicago Daily Tribune* emphasized how "suavely" he answered the questions being lobbed at him over the course of 30 hours by detectives and reporters. Even with three and four reporters simultaneously peppering him with questions about "love, philosophy, art, sports—relevant and irrelevant," she pronounces him "Caesar-like" in the manner in which he answered "each in turn rapidly enough to keep the questioner busy writing on his separate question." Leopold paused between answers only long enough to light a cigarette, she added, "for Nathan has smoked without stopping," before delivering another swift, decisive answer, "couched in judicial language, with perhaps a slightly cynical twist and a sudden smile."

**T**HE FIRST STATEMENT was recorded in the office of State's Attorney Robert Crowe at 1:35 a.m. on Friday, May 30. At this point in the transcript, Crowe has already been questioning Leopold since late Thursday afternoon and occasionally alludes to earlier conversations. Leopold denies having had any knowledge of the murder until running into one of his old teachers from the Harvard School on the day following Bobby Franks's disappearance. Present in the room, besides Crowe and Leopold, are Assistant State's Attorneys Joseph P. Savage and Milton D. Smith, Chief of Detectives Michael Hughes, and the shorthand reporter E.M. Allen.

**MR. CROWE: Q** What is your name?

**[MR. LEOPOLD:] A** Nathan F. Leopold Jr.

**Q** Where do you live?

**A** 4754 Greenwood avenue.

**Q** How old a man are you?

**A** Nineteen.

**Q** You were nineteen when?

**A** 19th of November.

**Q** Where were you born?

**A** Chicago.

**Q** Who was your father?

**A** Nathan F. Leopold.

**Q** What is his business?

**A** He is president of the Morris Paper House.

Crowe questions Leopold further about his family and his early education and then, having established that Leopold had attended the Harvard School for four years, asks him about teachers there, several of whom are still suspects in the case:

**Q** Were you acquainted with any of the present instructors?

**A** Yes, sir.

**Q** Name someone that you were acquainted with?

**A** Mr. M. Kirk Mitchell, Mr. Charles Edgar Pence, George Vauvel.

**Q** Do you know [Walter] Wilson?

**A** No, sir.

**Q** Or [Richard P.] Williams?

**A** No, sir.

**Q** They came after you left?

**A** Yes, sir.

**Q** What Mitchell, he occupies what position there?

**A** Assistant principal and professor in English.

**Q** He was a teacher of yours at one time?

**A** Yes, sir.

**Q** What did he teach? English?

**A** Yes, sir.

**Q** What else?

**A** That's all.

**Q** When was the last time you saw him?

**A** The last time I saw Mr. Mitchell was last Thursday.

**Q** And where?

**A** On Ellis Avenue, just south of 47th street.

**Q** Did you have a talk with him?

**A** Yes, sir.

**Q** What was the conversation?

**A** Mr. Mitchell said, after the greeting formalities, Mr. Mitchell said, "Have you heard about the Franks boy?" I said, "No." He said, "Do you know him?" I said, "No." I asked if he were a student of the Harvard. He said, "Yes;" he said he had been kidnapped the day before, and the rumor now was that his murdered body had been found and he himself would not believe it until he actually saw the body.

**Q** What time of day was that?

**A** It was about 5:15–5:30.

**Q** Had you heard anything about the Franks matter prior to that time?

**A** No, sir.

**Q** Up to that time you had heard nothing about the Franks matter?

**A** No, sir.

**Q** And you did not know Robert Franks?

**A** No, sir.

**Q** Did you know his brother?

**A** No, sir.

MITCHELL was one of three Harvard School teachers (the "Wilson" and "Williams" named in the transcript) rounded up by the police for questioning, based partly on their having the literary skills to write an extraordinarily educated-sounding ransom note. Mitchell was described to reporters by the principal as "Just a simple teacher who talks better English than most persons and whose voice and manner are a little more cultured and refined," which apparently fit detectives' profile of the kind of man who might have kidnapped Bobby in order to molest him. All three teachers were held without a warrant for five days and Mitchell left town immediately after his release, "broken down by his experiences" in custody, according to the *Chicago Daily News*. Fellow teacher and suspect Walter Wilson claimed that during his interrogation, police had beaten him with a heavy rubber hose, deprived him of sleep, and threatened to push him out a 15th-story window if he didn't confess, saying they would just tell everyone "that it was your guilty conscience that made you jump."

**Q** Did you know his father?

**A** No, sir.

**Q** Did you know any of the family?

**A** Yes, sir.

**Q** Did you know where they lived?

**A** Did I know where they live?

**Q** Yes.

**A** I don't believe so.

**Q** Do you now know where they live?

**A** Yes, sir.

**Q** How far is it from where you live?

**A** It is four blocks.

**Q** How far did you live from the school?

**A** A block and a half.

**Q** A block and a half from the school?

**A** Yes, sir.

**Q** Do you know a number of the pupils that go to the school?

**A** Yes, sir.

**Q** How did he [Mitchell] look when he left? How did he impress you?

**A** My judgment may be influenced by what I have heard since; but my impression is that he looked rather worried, that his color was not as good as usual, and his face looked longer than usual.

**Q** And you attributed that to what, if anything?

**A** At the time?

**Q** At the time.

**A** The fact that one of the pupils of his school had been murdered.

# 7
# Keener mentally than the average

## LEOPOLD AS "PRODIGY"

FREQUENTLY, Leopold's knowledge of 15 languages would be cited as evidence of his brilliance, but to Robert Crowe he can only name 13. Then he admits that amongst those he has studied, there are only five in which he is "more or less fluent": English, German, French, Italian, and Spanish. Later in the interrogation, he would further admit that for his unfinished project translating a fifteenth-century erotic work from the Italian, he had actually been working from a German translation of the Italian original because "my Italian is not anything to rave about." He had learned German, incidentally, at home, where it was still spoken in the family and by his childhood nursemaid.

**[MR. CROWE:] Q** When you graduated from the Chicago University [i.e., University of Chicago] you received the degree of—

**[MR. LEOPOLD:] A** Ph.B.

**Q** And the post-graduate you took was along what line?

**A** Comparative philology.

**Q** What does that mean, to the average citizen, who is not a college man?

**A** Study of comparative language.

**Q** You spent a considerable portion of your student days in studying the various languages?

**A** Yes, sir.

**Q** How many languages have you studied?

**A** Fifteen.

**Q** Can you name them?

**A** English, German, French, Italian, Spanish, Modern Greek, Russian, Hawaiian, Latin, Ancient Greek, Sanskrit, popular Latin, Hellenic Greek.

**Q** What is popular Latin?

**A** Popular Latin, otherwise known as vulgar Latin, is the Latin which was the speech of the common folks in the fourth and fifth centuries A.D., in the study of advanced languages.

**Q** The revival of Gaelic, you didn't speak Gaelic?

**A** No, I didn't have time. I discussed the matter with our Irish maid—Oscan Umbrian language.

**Q** What kind of language is that?

**A** Early dialects; dialects of languages that became obsolete in the Middle Ages.

**Q** Did you have any especial object in studying those languages?

**A** My father thought I was young enough to study just exactly what I pleased; and that was my choice.

## A NEW TYPE OF EDUCATED YOUNG MAN

The press found Nathan Leopold intellectually dazzling. The *Chicago Daily Tribune* called him a "student marvel." The *New York Times* called him "an advanced thinker." The *Chicago Daily News* called him a "prodigy" but actually used quotation marks around the term, and on May 30 ran a front-page story suggesting that Leopold was an example of a new "type" of educated young man: intellectually and financially gifted, morally and emotionally bankrupt. Yes, the *Daily News* pointed out, "The men with whom Leopold and Loeb have been associated are keener mentally than the average—they get better grades, but they also keep later hours. They are more brilliant to debate than the average, but they go in more strenuously also for gin and 'petting.'"

CONTINUED

CONTINUED

There were dangers, then, lurking where society might least expect, in the corridors and neighborhoods of the prestigious academic institutions where parents sent their children, expecting education to improve them. Instead, the *Daily News* suggested, these very institutions were now producing young men whose "conduct, like their thinking, is independent of conventions and taboos. They scorn the judgment of other students, glorying in their superior wealth, their sharper wits, their greater capacity for forbidden pleasures."

**Q** How many of these languages can you speak more or less fluently?

**A** About five.

**Q** And what are those?

**A** English, German, French, Italian, Spanish and Modern Greek,–well, not so much. I can order a beefsteak in any Greek restaurant.

**Q** And in most of the others you can read and write?

**A** No, I would not say that. I can read in all of them except possibly Russian and Sanskrit, without very much difficulty.

**Q** Have you any other line of study that you have studied?

**A** Yes, sir; ornithology.

**Q** You have made more or less of a specialty of it since then?

**A** Yes, sir.

**Q** Have you done anything besides study it, have you put it to any practical use?

**A** You mean have I published some?

**Q** No: have you put it to any practical use; have you taught?

**A** Yes, I have both taught and written.

**Q** When did you begin to teach?

**A** Began to teach in the spring of 1921.

**Q** And you have various classes?

**A** Yes, sir.

**Q** What is the course of instruction? What do you do?

**A** With my children, it is pure descriptive field ornithology, which means taking the kids out, teaching the methods of observation, teaching them what to look for in birds, familiarizing them with the species of birds which are common here; with my oldest class, which is about 90 per cent, every now and then I give them a little talk which might be called technical, such as might be called classification of birds.

**Q** You have three different classes now?

**A** Yes sir.

**Q** Class of children?

**A** Two classes of children.

**Q** And one of ladies?

**A** One of ladies.

**Q** The ladies are married ladies?

**A** Without exception.

**Q** Is there any significance in that, I mean the fact that they are all married?

**A** Merely that the ladies are of a certain age, one gets classes by getting different groups of friends, and of course, the unmarried ladies would not go around with the married ladies. I think my youngest student is considerably over thirty-five.

# 8
# Fake tortoiseshell spectacles, rather weak

## LEOPOLD FAILS TO DROP HIS GLASSES

AFTER QUESTIONING LEOPOLD about his familiarity with the area where Bobby Franks's body had been found and when Leopold had last visited that area (Leopold tells him a detailed version of the written account he had provided police on May 25), Robert Crowe raises the subject of the glasses.

**[MR. CROWE:] Q** Do you wear glasses?

**[MR. LEOPOLD:] A** No, sir.

**Q** Have you ever worn glasses?

**A** Yes, sir.

**Q** When did you first wear glasses?

**A** In October or November, 1923.

**Q** What was the occasion of your getting a pair of glasses?

**A** I had been suffering from a little nervous headache, which I thought might be attributable to eye strain, from the amount of reading I had been doing in pursuance of my studies. I went down to see Mr. Emil Deutsch, and he prescribed glasses for me.

**Q** That is—

**A** 30 North Michigan.

**Q** Where did you have the prescription filled?

**A** Almer Coe & Company.

**Q** How many pairs of glasses have you bought?

**A** One.

**Q** That pair was bought from—

**A** Almer Coe & Company, on the prescription of Dr. Deutsch.

**Q** Describe, as best you can, the pair of glasses that you bought.

**A** They were fake tortoiseshell spectacles, rather weak; that is as much as I can describe them. Is there anything you could suggest?

**Q** No; just your description. And you wore those when you read?

**A** Yes, sir.

**Q** You didn't wear them for sight?

**A** No, sir.

## A "USELESS CLEW"

Even as the press exploited the titillating possibility of millionaires' sons being secret murderers, the reality continued to seem unlikely. As the interrogations continued, the *Chicago Tribune* ran one story on May 30 in which family members called the accusation "too silly to discuss." On the same page was another story announcing—prematurely, as it turned out—that while everyone had expected that the spectacles found near the body would lead detectives to the murderer, this had proven false, since the spectacles had led police to Nathan Leopold, who had a perfectly good explanation for misplacing them: he must have lost them in the swamp near the culvert while he was bird-watching and never missed them. So though for the past 10 days the spectacles had been thought to be the most important "clew" to the murder case, and though "in fiction such clews always lead to the solution of the mystery," the *Tribune* said, "In fact they proved useless."

Leopold's glasses, which helped implicate him in the crime. They were preserved in the collections at the Chicago History Museum, where they are exhibited from time to time.

**Q** When did you stop wearing them?

**A** I think it was about in February, it might have been March.

**Q** And from that time on you have no recollection of having worn these glasses?

**A** No, sir.

**Q** When did you first talk to me?

**A** About three—five, this afternoon—yesterday afternoon.

**Q** That is Thursday afternoon?

**A** That's right.

Crowe reminds Leopold that in their initial conversation that afternoon, Leopold had assured him that his glasses were at home, but when Crowe allowed him to go home and search for them, he had not been able to produce them. Crowe then brings out the pair found near the body and asks whether Leopold thinks these are his. Leopold says, "I should think that they were." The glasses are then marked for identification with a notch in the bridge, and then Crowe asks Leopold:

**Q** Have you any idea how those glasses happened to be found at the scene of the crime?

**A** They probably dropped out of my pocket, in which I must have been carrying them, either Saturday or Sunday, May 17th or 18th.

**Q** You change your clothes many times?

**A** Yes, sir.

**Q** How many suits of clothes have you got?

**A** Eight.

**Q** How many do you wear? How many different suits do you wear when you are at home?

**A** Five.

**Q** You are in the habit of frequently sending these clothes to the tailor?

**A** Not my bird clothes; no, sir.

**Q** Do you send those?

**A** Yes.

**Q** About how often?

**A** It depends on how badly they need it; I don't stop to figure to think of what suit I wore the last time, and I take the first suit that is handy, and I may send the suit to the cleaner after each time that I had worn it, or I might be at home for months without it being sent to the cleaner.

**Q** Have you a bird suit for birding, or just an old suit?

**A** Just an old suit, four or five of them.

**Q** If you put your glasses in your pocket, you would put them in what pocket?

**A** My left breast pocket.

**Q** Left breast coat pocket?

**A** Left breast coat pocket, or possibly left vest pocket.

**Q** Which, generally, would you do?

**A** Generally I would put them in my coat.

**Q** Did you stumble or fall at this particular spot at any time?

**A** I do not remember.

**Q** You do not remember that?

**A** No, sir.

**Q** Will you put those in your left breast coat pocket and run and bend, and see whether they will drop out?

(Whereupon Mr. Leopold did as requested.)

**Q** Now, you have fallen to the floor twice?

**A** Yes.

**Q** The glasses are still in your pocket?

**A** Yes, sir.

**Q** You do not recollect of having fell at any time Saturday or Sunday?

**A** No, sir.

**Q** And you have a fairly good memory?

**A** I wouldn't swear to that; you mean ordinarily?

**Q** Ordinarily, yes.

**A** Yes, sir.

## 9
# A student of sexual perversion

### LEOPOLD'S INTEREST IN ARETINO

DETECTIVES HAD NOT ruled out the possibility that, despite the ransom demand, the real motivation behind the abduction and murder of Bobby Franks could have been sexual. The coroner's official pronouncement was that no molestation had taken place, though the wording of the report was ambiguous and Robert Crowe would stubbornly insist to the end that he thought sexual molestation had occurred (see chapter 64, page 236). But even if it hadn't, this didn't rule out the possibility that the murder had been an accidental or unintended result of an attempted assault gone awry. At this point in the transcript, fishing for evidence of Leopold's suspected "perversions," Crowe turns his questioning to the nature of Leopold's friendships with Loeb and another friend, Richard ("Dick") Rubel, and the fact that the three boys had a standing lunch date three times a week, one day at Leopold's house, one day at Loeb's house, and one day at the Drake Hotel, where Rubel lived with his family. The line of questioning veers toward Leopold's familiarity with the works of Pietro Aretino (referred to in the transcripts as "Aratino"), whose erotic works had scandalized sixteenth-century Rome.

**[MR. CROWE:] Q** And have you at any time spent any time studying works on perversion or degeneracy?

**[MR. LEOPOLD:] A** No, sir.

**Q** Have you ever read any Italian work on perversion or degeneracy?

**A** No, sir; not a work on perversion or degeneracy. You are no doubt referring to the works of Aratino. It deals with that, but they are not at all a study of it, they are merely incidental.

**Q** Who is Aratino?

**A** Aratino was one of the greatest figures of the cinquecento, in the 15th century. He had one of the most poisonous pens of any known to history, and received presents, as the story goes, from all crowned heads and great men of Europe, to prevail upon him not to write about them.

**Q** What works have you read?

**A** I have read his work "I Ragionamenti".

**Q** And what did that deal with?

**A** That is a narrative of two women in Rome, Nana and Antonina, in which Nana asks advice of Antonina what to make of hers, Nana's daughter. Antonina asks whether or not Nana has not, during her lifetime, been a nun, a wife and a courtesan.

**Q** A courtesan is a—

**A** A whore, a prostitute. Nana replies in the affirmative; and Antonina tells her that if she, Nana, will outline the life that she led in each of these three capacities, that

## AN OLD ITALIAN BOOK

With the contents of the interrogations leaking directly to a ravenous national press corps, another lurid angle began to unfold very publicly. The May 31 *Atlanta Constitution* reported that the questioning had turned to "a remarkable story of an unusual interest in sexual perversion taken by the group of which Leopold and Loeb were members." This article reported on Leopold's interest in translating "an old Italian book, which dealt with unusual forms of perversion," and noted that the pair of suspects "were known, even outside of the peculiar set with which they associated, as brilliant youths whose intellectual interests had taken strange turns."

she, Antonina, will be able to advise her. This Nana does, and her narrative forms the story; the story is in the form of a dialogue, question and answer.

**Q** What was the experience as a nun?

**A** As a very young girl, although not too young to have already had lovers, she entered into a nunnery. She finds there, instead of the religion and aestheticism which she expected, a spirit of unparalleled debauchery and sex intercourse.

**Q** What are some of the forms of sex intercourse that she relates?

**A** The use upon herself of a so-called dildo, which in this case was a glass, blown glass instrument made, I imagine, in the shape of a penis, manufactured in Murano, which is near Venice, in which warm water was inserted, and there is a description of one of the abbots having intercourse with a woman while another monk was practicing sodomy with him.

**Q** Putting the penis in the rectum?

**A** Correct. Several others are on the scene, masturbating in one form or another, and one or two couples, I believe, are practicing sex intercourse in the normal fashion.

**Q** In the normal fashion?

**A** Yes, sir.

**Q** That is men and women?

**A** Yes, sir.

**Q** What other forms of perversion did they indulge in in this nunnery?

**A** That is about all I can remember.

**Q** And as a wife what experience did she have?

**A** The part of the wife, as I told you, I only skimmed through. She is, of course, unfaithful to her husband, and has various experiences.

**Q** Some of them are acts of perversion?

**A** I believe so.

**Q** And as to the courtesan what occurred?

**A** That I know the least about.

**Q** But the first part, the nun, you read that with considerable care?

**A** First part of the nun, yes.

**Q** Now, did you ever contemplate translating that into English and publishing it?

**A** Yes, sir.

**Q** What was that?

**A** Sir?

**Q** What was that, what have you in mind with reference to that?

**A** A friend [Leon Mandel] and I were going to translate the I. Ragionamenti of Aratino into English with a very full notation and a very lengthy preface attempting some sort of a justification of Aratino by looking at him in the spirit of the times.

**Q** What were these notations going to be?

**A** Explanations of points which might not be perfectly apparent to all readers. Shall I give examples?

**Q** Yes.

**A** No one knows there is an allusion to a woman having a blue vein in her eye. This in the literature of the times appears to have been symbolic of virginity, as it was a superstition or belief that upon intercourse with a man this vein in a woman's eye, which at birth was blue, turned to red. That is one example.

**Q** What would be your notation on that?

**A** Just as I have given it, it would mark down the passage [about the] blue vein in the eye, and then say—I don't know just what form—the superstition in the middle ages, the color of a woman's vein changed.

**Q** Were there any others that you recall?

**A** It would give a notation on the manufacture of these so called ~~dildos at Murano~~ [this phrase is crossed out, with the phrase "fruits of Paradis at Murano" penciled in above] we would give the general geographical description of Murano and some of the manufactures for which it was known at the time, among which was glass blowing.

**Q** And fruits of paradise is referred to in the story where the artificial penis is?

**A** Yes, sir.

**Q** How did you intend to publish this, how did you intend to circulate it?

**A** We had no definite scheme, but we had expected to get some friend of ours to publish a very small little edition, two or three hundred copies, or subscriptions to be circulated only among people who had a legitimate interest in the literature of the times. Aratino has great literary value if one can get over the first feeling of revulsion and disgust, that is absolute filth.

**Q** In your judgment, he is about one of the filthiest Italian writers that you have read?

**A** Without exception.

**Q** Who was this friend that was going to help you publish this book?

**A** Leon Mandel, the second.

**Q** How old a man is he?

**A** Twenty-two.

**Q** And you were discouraged in this enterprise by—

**A** Professor [Ernest] Wilkins, now Dean of the colleges at the University of Chicago, head of the Italian Department.

**Q** When was it you had this project in mind?

**A** Last fall, October or November.

**Q** What else did this distinguished Italian write?

**A** He wrote a number of works, the thing for which he is most noted, perhaps, are a number of vile couplets in verse which he wrote for his friend, his name, I believe, was Romano, but I am not sure, who was very proficient in the art of steel cutting or wood cutting. This artist had put out a series of pictures depicting thirty-two ways of sex intercourse. These couplets made Aratino so famous that the expression now is "Thirty-two ways of Aratino," rather than Romano.

**Q** The thirty-two ways of sex intercourse included the old fashioned method or were they all perversion?

**A** I don't know, I have never seen the pictures.

**Q** You read the couplets?

**A** No, sir.

**Q** You never did?

**A** No, sir.

**Q** But there are thirty-two ways, thirty-two different forms of perversion?

**A** Yes, sir, according to Aratino.

**Q** How many forms of perversion do you know about?

**A** May I ask what you mean by perversion, whether you would include such things as the mutilation of people?

**Q** Perversion to me means the gratification of your passions.

**A** Sex passions?

**Q** Sex passions.

**A** I should say four or five.

**Q** What are they?

**A** Sodomy.

**Q** Sodomy is the putting of the penis in another person's rectum?

**A** Yes, sir.

**Q** Whether it is a man or woman?

**A** Yes, sir. ~~Conobingual~~ [this word is heavily blacked out, with the word "conolingual" penciled in above] method.

**Q** That means in vulgar language cock sucking?

**A** Yes sir. Here is one which I don't know the correct name, I have heard it spoken of as wind bagging.

**Q** Come back to where you left off.

**A** I told you the various ways of perversion I know of, I told you about the Conobingual method. Have I told you about wind bagging? This consists of insertion of the penis in the arm pit of either a man or a woman and causing discharge in the flange. Another of which I do not know the name, consists of placing the penis between two of the toes, then there is, of course, masturbation.

**Q** Well, that is self-abuse, practiced alike by girls and boys, then are there others that you know of?

**A** None that I know of until this afternoon.

**Q** Did you ever hear of a man going down on a woman?

**A** Yes, sir. I should include that under the ~~Conobingual~~ [again, this word is crossed out, with "Conolingual" penciled in above] method.

**Q** That embraces what?

**A** Cock sucking and cunt lapping.

**Q** Have you ever been the victim of a malicious story about your habits?

**A** Yes, sir.

**Q** You have been accused of what?

**A** I have been accused of sex perversion; I don't know specifically in what form.

**Q** With whom?

**A** With Dick Loeb.

**Q** And that report was spread pretty generally among your associates?

**A** Yes, sir.

**Q** How long ago?

**A** It was in June, 1921.

# 10
# He wasn't sober enough to go home
## LEOPOLD'S ALIBI

LEOPOLD'S ALIBI for the day and evening of Bobby Franks's disappearance rested on having been out most of the day driving around with Richard Loeb in the Leopolds' distinctively maroon-colored Willys-Knight car. He had rehearsed the details with Loeb but agreed the alibi would be used only if one of them were arrested within a week of the crime. Leopold had been taken into police custody eight days after the murder—but only seven days after the last stage of their ransom scheme had been abandoned. In the transcript, when he finally, under pressure, begins feeding Robert Crowe and the detectives details of the alibi, it doesn't occur to him that Loeb might do the math differently and fail to confirm what he is saying.

**[MR. CROWE:] Q** Do you remember Wednesday, the day the boy disappeared?

**[MR. LEOPOLD:] A** Yes, sir.

**Q** Give us an account of your movements that day.

**A** I rose about 7:15 A.M., then had breakfast, went out to school, had an eight o'clock class in the criminal law; at nine o'clock I had an hour off, if I remember correctly, visited a French class with a friend of mine, had a ten-o'clock class in agency, eleven o'clock—

**Q** Whose work do you study on agency?

**A** Wamble's Cases on Agency.

**Q** You don't follow the textbook system?

**A** No, sir. At eleven o'clock or shortly thereafter I went down town; had lunch at Marshall Field's grill.

**Q** Who were you with?

**A** Dick Loeb.

**Q** Richard Loeb?

**A** Yes, sir.

**Q** Have you seen him today?

**A** Yes, sir.

**Q** Where?

**A** I saw him at ten and eleven, at the University of Chicago, had lunch with him at the Windermere Hotel, was at his home until two-thirty. I saw him for a moment about one thirty this morning.

**Q** Over here [in the Criminal Court Building]?

**A** Yes, sir.

**Q** You have been with him frequently between last Wednesday and today?

**A** Yes, sir.

---

HAVE YOU SEEN HIM TODAY? Leopold and Loeb were both in police custody at this point. Sources disagree with each other—and with what Leopold says here—about what Leopold had done earlier in the day, but he was arrested on the afternoon of Thursday, May 29, and taken initially to the LaSalle Hotel for questioning, to avoid embarrassing his family by making the detectives' interest in him appear too serious. Loeb was picked up shortly afterwards and taken to another room at the hotel. As the questioning grew more serious, they were both moved to the Criminal Court Building, where they were held in separate rooms as the questioning continued. This segment of the interrogation was taking place in the early morning hours of Friday, May 30, so when Leopold refers to having seen Loeb "today" at the University of Chicago and at lunch, he's actually referring to the previous day— Thursday—which would prove to be the last day of his "normal" (i.e., free) life. His next glimpse of Loeb, he says, was at 1:30 a.m. in the Criminal Court Building—by which time they were both serious suspects.

**Q** You got to Marshall Field's, and you had your lunch, and you went out to Lincoln Park?
**A** Yes, sir.

**Q** And studied birds?
**A** Yes, sir.

**Q** Did you have anything to drink?
**A** Yes, sir.

**Q** What did you have?
**A** Had a little over a pint of gin, and about half a pint of Scotch.

**Q** You had the gin, and he had the Scotch?
**A** Yes, sir.

**Q** When you left there what was the condition of Loeb and yourself, when you left the park?
**A** I should say we might have been a little bit happy; neither of us was drunk.

**Q** He wasn't sober enough to go home ~~today~~ [this word is crossed out, with "to dinner" written in above]?
**A** No, that was on account of his breath.

**Q** And you had supper where?
**A** At the Cocoanut Grove.

**Q** After that, what did you do?
**A** After that, we went for a drive in my machine.

**Q** Where did you drive?
**A** Drove up and down 63rd street several times.

**Q** What was the purpose of your driving?
**A** Driving to find a couple of girls with nothing to do.

**Q** And you found them?
**A** Yes, sir.

**Q** Then what happened?
**A** Then we drove down Garfield Boulevard, almost to Western avenue, and back up to Jackson Park; parked the car just north and east of the Wooded Island.

**Q** Did you get out of the car?
**A** I had made a telephone call.

**Q** You had made a telephone call?
**A** Yes, home.

**Q** Telephoning your folks?
**A** Yes, sir.

**Q** Then what happened?
**A** Then we sat around in the car and had a few drinks, and couldn't come to any agreement with the girls; so we asked them to leave, and went to go home.

**Q** In other words, the girls—
**A** Wouldn't come across.

## GIRLS WITH MUDDY BOOTS

The May 30 *Chicago Tribune* described Nathan Leopold's questioning as "desultory," as if it were a tiresome formality everyone had to somehow get through. The paper quoted his alibi as saying, "We picked up a couple of girls and we took them riding with us. But they were of the kind that go home with their boots muddy and we made them do it."

# 11
# Ashes to ashes, and dust to dust

## LEOPOLD AS ATHEIST

LEOPOLD'S DECLARED ATHEISM would become part of the mythology of the case—interpreted by much of the public as a key to his moral degeneracy, but worn by himself as a badge of cool rationality. During the following exchange with Crowe during his interrogation, he asserts that his atheism dates back to the age of 11, though later he would explain it to psychiatrists as a reaction to the death of his beloved mother Florence, when he was 16—less than three years before the murder of Bobby Franks (see chapter 28, page 104)

**AN ADVANCED THINKER**

Sometimes press coverage illustrated as much about a particular newspaper as it did about the case. In the *New York Times*, too, Nathan Leopold's interrogation was page-one news on May 30, but minus the melodrama of the Chicago papers. Tersely, the paper characterized Leopold as "a student at the University of Chicago and an advanced thinker." It reported that he had admitted to ownership of the glasses and to "roaming about the prairie in the vicinity of the place where the Franks boy's body was found," and then concluded, somewhat redundantly, that "Examination developed the fact that he considered himself an advanced thinker and that he professed atheism."

**[MR. CROWE:] Q** Are you a member of any established church?

**[MR. LEOPOLD:] A** No, sir.

**Q** What if any religious belief do you entertain?

**A** None.

**Q** What is your idea of the existence of a God?

**A** I do not believe there is a God.

**Q** If you die, what becomes of you?

**A** Your ashes return to ashes, and dust to dust.

**Q** Is there any difference between my death and the death of a dog?

**A** No, sir.

**Q** In other words, when I die, I am dead all over?

**A** Naturally, dead.

**Q** There is no hereafter or any hope of return or reward or punishment?

**A** That is my belief.

**Q** For how long have you entertained that belief?

**A** Some seven or eight years.

**Q** You began to arrive at that conclusion between what ages?

**A** I should say around eleven.

**Q** And you have given some thought and study to that matter?

**A** Yes.

**Q** And you are what is popularly termed as an atheist?

**A** Yes, sir.

**Q** It is your belief, is it not, you expressed to me some time ago, that a God was created by the head of a tribe who was not powerful enough to punish all the crime and misdoings of his people, and he wanted them to believe that if anybody disobeyed him, after they died somebody with a longer beard or a bigger sword or bigger club would get them afterwards?

**A** That is a very plausible theory, so far as I know.

**Q** You express it somewhat better than I do; but substantially in that way?

**A** That is what my opinion is; but of course, it is only a theory.

**Q** The only way you can demonstrate that Christ exists is to die?

**A** Yes, sir.

# 12
# A falling out of
# cocksuckers
## THE INCRIMINATING LETTER

THE INTERROGATION then turns to the subject of the letter detectives had found in their search of Leopold's bedroom, which had tipped them off to the possibility of Leopold and Loeb being in a sexual relationship—which they in turn connected to the possibility of Bobby Franks's kidnapping having been sexually motivated. The Confessions includes the full text of the letter, with Robert Crowe reading it aloud to Leopold and stopping to ask for his clarification of various points. The text was also leaked to reporters, and all the Chicago papers quoted it verbatim (or slightly abridged for length), except that the phrase "a falling out of cocksuckers" was excised and left to readers' imaginations.

**[MR. CROWE:] Q** You have been pretty friendly with Rubel?

**[MR. LEOPOLD:] A** Yes, sir.

**Q** What is his first name?

**A** Richard.

**Q** And you have been very friendly with Dick Loeb?

**A** Yes, sir.

**Q** Have you ever had any trouble with Dick Loeb or Rubel recently?

**A** Any trouble?

**Q** Ever had any misunderstandings?

**A** Little ones, yes.

**Q** When?

**A** Well, I remember about last September or October, we had a little misunderstanding.

**Q** What was that about?

**A** Well, it was about a date for last New Year's Eve.

**Q** This was in October, you say?

**A** Yes; we had the date last spring, probably, in April or May.

**Q** For the following January?

**A** The following January first.

**Q** What was the misunderstanding in October?

**A** We had a date to go out together, and my statement is this: Something better came along, and he went with other parties, and left me in the lurch.

## THE AGE OF FLIPPERS AND FLAPPERS

To frame its slightly abridged account of the letter from Nathan Leopold to Richard Loeb the detectives had found in Leopold's room, the May 31 *Chicago Daily Tribune* described the friendship between Leopold and Loeb as springing from Leopold's loneliness as an isolated intellectual who, in this age of "flippers and flappers," preferred as companions "the tested great of the library for the temporarily famous of the campus." Yet in Loeb, he had found another youth of "unusual mental attainments." Together, the two had made many excursions together to watch birds, the paper claimed, and "thus watching birds and living with his friends of the book shelves and the stuffed specimens in his private museum, young Nathan esteemed his friend Richard more than do those who have many friends."

**Q** October; that wasn't the first of January?

**A** That is true, but most people, I guess, make dates for a year in advance for New Year's Eve.

**Q** Who told you in October he was going to change the plan?

**A** He did.

**Q** Who did?

**A** Dick. Isn't it Dick Rubel you are talking about?

**Q** Well, I don't know.

**A** Yes, Dick Rubel.

**Q** What misunderstanding and what words did you have about it?

**A** Do you want the entire circumstances?

**Q** Yes.

**A** Of course, I should give you my side of the story, naturally; of course, Dick Loeb and Dick Rubel and I have been pretty close friends for some time; we have palled around, the three of us, quite a bit. Last summer Dick Rubel was not in town; we made this date, we had decided definitely just what we would do, whether we would go to the Drake [Hotel] or something like that, or whether we would go to a cabaret; but anyhow, we knew we were going to be together. And this summer Dick Rubel went to Dick Loeb's home; and Dick Loeb at that time was friendly with a young lady who was quite young, and her best friend was also about her age; and Dick Loeb's girl's mother didn't want to let her go out on New Year's Eve, particularly alone with one couple, she would much prefer to have two; and they thought they would go out together with the two girls, they thought they could put it over on me and let it go at that, and I didn't like it very much, because I didn't think it was a very nice thing to do; and I had some words with Dick Rubel, and Dick Loeb about it; but it was all settled.

**Q** Did you write any letter to either one of them?

**A** Yes, I did; I wrote Dick Loeb a letter.

**Q** And the trouble was with Rubel and not with Loeb?

**A** The trouble originally was with Loeb; but I knew it was Loeb that was getting him to change his mind.

**Q** Did you ever commit any act of perversion on either one of these boys?

**A** No, sir.

**Q** Or they on you?

**A** No, sir.

**Q** You are positive of that?

**A** I am positive of that.

**Q** There wasn't any rumor around that you had?

**A** Yes, sir.

**Q** Of some act of perversion on Loeb?

**A** Yes, sir.

At this point Crowe shows Leopold the letter to Loeb detectives found in Leopold's bedroom.

**Q** Is that your handwriting?

**A** Yes, sir.

**Q** When did you write that?

**A** I think that is the letter which got to Dick Loeb, I don't know just the date, probably it is dated.

**Q** When?

**A** Wait a moment. I can remember the date; it was in the month of October.

**Q** This reads as follows: "Dear Dick: in view of our former relations, I take it for granted that it is unnecessary to make any excuse for writing you at this time, and still I am going to state my reasons for so doing, as this may turn out to be a long letter, and I don't want to cause you the inconvenience of reading it all to find out what it contains, if you are not interested in the subjects." Do you remember that?

**A** Yes.

**Q** "First I am enclosing the document which I mentioned to you today." What was that document?

**A** I'll be darned if I remember. Probably Dick might.

**Q** "Which I will explain later. Second, I am going to tell you of a new fact which has come up since our discussion, and which I am going to put in writing, what my attitude toward our present relation is, with a view of avoiding future possible misunderstandings, and in the hope"—

**A** May I read it to you? Probably I can decipher it, I probably can help you out.

**Q** "(Though I think it rather vain) that possibly we may have misunderstood each other, and yet clear this matter up.

"Now, as to the first: I wanted you this afternoon and still want you to feel that we are on an equal footing legally." What do you mean by legally?

**A** Well, that was just about a month after I had entered the law school, and I was pretty full up to the neck with torts.

**Q** "And therefore I purposely committed the same tort of which you were guilty, the only difference being that in your case the fact"—what was that tort?

**A** Well, I think in this discussion that we had had, I was sitting in Dick's automobile out at school, and against my will he took me down to his house in the automobile and refused to let me get out; false imprisonment, it was.

**Q** Did you commit the same one?

**A** I did, purposely.

**Q** That was just a case of one fellow driving along with the other fellow without his consent?

**A** I refused to let him out, and so forth; yes.

**Q** "The only difference being that in your case the facts would be harder to prove than in mine, should I deny them." How would it be easier to prove the facts in your case than to prove the facts in his?

**A** The other way around; I didn't drive him, but locked him in my room.

**Q** "The enclosed document should secure against changing my mind in admitting the facts if the matter should come up, as it would prove to any court that they were true." Were you figuring that you were going to have a lawsuit about this?

**A** Absolutely not. We were very formal; we had had a misunderstanding, and we were very formal about it.

**Q** "As to the second: On your suggestion, I immediately phoned Dick Rubel, and speaking from a paper prepared beforehand (to be sure of the exact wording) said, 'Dick when we were together yesterday, did I tell you that Dick (Loeb) had told me the things which I then told you, or that it was merely my opinion that I believed them to be so.'" What were those?

**A** The questions about the facts of how much Dick Loeb refused to get Rubel to change his date; and they tried to deceive me about having done it.

**Q** "I asked this twice, to make sure he understood, and on the same answer both times (which I took down as he spoke), showed that he did understand. He replied, 'No, you did not tell me that, Dick told you these things, but said that they were in your opinion true'.

"He further denied telling you subsequently that I had said that they were gleaned from conversation with you, and I then told him that he was quite right, that you never had told me. I further told him that this was merely your suggestion of how to settle a question of fact, that he was in no way implicated, and that neither of us would be angry with him at his reply (I imply your assent).

"This, of course, proves that you were mistaken this afternoon in the question of my having actually technically broken confidence, and voids my apology which I made contingent on proof of this matter." What confidence had you broken?

**A** Dick Loeb had told me something about Dick Rubel, some very inconsequential things, I have forgotten what now; it might have been almost anything; something deprecatory of Dick Rubel.

**Q** "Now, as to the third, last and most important question, when you came to my home this afternoon, I expected either to break friendship with you or attempt to kill you unless you told me why you acted as you did yesterday." What about that threat to kill him?

**A** That is common colloquialism, having a scrap might have killed him.

**Q** You are a student of law, you are a pretty fairly educated fellow, and pretty bright minded boy, as things go, aren't you?

**A** Yes, I think so.

**Q** "I expected to break friendship with you or attempt to kill you unless you told me why you acted as you did yesterday. You did, however, tell me; and hence the question shifted to the fact that I would act as before if you persisted in thinking me treacherous, either in act (which you waived, if Dick's opinion went with mine) or intention. Now, I apprehend, though here I am not quite sure, that you said that you did not think me treacherous in intent, nor ever had, but that you considered me in the wrong and expected such a statement from me. This statement I unconditionally refuse to make, until such time as I may become convinced of its truth. However, the question of our relations I think must be in your hands, unless the above conceptions are mistaken, inasmuch as you have satisfied first, then one and then the other requirement upon which I agree to refrain from attempting to kill you or refusing to continue our friendship. Hence I have no reason not to continue to be on friendly terms with you, and would under ordinary conditions continue as before.

"The only question then is with you; you demand me to perform an act, namely state that I acted wrongly. This I refuse. Now, it is up to you to inflict the penalty for this refusal—at your discretion, to break friendship, inflict physical punishment or anything else you like, or on the other hand to continue as before. The decision, therefore, must rest with you.

"This is all of my opinion on the right of way of the matter. Now, comes a practical question. I think that I would ordinarily be expected to and, in fact I do expect to continue in attitude toward you as before, until I learn rather by direct words or by conduct on your part which way your decision has been formed. This I shall do.

"Now a word of advice. I do not wish to influence your decision either way, but I do want to warn you that in case you deem it advisable to discontinue our friendship, that in both of our interests extreme care must be used. The motif of a 'falling out of cocksuckers?' "

**A** Refers to that very perversion, roughly.

**Q** Falling out of thieves; when thieves fall out, honest men get their dues?

**A** Of course, it is still from that adage.

**Q** Where had you heard the expression falling out of cocksuckers?

**A** I never had.

**Q** Is there any significance in that?

**A** It was exactly, that refers to the rumor which was spread about the two of us, as I mentioned in 1921, which was very prevalent, as a result of which Dick and I were very careful when we were alone together for over a year, in fact, we were very seldom alone together, and when we were, we took a chaperon along.

**Q** "Falling out of cocksuckers would be sure to be popular, which is patently undesirable"—you read it.

**A** (Reading) "—undesirable, and forms an unknown but unavoidable bond between us, therefore it is in my humble expedient, though our breach need be no less real in fact, yet to observe the conventionalities such as salutation on the street and the general appearance of at least not unfriendly relations on all occasions when we may be thrown together in public.

"Now Dick, I am going to make a request to which I have perhaps no right, and yet which I dare to make also for auld lang syne. Will you, if not too inconvenient, let me know your answer before I leave tomorrow, on the last count? This, to which I have no right, would greatly help my peace of mind in the next five days, when it is most necessary to me. You can, if you will merely call up my home before twelve noon, and leave a message saying 'Dick says yes', if you wish our relations to continue as before, and 'Dick says no', if not.

"It is unnecessary to add that your decision will, of course, have no effect on my keeping to myself our confidence of the past, and that I regret the whole affair more than I can say.

BEFORE I LEAVE TOMORROW: Leopold was traveling to Cambridge, Massachusetts, to deliver lectures for the Anthropological Society.

"Hoping not to have caused you too much trouble in reading this, I am,

"(For the present), as ever,

"Babe."

**Q** You have got two statements in there that you are failing to get even, though you and he do part, anyway for appearance's sake, that he pretend to be a friend of yours.

**A** Otherwise, there would have been a great deal of talk.

**Q** Cocksuckers falling out?

**A** Yes.

**Q** Don't you think that two young men of your standing and his standing, referring to a misunderstanding, and a parting of the ways between you, a falling out of cocksuckers is the same?

**A** That was in quotation marks, either actually or to be read as such; that is what I say would be the opinion of the talk, small talk, a great many of our friends, it seems we each, that we had a great number of friends, and one person who for reasons which we had tried to figure out, was decidedly malicious towards both of us, spread such a rumor as this, and as I say, we have tried to trace the source, and the most radical explanation I can possibly find is that possibly it is just an agreeable thing, associating among my friends, it may have been uttered in such a way in the presence of a number of people and in that way misinterpreted.

**Q** If a man called you a cocksucker what would you do?

**A** I would do my best to knock his block off under ordinary circumstances.

**Q** The same as if he called you a son of a bitch?

**A** Yes, if I thought he meant it.

**Q** I have heard the words son of a bitch being used as a term of endearment, but I never heard a man call another a cocksucker. You use pretty good language, you are a man of refinement, education, culture, come of a very honest family, the boys with whom you associate are all well bred boys, aren't they?

**A** Not in their conversation, it doesn't seem to be a part of good breeding nowadays.

**Q** Is it a habit among you boys to call each other cocksuckers?

**A** Sure.

**Q** They don't resent that?

**A** Certainly not. Hasn't an old friend ever come up to you and slapped you on the back and say, "Hello, you old son of a bitch," or "You old bastard," or something like that?

**Q** I say I have heard of a fellow being called a son of a bitch in terms of endearment, the fellow was only [this word is crossed out, with the word "always" penciled in above] smiling when he called it to me. There had been rumors that you were a cocksucker?

**A** Yes, sir.

**Q** Don't you think that that added fact would cause you to resent very sharply any fellow calling you a cocksucker?

**A** After I found it out, yes.

**Q** You knew that you had been charged with being a cocksucker several years ago?

**A** Yes.

**Q** So in the last two or three years you would resent very sharply anybody calling you a cocksucker?

**A** And supposing that rumor had been circulated among, say, two or three hundred of your intimate friends or your more intimate acquaintances, it was a habit and custom of society to use that term of endearment, what would be the effect of your flaring up and trying to knock the dickens out of a man that called you that?

**Q** It is pretty hard for me to be realizing anybody in a position of having a fellow circulate that rumor about me for several years and then persist in calling me a cocksucker.

**A** I haven't seen the man since that we have been trying to get, and I was talking about that, and I was trying to do everything in my power to knock Hell out of this man.

# 13

# This has got me pretty worried

## THE LINK TO THE UNDERWOOD PORTABLE TYPEWRITER

A MAJOR SCOOP

*Chicago Daily News* reporters James Mulroy and Alvin Goldstein—who also happened to be fellow students and friends with Richard Loeb at the University of Chicago—later won a Pulitzer Prize for their work on this case, not just for reporting on, but actually for helping to solve the crime. After Bobby Franks's disappearance, Mulroy was the first to talk to Sam Ettelson as Ettelson waited with Jacob Franks at the Franks home to hear more from the kidnappers, and when the newspaper sent Goldstein down to the funeral home where the body of the unidentified boy was taken the morning it was found in the culvert in Indiana, it was Mulroy who conveyed the news about the body to the family and suggested they send someone to see whether it was Bobby's.

Hearing that Nathan Leopold had been part of a law school study group whose notes he usually typed up, it was Goldstein who thought to ask a group member for the notes to see whether the type matched that of the ransom note. As the *Daily News* then reported in its triumphant scoop on May 30, "A typewriter expert was summoned into consultation by the police. After a microscopic examination of both samples, he tentatively announced that he thought one machine had produced both."

AFTER TWO ENTERPRISING *Chicago Daily News* reporters matched the type on the ransom note with the notes typed up by Leopold in his law school study group (notes that were referred to by the study group, and in the interrogation text below, as "dope sheets"), Leopold was forced to admit that he had in fact recently had an Underwood portable typewriter in his house. But he insisted that he had no idea where it had come from and that it must have belonged to one of the other boys in the group, which is why he could not explain where it was at that moment. So Robert Crowe had his detectives round up all the other boys, and the transcript shows Crowe and Assistant State's Attorney Joseph P. Savage, along with Assistant State's Attorney Robert McMillan and Police Captain William Schoemaker, bringing the study-group members into the room with Leopold one by one to confront him. Sam Ettelson, the friend of both the Franks and Leopold families who had initially thought Leopold's involvement with the crime preposterous, is also present at this session, and his exchange with Leopold toward the end makes it clear that they both see the noose beginning to tighten around Leopold's neck.

**[MR. CROWE:] Q** Now, Nathan, looking at the Underwood, Corona and Remington typewriters, which one would you say of the three is the portable that you worked on out at your room?

**[MR. LEOPOLD:] A** The Underwood.

**Q** You are quite sure of that, are you?

**A** Absolutely.

**Q** Well, look at that Underwood, now. Are you sure it was an Underwood that you worked on?

**A** Practically sure.

**Q** Do you remember whose typewriter that was, Nathan?

**A** I cannot; I have been trying like hell to.

**Q** Now, Nathan, what is that boy's name, [Maurice] Shanberg, that is one of the boys?

**A** Yes.

**MR. CROWE:** Have Shanberg come in.

(Whereupon Shanberg entered the room.)

**MR. CROWE:** Sit down, Shanberg. You know Nathan Leopold, Jr.?

**MR. SHANBERG:** Yes.

**MR. CROWE:** You and Nathan have always been good friends?

**MR. SHANBERG:** Well, always since at school, I met him at school.

**MR. CROWE:** Your first name is what?

James Mulroy (left) of the *Chicago Daily News*, who would later get the Pulitzer Prize along with Alvin Goldstein (right) for his work on this case. It was Mulroy who, having talked his way inside the Franks house on the morning after Bobby's disappearance, got a tip from his editor about the body in the Indiana morgue and convinced Ettelson that it was worth checking out, although no one yet had reason to believe that Bobby was not—as the kidnapper "Mr. Johnson" claimed—still alive.

**MR. SHANBERG:** Morris [should be "Maurice"].

**MR. CROWE:** Where do you live?

**MR. SHANBERG:** 843 Lafayette Parkway.

**MR. CROWE:** Now, Shanberg, during your law course at the University of Chicago, you had occasion to go over and work on the dope sheets with Nathan from time to time; is that right?

**MR. SHANBERG:** Yes.

**MR. SAVAGE:** And there was yourself and—

**MR. SHANBERG:** There was three more fellows.

**MR. SAVAGE:** Who were the three more?

**MR. SHANBERG:** Mr. [Arnold] Maremont, [Howard] Oberndorf [should be "Obendorf"] and [Lester] Abelson.

**MR. SAVAGE:** And the five of you folks worked together over there on various dope sheets, and one in particular was the equity work; is that right?

**MR. SHANBERG:** Yes.

**MR. SAVAGE:** By dope sheet, you mean that is preparatory work?

**MR. SHANBERG:** Briefing the course as a whole.

**MR. SAVAGE:** Now, do you remember at any time, Shanberg, of seeing a typewriter, a portable typewriter over at Nathan's house?

**MR. SHANBERG:** Only on one occasion; that was the last time I was there.

**MR. SAVAGE:** Prior to working on that portable typewriter, you worked with this Hammond typewriter; is that right?

**MR. SHANBERG:** Yes.

**MR. SAVAGE:** And who operated the typewriter?

**MR. SHANBERG:** Mr. Leopold, except on occasions when Mr. Leopold went to the phone.

**MR. SAVAGE:** And then Mr. Maremont operated it?

**MR. LEOPOLD:** Pardon me, I don't know if you were there, Shanberg, but I think on other occasions Mr. Maremont operated the typewriter.

**MR. SHANBERG:** Yes.

**MR. LEOPOLD:** Yes.

**MR. SAVAGE:** Now, looking over the typewriters that are sitting on the desk there, which one would you say of the three was the one that was used there after you stopped using the Hammond?

**MR. SHANBERG:** I think that one (indicating) is the one that resembles it most closely.

**MR. SAVAGE:** Referring to the Underwood?

**MR. SHANBERG:** Yes.

**MR. SAVAGE:** Now, did you ever own a typewriter, Mr. Shanberg?

**MR. SHANBERG:** No.

**MR. SAVAGE:** Did you ever bring one over to Nathan's house?

**MR. SHANBERG:** No, sir.

**MR. SAVAGE:** Nathan, is there anything that you want to ask Shanberg that may refresh his memory in some way as to the typewriter?

**MR. LEOPOLD:** Where was the Underwood the last time it was used, that one time?

**MR. SHANBERG:** That was the only time that we worked downstairs there; I cannot say whether that was down there or not—

**CAPT. SCHOEMAKER:** Just answer the question that he put to you.

**MR. SAVAGE:** Well, the time that he was there and they worked with the Underwood, it was downstairs on that table?

**MR. SHANBERG:** Yes, in one corner of the room.

**MR. SAVAGE:** Now, Nathan, is there anything that you can think of that may refresh Shanberg's mind, so that he would have a recollection as to the time you were doing that, or where you got the typewriter from?

**MR. LEOPOLD:** No, except that he says that was the first time that we doped equity. It must have been sometime between January—well, it must have been some time between February first and March 15th.

**MR. LEOPOLD:** That is all I have.

**MR. SAVAGE:** All right, Shanberg; will you move out, please?

**CAPT. SCHOEMAKER:** You see this, here (indicating)?

**MR. SHANBERG:** Yes.

**CAPT. SCHOEMAKER:** You remember that was written in Leopold's house?

**MR. SHANBERG:** Yes, sir.

**CAPT. SCHOEMAKER:** And who wrote this?

**MR. SHANBERG:** Mr. Leopold.

**CAPT. SCHOEMAKER:** And he wrote it on a portable?

**MR. SHANBERG:** Portable typewriter.

**CAPT. SCHOEMAKER:** Where is that machine at, Leopold?

**MR. LEOPOLD:** I have no idea.

**CAPT. SCHOEMAKER:** Well, what became of it?

**MR. LEOPOLD:** I don't know.

**CAPT. SCHOEMAKER:** You had it, didn't you?

**MR. LEOPOLD:** Yes.

**CAPT. SCHOEMAKER:** Well, what did you do with it?

**MR. LEOPOLD:** I didn't do anything with it.

**CAPT. SCHOEMAKER:** Well, where is it?

**MR. LEOPOLD:** I don't know.

**CAPT. SCHOEMAKER: Q** Whose is it?
**A** I don't know.

**Q** You don't know; well, you will get that machine, see?
**A** All right; but I don't know where it is.

**Q** Well, you will get it, or we will get it.
**A** All right.

**CAPT. SCHOEMAKER:** Well, that ends that.

(At this point <u>Arnold Maremont</u> entered room.)

One by one, the rest of the study-group members are brought in: after Maremont, Abelson, then Obendorf. Each is asked in front of Leopold to look at the three sample typewriters on the desk—a Corona, a Remington, and an Underwood portable—and identify the machine the notes were typed on. Each is asked whether he owned or has ever brought to Leopold's house a portable typewriter, and Leopold is given a chance to question each of them in turn. The tone up to that point seems polite, even cordial, but when all the study-group members have left, it grows more antagonistic as the interrogators' frustration with Leopold begins to boil over and Schoemaker springs an incriminating piece of information he's gotten from the family maid.

**CAPT. SCHOEMAKER:** How long did you have that portable in your house?

**MR. LEOPOLD:** I believe several weeks.

**CAPT. SCHOEMAKER:** Well, it is still there, as far as you know?

**MR. LEOPOLD:** As far as I know, except I have not noticed it.

**CAPT. SCHOEMAKER:** You never got rid of it in any way?

**MR. LEOPOLD:** No.

**MR. SAVAGE:** Nathan, I asked you to tell me the names of the boys, and you did; and we have made a check on that, now. Now, you are satisfied from our check that none of those boys are the ones that brought that machine to the house?

**MR. LEOPOLD:** Unless they are scared to death.

**MR. ETTELSON:** Why should they be scared?

**MR. LEOPOLD:** It is a pretty nasty thing to be tangled up in.

**MR. ETTELSON:** Well, they are not tangled up in it.

**MR. LEOPOLD:** Three or four of them are positively nervous.

**MR. ETTELSON:** They are not more nervous than you are; I think you are the most nervous in the bunch.

**MR. LEOPOLD:** Well, I am nervous. I don't think Arnold was nervous, but I thought Howard was nervous and I think Shanberg and I think Abelson was.

**MR. SAVAGE:** Nathan, I understood you to say that the typewriter had been taken out again by the boy that brought it in.

**MR. LEOPOLD:** That was my assumption.

**MR. SAVAGE:** You just assumed that?

**MR. LEOPOLD:** Yes.

**MR. SAVAGE:** You don't know whether it was actually taken out or not?

**MR. LEOPOLD:** No, I do not.

**MR. SAVAGE:** Or you don't know when it was taken out, if it ever was taken out?

**MR. LEOPOLD:** No, I don't.

**MR. SAVAGE:** Do you ever remember the typewriter coming in?

**MR. LEOPOLD:** I do not.

**MR. SAVAGE:** Do you remember under what circumstances it could have come into the house?

**MR. LEOPOLD:** Only those I named, I cannot think of any other possible circumstances.

**MR. SAVAGE:** It would hardly come into the house without some comment at the time the machine was brought there; what I mean is, that one would hardly come in and leave a typewriter at your home without saying something about it, or message?

**MR. LEOPOLD:** I should not think so.

**MR. SAVAGE:** So, keeping that in mind, can you recollect the time that the machine was brought into your house?

**MR. LEOPOLD:** I am absolutely unable to, Mr. Savage; I have tried my very hardest.

**[CAPT.] SCHOEMAKER:** Just a moment. You have got a maid in your house, haven't you?

**MR. LEOPOLD:** Yes.

**CAPT. SCHOEMAKER:** Named Elizabeth [Sattler], isn't she?

**MR. LEOPOLD:** Yes.

**CAPT. SCHOEMAKER:** And Elizabeth is a good, truthful girl, isn't she?

**MR. LEOPOLD:** So far as I know.

**CAPT. SCHOEMAKER:** She wouldn't lie, would she?

**MR. LEOPOLD:** No.

**CAPT. SCHOEMAKER:** Did she ever see this portable machine, that you know of?

**MR. LEOPOLD:** Not that I know of, but I supposed she has seen it.

**CAPT. SCHOEMAKER:** I suppose she has, because she told me she had, when I talked to her today.

**MR. LEOPOLD:** I see.

**CAPT. SCHOEMAKER:** And she said it was there two weeks ago, she seen it, this portable machine?

**MR. LEOPOLD:** Yes?

**CAPT. SCHOEMAKER:** With you.

**MR. LEOPOLD:** Yes?

**CAPT. SCHOEMAKER:** She seen it with you, two weeks ago.

**MR. LEOPOLD:** Yes.

**CAPT. SCHOEMAKER:** So where is the machine? That is all I want to know.

**MR. LEOPOLD:** I would like to know, too. It is probably in the house.

**CAPT. SCHOEMAKER:** Yes, probably in the house.

**MR. LEOPOLD:** Does she know where it is now?

**CAPT. SCHOEMAKER:** I don't know. She said you had it. She is not planting the machine any place, it was in your hands.

**MR. SAVAGE:** Nathan, can you say here now where that machine could possibly be in the house?

**MR. LEOPOLD:** There are only about four or five likely places in the house where it could be.

**CAPT. SCHOEMAKER:** Mark those down.

**MR. LEOPOLD:** The first would be upstairs, in my suite.

**CAPT. SCHOEMAKER:** And then in his room on the second floor.

**MR. LEOPOLD:** Yes.

**CAPT. SCHOEMAKER:** And then in his closet.

**MR. LEOPOLD:** Yes.

**CAPT. SCHOEMAKER:** And then in the telephone room.

**MR. LEOPOLD:** Yes.

**CAPT. SCHOEMAKER:** And where else?

**MR. LEOPOLD:** That is all.

**CAPT. SCHOEMAKER:** Now, listen; when Elizabeth told me that you had that portable typewriter two weeks ago, is that true?

**MR. LEOPOLD:** If she says so, it probably is. I don't recollect.

**CAPT. SCHOEMAKER:** Well, my God, didn't I tell you she said so?

**MR. LEOPOLD:** Yes.

**CAPT. SCHOEMAKER:** Well, is it true?

**MR. LEOPOLD:** I suppose it is.

**CAPT. SCHOEMAKER:** If you had it two weeks ago, what were you doing with it two weeks ago?

**MR. LEOPOLD:** Probably operating.

**CAPT. SCHOEMAKER:** Probably operating?

**MR. LEOPOLD:** Yes.

**CAPT. SCHOEMAKER:** Where at?

**MR. LEOPOLD:** I don't know.

**CAPT. SCHOEMAKER:** Why, you are an absent-minded boy?

**MR. LEOPOLD:** Certainly not; but I don't happen to remember the occasion.

**CAPT. SCHOEMAKER:** You lose your memory, do you?

(No response.)

**MR. SAVAGE:** I am going to give you credit for one thing: I think you have got the most remarkable memory of any man I ever came in contact with, for age or otherwise. Now, I sat and listened to you yesterday go back three and four weeks, and in detail minutely describe your actions as to just what you had done day in and day out, what you did this day and what you did that day, and in detail. Can't you think, Nathan, where that typewriter came, how it happened to come into the house, and how it happened to go out, or whether it is still there?

**MR. LEOPOLD:** I think very probably that if I had been present when the typewriter was brought in the house and when, if a remark was made about it, that I should probably remember it, yes; but—

**MR. SAVAGE:** Well, Nathan, you know, even if you weren't present, there would be something come up there in the way of a letter or note or telephone conversation, or something else, telling you that the typewriter was there; and you are not one who will forget dates or times or anything else.

**MR. LEOPOLD:** No. I will tell you, this has got me pretty worried.

**MR. ETTELSON:** Well, I think it would worry you a little bit.

**MR. LEOPOLD:** I am sorry, I am doing the best I can. I don't remember when or how that typewriter got in or out.

**MR. ETTELSON:** I think you are doing the best you can. The question is, whether you are doing well enough.

There is one more exchange about the typewriter, in which Leopold suggests that his friend Leon Mandel—with whom he worked for a while translating the Aretino materials before that book project was abandoned—might have been the person who brought the typewriter into his house. But Mandel left for Europe on his honeymoon in early May, and the maid said she saw the typewriter in the Leopold house within the past two weeks; Crowe therefore points out to Leopold that Mandel couldn't possibly have taken the typewriter away in the past two weeks if he's in Europe on his honeymoon.

**[MR. ETTELSON:] Q** And if you fellows and the maid don't know a damned thing about it, the chances are nobody ever came and got it?

**[MR. LEOPOLD:] A** Absolutely.

**Q** That machine ought to be there now?

**A** It ought to.

**Q** The fact that that letter that Franks got was written on the same machine that some of your stuff was written on, and the fact that experts say that the same person wrote it might be a damned good reason for you in losing that machine.

**A** Certainly.

**Q** And knowing nothing about it?

**A** Certainly.

# 14
# He is a liar or mistaken

## LOEB IN DENIAL

S VEN ENGLUND, the Leopold family's chauffeur, went down to the Criminal Court Building to talk to State's Attorney Robert Crowe fully expecting that his testimony would exonerate Leopold. How could Leopold have driven the murdered boy's body down to a field in Indiana if Englund could swear that he had in fact left the car home all day so that Englund could fix the brakes? He—and Leopold's family—was unaware that the story Leopold had told his questioners about the day of the murder involved driving around town most of the day in Leopold's maroon Willys-Knight automobile. After Englund's statement, Crowe realizes that their alibi was false, and at 1 a.m. on Saturday, May 31, he confronts Loeb—who has been under questioning in a separate room—with this information. Loeb turns pale but, for the moment, continues to stonewall. Although detectives had been interrogating him prior to his confession, there is no known transcript of those interrogations. The confession below is the full text of Loeb's first recorded statement. Assistant State's Attorney Joseph P. Savage and Chief of Detectives Michael Hughes are also in the room, along with shorthand reporter E.M. Allen.

**MR. CROWE: Q** Now, Loeb, you told me that Wednesday, you drove down town Wednesday, the 25th [should be the 21st], you drove down town with this young fellow Leopold, in his car, that is a sport model, it is a red car with a tan top, a Willys-Knight?

**[MR. LOEB:] A** Yes.

**Q** You left the school around eleven o'clock?

**A** Yes, sir.

**Q** Or some time after eleven, between eleven o'clock and noon, and you had lunch at the grill room at Marshall Field's?

**A** Yes, sir.

**Q** Yes or no?

**A** Yes.

**Q** Then you went out to Lincoln Park?

**A** Yes, sir.

**Q** And that all the driving you did this day was in this car?

**A** Yes, sir.

**Q** You didn't have a car yourself, did you?

**A** No.

**Q** You didn't drive any that day?

**A** No.

**Q** Have you got a car in your family that is a weather-beaten green?

**A** Well, my mother has a Cadillac, yes.

**Q** A Cadillac; and that is a sort of a green?

**A** Yes.

**Q** Isn't it a fact that shortly after one o'clock P.M. you drove up in the Cadillac, you driving it and Leopold driving the red car, drove to his garage; you saw the man just went out [referring to Sven Englund, who was leaving the offices]; yes or no?

**A** Yes.

**Q** Who was he?

**A** Pardon me; that "yes" was to your question that I saw the man go out.

**Q** Who is he?

**A** He is Leopold's chauffeur.

GREEN CADILLAC: Detectives did not yet realize that the green car in which Englund had seen Loeb was one that had been rented for the purpose of committing the murder so the vehicle would not be traceable to either household.

**Q** Now, isn't it a fact that Wednesday, May 21st, some time between one and a quarter after one you drove up to that garage, to Leopold's garage, you driving your mother's car, that green Cadillac, he driving the red car, and that he said to the chauffeur "The brakes squeak so much here, I want you to fix them;" he says, "I can put some oil on them and you can use the emergency, and if you are careful you will not run into anybody," and he said, "I will not run into somebody I have had that brake squeak", and you turned the car over to the chauffeur and got into your car and drove away?

**A** No.

**Q** That is not a fact?

**A** No.

**Q** If this chauffeur says so, he is a liar?

**A** Yes.

**Q** Although he has a particular reason for remembering?

**A** It is not a fact.

**Q** If the chauffeur took the car in and oiled it up, oiled the brakes and fixed it up, that would make an impression on his mind, wouldn't it?

**A** Yes.

**Q** If he says that is a fact, he is a liar or mistaken?

**A** I didn't get that.

**Q** He is a liar or he is mistaken?

**A** Yes.

**Q** Then if he has an additional reason for remembering the particular day, what would you say to that?

**A** I would say he was still a liar or mistaken.

**Q** Didn't you boys come back then somewhere around ten o'clock in the evening, and take that ~~old~~ [this word is crossed out, with the word "red" penciled in above] car out?

**A** When is all this?

**Q** Wednesday, May 21st, the date this boy disappeared; that is not true?

**A** No.

**Q** This chauffeur is mistaken?

**A** Yes.

**Q** Do you and Leopold belong to the same fraternity?

**A** No.

**Q** You are not fraternity brothers?

**A** No.

**Q** Did I ask you last night about the letter he wrote you in which he said it wouldn't do for cocksuckers to fall out?

**A** Yes, sir.

LAST NIGHT: This is in reference to the unrecorded interrogations.

**Q** What significance did you attach to that?

**A** Purely the fact that he wanted to save—that a rumor had gotten around that he was a cocksucker.

**Q** What difference would that make if there had been a rumor he had been a cocksucker and you and he had fallen out and you had quit talking to him, what difference would that make?

**A** We did everything in our power to avoid any possible scandal in regard to that thing for two years since it happened. That was three years ago when this rumor started, for two years we were very careful never to be alone together, to be seen alone together any place or to be alone together any place where we could be seen. We were careful if we wanted to go to a theater on a particular evening we would be careful to have somebody come along, purely and simply on the advice of my brother, who had told me to be careful and not to see too much of Leopold and if I did to be sure there was somebody else around.

**Q** Wasn't that an intolerable condition to exist, two fellows that were very friendly and wanted to be together and would be together without the world suspecting they were cocksuckers, and you had to have a chaperone all the time?

**A** No, it wasn't necessary.

**Q** Wouldn't it be much better for you to break off and say, "Now, there is a lot of suspicion as to our relations here, you better go your way and I will go my way and that will end all this talk and let's forget it?"

**A** We never did that, but for quite a while we saw very little of each other. It was just due to the fact that we happened to be going to the University of Chicago and that we were thrown together a great deal, it was much more pleasant.

(Confession)

# S T A T E M E N T

## o f

## N A T H A N   F .  L E O P O L D , JR.,

Made in the office of the State's Attorney of Cook County,
Criminal Court Building, Chicago, Illinois, on Saturday,
May 31, 1924, at 4:20 A. M.

- - - - - - - - - - - - - - - - - - - - - - - - - -

Present:   Joseph P. Savage, Assistant State's Attorney;

Michael Hughes, Chief of Detectives;

E. M. Allen, Shorthand Reporter.

- - - - - - - - - - - - - - - - - - - - - - - - - -

MR. SAVAGE:   Q  What is your name?

A  Nathan F. Leopold, Junior.

Q  And your address?  A   4754 Greenwood Avenue.

Q  And your business?    A    Student.

Q  Student at what school?

A  University of Chicago Law School.

Q And you have attended the University of Chicago
Law School for how long?  A   For nine months.

Q  Prior to that time, what school did you attend?

A  University of Chicago.

Q  And for how long during that period?   A    For a
year.

Q  And prior to that?    A    University of Michigan
for a year; prior to that University of Chicago for a

1.

The first page
of Leopold's
confession.

# 15
# We intended to murder him

## LEOPOLD'S ACCOUNT OF THE MURDER

SHORTLY AFTER INTERROGATING him about the Willys-Knight car, the team of questioners succeeded in convincing Loeb that he was cornered. According to his own later account, before he confessed, Loeb requested an attorney—a request Robert Crowe appears simply to have ignored. He also later claimed that Crowe had assured him that if he came clean, he could be saved. Once Leopold was informed that Loeb had broken down and told Crowe details about the murder only Loeb could possibly have known, he too begins to talk. Though it begins 20 minutes after Loeb's, Leopold's confession appears first in the document, with Assistant State's Attorney Joseph P. Savage and Chief of Detectives Michael Hughes questioning him and E.M. Allen taking shorthand. Crowe appears to have been going back and forth between the two rooms.

**MR. SAVAGE: Q** What is your name?

**[MR. LEOPOLD:] A** Nathan F. Leopold, Junior.

**Q** And your address?

**A** 4754 Greenwood Avenue.

**Q** And your business?

**A** Student.

**Q** Student at what school?

**A** University of Chicago Law School.

**Q** And you have attended the University of Chicago Law School for how long?

**A** For nine months.

**Q** Prior to that time, what school did you attend?

**A** University of Chicago.

**Q** And for how long during that period?

**A** For a year.

**Q** And prior to that?

**A** University of Michigan for a year; prior to that University of Chicago for a year; prior to that Harvard School for five years; prior to that, Douglas School for four years; prior to that, Spade School for two years.

**Q** How old are you, Nathan?

**A** Nineteen.

**Q** What is the date of your birth?

**A** November 19, 1904.

**Q** Have you any brothers, Nathan?

**A** I have two brothers.

**Q** What are their names?

**A** Foreman and Samuel Leopold.

**Q** And you have one other—

**A** Cousin who lives with us, Adolph Ballenberger.

**Q** Your father's name?

**A** Nathan F. Leopold.

**Q** What is his business?

**A** Morris Paper Mills.

**Q** Now, Nathan, I just want you to go on in your own way and tell us the story from the beginning, tell us the whole thing.

**A** When we planned a general thing of this sort, it was as long ago as last November, I guess, at least; and we started on the process of how to get the money, which was much the most difficult problem. We had, oh, several dozen different plans, all of which were not so good, for one reason or another. Finally [we] hit upon the plan of having the money thrown from a moving train, after the train had passed a given landmark. The landmark we finally chose was the factory of the Champion Manufacturing Company at 74th street and the I.C. [Illinois Central] Railroad tracks.

The next problem was the system of notification to the father. We originally planned a number of relays, in other words, the man was to receive a special delivery letter telling him that his son had been kidnapped and would be held for ransom, to secure ten thousand dollars in denominations as follows: Eight thousand dollars in fifty-dollar bills; two thousand dollars in twenty-dollar bills. He was to get old, unmarked bills, whose numbers were not in sequence. These he was to place in a cigar box, securely tied, wrapped in white paper; the ends were to be sealed with sealing wax. The reason for that was to give him the impression that the box would be delivered personally to a messenger of the real executives of the plan. He was then to receive a phone call at about one or two o'clock in the afternoon, instructing him to proceed to a "Help-Keep-The-City-Clean" box, whose location was to be definitely given; then he was to find another note which would instruct him to proceed to a drug store which had a public phone booth; he was to be called at this phone booth, the drug store being very near the I.C. tracks and given only just enough time to rush out, buy a ticket and board a through train without allowing him enough time to instruct detectives or police where he was going. In the train he was to proceed to the rear car, look in the box left for telegraph blanks for another letter. This letter instructed him to go to the rear platform of the car, face the east and look for the first large red brick factory adjacent to the tracks, which had a black water tower rearing a white inscription, "Champion". He was to count two or three after that, and then throw the box as far to the east as he could.

The next problem was getting the victim to kill. This was left undecided until the day we decided to take the most likely looking subject that came our way. The particular occasion happened to be Robert Franks. Richard was acquainted with Robert, and asked him to come over to our car for a moment. This occurred near 49th and Ellis avenue. Robert came over to the car, was introduced to me, and Richard asked him if he did not want to ride home.

Dear Sir:

Proceed immediately to the back platform of the train. Watch the east side of the track. Have your package ready. Look for the first <u>LARGE</u>, RED, BRICK factory situated immediately adjoining the tracks on the east. On top of this factory is a large, black watertower with the word CHAMPION written on it. Wait until you have COMPLETELY passed the south end of the factory - count five very rapidly and then IMMEDIATELY throw the package as far east as you can.

Remember that this is your only chance to recover your son.

Yours truly,

GEORGE JOHNSON

Loeb did actually plant this letter of instructions in the telegraph box of a train bound from Chicago to Boston, as planned, but the rest of the ransom scheme was abandoned after Bobby's body was found and identified, and the train left Chicago with the note, but without Franks on board. It was discovered accidentally on May 31, by an electrician for the Pullman Company, when the train was being inspected in the Mott Haven Yard in New York.

**Q** Richard who?

**A** Richard Loeb. He replied, no, but Richard said, "Well, get in a minute, I want to ask you about a certain tennis racket." After he had gotten in, I stepped on the gas, proceeded south on Ellis avenue to 50th street. In the meantime Richard asked Robert if he minded if we took him around the block; to which Robert said "No."

As soon as we turned the corner, Richard placed his one hand over Robert's mouth to stifle his outcries, with his right beat him on the head several times with a chisel, especially prepared for the purpose. The boy did not succumb as readily as we had believed, so for fear of being observed, Richard seized him, pulled him into the back seat. Here he forced a cloth into his mouth. Apparently the boy died instantly by suffocation shortly thereafter.

We proceeded out to Calumet Boulevard in Indiana, drove along this road that leads to Gary, being a rather deserted place. We even stopped to buy a couple of sandwiches for supper.

**Q** Where?

**A** On Calumet Boulevard at, I guess, 132nd street. The body was covered by an automobile robe which we had brought along for the purpose. We drove around up and down this road, then proceeded over the path which leads out toward Hegewisch from 108th and Avenue F to the prearranged spot for the disposal of the body.

We had previously removed the shoes, socks and trousers of the boy, leaving the shoes and the belt by the side of the road, concealed in the grass.

SHOES, SOCKS AND TROUSERS: This description of undressing the body in two stages struck Crowe as especially disturbing. Despite the coroner's opinion, he maintained in his closing argument that it strongly suggested sexual molestation (see chapter 64, page 238).

Having arrived at our destination, we placed the body in the road, carried it to the culvert where it was found. Here we completed the disrobing; then in an attempt to render identification more difficult, poured hydrochloric acid over the face and body. Then we placed the body into the drain pipe, pushed it in as far as we could. We gathered up all the clothes, placed them in the robe.

Apparently at this point the glasses fell from my pocket.

I carried the robe containing the clothes back to the automobile, a distance of some 300 yards, one of the socks apparently dropping from the bundle.

We then proceeded north to 104th and Ewing avenue, from where I telephoned my folks, telling them that I should be a trifle late in arriving home. We then drove to 47th and Woodlawn, and from there I telephoned the Franks home. I spoke to Mrs. Franks and told her that my name was George Johnson; that her boy had been kidnapped but was safe, and that further instructions would follow.

In passing 55th street, we had mailed the special delivery letter, which had been completed except for the address, which I printed on. After taking my aunt and uncle home, I returned to my home, and after my father had retired, Richard and I proceeded to his home, where we burned the remaining clothes, hid the robe and washed the more obvious bloodstains from the automobile.

CHICAGO TIME: Although the city of Chicago adopted daylight savings time in 1920, trains continued to run on central standard time all year round. The murder took place during daylight savings time, thus "Chicago time" is one hour ahead.

Then I parked the automobile near my home. The next day at two-thirty Central time, or three-thirty Chicago time, we were down at the Illinois Central station at 12th street. Here Richard bought a ticket to Michigan City on the three o'clock train, entered the train and deposited the letter in the telegraph box.

In the meantime, I called the Franks' home, told Mr. Franks to proceed immediately to a drug store at 1465 East 63rd street, and to wait at the more easterly of the two public phone booths for a telephone call. I told him a Yellow cab would be at his door to take him; I repeated the number twice, and he asked if he couldn't have a little more time, to which I replied no, it must be immediately.

About the time I was finished, Richard had returned from the train, and he started out south intending to call the drug store from Walgreen's drug store at 67th and Stony Island.

We chanced to see a newspaper lying on the stand with headlines, "Unidentified Boy Found in Swamp." We deliberated a few moments as to what to do, Dick thinking that the game was up. I, however, insisted that it could do no harm to call the drug store. This I did, but was told that no Mr. Franks was in the building.

We then went to 60th and Stony Island, another drug store, and again telephoned. We met with the same reply; then gave it up as a bad job, and returned the car to the place where it had been rented. Our original plan had included a relay which was to send Mr. Franks to a "Help-Keep-The-City-Clean" box at the corner of Vincennes at Pershing; but we had difficulty in making the envelope stick to the cover of the box as we intended, and hence decided to eliminate this relay.

Thursday, immediately after dinner, we drove the car to our garage, started to clean up the rest of the blood stains. Our chauffeur, Sven Englund, noticed us, and came out to help; whereupon Richard told him it was merely some red wine which had been spilled.

**Q** Who did clean it up?

**A** Dick did most of it, and I helped him.

**Q** Is there anything else you can think of at this time?

**A** No.

Savage continues to question Leopold about various details of the murder. The only questions about motive come at the very end of the session:

**[MR. SAVAGE:] Q** You at no time struck Robert Franks at all?

**A** No, sir.

**Q** You at no time choked him?

**A** No, sir.

**Q** At the time you conceived kidnapping some young fellow around there, did you intend to murder him, what was your intention, to murder him first and hide the body?

**A** No, we intended to murder him.

**Q** Your intentions were to murder him and hide the body and collect the money afterwards?

**A** Yes.

**Q** That was the general plan?

**A** Yes.

**Q** Why did you conceive that idea? Why did you intend to murder him?

**A** Because he couldn't expose us.

**Q** What did you intend to do with the money, the ten thousand dollars, when you collected it?

**A** Hide it away, either in a safety deposit box or some other safe place, for a year, and then spend it very carefully.

**Q** That was the agreement reached between you and Richard?

**A** Yes.

**Q** When Richard hit Robert first, was it down in the tonneau of the car, the bottom of the car, or was it on the seat he choked him?

**A** It was on the seat; Robert was sitting on the front seat, Dick was in the back seat.

**Q** Robert was sitting in the front with you?

**A** Yes; and Dick sort of leaned over and put his hand over his mouth, like this.

**Q** Did he pull him back in the rear?

**A** Not until later.

**Q** After he cracked him on the head, did he fall down then, Robert?

**A** No, he struggled.

**Q** Now, then, since you have been here with the Chief and the Assistant State's Attorneys and the other police officers, no one has abused you in any way, have they?

**A** No, sir.

# 16
# That is all I have to tell about the murder of Robert Franks

## LOEB'S ACCOUNT OF THE MURDER

### THE JAZZ-LIFE

In her colorful postcon-fession story for the June 1 *Chicago Sunday Tribune*, Maurine Watkins once again dis-played her considerable gifts as a dramatist. She pointed out that "'Loeb' as the name of a mur-derer falls strangely on Chicago ears," and then recounted the immi-grant family's dramatic rise from rags to riches in the United States. She claimed that Albert Loeb was so proud of his son's academic success at the University of Michigan, where at age 18 he was the youngest graduate ever, that he built Richard Loeb a miniature nine-hole golf course in the backyard of their Ellis Avenue home, and "there young Loeb 'went around' with his friends. And in that same yard he played tennis with young 'Bobby' Franks!"

Now, with Albert Loeb confined to his bed, and Anna Loeb "weeping alone," Watkins asked her readers why young men with such great advantages would have committed such a crime: "Were they bored by a life which left them nothing to be desired, no obstacles to overcome, no goal to attain? Were they jaded by the jazz-life of gin and girls, so that they needed so terrible a thing as mur-der to give them new thrills?"

**L**OEB'S CONFESSION begins by recounting the preparation that went into the crime—how the pair set up a fake bank account at the Hyde Park State Bank (see image on page 66) under the name Morton D. Ballard and used it to rent a dark green Willys-Knight car so that they would not have to use Nathan Leopold's highly recognizable maroon one. On the day before the murder, according to the transcript, he purchased rope and a chisel, while Leopold obtained a bottle of hydrochloric acid. At Leopold's house, Loeb dictated the ransom note and other commu-nications to the as-yet-unknown victim's father, based on drafts they had composed together a few days before. Leopold typed these on an Underwood portable typewriter. This excerpt begins with Loeb's account of the afternoon of Wednesday, May 21, as they slowly cruised around the neigh-borhood near the Harvard School in their rented car, looking for a victim. The shorthand reporter, F. A. Sheeder, recorded that the interrogation was performed by Assistant State's Attorney John Sbarbaro and detective William Schoemaker.

**[MR. SBARBARO:] Q** Now, you are down there on Ingleside avenue waiting for the kids to come out of the Harvard School?

**[MR. LOEB:] A** Yes. I walked over to the Harvard School to reconnoiter.

**Q** And that is about what time?

**A** Just about two-twenty.

**Q** You are over there for the purpose of reconnoitering?

**A** Yes, sir.

**Q** Go ahead.

**A** I talked to a fellow by the name of Cease [should be "Seass"; he is referring to James Seass, a part-time Harvard School instructor].

**Q** Who is this man Cease?

**A** He is the tutor who takes out the children.

**Q** After classes?

**A** In the afternoon, to supervise their play. I talked to him for a few moments, and then talked to a young boy by the name of—

**Q** What did you talk to Cease about?

**A** I don't remember.

Court evidence comparing Richard Loeb's signatures on documents related to his personal Hyde Park State Bank account (bottom) to his signature as "Morton D. Ballard" on the fake bank account (top) that he set up in order to rent the Willys-Knight car under the fake name (rental agreement on facing page).

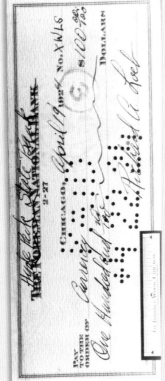

NAME                      ADDRESS          *Peoria, Ill.*

*Morton D. Ballard* 302 Elm St.

BELOW PLEASE FIND DULY AUTHORIZED SIGNATURES, WHICH YOU WILL
RECOGNIZE IN THE PAYMENT OF FUNDS OR THE TRANSACTION
OF OTHER BUSINESS ON OUR ACCOUNT

SIGNATURE     *Morton D. Ballard*

SIGNATURE

SIGNATURE

BUSINESS

DATE    *5-7-24*

INTRODUCED BY

## HYDE PARK STATE BANK
S. W. CORNER 53RD ST. & LAKE PARK AVE.

CHICAGO              1M-1-24

---

NAME       Richard A Loeb,     ADDRESS     *5017 Ellis Av*

BELOW PLEASE FIND DULY AUTHORIZED SIGNATURES, WHICH YOU WILL
RECOGNIZE IN THE PAYMENT OF FUNDS OR THE TRANSACTION
OF OTHER BUSINESS ON OUR ACCOUNT

SIGNATURE     *Richard A. Loeb*

SIGNATURE                 *Oakland 4270*

SIGNATURE                 *Student*

BUSINESS

DATE    *Sept 28 23*           INTRODUCED BY          *485*

## HYDE PARK STATE BANK
S. W. CORNER 53RD ST. & LAKE PARK AVE.

CHICAGO

---

## HYDE PARK STATE BANK
2-210   No. *BWLS*

CORNER OF 53RD ST. & LAKE PARK AVE.

CHICAGO, *April 15*    1924

PAY TO THE ORDER OF *Cash*            $5 00/100

*Five and* 00/100                  DOLLARS

MEMBER
FEDERAL RESERVE
SYSTEM             *Richard A. Loeb*

Nº 4629

# Lease Agreement

*Ex B Ident*

THIS AGREEMENT, Made this ___9th___ day of ___May___, 192_1_, by and between

RENT-A-CAR COMPANY, a corporation, hereinafter referred to as the Lessor and ___Morton W. Ballard___

whose address is (business) ___203 Illinois St. Peoria___, (residence) ___302 Elm St. Peoria___

hereinafter referred to as the Lessee,

WITNESSETH:

That the Lessor hereby leases to the Lessee certain automobiles described in "Exhibit A," which is attached hereto and made a part of this lease. It is the intention of the parties hereto that this lease and all of its terms and provisions shall be continued in effect, covering any number of cars leased to Lessee, the rates, description of car and equipment to be set out in an exhibit, which for convenience is referred to as "Exhibit A."

In consideration of One Dollar and other good and valuable considerations, the receipt whereof by each to the other in hand paid is hereby acknowledged, and as a further consideration for this agreement the Lessee is to deposit certain sums of mony described particularly in "Exhibit A," which sums of money so deposited shall be held by the Lessor as a cash guaranty of the faithful performance of this lease and/or as a partial indemnity to the Lessor against careless and improper use of any automobile leased by the Lessee while the same is in the custody or control of Lessee. In the event this agreement is faithfully performed by the Lessee and the automobile or automobiles are not injured or damaged, and the rental is fully paid, then and in that event the moneys so deposited shall be returned to Lessee upon the surrender of the said automobile or automobiles; otherwise, Lessors may apply said deposit, insofar as is necessary, to indemnify the lessor of and from any loss, cost or damage, but this provision shall not be construed as preventing the Lessor from collecting from Lessee any damage in excess of the amount of said deposit.

First: That L...                                                                                          gaged, encumbered or
repaired, or in any w...                                                                              for hire; or allow or
permit said automobil...                                                                             ss; or allow or permit
any person other tha...                                                                              permit said automobile
or automobiles to be...                                                                              without first obtaining
Lessor's consent so t...                                                                              

Second: Less...                                                                                        ge, Liability and twenty-five dollars deducti...                                                                            ering Lessee only. In
the event of a collisio...                                                                            maged or Fifty dollars
if any other make o...                                                                                rs to other make cars
while in Lessee's (yo...                                                                              sult from intoxication,
reckless driving, spee...                                                                             (you) is liable for the
full amount of dama...                                                                                ds, attorney fees and
court costs. Said as...                                                                               y illegal purpose, or if
car is abandoned afte...                                                                              s not to cover damages
caused by freezing r...                                                                               ply of suitable lubrica-
tion ... more than f...                                                                               his agreement shall be
stolen lessee hereby...                                                                               sor at once and shall
remain with the car u...                                                                              see hereby agrees that
he will immediately n...                                                                              a sworn statement as
to whom, where and f...                                                                               this agreement and in
the event the insuran...                                                                              that the same was not
locked, lessee hereby...                                                                              len.

Third: Lessor...                                                                                       r person or persons.
Fourth: In th...                                                                                       s and addresses of all
parties participating...                                                                              riting and in case any
suit is commenced ag...                                                                               ately in writing.

(RENT-A-CAR COMPANY)    **Morrison Hotel**
                        **IDENTIFICATION CARD** Nº **4629**

Name    *Morton W. Ballard*    **Ballard**
Res. Address  *302 Elm St Peoria*    Phone *802 J*
Bus. Address  *203 Illinois St.*    Phone *15 W*
Occupation  *Salesman*
Age *23* Height *5* ft. *6½* in. Weight *140* lbs. Eyes *Gray* Hair *Black*
Customer's Signature  *Morton W. Ballard*
O. K. for RENT-A-CAR, SERVICE
By  *A. Mae B.*

Fifth: Lessee agrees carefully to examine every automobile and equipment before taking the same and agrees not to take the same unless from such examination he... ...d order and repair with five servi..able tires. Lessor agrees to maintain said car in repai... ...or tire, caused by ordinary wear and tear; pro-vided, however, such repairs are to be mad... ...or; otherwise Lessor assumes no liability for said repairs.

Sixth: Lessor reserves the right to terminate this lease at any time when, in its sole judgment, any automobile leased hereunder is receiving improper or unusual usage and in such event Lessor may retain the deposit to apply toward the rent, damage, etc.

Seventh: Time, prompt payment, and careful use of any automobile leased hereunder are the essence of this lease. Lessee agrees that he has no interest in, to or respecting any automobile herein leased or any part thereof; that title thereto is, and at all times shall be and remain in the Lessor and the Lessor shall have the right to sell said automobile subject to this lease; or to assign this lease or encumber the same; that in the event a construction of this lease becomes necessary, it is to be construed as having been made, executed, delivered and fulfilled in accordance with the laws of the State of Illinois.

Eighth: Lessor reserves the right to terminate this lease by giving Lessee notice by registered mail to said effect, which notice shall be sent to the address specified in this lease as Lessee's address, and in the event said automobile is not delivered to Lessor within two hours after the receipt of such letter (or Lessor may make demand for said automobile, by telephone or otherwise) Lessor may take possession of any car leased hereunder, without notice or demand, with or without process of law, and for said purpose may enter the premises of Lessee and retake possession of any automobile leased hereunder, and Lessee agrees to pay Lessor all costs and expenses for pursuing and searching for said automobile, including reasonable attorneys' fees.

Ninth: This contract states the full understanding of the parties in connection with the leasing of every automobile leased hereunder and no officer, agent or employe of Lessor has any authority to vary, alter, amend, or cancel any clause of this lease or to add or change any clauses herein unless it is done in writing and under the hand and seal of the proper officers of Lessor.

Tenth: Lessee hereby irrevocably constitutes any attorney of any court of record to appear for him and in his behalf, in any court, at any time hereafter, and confess a judgment without process in favor of the Lessor, for such amount as may appear to be unpaid thereon, together with all costs and reasonable attorneys' fees, and to waive and release all errors which may intervene in any such proceedings and consent to immediate execution on said judgment, hereby ratifying and confirming all that said attorney may do by virtue thereof.

Eleventh: Nothing contained in this lease shall be construed as authorizing or permitting the said Lessee to have any work done or labor performed or parts or material furnished to any car at Lessor's expense.

**IN WITNESS WHEREOF,** this agreement was signed and sealed by the parties hereto the day and year first above written.

_____*Morton W. Ballard*_____                  RENT-A-CAR COMPANY

_____                          By *A. Mae F. Burney*
*Customer sign here*      Lessees.                        Lessor

LEVINSON was a classmate of Loeb's younger brother, Tommy, who would have made an appealing target, since at age nine he was young and small and his father, Salmon Levinson, was a prominent Chicago attorney who would have been able to pay the ransom.

**Q** Then you talked with whom else?

**A** With a little boy by the name of Levinson, John Levinson, whom I know. I just asked Levinson about his baseball game, and so forth and so on.

I left Harvard School, then, that is, I left—pardon me, I left the back, the playground where I had been talking to Cease and to Levinson, and went out in front of the Harvard School, where I met my little brother, who attends that school. I talked to him for a short time, and then Leopold came down Ellis Avenue on the west side of the street, and whistled for me to come over. He walked down the alley leading to Ingleside, the same alley near which the car was parked, and told me that there were some children playing on Ingleside avenue that he thought may be possible prospects.

**Q** For kidnapping?

**A** For kidnapping, yes. We decided, however, not to get them, and walked down Drexel Boulevard to where we saw a group of children playing on a vacant lot at the corner, –the southeast corner of Drexel and 49th street. We watched these boys and noticed that Levinson was amongst them.

**Q** What is his first name? John Levinson?

**A** I think so. We went back to the car, got the car and drove to the west side of Drexel, opposite to where the children were playing. We looked to see if we could recognize them from that distance, but it was very difficult; so we walked down to 50th street, and around 50th street through an alley where we could watch them more closely. Even from there, however, it was impossible to watch them very closely unless we showed ourselves; so we decided to go back to his car, drive over to his house and get a pair of bird glasses.

**Q** You mean field glasses?

**A** Well, yes, field glasses, –and watch the children through the field glasses. This we did. While he was getting the field glasses I went to a drug store on the corner of 47th and Ellis, where I looked up the address of Mr. Levinson, so that we would be able to tell where John lived. I incidentally bought a couple of packages of Dentyne chewing gum at that drug store.

I picked Leopold up immediately after that with the field glasses, and we went over to the same place on Drexel Boulevard. We watched the children some more through the field glasses, and noted that Levinson with a group of some of the other children went down the alley way out of sight. We didn't think that he had gone home, so remained watching. But when, after quite a while, he didn't show up, we came to the conclusion that he might have gone home.

I went to look for him in the alley, but didn't see him, and saw Cease leaving with the rest of his children.

We then went to a corner lot at the corner of 48th and Greenwood, the northeast corner, where John Coleman [he appears to mean Clarence, not John, Coleman] and Walter Baer's sons were playing baseball. We watched them for a little while, then went down to see if Levinson had gone home, passed his house and found that he was not there or playing on the street. We returned down Lake Park avenue, passed the lot where the Coleman boy was playing, and went into Leopold's house to watch the children play from one of the windows there. We didn't stay there long, but left, and drove down Drexel to go past this lot where Levinson had been playing; turned, and went down Hyde Park Boulevard, turned and went north on Ellis avenue. All this time I was driving. We proceeded north on Ellis avenue until we caught a glimpse of Robert Franks, coming south on the west side of Ellis avenue. As we passed him, he was just coming across or past 48th street. We turned down 48th street and turned the car around, Leopold getting into the back seat. I drove the car, then, south on Ellis avenue, parallel to where young Franks was, stopped the car, and while remaining in my seat, opened the front door and called to Franks that I would give him a ride home. He said no, he would just as soon walk; but I told him that I would like to talk to him about a tennis racket; so he got in the car.

We proceeded south on Ellis avenue, turned east on 50th street, and just after we turned off Ellis avenue, Leopold reached his arm around young Franks, grabbed his mouth and hit him over the head with the chisel. I believe he hit him several times, I do not know the exact number. He began to bleed and was not entirely unconscious, he was moaning. I proceeded further east on 50th, and turned, I believe at Dorchester. At this point Leopold—

**Q** What time was it?

**[MR. LOEB:] A** This was around five o'clock, I don't know the exact time. At this time Leopold grabbed Franks and carried him over the back of the front seat and threw him on a rug in the car. He then took one of the rags and gagged him by sticking it down his throat, I believe. We proceeded down Dorchester, and then at Leopold's direction drove into the country. I think we drove either out Jeffery Road or South Shore Drive; I think it was Jeffery Road, I am not acquainted with the district out there, and drove slowly at his directions, and that plus the fact of my excitement, accounts for my not being able to tell any of the places where we drove. However, we drove until we were at a deserted road which led off the main road somewhere before the Indiana line. We turned down this road, but it was only for—it was only a road for a short distance, and ended in a blank. This Leopold knew, but wanted to take it, because it was so deserted.

We turned around; and as we turned around he, seeing that Franks was unconscious, climbed into the front seat. Up to that time he had been watching him from the back seat. He had covered him up with the robe that we had brought along, the robe also belonging to Leopold. We then drove further south on the main highway, until we turned at a road which I believe leads to Gary. We went down this road a way, and then turned off the road on another deserted road, this deserted road leading north. We followed that for only a short distance, then turned down another deserted road leading west. We stopped the car, got out, removed young Franks' shoes, hid them in some bushes and removed his pants and stockings, placing them in the car. We did this in order that we might be saved the trouble of too much undressing him later on. We also left his belt buckle and belt with the shoes, not in the same place, but very near there.

We then proceeded to drive around back and forth and back and forth.

**Q** Waiting for it to get dark?

**A** Waiting for it to get dark. We stopped at a little sandwich shop on the road, and Leopold got out and purchased a couple of redhot sandwiches and two bottles of root beer. We then kept driving more and more, until it was fairly dusk.

Then Leopold wanted to make a phone call—the phone call had nothing to do with the Franks case—he made this phone call from a drug store situation on the northeast corner of one of the intersecting streets meeting this main highway, the name of which I do not know.

FRANKS WAS UNCONSCIOUS: In Leopold's account, he says he believes Bobby died "instantly" by suffocation as soon as the rag was stuffed into his mouth.

SAVED THE TROUBLE: As previously noted, Crowe believed this account of undressing the body in two stages suggested some sexual motivation, and in Loeb's narrative it is not clear whether Bobby was at this point dead or unconscious.

PHONE CALL: Leopold was calling his sweetheart, Susan Lurie, to confirm a date with her.

The important thing is that I parked the car on this side street facing west, parallel to the tracks. The driver's seat is on the left of the car. Therefore, I was nearest to the drug store. He got out of the car, went to the drug store and made his phone call. In returning, he came straight to the car, so that he hit the door that I was sitting at, rather than the door next to the vacant seat, and he said, "Slip over and let me drive for a while", which I did.

He drove the car. We again proceeded down the thoroughfare, waiting for it to get dark. I remember we turned up one road which he said led to Indianapolis, and then back again, and finally he drove the car to a place where he knew which was near this culvert. We had both investigated the culvert on a previous journey out there some weeks before.

**Q** When you had planned it, you mean?

**A** Yes. We dragged the body out of the car, put the body in the robe and carried it over to the culvert. Leopold carried the feet, I carried the head. We deposited the body near the culvert, and undressed the body completely.

Our original scheme had been to etherize the boy to death.

**Q** Where did you pour the hydrochloric acid on him?

**A** Right there. The scheme for etherizing him originated through Leopold, who evidently has some knowledge of such things, and he said that that would be the easiest way of putting him to death, and the least messy. This, however, we found unnecessary, because the boy was quite dead when we took him there. We knew he was dead, by the fact that rigor mortis had set in, and also by his eyes; and then when at that same time we poured this hydrochloric acid over him, we noticed no tremor, not a single tremor in his body; therefore, we were sure he was dead. Leopold put on his hip boots, taking off his coat in order to do this, and took the body and stuck it head first—

**[CAPT.] SCHOEMAKER:** Was it dark at that time?

**[MR. LOEB:] A** Yes. Stuck it headfirst into the culvert. I might say that at this time it was fairly dark, but still not pitch black, so that we were able to work without a flashlight.

**MR. SBARBARO: Q** How far did you have to carry the body, from the time you got off the machine until you dropped it down into or near the culvert?

**[MR. LOEB:] A** I should say about a city block and a half; I don't know.

**Q** How did you carry it, in this blanket?

**A** In the blanket, yes. That is we had the blanket in sort of, as you might use a stretcher.

**Q** Well, then you put the body right down into the culvert?

**A** Yes.

**Q** And you poured your hydrochloric acid on it?

**A** Before we put it down in the culvert.

Chicago History Museum, DN-0077990

Crowe (left foreground) shows off the mangled Underwood portable typewriter, which was recovered from the Jackson Park lagoon by divers.

**Q** And then what did you do?

**A** Then I went to the opposite side of the culvert, where the water runs out, and where you can get at the water very easily, where I washed my hands which had become bloody through carrying the body.

**Q** The head had bled very freely?

**A** Yes, the head had bled quite freely, I wouldn't say very freely, but quite freely. There was quite a bit of blood; the blanket or robe was quite saturated with blood. We then left, taking the robe we used, as also the clothing of young Franks, and we started homeward, and Leopold stopped to call up his folks and to tell them that he would be slightly detained. This I should judge was about nine o'clock. We then stopped at a drug store somewhere in the neighborhood, where I looked up the address of Jacob Franks and the telephone number, and at the same time Leopold printed the address on the envelope.

Sbarbaro and Schoemaker continue to quiz Loeb about what he did in the days immediately following the murder, and eventually Loeb accounts for the mysteriously missing Underwood portable typewriter:

**[MR. LOEB:]** Late Saturday night, around two o'clock, I met Leopold at a restaurant next to the garage, the Fashion Garage at the corner of 51st and Cottage. He had this car, and we took his car in which he had placed his typewriter, the Underwood portable typewriter, upon which the letters had been written, and we took the typewriter out of the back trunk, brought it into the front seat, and I took a pair of pliers and pried off the keys, just the very tips of the keys, where the imprints would show. We took these keys in a little bundle and threw them off the bridge in Jackson Park, situated near the golden statute [should be "statue"] of Liberty. Then we took the typewriter intact with case, and threw it off the bridge leading to the outer harbor. In other words, the bridge, the big stone bridge with the pyramid effect at all four corners of the bridge; it is the bridge leading to the outer harbor. The typewriter was thrown on the east side of the bridge.

The robe was then taken from its hiding place. We went over to Leopold's garage and got some gasoline, took the robe out on South Shore Drive, on a little side street connecting with the South Shore Drive, and saturated the robe with gasoline and set fire to it.

That is all I have to tell about the murder of Robert Franks.

**[MR. SBARBARO:] Q** And this statement that you have just made has been made of your own free will?

**[MR. LOEB:] A** Yes. I just want to say that I offer no excuse; but that I am fully convinced that neither the idea nor the act would have occurred to me, had it not been for the suggestion and stimulus of Leopold. Furthermore, I do not believe that I would have been capable of having killed Franks.

This statement is made of my own volition.

# 17
# It was he who did the act
## LEOPOLD'S CORRECTIONS OF LOEB

IMMEDIATELY FOLLOWING their separate confessions, made in separate rooms, Leopold and Loeb were brought together in a room so that their respective confessions could be read aloud to both of them, giving each a chance to refute anything the other one had said. They did not, as the *Chicago Daily News* reported, "dictate jointly their real confession." In fact, their separate confessions agree in all but the most minor details—except that each vehemently insists the other had physically committed the murder.

At this point, the room was crowded. Shorthand reporter E.M. Allen listed 13 other witnesses besides himself, including State's Attorney Robert Crowe; Assistant State's Attorneys Joseph P. Savage, John Sbarbaro, and Robert McMillan; Chief of Detectives Michael Hughes, Captain Schoemaker, and several other detectives; and Sam Ettelson.

**MR. LEOPOLD:** I have some corrections.

In the first place, the date as given by Mr. Loeb is about a month or two at the most before the crime took place. As I remember it quite distinctly, we started planning this thing as early as November, 1923. ⟶ NOVEMBER, 1923: He is referring to the date Loeb said they had begun planning the crime.

In the second place, the suggestion was his, not mine.

In the third place, the Rent-a-Car is at 14th and not 16th street. The little restaurant to which he refers is also at 13th, not 1538 Wabash. The hardware store to which he refers is not at 47th, but between 55th and 56th, on Cottage Grove avenue.

I did not bind the chisel with tape; he did. The hip boots were not my brother's, but mine. The place that mentioned getting the car was at 14th and not 16th street.

At the time the Franks boy entered our car, I was driving, not Mr. Loeb, and Mr. Loeb was in the back seat. It was Mr. Loeb struck him with the chisel, and not I.

The phone call to my father's, I think, was made at nine-forty-five.

**MR. SAVAGE:** Where did you phone from?

**MR. LEOPOLD:** At 104th and Ewing avenue. Mr. Loeb I think went home at one o'clock, instead of at ten-thirty; as he seems to think.

**MR. LOEB:** No, I never said that; I said I went to your house at ten-thirty.

**MR. LEOPOLD:** Then I misunderstood. And as far as that suggestion is concerned, again, I am sure it was Mr. Loeb that made it, and it was his plan, and it was he who did the act.

**MR. CROWE:** Outside of that, the statement is correct?

**MR. LEOPOLD:** Correct.

## THE BOYS DEFLATE

"[T]heir confidence, their astounding aplomb had deserted them at dawn today," said the May 31 *Chicago Daily News*, "when daylight began creeping through the dusty windows of the Criminal court building to reveal the climax of the terrible drama." The paper reported that Richard Loeb, "lately so cocksure," now sat slumped in a chair, stammering and gasping out his confession. Meanwhile Nathan Leopold, "ashen, haggard," was making his confession in another room.

Brought together in one room to listen to one another's confessions, the paper claimed, "They cursed each other, shouted hysterical charges and denials and threats. Then the cold truth of their ax [the intended word would seem to be "acts"] sobered them. They sat shaken and beaten to dictate jointly their real confession."

Q   Richard who?

A   Richard Loeb.   He replied no, but Richard said,
"Well, get in a minute, I want to ask you about a
certain tennis racket."   After he had gotten in,
I stepped on the gas, proceeded south on Ellis avenue
to 50th street.   In the meantime Richard asked
Robert if he minded if we took him around the block;
to which Robert said "No."

As soon as we turned the corner, Richard
placed his one hand over Robert's mouth to stifle his
outcries, with his right beat him on the head several times with a chisel, especially prepared for the
purpose.   The boy did not succumb as readily as we had
believed, so for fear of being observed, Richard
seized him, pulled him into the back seat.   Here he
forced a cloth into his mouth.   Apparently the boy
died instantly by suffocation shortly thereafter.

We proceeded out to Calumet Boulevard in
Indiana, drove along this road that leads to Gary,
being a rather deserted place.   We even stopped to
buy a couple of sandwiches for supper.

Q   Where?

A   On Calumet Boulevard at, I guess, 132nd street.

5  The body was covered by an automobile robe which we

19

Loeb's account
of the murder,
in which he
is driving and
Leopold commits
the murder—
though it isn't
clear at what
point Bobby
actually dies.

        We proceeded south on Ellis avenue, turned
east on 50th street, and just after we turned off
Ellis avenue, Leopold reached his arm around young
Franks, grabbed his mouth and hit him over the head
with the chisel.   I believe he hit him several
times, I do not know the exact number.   He began to
bleed and was not entirely unconscious, he was moaning.
I proceeded further east on 50th, and turned, I believe at Dorchester.   At this point Leopold —

Q  What time was it?

A This was around five o'clock, I don't know the
exact time.   At this time Leopold grabbed Franks
and carried him over back of the front seat and threw
him on a rug in the car.   He then took one of the
rags and gagged him by sticking it down his throat, I
believe.   We proceeded down Dorchester, and then at
Leopold's direction drove into the country.   I think
we drove either out Jeffery Road or South Shore Drive,
I think it was Jeffery Road, I am not acquainted
with the district out there, and drove slowly at his
directions, and that plus the fact of my excitement,
accounts for my not being able to tell any of the places
where we drove.   However, we drove until we were at
a deserted road which led off the main road some-

94

# 18
# I have been made a fish
## LOEB'S CORRECTIONS OF LEOPOLD

**WHO DONE IT?**

Despite the astonishing detail in which both Nathan Leopold and Richard Loeb were willing to describe the murder, the obvious question remained for the press and the public: which one of them had actually killed Bobby Franks? In a bit of fanciful dialogue—clearly belied by the interrogation transcript—the June 1 *Chicago Daily Tribune* reported that the issue had been resolved:

"'You hit him first, Dick,' Leopold said.

"'No, Babe, don't you remember? I was driving. I couldn't have hit him first because he was in the back seat with you? I was the one that called him by name and got him into the car. You didn't know him. Don't you remember?'

"'That point was cleared up.'"

T HE *TRIBUNE*'S DRAMATIC (and imaginary) dialogue notwithstanding, Leopold and Loeb most certainly did *not* clear up the point of who had actually committed the murder. In his real refutation of Leopold's accusation, preserved in the Confessions, Loeb's agitation on the subject makes him nearly incoherent, and Leopold continues to deny that he could possibly have committed the crime himself. Loeb is also furious at "having been made a fish"—in other words, feeling betrayed—by Leopold's use of the alibi about driving around and drinking, which they had both agreed in advance not to use if questioned more than a week after the crime; later than that, they were just supposed to have "forgotten" what they'd done that day.

Had Leopold not used the alibi, Loeb seems to be suggesting here, the chauffeur's testimony could not have tripped them up. Leopold in turn blames Loeb for being the one to break down and confess. On June 2, the *Chicago Daily Tribune* would describe them as being "open enemies" and report that as they went about, "a detective or two" had to be placed in between them. Leopold tells this whole story many years later in his book *Life Plus 99 Years*, explaining that "our subconscious desires determined our respective interpretations in advance: each of us chose that interpretation which most nearly accorded with what he had wanted in the first place," and then adding "What a rotten writer of detective stories Life is!"

**MR. LOEB:** There are certain corrections that Leopold has made in mine that are not important, such as 14th street, and the boots being his instead of his brother's, which don't amount to a damn—I mean, it don't make any difference, they are not important, and do not affect the case.

However, I would like to say this: In the first place, he says that that chisel was wrapped by me. It was wrapped by him, and wrapped by him in Jackson Park. He brought it and put it in the car, and he wrapped that chisel while waiting there in Jackson Park, in that little nine-hole golf house. All right.

In the second place, he mentioned that the idea of the thing, that the main thing was to get the place and the means of throwing that package, and he struck on that thing in the train, and he—that was his idea; but he doesn't mention the method of the killing, that he had that very well conceived and planned out, as evidenced by the ether in the car, which was absolutely the notion that he followed through. The boy was to be etherized to death; and he was supposed to do that, because I don't know a damn thing about it, and he does. He has a number of times chloroformed birds, and things like that, and knows ornithology, I don't know a damned thing about that.

He said the time was November, when the idea was first conceived. Well, now, I don't know exactly; I believe I said two months in my statement. I know right well it was not November, it might have been a little bit longer than two months, it might have been two and a half months, but it certainly was not any longer than that. [ . . . ]

So there are one or two other things. In the first place, I never touched that body after the hydrochloric acid was poured on that body. After the hydrochloric acid was poured on that body, you stepped into that culvert with your boots on, and you took hold of the feet and gave the body a push, and the body splashed in there, and it splashed on your pants, too, and you were worried about it.

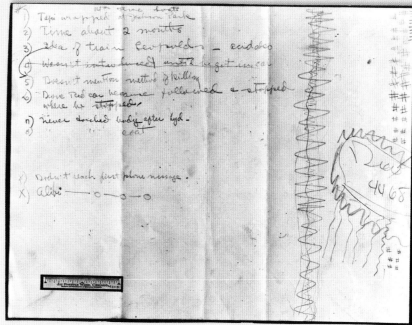

Northwestern University Archives

The notes Loeb was making as Leopold's confession was being read aloud to him (along with his doodles) are preserved in an evidence photo.

**MR. CROWE:** Who hit him with the chisel?

**MR. LOEB:** He did.

**MR. CROWE:** Who is he?

**MR. LOEB:** Nathan Leopold, Junior. He was sitting up in the front seat—I said he was sitting up in the front seat—I mean I was sitting up in the front seat. That is obviously a mistake, I am getting excited. This Franks boy got in the front seat. Now, he was a boy that I knew. If I was sitting in the back seat, he would have gotten into the back seat with me. He was a boy I knew, and I would have opened the door and motioned him in that way. As it was, he got in the front seat with me, because I knew the boy, and I opened the front door. He didn't see Babe until he was inside the car. He said at some place I introduced him to this Franks boy and then took him into the car. I took him in the car, and when he got in the car I said, "You know Babe, this is Babe, Franks."

And then, one other thing I wish to point out. I have been made a fish right along here. Now, this story that you speak of in your testimony, this story of the finding—of all this alibi of these women and being drunk in the Cocoanut Grove, and everything, we planned that definitely, it was definitely decided that the story was not to go after Wednesday afternoon, which would be a week after the crime, we were to forget our story, we were to just say that we didn't know what we were doing, and that there was no evidence. We felt that you were safe with your glasses after a week had passed, that your glasses being out there would not necessitate an airtight alibi, because we didn't figure anything else, and we figured that would be safe enough after a week not to know exactly where you were on that particular Wednesday afternoon.

**MR. CROWE:** Who felt that?

**MR. LEOPOLD:** I told the same story exactly here to Mr. Savage.

**MR. CROWE:** All right.

**MR. LOEB:** When you came down Thursday, and you told another story, which you had agreed not to tell, I came down to Mr. Crowe, and he questioned me, and questioned me about my actions and everything else, and I denied being ever drunk,

I denied being with you, Leopold, and I denied being up at the Cocoanut Grove; and those things put together made me absolutely certain that you had told the story you should not have told.

Then he started to talk about the park, about being out at Lincoln Park; he mentioned parks, he brought it around, but I knew what he was driving at, it was Lincoln Park; and when he did that, I stepped in to try to help you out. I think it is a damned sight more than you would have done for me. I tried to help you out, because I thought that you at least, if the worst comes to the worst, would admit what you had done and not try to drag me into the thing in that manner.

Well, now, that is all I have got to say.

**MR. SAVAGE:** Have you got anything to say to that?

**MR. LEOPOLD:** Yes, I have.

**MR. SAVAGE:** Nathan wants to say a word.

**MR. LEOPOLD:** His correction about what car I was driving down I think is correct. The others are all absurd, outright lies. He is trying to get out of this himself.

I can explain to you myself exactly how I opened the door to let the Franks boy in, and he got up from the back seat, leaned over forward and spoke to the boy from the back. I was driving the car, I am absolutely positive.

The reason for changing that story was, as you remember, when you first questioned me as to my actions, I was very indefinite, and I was urged to remember, quite strongly, what I had been doing; and I am sorry that you were made a fish and stepped into everything and broke down and all that. I am sorry; but it is not my fault.

All the rest of the corrections he made, with the exception of that one of the car, are lies.

**MR. CROWE:** Now listen, boys.

**MR. LEOPOLD:** Yes.

**MR. CROWE:** You have both been treated decently by me?

**MR. LEOPOLD:** Absolutely.

**MR. CROWE:** No brutality or no roughness?

**MR. LEOPOLD:** No, sir.

**MR. CROWE:** Every consideration shown to both of you?

**MR. LEOPOLD:** Yes, sir.

**MR. CROWE:** Not one of you a complaint to make, have you?

**MR. LEOPOLD:** No, sir.

**MR. CROWE:** Have you, Loeb?

**MR. LOEB:** No.

# 19
# I told Mrs. Franks her son had been kidnaped

## LEOPOLD REENACTS THE PHONE CALL

CROWE TOOK Leopold and Loeb on several extraordinary field trips to gather evidence for his case against them, and—still without legal counsel—they cooperated fully. On the morning of Saturday, June 1, following the all-night ordeal of the confessions, they traveled in a caravan of seven cars, escorted by 40 detectives, as well as reporters for the Chicago papers. At the drugstore where he had waited for a phone call from the Rent-A-Car company so that he could vouch for Leopold's phony identity, Loeb was identified by the owner and promptly fainted. (Leopold, still furious at him, remarked contemptuously to a *Tribune* reporter, "If I had thought he ever would squawk I'd be in this alone.") They showed detectives where they had hurled Leopold's typewriter into the Jackson Park lagoon, and a diver was summoned to look for it. They led them to the field where they thought they had hidden Bobby Franks's shoes, which were later found by the detectives and positively identified by Bobby's brother, Jack. The Confessions chronicles a visit made late that same Saturday night to the Walgreens at 1200 47th Street (no longer in existence) from which they had made the first phone call informing Flora Franks that her son had been kidnaped, and where they are asked by the detectives to reenact the scene exactly, squeezing themselves together into the tiny phone booth as they had on the night of the murder.

AT WALGREEN'S DRUG STORE, AT 1200 EAST 47TH STREET, AT 10:25 P.M.

**MR. SBARBARO:** What time was it when you were in this drug store?

**MR. LEOPOLD:** Approximately 10:25.

**MR. SBARBARO:** Did you purchase a slug [a substitute coin, to be inserted in the phone to make a call] at the counter?

**MR. LEOPOLD:** Yes.

**MR. SBARBARO:** Was it at that time you called the Franks residence?

**MR. LEOPOLD:** Yes.

**MR. SBARBARO:** Did you call, yourself?

**MR. LEOPOLD:** I did.

**MR. SBARBARO:** And was Richard Loeb here with you?

**MR. LEOPOLD:** He was.

**MR. SBARBARO:** Where was he standing when you called Franks?

**MR. LEOPOLD:** In the phone booth with me.

**MR. SBARBARO:** He was inside the phone booth with you?

**MR. LEOPOLD:** Yes.

**MR. SBARBARO:** Indicate which phone booth it was, will you?

**MR. LEOPOLD:** I will; this one (indicating).

**MR. SBARBARO:** And will you indicate which way you were faced?

**MR. LEOPOLD:** We just crowded in and closed the door this way (illustrating).

**MR. SBARBARO:** Dick, come over here and show us just what position you were standing when Nathan called the Franks home.

**MR. LOEB:** I don't remember–

**MR. LEOPOLD:** Dick was standing this way (indicating), about here; and you closed the door (addressing Loeb).

**MR. LOEB:** I remember distinctly closing the door, it was hard to close.

**MR. SBARBARO:** You recall having some difficulty about closing the door?

**MR. LOEB:** Yes.

**MR. SBARBARO:** How many times did you call the Franks residence from this place, and what did you say?

**MR. LEOPOLD:** I told Mrs. Franks her son had been kidnaped; that my name was George Johnson; that her boy was safe, and that she would hear what to do in the morning; and I hung up before she had a chance to say anything.

# 20
# It is the duty of a parent to stand by his child

## A VISIT FROM LEOPOLD'S FATHER

THE CONFESSIONS RECORDS Leopold's first face-to-face encounter with his father following his admission that he and Loeb had committed the murder. Leopold Sr. had requested the opportunity for a private talk with his son—who as yet has had no access whatsoever to legal counsel. Robert Crowe intends to keep it that way as long as possible—especially until psychiatrists have had a chance to evaluate Leopold and Loeb in order to eliminate the possibility of an insanity defense. "The state's attorney's office summarized the situation this way," said the June 2 *Chicago Daily Tribune*. "'If your father had $10,000,000 he'd spend at least $5,000,000 to prevent your being hanged. The fathers of these boys have an estimated combined fortune of $15,000,000, and we suppose it will be millions versus the death penalty.'"

To forestall the predicted insanity defense, Robert Crowe rounded up three of Chicago's most prominent "alienists"—the term that was then used for psychiatrists who assessed the mental competency of accused killers to stand trial. Hugh T. Patrick was past president of the American Neurological Association and professor emeritus of nervous and mental diseases at Northwestern University Medical School; Archibald Church was the head of Northwestern's Department of Nervous and Mental Diseases and the author of a well-known textbook on mental illness; and William O. Krohn, whose PhD in psychology was from Yale University, had coauthored a definitive textbook called *Insanity and Law: A Treatise on Forensic Psychiatry*. As the following exchange shows, they were already present in the state's attorney's office when Leopold's father was allowed his first, very brief exchange with his son after the confession. Among the others also present were Crowe; Assistant State's Attorneys Sbarbaro, Savage, and Smith, and detectives Hughes and Schoemaker.

**MR. CROWE:** Just sit down, Mr. Leopold; I will have the boy brought in.

**DOCTOR PATRICK:** Mr. Leopold.

**MR. LEOPOLD, JUNIOR:** Hello, Dad.

**MR. LEOPOLD, SENIOR:** Hello, my son. Could I talk to this boy myself, privately?

**MR. LEOPOLD, JUNIOR:** I would like to talk to my father alone.

**MR. CROWE:** Just at this particular time I cannot do it.

**DR. PATRICK:** I am Doctor Patrick, Son.

**MR. LEOPOLD, SR.:** Is that true, Mr. Crowe, that a parent may not have the opportunity to talk to his child?

**MR. CROWE:** I want to give you an opportunity to talk to him and ease your mind as to the boy's wellbeing. In fact, he is not being abused, and so on; but at this particular time I do not think it is proper for me to permit two of you to talk together. They do in jail on certain days, that is allowed to them. You appreciate that I don't like to be harsh.

### "OUR BABY ISN'T DEAD"

While the revelations from the confessions were playing out sensationally across the newspapers, the private devastation within the three families was only just beginning to unfold. The May 31 *Chicago Daily Journal* reported that Nathan Leopold Sr. was still in complete denial about his son's confession. "That's a lie," he told their reporter. "[T]hat boy can not be guilty. I am not ready to discuss the case at this time, but I am sure that the boys never harmed the Franks child. It can not be true."

The *Chicago Daily Tribune*, meanwhile, described the scene on the 5000 block of Ellis Avenue, bookended on the southeast corner by the Loeb mansion and on the northwest corner by the Franks house. "Automobiles were passing [the Loeb house], slowing down while their occupants gazed along the driveway to the porte cochere. A half minute more and they were

CONTINUED

CONTINUED

staring again, this time at the house of Franks. On the sidewalk stood groups of curious pedestrians."

That afternoon, Jacob Franks had identified the shoes found in the swamp where Nathan Leopold and Richard Loeb had hidden them as Bobby's. He said he had been with Bobby at Marshall Field's a few weeks before when Bobby picked them out. In the June 1 edition of the *Tribune*, he said that Flora Franks was still absolutely unable to accept the loss of her son.

"She keeps saying that our baby isn't dead," Franks said. "She keeps saying that they are only hiding him. She believes that Robert will come back to her."

Chicago History Museum, DN-0078038

(Seated, left to right) Jacob Loeb, Nathan Leopold Jr., Richard Loeb, and Nathan Leopold Sr. on June 2, 1924, when the families were first allowed contact after the confessions and the examination by the state's psychiatric experts.

**MR. LEOPOLD, SR.:** Mr. Crowe, he may tell me things in my presence that he might be diffident about telling when others are present. In other words, if I ask him of the treatment he got, he might hesitate to answer when these people around here have been working on him, and he might tell me things that might be private in that respect.

**MR. CROWE:** He can tell all that to you tomorrow.

**MR. LEOPOLD, SR.:** He might be fearful of it, might be fearful that something might come up.

**MR. CROWE:** When he has an interview with you alone, he can tell you all those things. If he has got anything now, he can tell it. I did want you to see him, so you could assure yourself that the boy was all right. In other words, I appreciate the state of your mind at this particular time, and I do not want to make it any harder for you.

**MR. LEOPOLD, SR.:** Of course, you realize, I suppose, all the men that have children, it is the duty of a parent to stand by his child.

**MR. CROWE:** Absolutely; and it would not be natural that you did not.

**MR. LEOPOLD, SR.:** I want him to get every opportunity that everybody else would get under similar circumstances. If he is entitled to counsel, he should have it. If it is not proper for him to talk without counsel, then my advice to him would be not to talk. Is that correct? That is what you would tell a son, isn't it? That also includes any doctors. In other words, if you have constitutional rights, they should be accorded you.

Crowe at this point apparently rebuffs him and allows the psychiatrists to begin their examination.

# 21
# Pure love of excitement, or the imaginary love of thrills

## WHY THEY DID IT

Aᴛ ᴛʜɪs ᴘᴏɪɴᴛ in the transcript, Leopold and Loeb have still not seen an attorney who might have warned them not to cooperate with the examination, so their responses to the questions are still relatively unguarded. The interview recorded in the Confessions begins innocuously with small talk about Leopold's interest in ornithology, but eventually the doctors confront both boys directly about their motives in the murder.

**MR. CROWE:** Mr. Loeb, do you know the difference between right and wrong?

**MR. LOEB:** Yes, sir.

**MR. CROWE:** You think you did the right thing in this particular matter?

**MR. LOEB:** In the Franks case?

**MR. CROWE:** Yes.

**MR. LOEB:** Absolutely not.

**MR. CROWE:** And you know it is wrong to kidnap a boy?

**MR. LOEB:** Yes, sir.

**MR. CROWE:** What is your idea about right or wrong of getting a boy and kidnaping him?

**MR. LOEB:** It is wrong, sir.

**MR. CROWE:** You know the consequence of this act, don't you?

**MR. LOEB:** Yes.

**MR. CROWE:** What was the reason you told other stories as to your movements on that day?

**MR. LOEB:** Well, in the first place, for fear of detection myself; but I think that the main thing that had been running through my mind all through this case, all through the questioning, has been the condition of my folks, and that is especially so because my father is very sick. That has just gone through my mind. I think I have told them now enough afterwards.

**MR. CROWE:** It is the attendant disgrace that accompanies this?

**MR. LOEB:** In relation to my folks.

**MR. SAVAGE:** And you feel remorse for them?

**MR. LOEB:** Yes, sir.

**LEGALLY INSANE?**

The lead story in the June 2 edition of the *Chicago Daily Tribune* explained to readers that there were two questions that would determine the relevance of an insanity defense under Illinois law: the first was whether the defendants had the power to distinguish between right and wrong in regard to the act they had committed, the second was whether they had the power of choice in either refraining from committing, or deciding to commit an act they knew was wrong.

Without specifically attributing the comment to any one of the three alienists who had spoken to Nathan Leopold and Richard Loeb on behalf of the state, the *Tribune* quoted one of them as saying,

"So far I have seen no signs of any mental disorder or disease in either. I asked Loeb: 'Did you at any time feel like backing out of that murder?' and he replied, 'I did, but I didn't want to be called a quitter.' . . .

"Neither yet understands the significance of their act. They have not been alone and they have been treated too kindly. When the time comes that each is alone in a cell and given opportunity to think I believe they will go to the depths of despair."

**MR. SAVAGE:** When was the first you felt it?

**MR. LOEB:** I felt sorry about the thing, about the killing of the boy—oh, well, that very night. But then the excitement, the accounts in the paper, the fact that we had gotten away with it and that they did not suspect us, that it was given so much publicity and all that sort of thing, naturally went to the question of not feeling as much remorse as otherwise I think I would have. I think if that thing had not appeared in the papers, if people had not come to me and said, "The fellow who did that was crazy, the fellow who did that was insane," if people would not come up, you know, and say that, things like that, I think I would have felt a great deal more remorse. I think since I have spent some time alone these last two or three days it has dwelt on my mind a great deal; not the question of my folks, about me, and the disgrace has not been the only thing I thought of.

**DR. KROHN:** Had you any feeling of detracting or giving up the scheme?

**MR. LOEB:** No, sir, I don't think so.

**DR. KROHN:** You always felt as if you were going to go right through with it?

**MR. LOEB:** Yes, sir. I could tell you the truth, sir, I have a sort of feeling that maybe I had a feeling of that sort. Do you mean that I expressed it or that I felt it?

**DR. KROHN:** No, that you really felt it?

**MR. LOEB:** Yes, I really think that I did.

**DR. KROHN:** Didn't want to be called a quitter.

**MR. LOEB:** Yes, that's just it. I have always hated anybody that was a coward.

**DR. KROHN:** You realize now, though that you had the power to refrain from doing it?

**MR. LOEB:** Yes, sir.

**DR. KROHN:** You could have refrained from doing a wrong thing?

**MR. LOEB:** Yes, sir.

**DR. KROHN:** You had the power of will and choice to decide whether you would do it or not?

**MR. LOEB:** Yes, sir.

**DR. KROHN:** You had that all the time?

**MR. LOEB:** Yes, sir.

**DR. KROHN:** There was no feeling on your part of failure to work out a certain scheme or anything else about doing it?

**MR. LOEB:** No, sir.

**DR. KROHN:** You had full control of doing it?

**MR. LOEB:** Yes, sir.

**DR. PATRICK:** I think this question has been probably asked before; but looking back at the very beginning of this thing again more or less vaguely, perhaps, what was your incentive, what did you have in mind to get things started, from the very beginning? Perhaps you don't remember.

MR. LOEB: I felt sorry about the thing, about the killing of the boy— oh, well, that very night. But then the excitement, the accounts in the paper, the fact that we had gotten away with it and that they did not suspect us, that it was given so much publicity and all that sort of thing, naturally went to the question of not feeling as much remorse as otherwise I think I would have.    I think if that thing had not appeared in the papers, if people had not come to me and said, "The fellow who did that was crazy, the fellow who did that was insane," if people would not come up, you know, and say that, things like that, I think I would have felt a great deal more remorse. I think since I have spent some time alone these last two or three days it has dwelt on my mind a great deal; not the question of my folks, about me, and the disgrace has not been the only thing I thought of.

Perhaps the most shocking— and infamous—passages in the Confessions were the ones that established the lack of remorse either Leopold or Loeb seemed to feel about taking Bobby Franks's life, and that asserted a motive that would forever label them as the "Thrill Killers." Here we see a passage on the subject from Loeb's account and then from Leopold's (bottom).

state of mind, the thing that prompted Dick to want to do this thing and prompted me to want to do this thing was a sort of pure love of excitement, or the imaginary love of thrills, doing something differ- ent; possibly,as the Doctor here suggested the satis- faction and the ego of putting something over, as the vernacular has it.    The money consideration only came in afterwards, and never was important, the getting of the money was a part of our objective, as was also the commission of the crime; but that was not the exact motive, but that came afterwards.

MR. CROWE: You wouldn't take ten thousand dollars out of my pocket,if I had it?

MR. LEOPOLD, JR: It depends on whether I thought I could get away with it.

**MR. LOEB:** I don't know. That's the one thing, you know when this thing comes up and I feel this way, I feel so sorry, I have asked myself that question a million times: How did I possibly go into that thing, how did I do it?

**DR. PATRICK:** You cannot trace the original nucleus of it, can you, Mr. Leopold?

**MR. LEOPOLD:** Yes, sir, I think I can, I think it will be to my disadvantage to do so; but again have enlisted Mr. Savage's help and he tells me to come out and just tell the whole thing. There is no question of being swayed by momentary excitement at all; I am sure, as sure as I can be of anything, that is, as sure as you can read any other man's state of mind, the thing that prompted Dick to want to do this thing and prompted me to want to do this thing was a sort of pure love of excitement, or the imaginary love of thrills, doing something different; possibly, as the Doctor here suggested the satisfaction and the ego of putting something over, as the vernacular has it. The money consideration only came afterwards, and never was important, the getting of the money was a part of our objective, as was also the commission of the crime; but that was not the exact motive, but that came afterwards.

**MR. CROWE:** You wouldn't take ten thousand dollars out of my pocket, if I had it?

**MR. LEOPOLD:** It depends on whether I thought I could get away with it.

## 22
# I never read that
### LOEB DENIES PLAGIARIZING THE RANSOM NOTE

FROM THE MOMENT the case had first hit the newspapers, the literary quality of the ransom letter had been considered a clue to the possible identity of the killer. Its resemblance to a note that had appeared in a recent issue of *Detective Story Magazine* had been widely publicized (see chapter 2, page 9), suggesting that the Franks letter had essentially been plagiarized from the fictional kidnapping. But for the record—though it was never picked up by the papers—Loeb denies to Robert Crowe ever having looked at the issue in question and attributes primary authorship to Nathan Leopold.

**MR. CROWE:** Do you remember that letter, Mr. Loeb, that appeared in some detective magazine?

**MR. LOEB:** I never read that.

**MR. CROWE:** But you have seen the letter in the paper?

**MR. LOEB:** Yes, sir.

**MR. CROWE:** What magazine did that appear in?

**MR. LOEB:** A Detective Story Magazine.

**MR. CROWE:** You got that magazine, didn't you?

**MR. LOEB:** I got the magazine, I subscribed for it, I believe, two years ago. It was my first year up at Michigan. I also bought the magazine my first and second year in Chicago quite often; I however recently have not read that magazine, but I have always been interested in mystery stories and detective stories, and all light literature of that sort. It is only natural, because I don't take to heavy literature; my reading of fiction is practically entirely confined to that sort of stuff, the light fiction, and some of the short mystery stories, and that type of fiction has always appealed to me a great deal.

**MR. CROWE:** You hadn't seen this magazine, the particular copy?

**MR. LOEB:** Not this year. I read this magazine, I believe, twice.

**MR. CROWE:** You hadn't read this letter prior to that?

**MR. LOEB:** No.

**MR. CROWE:** The letter in this case was sent to Franks' house written in very good English; the punctuation is perfect, and it would be the work of an educated person.

**MR. LOEB:** Yes, sir.

**MR. CROWE:** There was a letter published in a detective magazine we have just been talking about that this might be based on.

**MR. LEOPOLD, JR:** I want to ask Mr. Loeb a question or two, if I may. Dick, when did you start reading the Detective Magazine; do you remember about that?

## SUCH A FINE KID
Maurine Watkins was not the only verbal coloraturist to embellish journalistic accounts of developments in the case. *Chicago Tribune* writer Morrow Krum was one of the reporters riding along with Loeb and police detectives as they toured locations relevant to the crime following the confessions. Krum portrayed Loeb as swinging wildly from arrogant self-assurance to complete despair during the course of the expedition, beginning with—as Krum reported it on June 2—Loeb's assertion that "This thing will be the making of me."

"'I'll spend a few years in jail and I'll be released,' Loeb said confidently. 'I'll come out to a new life. I'll come out and I'll work hard and I'll amount to something—make a career.'"

When a detective then reminded Loeb that he had "taken a life, you've killed a boy," Loeb was said to plunge into a florid fit of remorse, recalling "the sight of that happy little boy [Bobby Franks], swinging down the sunlit sidewalk, swaying from side to side in his happiness, his innocence. I have thought of that several times. He was such a fine kid. His little tennis raquet, no I guess he didn't have the raquet as we dragged him into the car, but O his face, the sunlight, the happiness in his eyes."

**MR. LOEB:** Oh, quite a while ago. It is four or five years ago.

**MR. LEOPOLD, JR:** It couldn't have been five or six years ago.

**MR. LOEB:** Probably not.

**MR. LEOPOLD, JR:** It surely wouldn't have been over ten years ago.

**MR. LOEB:** No.

**MR. LEOPOLD, JR:** Do you think you have a more keen interest in mystery stories and detective stories than the interest that is shown by most boys of our age?

GOVERNESS: Loeb appears to be referring to Emily Struthers, who would subsequently become a subject of great interest to the defense psychiatrists (see chapter 37, page 129).

**MR. LOEB:** Yes, I think I have. When I was a boy until the age of fourteen or about, I think, around there until some time later, I had a governess. This governess was originally with me, and then my little brother, who was younger, then had her as a governess. She elicited great care over me, and as a child she read to me out loud, always took very fine literature. I remember the stuff I read as a child is about fifteen times deeper and superior literary style to the literature I have read during the last four or five years.

**DR. KROHN:** For instance, what?

MICHAEL ANGELO'S LIFE: Loeb is referring to *The Life of Michael Angelo* (Michelangelo) by Herman Grimm, originally published in 1865.

**MR. LOEB:** For instance, "Quo Vadis," the works of Dickens, Michael Angelo's by Grimm; I think she gave me Michael Angelo's Life, by Grimm, on something like my tenth birthday, and read it to me at that age. I enjoyed it; she read it very well, and everything like that. But I probably had the looks that I was tired of it. Furthermore, I have followed in college history courses to the exclusion of almost everything else. In history courses you have to do a great deal of reading, and a lot of the reading is very deep; for instance, if you take a mathematical course, or some sort of course, the usual reading which you do is very limited; and I had to read a whole mass of stuff, and when I came to read for pleasure, I used to pick on something light; and that is how I account for my interest in that sort of thing.

**MR. CROWE:** Let me ask this question: Who typed this letter?

**MR. LEOPOLD, JR:** I did, sir.

**MR. CROWE:** That is the letter to the Franks people.

**MR. LEOPOLD, JR:** Yes, sir.

**MR. CROWE:** Who composed it?

**MR. LEOPOLD, JR:** I composed it, jointly.

**MR. CROWE:** How about that?

**MR. LOEB:** That is, to a certain extent, true. The first part of that letter was typewritten, written on Leopold's stationery; we sat down there and he type-wrote it. It is quite obvious, it is quite natural that a man who would write the letter, whether he was writing it or typewriting it, he did most of the composing, Leopold asking "Shall I say this", and "Shall I say that?" And I saying, "Yes," or making some corrections. It was done jointly, and I really think the majority of the letter was written and the conversation was entirely Mr. Leopold's.

**MR. LEOPOLD, JR:** Didn't I make some changes at your suggestion?

**MR. LOEB:** There were some changes, yes.

# 23
# No man could feel happy

## ETTELSON CONFRONTS LEOPOLD

THE CONFESSIONS CONCLUDES with a conversation between Sam Ettelson and Leopold recorded as having taken place at 1 a.m. on Sunday, June 2, in the state's attorney's office. The exchange is interesting for two reasons. First, because it contradicts reporting by the papers and others writing about the case that Jacob Franks did not yet know about the death of his son when he took the second phone call from "George Johnson." Second, because Ettelson himself had apparently answered that second phone call. He had been with the Franks family almost from the first moment they realized Bobby was missing, offering strategic, legal, and emotional support, and that afternoon he was screening their phone calls. But Ettelson was a friend of the Leopold family as well as the Franks family. It is still clearly hard for him to grapple with the news that the terrifying George Johnson, who had cold-bloodedly murdered his close friend's child, had been Leopold all along.

**MR. ETTELSON: Q** You telephoned to Mr. Franks' home about 3:35 Thursday, or 3:30 Thursday?

**[MR. LEOPOLD:] A** Yes.

**Q** That was May 22nd?

**A** Yes.

**Q** This year?

**A** Yes.

**Q** Now, who answered the phone?

**A** You did.

**Q** Did you recognize the voice?

**A** No, sir.

**Q** How did you know?

**A** I read the newspaper account of it.

**Q** Well, someone answered the phone?

**A** Yes.

**Q** And you say it was I?

**A** Yes.

**Q** Well, then, what happened?

**A** I said, "Hello," you said "Hello". I said, "Is Mr. Franks in?" You said, "Who wants him?" I said, "Mr. Johnson wants him." "Who is that?" I said, "George Johnson"; and you said, "Just a minute." Somebody else came to the phone—at least, there was a pause, I don't know, they came back, and somebody said, "Hello." I said, "Mr. Franks?" He said, "Yes." I said, "This is George Johnson speaking, and there will be a Yellow cab at your door in ten minutes", and to get into it and proceed immediately to the drug store at 1465 East 63rd street. I remember it, you asked me what that first sentence was about the Yellow cab, and I repeated it. He said, "Now, can't I have a little bit more

## LEOPOLD'S SWEETHEART

Among those in the intimate circles of Nathan Leopold and Richard Loeb who were struggling with disbelief in the aftermath of the confessions was Susan Lurie, Leopold's apparent sweetheart, who was in her senior year at the University of Chicago, studying philosophy. *Chicago Daily Tribune* reporter Morrow Krum described her in the June 2 edition as having a "slender dainty figure," with brown hair, black eyes, and dimples that "played in each cheek." In an exclusive interview with Krum, she revealed that she had gone on two dates with Leopold between the time of the murder and his arrest. The first had been the Friday night after the murder, when, she said, "he seemed gay." They danced and were happy "and he did not once mention the sensation that was sweeping over the city. . . . I have had trouble making myself believe even now that he is guilty."

CONTINUED

time?" I said, "No you can't have any more time; you must go immediately", and I hung up the phone.

**Q** Didn't he say something had come up that made it necessary for him to have a few hours?

**A** He may have, but I didn't hear it.

**Q** Didn't he say something about—

**A** No, the only question he asked me, "Couldn't I have a little more time?" I said, "No, sir."

**Q** You see, at the noon time he got news of the death of his boy.

**A** He didn't have it then, did he?

**Q** I sent Ed Gresham [Mrs. Franks's brother] out with two of the newspaper boys [to identify the body] and told him to call up at the Franks residence and just use one word if it was Robert's body, say "Yes", and if it was not say "No", because I didn't want the mother to get it, because they had an extension phone.

He called up and said, "Hello, Sam", and I said, "Yes." "Well," he said, "Yes." So then the receiver was hung up, and I proceeded to tell Mr. Franks; I said, "Jake, it looks to me as if the worst had happened." And he said, "What do you mean?" I said, "Your boy is dead." So just three minutes after that time you called up, and that is why he was so nervous.

**A** He was perfectly calm.

**Q** Well, maybe you think so, but he wasn't. One o'clock—two o'clock—three o'clock—three-thirty. Now, I got the message from Ed Gresham, the boy is dead, and I proceeded to tell this to Franks, "It looks pretty bad", and the next sentence was, "It looks as if the worst had happened," and he said, "What do you mean?" I said, "That your boy is dead." Now, you don't think that if a telephone call came to the father who thought his boy was alive and who expected to get him back, that he wouldn't be a little upset with that news, do you?

**A** Of course not.

**Q** So when you gave the number, he didn't quite get the number, and so he said, "Repeat it", and you hung up.

**A** No, sir; I repeated the even number twice.

**Q** Well, he didn't get it; all he got was—what was it, thirteen or fourteen?

**A** Fourteen, 1463.

**Q** Well, all he got was the fourteen.

**A** I was under the impression that the phone call telephoning the boy was dead came between my phone call and the arrival of the Yellow cab.

**Q** The papers didn't have it right; because within five minutes of the time I gave my news of the death of the boy, this call came from Johnson—Nathan Leopold, in other words. So no man could feel happy.

**A** Well, I am surprised at the complete calmness of the voice.

**Q** Well, let me tell you something—

**A** I was a lot shakier than he.

**Q** What do you mean?

**A** The only reaction I had in the whole case was when I stepped in the telephone booth and called that number, my voice quivered.

**Q** Well, what was the reaction?

**A** Well, I didn't just have complete control of myself.

CONTINUED

Even more disturbing, though, was the lunch they'd had together on the day before Leopold's arrest. Leopold, she said, had bought a newspaper, spread it on the table, and begun discussing the Franks murder with her. She had said that it would be a good joke if he went to the police and confessed to the crime, to which he replied that it would be a perfect joke and she would collect the $10,000 reward for identifying the killer. "He laughed gayly over that."

"Her voice was low," Krum reported. "Appreciation of the fact that she had been with a murderer was in her eyes."

# PART III

# The Hulbert-Bowman Report

# 24
# A perfect case for the death penalty

## CLARENCE DARROW CALLS IN THE ALIENISTS

**EVERY POSSIBLE KINDLINESS**

At the end of the exhausting weekend that produced the confessions and the additional corroborating evidence from the macabre field trip reconstructing the crime, State's Attorney Robert Crowe had no doubts about his "hanging case."

"I have never heard of a case so complete," Crowe was quoted as saying in the June 6 *Chicago Herald and Examiner*. "There is nothing missing. It's a perfect case for the death penalty."

Crowe emphasized that the defendants' confessions had been made freely and without duress. In fact, he elaborated, "I was afraid I would be criticized for treating these prisoners too well. Before they confessed they were fed and housed at the best hotels. The bill for them for one night at one hotel was $102. While they were having every possible kindliness, I and other investigators were eating sandwiches or nothing. I had no food from Friday morning until Saturday morning."

**S**O OVERWHELMING was the evidence against Nathan Leopold and Richard Loeb that the only remaining mystery in the case appeared to be: *Why?* What had driven such promising, brilliant, well-brought-up young men to commit such an unimaginably cruel and senseless crime? No one seemed quite able to accept the explanation offered by Leopold and Loeb themselves: that the whole thing had been dreamed up, carefully planned over several months, and coldly executed based on "a pure love of excitement, or the imaginary love of thrills, doing something different."

The newspapers scrambled to find "experts" to make sense of things. The June 2 *Chicago Daily Journal* credited "the boys at the University of Chicago" with coining the term "Dementia Jazzmania" to denote a disease "that peps up the ego of the individual until he imagines he is mentally what Jack Dempsey is physically, a super-self, able to outwit all other persons in the commission of crime and to outthink the rest of the world in avoiding its detection." Also on June 2 the *Chicago Daily Tribune* quoted a "Jewish Spokesman" who blamed the crime on the abandonment of Jewish values in the Leopold and Loeb families, as in the families of the United States's other "hundreds of thousands of rich Jews who don't know what to do with their money, and who let their children grow up without any feeling of Jewish responsibilities." The June 9 *Chicago Herald and Examiner* had "Psychologist and Character Analyst" Charles A. Bonniwell diagram the features of both boys' mouths, to prove how Loeb's lack of "will power" could be clearly read in his narrow, weak lips, while Leopold's "thick and beefy" lips suggested his "desires would more than likely be gross." The families, who had encouraged their sons to cooperate fully with detectives—never imagining for a moment that they could possibly be guilty—realized too late that by not insisting on legal counsel during the interrogation they had handed the state's attorney a virtual death sentence.

There was perhaps one attorney in the United States with both the skill and the nerve to take on a case this unpopular and apparently doomed. And as it happened, Clarence Darrow and his wife, Ruby, were fast asleep in their Chicago apartment in the wee hours of June 2 when Loeb's uncle Jacob and Nathan Leopold Sr. frantically rang the doorbell. They barged past Ruby to the bedroom, where they demanded that a very startled Clarence defend the boys. They would pay him any fee he asked for, they said—the families' combined net worth being at least $15 million, according to the papers.

Darrow had known the Loeb family for years, and he was shocked to hear that Loeb had confessed to this murder that was mesmerizing the nation. But it wasn't personal loyalty that persuaded him to take the case, he said later. He had made his name defending underdogs, often at substantial risk to his own career, but usually because he saw in their predicaments a chance to advance social justice. A passionate debater at heart, he was brilliant at winning over juries with a unique mixture of down-home folksiness and soaring eloquence; his closing arguments were often published, popularly read, and widely influential. He fiercely opposed the death penalty, and in Leopold's and Loeb's confrontation with a state's attorney who had publicly declared he had a "hanging case," he saw a very high-profile forum in which to make his argument.

The most obvious defense available to the boys was insanity. To the general public, this idea was nearly self-evident: by definition, wouldn't you have to be crazy to do what Leopold and Loeb had done? But to be recognized as legally insane, the defendants would have to be shown (1) not to be capable of distinguishing between right and wrong and (2) not to be capable of refraining from committing an act they knew was wrong.

> To be recognized as legally insane, the defendants would have to be shown (1) not to be capable of distinguishing between right and wrong and (2) not to be capable of refraining from committing an act they knew was wrong.

As part of the interrogation, Crowe had already called in alienists who would be prepared to declare the boys unquestionably sane. So the first move by Darrow and his defense team was to scour the country for prominent psychiatrists who could look for grounds to dispute that.

## SUSPECTED MENTAL KINKS

The idea that science could help unravel the mysteries and irrationalities of human behavior was an extremely progressive one in 1924. Psychoanalysis was still in its infancy—and though Sigmund Freud personally declined an invitation from publisher William Randolph Hearst to travel to the United States and analyze Nathan Leopold and Richard Loeb himself, a case can be made that it was his influence on the alienists who did examine them and whose theories about their behavior were publicized during the court case that brought Freudian theory into mainstream consciousness.

Given that Leopold and Loeb had suggested to interrogators that the murder of Bobby Franks had been, for them, a kind of scientific experiment, reporters delighted in the idea that the tables were about to turn and the murderers were themselves to become the subjects of experiments, during "tests on which their lawyers rely to save their necks."

Evoking a kind of Frankensteinian scenario, the June 13 *Chicago Daily News* reported that "The laboratory was the former death cell in the county jail, now used for various extraordinary purposes; the scientists, two psychiatrists—Dr. [Karl] Bowman of the Boston psychopathic hospital, brought here to direct examinations of the young kidnaper-murderers, and Dr. Harold S. Hulbert of Chicago."

It was explained that all this scientific testing of the defendants would show that "despite their brilliance in college certain functions of the mind have been affected by physical flaws." And, since Bowman specialized in studying the influence of the ductless glands on human behavior, he would be applying specialized testing "to try to determine whether any of these glands has caused the suspected mental kinks in his subjects."

# 25

# IN RE: NATHAN LEOPOLD, JUNIOR

## THE SCOPE OF THE PSYCHIATRIC REPORTS

CLARENCE DARROW hoped that either the most modern theories of psychotherapy or of biochemistry—specifically the study of glands suspected of influencing human behavior—might help explain the crime. He hired Karl Bowman, the chief medical officer at the Boston Psychopathic Hospital and a noted expert in the "ductless glands," to come to Chicago to make a thorough examination of Leopold and Loeb.

"The thyroid and parathyroid glands in the neck, the thymus in the chest, the pituitary and pineal glands in the head, the gonads or sex glands all belong to this group," a medical expert explained to the *Chicago Daily Tribune*, "and it is apparent that the defense hopes to be able to prove that some fundamental disorder or failure to function of these glands caused a mental condition in which Leopold and Loeb killed Robert Franks."

Harold Hulbert, a young Chicago neuropsychiatrist in private practice, was hired to assist Bowman in his examinations. Together with a succession of other prominent psychiatrists summoned from the East Coast over the course of the next several weeks, Hulbert and Bowman produced reports on both Leopold and Loeb containing extraordinarily detailed portraits of each boy's upbringing, physical condition, education, fantasy life, sexual experience, and thoughts about the crime. The excerpts in this section are taken directly from Hulbert's own copies of the reports, now part of the Harold S. Hulbert Papers in the Northwestern University Archives.

Most of the contents of these reports—with the exception of some of the extremely sexually explicit material—made their way into the newspapers. Darrow claimed they had been stolen from his office and that, realizing they were about to be published by one paper, he then gave them to the others to be "fair," but it's also possible that Darrow simply leaked them because he had shrewdly calculated that the intimacy of the material might help humanize the defendants in the popular imagination. It is certainly true, as historian Paula Fass observed, that the newspapers' obsessive coverage of and speculation about every detail of the lives of the two murderers completely eclipsed any focus on the life of the boy they had killed.

### IN RE: NATHAN LEOPOLD, JUNIOR

The following examination of Nathan Leopold, Junior, was made at the request of his family, through his attorneys, Messrs. Clarence S. Darrow, Benjamin C. Bachrach and Walter Bachrach, in order to determine whether or not insanity was a justifiable plea for defense, he being accused of and admitting the murder of Robert Franks, on May 21, A.D. 1924.

The examination covered a period of [eight] days, namely, from June 13, 1924 to June [21st] 1924, inclusive. It has included not only the mental and physical examination, but also numerous interviews with members of the family and others who have been more or less intimately acquainted with him, for the purpose of taking an accurate history and studying the case from every possible angle. The examination included a physical, a neurological and endocrine and X-ray examination and clinical laboratory examinations, and an exhaustive psychiatric study.

The examination of the patient took place at the Cook County Jail, in Chicago.

Brothers BENJAMIN AND WALTER BACHRACH were both prominent Chicago attorneys, brought to the defense team by the Leopold family, as Darrow was brought by the Loebs.

# 26
# I am small, my heart is pure

## THE BRILLIANT BABY LEOPOLD

### THE JEWISH ANGLE

Calling the Franks murder "one of the most important crimes on record," the June 2 *Chicago Daily Tribune* noted that one of its most significant aspects was that "The three principals in the tragedy are of one race. The Franks boy, Leopold and Loeb are all Jews." Thus, the *Tribune* had invited Dr. S. L. Melamed, the editor in chief of the *Jewish Courier*, to analyze the Jewish angle of the case.

Fearing an anti-Semitic backlash in which the public might hold the whole Jewish population responsible for the crime, Melamed firmly asserted that the real "Jewish tragedy" of the Franks murder lay in the fact that the Leopold and Loeb families had abandoned all their Jewish beliefs and practices.

"If the parents of these two boys had given the children a Jewish education, if the boys had borne on their shoulders individual responsibility, if they had interested themselves in Jewish problems, if their hearts had bled for their people, if they had been consciously Jewish with Jewish souls, they would certainly not have devoted

CONTINUED

LEOPOLD'S SAGA OF brilliant overachievement began in infancy, according to information collected by the doctors. Early milestones recorded in his baby book—taking his first step at three months, speaking at four months—seem to defy nature and suggest how invested the family must have been in Leopold's identity as a precocious, overachieving child.

The delivery was normal. The baby was breast fed. [Leopold] was a very wakeful baby.

His baby book shows the following data: He was born on Saturday, the nineteenth of November, 1904, at 3:55 P.M., at 3223 Michigan Avenue, Chicago, and weighed six pounds and four ounces. He sat at an open window at three months. He first laughed at four weeks, and he first laughed aloud at twelve and a half weeks. He took his first step at three months, namely, on February 24th. He wore his first shoes in July. He spoke his first word at four months and three weeks, saying: "Nein, Nein, Mama".

[. . .] He was bright, alert, and had a very marked affection for his Mother. From the age of one year on, he had a very marked development of the hair of the head. His facial expression at times is rather effeminate, and there are two pictures showing him dressed as a girl in costume where one would not notice anything unusual.

[. . .] When he was three years old, on the nineteenth of November, 1907, he said his first prayer:

"Ich bin klein, Mein herz is rein".

(I am small, my heart is pure).

[. . .] He has occasional headaches which he attributes to constipation. They are usually frontal in character but are sometimes occipital. He always has headaches when he has fever. He thinks headaches may have been due somewhat to eye strain, and he has had glasses prescribed for his eye condition. (He smiles sardonically when mentioning this, and says, "I wish I had not gotten them"). [This sentence is underlined in pencil and starred in the original transcript.]

(LEOPOLD)

was three feet four and one-half inches tall.

At six years he weighed forty-two pounds.

At seven years he weighed forty-three pounds
and was three feet ten inches tall.

At nine years he weighed fifty-four pounds.

At ten years he weighed sixty-five pounds and
was four feet two inches tall.

At eleven years he weighed sixty-eight pounds
and was four feet three inches tall.

At thirteen years he weighed eighty-five pounds,
and was five feet tall.

When he was three years old, on the nineteenth
of November, 1907, he said his first prayer:

"Ich bin klein, Mein herz ist rein".

(I am small, my heart is pure).

He was circumcised on the fifteenth day.

He was a chubby infant.   He grew to be a tall
boy,   but not strikingly thin,   in spite of his height.

The patient had measles when five years of
age, but as far as known, he recovered completely.  Until the age of 9, he was liable to gastro-intestinal
disturbances which were manifested by fever, headache and

-7-

(LEOPOLD)

CONTINUED

their entire time to 'pleasure and good times' and would not have had the possibility of going wrong," he argued.

The novelist Meyer Levin—a classmate of Nathan Leopold's who would decades later publish the blockbuster novel *Compulsion*, based on the murder—offered his own cunning, somewhat sly interpretation of the Jewish implications of the crime, an interpretation that alluded to the kind of emphasis on overachievement and precocity that he identified with the Jewish community (of which he was part). His 1949 memoir, *In Search*, speculates that "beneath the very real horror that the case inspired, the horror of realizing that human beings carried in them murderous motives beyond the simple motives of lust and greed and hatred, beneath all this was a suppressed sense of pride in the brilliance of these boys, sympathy for them in being slaves of their intellectual curiosities, a pride that this particular new level of crime, even this should have been reached by Jews."

The section of the Hulbert-Bowman Report transcribed in part on the facing page, including Leopold's first prayer.

# 27
# The governess

## DESPITE HIS MEANNESS

It is not clear where Pauline Van den Bosch fit into the sequence of Nathan Leopold's governesses. In the June 4 *Chicago Daily Tribune* she said that she was in the household from 1916 to 1918, the years when Leopold would have been 12 to 14—though the psychiatrists in their report claim that after Sweetie, who would have been the previous governess, left the household, there were no further governesses. The psychiatrists don't seem to have tracked Van den Bosch down to ask about her tenure in the household or include her thoughts in their report, but she was widely quoted in the newspapers. She said in the *Tribune* that she loved Nathan best of the three Leopold children "despite his

CONTINUED

A T THE ANNUAL meeting of the American Psychiatric Association, which happened to convene in Atlantic City, New Jersey shortly after the sensational confessions, the consensus of delegates, as reported in the June 5 *Chicago Daily Tribune*, was that "The real responsibility for the tragic careers of Nathan Leopold Jr. and Richard Loeb of Chicago, millionaire self-confessed slayers of 14 year old Robert Franks, rests with their parents." Ironically, it was to this convention that Clarence Darrow sent attorney Walter Bachrach, seeking additional alienists for their cause, and by the time the Hulbert-Bowman Report was finalized, the defense team had carefully absolved the families (who had, of course, funded the activities of the psychiatrists and the writing of the report).

Blame for the boys' upbringings had been shifted in both cases entirely to their governesses, whose faults are inventoried in exquisite detail. Nathan's account of his relationship with "Sweetie" in the following excerpt is indeed disturbing, if the details are trustworthy as reported; on the other hand, the misogyny and class bigotry of the report's authors come through clearly, for example, in their comments about how Sweetie's feeblemindedness is proved by her vulgar taste in clothing.

The patient [Leopold] had a nurse during his first six months. When she left he was taken care of by a Governess by the name of Marie Giessler, who was familiarly known as Mimie, who stayed until the patient was five or six years of age. She left because she was getting old. She was a German woman and talked in German, so that in his early childhood he was a bi-linquet [should be "bilingual"] who later made use of his knowledge of German to give him some advanced credits in school.

According to the patient, his next Governess was a little Irish Catholic girl, named Paula who stayed for a period of about six months, and who had quite an influence over the patient at that time. "She told me the lives of the saints. I was very anxious to learn". These were the minor saints largely. She fell in with his previous study of cataloguing the churches in the neighborhood where he lived.

His next governess was Miss Mathilda Wantz, an Alsatian who came direct from Alsace and spoke no English. A week after she arrived the family took a trip to Colorado Springs. The patient started to instruct her in the English language and derived great pleasure in telling her incorrect statements which would get her into embarrassing situations. For instance, he told her that "Go to hell" meant "Good morning". This governess stayed until the patient was twelve years of age. She was homely, suspicious, had a violent temper and was continually getting into scrapes with other people. "She had a very great influence over my brother and myself. She displaced my mother. She was a scheming woman, who used the children as a barrier to shield herself." The patient's nickname for her was "Sweetie". "I was thoroughly devoted to her".

Sweetie occasionally bathed in the same bath tub, at the same time with Sam [Leopold's brother], on the nights when the family were away and then went to bed with him. She played with his penis. She encouraged him to wrestle in bed with her. Once when he was lying on her he got an erection. He did not insert it. He did not know about insertion. This erection hurt him by "straining the cords". She also bathed and was more or less familiar with Nathan Leopold, Junior, the patient, although the patient cannot recall it. She showed the boys her menstrual sanitary napkins. She encouraged and permitted the boys to examine her from head to foot in her undressing closet. She was well built but tall, She often said to the boys that their mother wished that she, the mother, had a figure like hers, Sweetie's. She called her breasts "ballen". The German word translated in English means balls, but the boys felt there was no significance in this word balls to testicles, rather that the breasts were round of themselves. Another name for her breasts that she taught them was Titti-Cock-i-Zay which was the name of a Lake in Switzerland. She called her nipples "ehrdbaren" which in English means strawberries. The patient remembered the nickname for the nipples but does not remember the rest. She was a girl afraid of having children and therefore said that she was afraid of grown up men. (It is interesting to know that her present address in Alsace is number 9 Rue de Bambino, Strassburg, which means in Italian "street of the children".) She has never married. Steps have been taken to ascertain if she has ever been adjudged insane or feeble minded, in the old country. Sweetie had no middle initial and one time Sam said to her that her name was Mathilda H. Wantz, whereupon she got a flare of bad temper, which lasted for some time. The boys and Sweetie had developed the phrase, that "she's an H" which means that the maid Kittie was Heifisch or shark. The shark has a large mouth like a gash. Sweetie said Kittie was a "Hore" and was gashed, so when either of the boys or Sweetie speak of Kittie saying "she is an H", they mean that Kittie is a "hore". Sweetie would not let the boys talk to any of the other employees in the ménage and was extremely jealous of the other servants. Sweetie could be made to cry if the boys would use this phraseology: "I will have nothing more to do with you, you go to hell". There seems to be an unconfirmed idea that Sweetie would encourage and permit Nathan to use his penis on her by inserting it between her legs while she was lying on her face and he was lying on her back. The patient recalled definitely that she encouraged him to wrestle with her, and she held this out, the permission to wrestle with her, as a reward for his good conduct. One time the patient was lying down across his bed, with her head or his feet on his brother's bed. He was slightly ill at the time. This governess came into the room and jerked the beds apart and just at this moment the patient's mother came into the room. She was indignant at this familiarity or she was indignant of this treatment of her son. In either case Tillie was discharged at once and she is now living in the old country as mentioned. It was somewhat recognized in the family

CONTINUED

meanness," and that as a boy he had had "a mania for killing and collecting birds for a little museum which he kept at his home."

She recalled an afternoon when Leopold had shot at a bird on the lawn "and the shot narrowly missed the nurse at the Schaffner home, near by. I upbraided him and tried to tell him of the consequences of such carelessness."

"'I should give a damn,' was his answer."

She said she hoped they wouldn't hang him, but, she said, "I think it would be best if they would confine him for the remainder of his life at hard labor—something that would dull his too brilliant mind."

that she wasn't a good influence over the boys. An example is that once when seven years of age, when he was sick, the patient borrowed a stamp collection from a neighbor boy to compare with his own stamp collection. He found in his friend's book several duplicates of stamps which he himself did not have. He stole these stamps, aided and abetted by his governess. When the family found out about it later the stolen stamps were returned. She held over his head the threat to expose him for a while. From talking with the family the impression is gained that this woman would now be diagnosed as a feeble minded person. This impression is confirmed somewhat by comments on her dress. For example she greatly enjoyed sewing brilliant red ribbon bows in more or less profusion over her dress. She told the boys that this was beautiful, and once they asked their mother why she didn't dress in the same beautiful manner, when as a matter of fact, Mrs. Leopold and her sister, Mrs. [Birdie] Schwab were very gentile ["gentile" is used in the original transcript] ladies and had very excellent taste in women's dress.

The Psychiatric importance is that this woman of very peculiar mentality was so close to the boys, especially the patient, that the boys took her abnormal ideas as normal, because of "primacy, frequency and intensity". The patient had no other governesses.

# 28
# Happiness is a perfume

## LEOPOLD'S MOTHER

IN ADDITION TO bearing two other healthy sons—Leopold's older brothers, Foreman ("Mike") and Samuel—his mother had suffered three miscarriages. During her pregnancy with Nathan she developed nephritis (an inflammation in the kidneys) and was confined to bed. She remained an invalid for the next 17 years, until she died. In the psychiatric narrative, Leopold's feelings of guilt and loss help show his otherwise incomprehensible lack of empathy and morality to be a response to his tragic early bereavement.

[Leopold] states that his mother was beautiful, loving, lovable and kind. As a small child he thought that she had a temper, but now he wonders why he should have thought so. His mother was charitable, kind, extremely considerate and the champion of the weak. She hated to have her children separated from her, but was stoical when her sons went away to war. She had good common sense, but was not brilliant. She was rather poor at figures. She was a fair linguist. She had very little ability with music. When a girl she had displayed great histrionic ability. With regard to her attitude toward the patient, "she was disgustingly and inordinately proud of me." The patient felt rather mixed emotions towards this attitude of his mother's. The patient found that it was rather easy to persuade her when he wished to alter her opinion. She was very conscientious. Every letter that she wrote to the patient she would end up telling him to watch his bowel movements and to brush his teeth.

She was idolized by all who knew her. She was interested in a great many philanthropies, her favorite motto was "Happiness is a perfume you cannot sprinkle on others without getting a few drops on yourself".

As he grew older the patient became more attached to his mother. He does not seem willing to admit that there was any extreme attachment to his mother, and takes the view that it was simply a rather normal love for a mother who was infinitely above the average mother. For the last three years, before her death, he knew that her nephritis was a complication of her last pregnancy, namely the one when he was born. This worried him and depressed him very much. He felt after she died, that he was the cause of her death, that he was here instead of her. He visited the cemetery often. Almost always he used to visit with her before going out on an expedition to go birding. He regarded his mother and her sister Aunt Birdie (Mrs. Schwab) as two bodies with one soul. It is noticed that these ladies have lived side by side ever since the first of them became married and that Aunt Birdie is now the manager of the Leopold household, tending to her own household duties as well. The patient states that after his Aunt Birdie took charge of the household he tended to think of her to a certain extent as replacing his mother. His brothers apparently noticed this and reproached him for this.

The patient states that there have been two experiences in his life which have completely altered his philosophy of life and changed his general attitude toward

---

1 Fass was mistaken; Leopold's mother Florence died when he was just a month short of his 17th birthday, in 1921.

## THE LOSS OF BOBBY

Due to the detailed questioning by Karl Bowman and Harold Hulbert, an enormous amount of information about the childhoods of both Nathan Leopold and Richard Loeb has been preserved. Outside the walls of the jail where they were being held their celebrity continued to grow. A reporter from the *New York Herald Tribune*, for instance, noted on June 4 that Leopold hoped someday to write about his prison experiences. The reporter even compared him to Oscar Wilde—inserting little tidbits from "The Ballad of Reading Gaol" into the story.

On the other hand, any clear picture of Bobby Franks, the victim, dissolved into brief, sentimental—and only occasional—references to "that poor little lad," and, as coverage of the case continued, mostly disappeared.

As historian Paula Fass has written, "The Hulbert-Bowman Report did not explain away the death of the Franks child, but it substituted the troubled bodies and childhoods of the killers for the tragic loss of Bobby and the remainder of his childhood. One could hardly read Hulbert and Bowman's reports and not be affected by the fragile loneliness of Leopold's childhood, scarred by feelings of physical inferiority, the sexual abuse of a governess, and the loss of this mother when he was fourteen."[1]

mankind. His boyish philosophy was that a man was good until he was proven otherwise, now he is cynical and has few friends. The reason he has few friends is because a friend could hurt him so much that he does not wish to take the chance of this occurring. He says that as a burnt child shuns the fire, so he shuns making friends because they might hurt him. Everything now he says he does from a purely selfish motive. His mother's death is one of the things which has so altered his feelings. He feels that if his mother who was such a good and exceptional person had to suffer so much in this world, and that if God took her away from this world when she was needed here, then that God is a cruel and senseless God and he does not care to worship him. "After my mother's death I realized that if I could kid myself into the belief that there was a life hereafter I would be happier, but I felt I must be intellectually honest." [. . .] He feels that there is not such things as an inherent right or wrong and that justice has no objective existence. He feels that the only wrong he can do is to make a mistake and his happiness is the only thing in life that matters at all to him. [. . .] When he is questioned about whether he has contemplated suicide as a way out of his present difficulty he states that he will not commit suicide, first because of his duty to his family,–that he must do as they say, and second because the trial will be intensely interesting and he will learn a good deal and enjoy it. In this connection he hopes to see the physician's report made at the end of the examination. He states that he is not despondent nor is he downhearted. (The possibility of suicide must always be borne in mind in this case.)

(LEOPOLD)

his mother, and takes the view that it was simply a
rather normal love for a mother who was infinitely
above the average mother.  For the last three years,
before her death, he knew that her nephritis was a complication of her last pregnancy, namely the one when
he was born.  This worried him and depressed him very
much.  He felt after she died, that he was the cause
of her death,  that he was here instead of her.  He
visited the cemetery often.  Almost always he used to
visit with her before going out on an expedition to
go birding.  He regarded his mother and her sister
Aunt Birdie (Mrs. Schwab) as two bodies with one
soul.  It is noticed that these ladies have lived side
by side ever since the first of them became married
and that Aunt Birdie is now the manager of the Leopold
household,  tending to her own household duties as well.
The patient states that after his Aunt Birdie took
charge of the household he tended to think of her to a
certain extent as replacing his mother.  His brothers
apparently noticed this and reproached him for this.

    The patient states that there have been two
experiences in his life which have completely altered

-45-

(LEOPOLD)

From the 45th page of
the Hulbert-Bowman
Report. Though
Leopold's lack of normal
human feeling became
one of the dominant
aspects of his public
persona, the early
death of his mother was
something that appeared
to haunt him for the rest
of his life (see chapter
75, page 288).

# 29
# Never been attracted to the opposite sex

### LEOPOLD'S LOVE LIFE

## Puppy Love

What Nathan Leopold told Karl Bowman and Harold Hulbert about his negative feelings toward women is directly contradicted by the account he wrote many years later of this period of his life. In *Life Plus 99 Years*, he writes gushingly about his feelings for Susan Lurie, the University of Chicago student he was seeing at the time of the murder. Referring to her by the pseudonym "Connie," he recalled that "I was head over heels in love. Puppy love, if you like, but somehow it doesn't seem like puppy love when you're a puppy. . . . She was far more beautiful than any other girl I'd seen, and far more intelligent—she was graduating from the university in June."

He recalled the last time he saw her as having been on the Sunday after Bobby Franks's murder, when he took her canoeing on the Des Plaines River: "We found the perfect nook, a grassy glen surrounded by thick woods. Here we beached the canoe. Connie had brought the blue vellum-covered volume of French poetry I had given her for her birthday the week before. And as she read the liquid verses to me, I laid my head in her lap." Leopold recalled this afternoon as "the happiest of my life." That was May 25, the same day several hundred gawkers gathered outside the Franks home back in Hyde Park to watch eight of Bobby's young classmates carry his casket to the hearse for the ride to his final resting place in the family mausoleum at Rosehill Cemetery.

Susan Lurie, who was dating Leopold at the time of the murder, and State's Attorney Robert Crowe. Lurie was brought in for questioning during the trial.

Chicago History Museum, DN-0077611

THE HULBERT-BOWMAN REPORT includes a short section, "LOVE LIFE," and a much longer one, "SEX LIFE," chronicling Leopold's sexual development, experiences, and fantasies in minute detail. Based on their interviews, the psychiatrists are unequivocal in stating that Leopold "has never been attracted towards the opposite sex," entertaining the idea of marriage only narcissistically, as a means of ensuring that his "germ plasm" will live on.

From "LOVE LIFE":

The patient [Leopold] has never been attracted towards the opposite sex and has never had any real love affair. He has always tended to look down upon woman and despise them because he has felt them inferior intellectually. He did not have the average puppy love affairs of the growing boy. He looked for a girl because his friends did it. It was the thing to be done. He never looked forward with much emotion to marrying. He thought that he would probably marry and have children but he never picked out any definite girl or any definite ideal as a possible subject. Because of his lack of sex attraction towards women he wondered if he would be able to satisfy his wife and whether he should marry. He is not engaged or in love with any girl at the present time.

From "SEX LIFE":

The patient later slightly contradicts himself about his ideas for marriage and early love affairs, and states that he has definitely planned to marry and have children. In his idea the germ plasm is the only type of immortality there is. He has felt that his children will be superior to the average. With regard to children he hoped to have three. First a boy, then a girl and then another boy. In raising his children he would never allow taboos to spring up or impose such fictions as Santa Claus upon them. He then hastens to add that if the children's mother were very insistent upon telling the children there was a Santa Claus he would consent to that. He would send his children to Sunday school until they were eleven or twelve years of age and then allow them to decide for themselves.

# 30
# King and slave
## LEOPOLD'S FANTASY LIFE

### Leopold's Later Denial

Clarence Darrow unquestioningly incorporated Karl Bowman and Harold Hulbert's king-slave narrative into his defense case, but like so much in the psychiatric reports, it may not be accurate. In his book *Leopold and Loeb: The Crime of the Century*, Hal Higdon wrote that 36 years later, while being deposed for his lawsuit against the author of the book *Compulsion*, Nathan Leopold validated almost all the contents of the transcript of the 1924 court case, but when asked if it was true that in his king-slave fantasies he was the slave 90 percent of the time, he became visibly angry and snapped, "That's not true!" The attorney then read him the passage in this chapter from the Hulbert-Bowman Report, after which he again insisted, "Drs. Bowman and Hulbert were mistaken."

IN THE WEEKS following the crime, the press embellished the general impression they had formed initially that Leopold was the Evil Misfit Genius who held Richard Loeb—the Good-Natured Fraternity Boy—under his spell and drove him to commit a crime which otherwise he might not have gotten involved in. When leaked to the press, the Hulbert-Bowman Report turned that impression on its head, revealing Leopold's salacious fantasies about a king and his slave in which (according to the psychiatrists) Leopold imagined himself to be in the slave role 90 percent of the time, with his "companion" (i.e., Loeb) in the role of king. For the psychiatrists, this dovetailed neatly with Loeb's fantasies of being a master criminal who needed a worshipful follower to help him carry out the brilliant crimes he liked to plan, so that Loeb became the driving delinquent force and Leopold the nerdy but obedient sidekick.

REVERIES OR PHANTASIES

When five years old the patient [Leopold] first saw his brother who had been to military school in a uniform. He idolized his oldest brother. He was greatly impressed by the uniform and the idea of having a body of men under command appealed to him intensely. He commenced to construct phantasies, which he indulged in, before going to sleep at night. His earliest phantasy was that of "King and Slave."

In this phantasy of King and Slave the patient was sometimes the Slave and sometimes the King but he usually preferred to play the role of the Slave and figures that in ninety percent of his phantasies he occupied the role of Slave. The phantasy had a great many variations which he would develop from time to time. His first account of the phantasy was there was a King who had a Slave who was intensely devoted to him. This Slave was the strongest man in the world. In some way or other, and the way frequently varied, he saved the life of the King. The King was very grateful and wanted to give him his liberty but the Slave refused. The Slave was usually comfortable as regards his living conditions, but occasionally in some of the phantasies, would be in a cell.

There were often "Kings' Banquets", where each King brought his body Slave along to serve him. The Slaves were all chained but the patient was only chained with a tiny gold chain which he could easily have broken.

When the patient was a Slave he was always very good looking and very strong. Often times there would be combats when a champion would be picked from each

(LEOPOLD)

## REVERIES OR PHANTASIES

When five years old the patient first saw his brother who had been to Military school in a uniform. He idolized his oldest brother. He was greatly impressed by the uniform and the idea of having a body of men under command appealed to him intensely. He commenced to construct phantasies, which he indulged in, before going to sleep at night. His earliest phantasy was that of "King and Slave". He tried at times to actually play out this phantasy, but never succeeded in doing it and it did not seem to work. He therefore confined himself to the level of imagery without much effort to act out his ideas.

In this phantasy of King and Slave the patient was sometimes the Slave and sometimes the King but he usually preferred to play the role of the Slave and figures that in ninety percent of his phantasies he occupied the role of Slave. The phantasy had a great many variations which he would develop from time to time. His first account of the phantasy was there was a king who had a Slave who was intensely devoted to him. This Slave was the strongest man in the

(LEOPOLD)

From the "King and Slave" section of the Hulbert-Bowman Report.

side to settle a question. The patient would be selected to represent his side and would always win. The patient kept a very logical mind with all of the phantasies and was often much disturbed because he couldn't work out his phantasies logically and because there seemed to be objections. For instance, he states that in one phantasy there would be thousands of men armed with guns trying to overpower him but he would kill them all off. Then his reasoning would assert itself and he would inquire how it would be possible that one of these thousands of armed men should have managed to shoot and kill him. This phantasy was so illogical and impossible to him that he would give it up.

In another phantasy the King would be holding Court and the patient, as his Slave, would be lying at his feet. Some one would endeavor to murder the King, but the patient would prevent him.

In the summer of 1916, when not quite twelve, the patient went to a summer camp. It was here that he first made an attempt to fit any of his companions or his associates into these phantasies. The Counsellor in his tent, William M_____ was a well developed and to his mind, at that time, a very good looking boy of eighteen. The patient proceeded to fit him into the position of Slave. At this time his phantasy was a nightly occurrence. He would lie on his side or stomach, with his arms under the pillow, hugging the pillow. He would experience a certain odor which would be partially from the pillow and partially from his own body and which he regarded as extremely pleasant.

He developed a great love of symmetry in the human form at this time. He continued to develop his phantasies. A later development was that the King would get the Slave when he was a boy or even as a baby, at least before he was ten or twelve years of age and before he was completely developed physically. Then the King would find the boy being beaten by cruel slave drivers, dirty, neglected and sick. He would take the boy for his Slave. After the Slave had saved his life, the King would try to give the Slave his liberty but the Slave would refuse, saying that the King had saved his life. The King would say that this had caused no effort on his part and therefore he was entitled to no particular gratitude. The Slave, however, would persist that this made no difference and would refuse to accept his liberty.

HART SCHAFFNER & MARX TYPE: As pictured in 1920s advertisements for the Chicago men's clothiers, the "Hart Schaffner & Marx type of individual" would have embodied what we would call the ideal Ivy League, WASP, or preppy man.

As time went on the patient would add other good looking boys to his list of slaves. His phantasy has proceeded up until about a year ago. His ideal for the Slave has been a man who was large, muscular, or beautiful and with practically the conventional type of face. The Hart Schaffner & Marx type of individual illustrates pretty much his ideal.

The phantasy has developed certain variations in that there was a chief Slave named Bill, who would own two or three Slaves himself. These Slaves in turn would own two or three more and so on down. The King, however, would own all of them.

During the past two or three years he has fitted his closest companion [Loeb] into this King-Slave phantasy. At first this companion had not seemed very good looking to him but after a while became the patient's ideal of good looks. He commenced to think that his companion was more athletic than he actually was, and then phantasied him as an ideal athlete although this was far from the truth. This companion told the patient of receiving wonderful marks at school. Although the patient knew this was not the truth, he would not allow himself to believe that his companion was not getting perfect marks. He felt that his companion was much more brilliant and much more intellectual than he was.

Some time in 1922 or 1923 he made a table or chart for the perfect man. His companion received a score of ninety, the patient received a score of sixty-two and his other friends received scores of about thirty to forty. "At this time there was an almost complete identification of myself with _____ the companion. It was a blind hero worship."

The phantasies continued and the patient continued to consider every boy who appealed to him as eligible for the part of Slave.

The phantasy took the turn that he bought these Slaves and when the Slaves were bought they were always branded with a crown or seal on the inner calf of the right leg. The setting for this branding was often the locker room of the gymnasium of the Harvard School. ————————————————————→ HARVARD SCHOOL: The school both Leopold and Bobby Franks had attended.

The patient went on to develop a very elaborate phantasy involving himself and his companion with others in this phantasy. In this phantasy they would be taking a sea voyage and would be wrecked on an unknown island. The patient would be the only one that could speak the natives' language. A piano was saved from the wreck and the patient was the only person able to play upon it. No one in this island knew anything of music. The people in this island were divided into two groups—Nobles and Slaves. Because of his ability with the music the patient was made a Noble. He then bought a certain one of his companions to be his Slave. Often he would phantasy this companion had been the property of some one else and had been very sick and he would then nurse this companion through his illness. He would generally give this companion his choice of three things.

First: Liberty, in which case the brand mark on the inner calf of his right leg would be obliterated and he would be set free. He would, however, be at the mercy of the first lord (Noble) that saw him, who could take him for his Slave.

Second: To remain as his personal Slave in every sense of the word.

Third: To sell him to some other Noble. He would develop this phantasy so that his companion should receive worse treatment elsewhere than with him, and that therefore his companion would not be desirous of leaving him.

On this island there were two words which were specially used as terms of endearment. These words were "pussy" and "kitten".

The patient mentions that he has always been very fond of cats, and that as a small child he used to play that he was a kitten.

The patient indulged in this last mentioned phantasy over a considerable period of time and on very many occasions, proliferating it and varying it in various directions.

The patient is not spontaneous over the narrative of any of his phantasies, if any, in jail.

## A WARNING TO PARENTS

On July 28, the day that the contents of the psychiatric reports leaked into newspapers across the nation, Ben B. Lindsey, judge of the Juvenile Court of Denver and, "for a quarter of a century one of the world's foremost authorities on juvenile problems," contributed an analysis of the case to the July 28 *Los Angeles Times*, which was also syndicated to other papers through the North American Newspaper Alliance. He declared the crime to be symptomatic of a "modern mentality and modern freedom of youth, with the misunderstandings between parenthood and childhood."

Its causes, he warned, lurked in the very condition of modern youth. "The indifference to the rights of others in the stealing of automobiles, in joyrides, jazz parties, petting parties, freedom in sex relations and the mania of speed on every turn."

While Nathan Leopold and Richard Loeb should of course be held accountable for the "grewsome" crime they had committed, parents should understand that they had "drifted into the dangers that certain adult minds have made for all misdirected youths. Thus in Loeb and Leopold we find two childhood wrecks, beating against the rocky mental shores of the Schopenhauers and the Nietzsches, with their pessimism, their atheism, their materialism, to which is added the filthy sex eroticism of the sixteenth century."

# 31
# Partners in crime

## DEEDS LEOPOLD AND LOEB HAD
## PREVIOUSLY COMMITTED TOGETHER

L EOPOLD AND LOEB both told the psychiatrists about a series of "delinquencies" they
had committed together. Leopold said this had begun around the time he was 15—the same
time he started drinking alcohol and "commenced to go about with women." Loeb, he said, first
convinced him to cheat at cards, and he asserted that he had gone along without getting any great
thrill or satisfaction from it. "On the other hand, there doesn't appear to have been the slightest
feeling of guilt or remorse," the doctors noted. Though he followed Loeb to the University of Michigan for one year of his college education, he discovered that his friend avoided him there, telling
him that "there were rumors of homo-sexual relationship between him and the patient, and while
[Loeb's fraternity brothers] didn't believe this rumor at all, they felt that it would be an advisable
thing for him not to be seen much in the patient's company." But once they had both returned to
Chicago, the increasingly ambitious "delinquencies" resumed. They stole several cars together.
Sometimes, after drinking, they would drive around and throw bricks through the windows of other
cars. They turned in fake fire alarms and set at least one real fire, pouring gas all over a shack in
a vacant lot and then lighting it. A planned robbery of a friend's wine cellar fell through when they
couldn't get into the house. Then in November of 1923, Loeb suggested they rob his old fraternity
house at the University of Michigan late one night following a football game on campus, when the
presence of visitors on campus might distract from their activities.

They carried with them two flashlights, two loaded revolvers, rope to tie up
anybody who might interfere. The patient's [Leopold's] companion [Loeb] carried
a chisel wrapped with tape with which to hit anybody over the head who might
discover them. The patient carried one of the loaded revolvers. He says that
if anybody had recognized him he would have shot to kill. The robbery of his
companion's fraternity house went off quite successfully. They took everything
they could find of value, and a number of things of no special value, merely to make
it more unpleasant for the fraternity boys. The patient picked up a typewriter and
brought it along. He had no specific purpose for taking it, but seeing it there, he
simply picked it up and brought it along.

The patient's companion apparently lost his nerve a little, and didn't desire to rob
the second fraternity house, but the patient insisted that that was in the agreement,
and that they should go through with it. They accordingly drove over to the second
fraternity house, but on entering they discovered that the occupants were sleeping
on the second floor, and they could hear someone snoring. As had been previously
agreed, they did not go further with this robbery, but left the house immediately.
They did, however, pick up a camera which was in the hallway, and took it with them.
They then drove home in the car and arrived safely, and no one suspected them of
being implicated.

This was the
infamous
UNDERWOOD
PORTABLE
TYPEWRITER
that was later used
to write the Bobby
Franks ransom
note and whose
presence in his
house Leopold
would have so much
trouble explaining to
the police.

# 32
# For Robert's sake

## THE FATAL PACT, PART I

**THE PARTY IS NOW IN JAIL**

On June 11, 1924—the day a "fatal pact" between Nathan Leopold and Richard Loeb was set to expire when Leopold boarded the *Mauretania* for his planned summer trip to Europe—five ocean liners left New York to cross the Atlantic. As was customary in the days when an ocean crossing was still considered a prestigious high-society event, the *New York Herald New York Tribune* reported on notables among the passenger lists of all five ships.

Among the passengers on the French liner *Paris* were Mrs. W.K. Vanderbilt, a prominent socialite and the estranged wife of William Kissam Vanderbilt II, and one Maurice C. Blake, "formerly of St. Mark's School," who "said college men would

CONTINUED

O N THE DRIVE home from the burglary at Ann Arbor, Leopold and Loeb quarreled, but both apparently worried that ending their relationship could be dangerous should the other divulge anything about the criminal and/or intimate acts they had committed together. Instead, they wound up formalizing the terms of their relationship with a pact, described in this section of the report.

The pact would expire as of June 11, when Leopold was scheduled to sail to Europe with his friend Abel Brown on the *Mauretania*. Leopold claimed that he had hoped to drag the planning of the kidnapping out long enough to escape to Europe without actually carrying it out. Instead, he wound up literally missing the boat, being confined to much less luxurious quarters in the county jail. Officials of the Cunard steamship line confirmed that he had purchased a ticket, which they cancelled.

The Hulbert-Bowman Report does omit one aspect of the pact: the sexual rewards Loeb granted to Leopold in return for obedience to his commands. This information was revealed to the judge and attorneys at the court hearing by William Healy, another alienist hired by the defense (see chapter 54, page 191).

While the patient and his companion were driving home from the robbery of the fraternity house at Ann Arbor in November, 1923, they had one of their worst quarrels. They had been drinking at the time. They made various accusations against each other, and for a time it appeared as if their friendship would break up. However, they both apparently felt that a great deal was to be gained from their friendship, and both were apparently somewhat afraid of dissolving the friendship; each feared that the other might betray him or harm him in some way. Finally they compromised on a very definite pact whereby the friendship was to be continued. Under this contract the patient [Leopold] was to be absolutely under the orders of his companion [Loeb], except that his companion should not give him any commands which would make him appear ridiculous or get him into any difficulty with his family. These commands were not to apply to minor points, and in order that the patient should know when his companion was giving him a command, which must be obeyed, according to their pact, it was arranged that his companion should say "For Robert's sake" whenever he was making a demand of the patient, under the terms of their friendship. This relationship was to last until the patient went to Europe in the summer of 1924.

On this return trip from Ann Arbor the patient's companion first broached the question of kidnapping a boy and securing ransom. The patient was not especially desirous of doing this, but agreed to it according to the terms of their friendship. His companion worked out a great many ideas and plans, whereas the patient did not take a very active part in building up the scheme. He made numerous impossible suggestions, purely with the idea of delaying the plan, and states that he didn't think the plan would ever be executed, and that he would delay things so that the plan couldn't be carried out before the time for him to go to Europe. On the other hand, he did make several very practicable suggestions which were of value in perfecting their plan. They spent a great deal of time discussing these plans. They probably met at least two or three nights a week, drank some, and talked over their plans. The patient had no real objection, or no moral scruples, against carrying out this scheme. He merely felt it was dangerous, and that he would derive no pleasure from it, therefore, he rather preferred not to participate in it. His companion, however, was quite insistent, and the plans seemed to work out rather more quickly than the patient had anticipated, so that by the early spring of 1924 all was ready.

CONTINUED

follow him later to be assistants at the summer camp for American boys on Lake Bourget, France." The newspaper article specifies that the college men were associated with Yale, Harvard, Princeton, and Dartmouth.

Traveling on the *Mauretania* were John Tiller, "trainer of British dancing girls"; Herman Irion, general manager for Steinway & Sons; and celebrity pro golfers Walter Hagen, Johnny Farrell, Abe Espinosa, and Gil Nicholls, who were bringing golf equipment on board "so that they may practice shipboard."

The article notes that "Nathan F. Leopold Jr., held for the murder of Robert Franks, in Chicago, was booked to sail on the Mauretania. Cancellation of his passage reads: 'The party is now in jail.'"

Leopold's passport application (reproduced on the next three pages) had been approved on April 28, less than a month before the murder. Signed by his father, as well as himself, it states that he planned on traveling in the British Isles, France, and Italy—and confirms that he planned to leave on June 11. Here we see the application and the affidavit signed by Nathan Leopold Sr. (facing page).

## FORM OF AFFIDAVIT FOR A RELATIVE.

Personally appeared before me, a Notary Public, one *N. F. Leopold* who on oath says:

That *he* is the *father* of *Nathan F. Leopold Jr.* who is an applicant for an American passport, and that the said *Nathan F Leopold Jr.* to *his* personal knowledge, was born in *Chicago, Ill* on or about *Nov. 19, 1904*

The affiant bases *his* knowledge upon the following facts:

*That the applicant is his son*

*I hereby give my son permission to travel in Europe*

*N. F. Leopold*
(Signature of affiant.)

*Manufacturer*
(Occupation.)

*1517 Conway Bldg - Chicago, Ill.*
(Address.)

Subscribed and sworn to before me this *4* day of *April* 19*24*

*Chas N Morris*
Notary Public.

[SEAL.]

Paragraph 6 of the "Rules governing the granting and issuing of passports in the United States," promulgated by the President on January 24, 1917, reads:

"NATIVE CITIZEN.—An application containing the information indicated by rule 5 will be sufficient evidence in the case of a native citizen; except that a person born in the United States in a place where births are recorded will be required to submit a birth certificate with his application. If a birth certificate is not obtainable, the application must be supported by an affidavit of the physician who attended the birth or affidavits of parents or other reputable persons having actual knowledge of the applicant's birth in this country."

1—985

(Date of departure.)

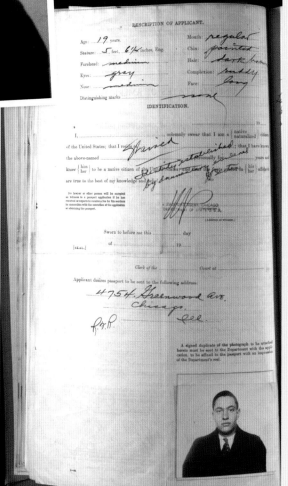

Leopold's passport photo (above) and a page from his application (right).

# 33
# Rope

## SHARING THE GUILT OF THE CRIME

### Hitchcock's Macabre and Tedious Thriller

Initial reviews of Alfred Hitchcock's film *Rope* after its 1948 release were mixed. Mae Tinee's[1] review for the *Chicago Daily Tribune* curiously doesn't reference the Leopold and Loeb murder, even though it would still have been a vivid memory for a huge proportion of the paper's Chicago readership. The review said, "If Mr. Hitchcock's purpose in producing this macabre tale of murder was to shock and horrify, he has succeeded all too well, and I'm glad the Chicago censors have decreed that no child may see it." *New York Times* reviewer Bosley Crowther found it tedious and macabre and said that "time could be better spent than by watching a waspish cocktail party in a room with a closely present corpse, placed there by a couple of young men who have killed for a thrill and nothing more." Norbert Lusk, writing in the *Los Angeles Times*, observed that "Mr. Hitchcock appears to have had a double aim: first, to shock by the cold-bloodedness of his murder story; second, to show off."

While the plot was only very loosely based on the Leopold and Loeb case, it immortalized some of the most popular tropes to become associated with the story in the collective consciousness, most notably the murderers' use of Nietzsche's concept of the Übermensch to justify actions outside the bounds of common morality.

---

THE EXACT NATURE of the ties that bound Nathan Leopold and Richard Loeb together has always been of intense interest—to the psychiatrists who examined them, to the media and the general public who followed their revelations in enormous detail, and to many of the writers, filmmakers, and others who have chronicled and reimagined the case in the decades since. They were symbolized artistically in *Rope*, first a play, then an Alfred Hitchcock film, in which two young men attempt to commit "the perfect crime" by jointly strangling a former classmate, each holding onto one end of the rope. As the psychiatrists report here, this was in fact the original plan for Bobby Franks's murder.

The earlier plan had been to kidnap a particular boy, whom the patient's companion [Loeb] did not like. This, however, was soon given up, for two reasons; first, the boy was large and strong, hence he would be difficult to capture and overcome; second, this particular boy was away to school.

They then decided to secure any small boy whom they knew to have wealthy parents, to lure him into an automobile, to knock him senseless by hitting him over the head with a taped chisel, to then take him to a secluded spot, there to strangle him with a piece of rope, then pour hydrochloric acid over the face, the penis and any identifying scars, to strip off all clothing, and to push the body deep into a funnel shaped culvert through which the water flowed, expecting the body to entirely decompose and never be found.

The patient suggested that they secure a girl instead of a boy and that [Leopold] rape her before they killed her. When asked why he suggested this he said that "it was the thing to do", and that this would also bring up his phantasy of [a] French girl being attacked by the German soldiers, and hence he would derive a great deal of pleasure from it. The patient's companion objected to this idea, so it was discarded.

---

1 Mae Tinee—a pun on "Matinee"—was the pseudonym for multiple *Tribune* film reviewers. At one point, Maurine Dallas Watkins was among them, though it seems unlikely she would have written this one, since by the 1940s, after a stint in Hollywood, she had retired to Florida. And in any case, the tone is much too priggish for someone who had taken so much delight in her original reporting on this "macabre tale of murder."

The reason why they agreed to strangle the victim with a rope was that, to their minds, that would make them both equally guilty of the crime. It was not with any idea of close friendship or brotherhood; but rather the opposite. The patient did not like the idea of strangling the victim, and suggested chloroforming him, but his companion would not agree to this. [. . .]

The patient described in detail the carrying out of the kidnapping and the murder. He told how the victim was lured into the automobile, hit over the head with a taped chisel and knocked unconscious. It was necessary to hit the victim several times over the head, and he bled some. This upset the patient a great deal. He said to his companion, "my God, this is awful"! He experienced a sinking feeling in the pit of his stomach, his hands trembled, and he lost some of his self-control. His companion, however, was quite cool and self-possessed; he laughed and joked, and helped the patient to get back his self-control. They then proceeded to a spot near the culvert. They picked the boy up and carried him several hundred yards to the culvert. They discovered that he was quite dead, and there was no necessity for strangling him. They then stripped the body of all clothing and poured hydrochloric acid over the face, the penis, and the abdominal scar.

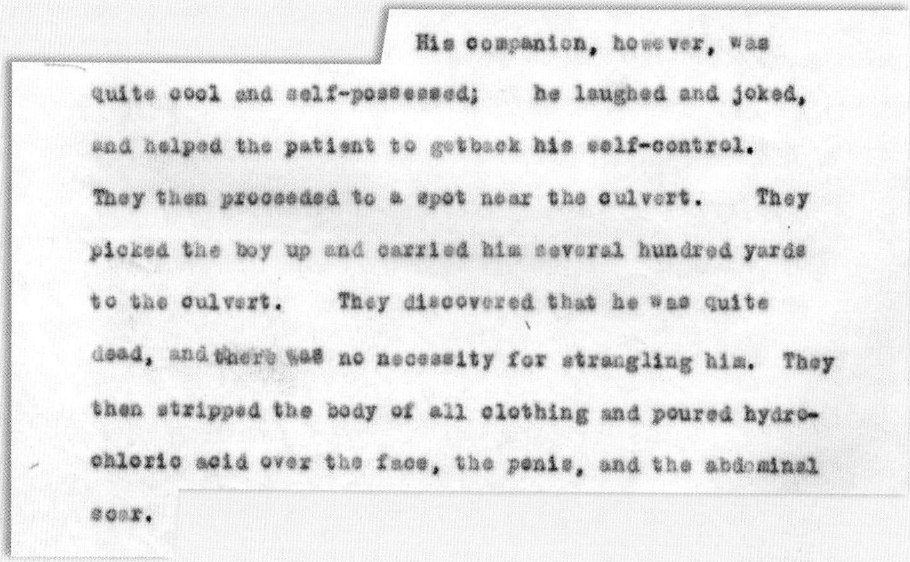
His companion, however, was quite cool and self-possessed; he laughed and joked, and helped the patient to getback his self-control. They then proceeded to a spot near the culvert. They picked the boy up and carried him several hundred yards to the culvert. They discovered that he was quite dead, and there was no necessity for strangling him. They then stripped the body of all clothing and poured hydrochloric acid over the face, the penis, and the abdominal scar.

A clipping from the Hulbert-Bowman Report, transcribed above.

Northwestern University Archives

# 34
# No question of remorse or guilt

## LEOPOLD DECLARES HIMSELF LEGALLY SANE

AFTER WEEKS of examination, the alienists asserted in their official report that they had found no support for the idea that Leopold could be declared insane—at least in legal terms. On the contrary, in the days between the murder and his arrest, he had passed with flying colors the law exams that he hoped would gain him admission to Harvard Law School, and—had his connection to the Bobby Franks murder never been discovered—would in all likelihood have become an outstanding attorney.

The patient [Leopold] denies any feeling of remorse at having committed this crime. He states that he has no feeling of having done anything morally wrong, because he doesn't feel that there is such a thing as morals, in the ordinary sense of the word. He maintains that anything which gives him pleasure, is right, and the only way in which he can do any wrong is to do something which will be unpleasant to himself.

He does not think that he is insane. He states that he knew what he was doing at the time, and he knows what the law says in regard to this.

Asked whether he would commit another such crime if he were certain that he could escape detection, he replied, "I wouldn't commit another such crime, because I realize that one can never be sure of escaping detection." He feels that this would be the only reason that would keep him from another such attempt; that there would be no question of remorse or guilt entering into the thing.

He denies that he got any pleasure from committing the crime, and says that he does not enjoy seeing people suffer. On the contrary, he insists that it is unpleasant to him to witness people suffering physical pain. He doesn't feel that this is sympathy on his part, but merely it is unpleasant, and he doesn't like to see it. He states that he is rather fond of small children; that he has always wanted to take a crying child into his arms and comfort it, and that on such occasions he almost notices "a function of my lachrymal glands."

"A FUNCTION OF MY LACHRYMAL GLANDS": By which Leopold means he almost cries.

While in the jail the patient has clearly been under considerable emotional tension, and is rather irritable at times. The newspaper report that he is a cold-blooded scientist, with no emotion and entirely unconcerned, is completely wrong. The patient, ordinarily is able to make a calm and self-possessed appearance, and before the reporters and visitors seems perfectly self-possessed and unconcerned. On the other hand, when he does not feel the need for doing this, and when he is talking frankly with people, and no longer posing, he shows a good deal of irritability and nervous tension. [ . . . ]

## ALLEGATIONS OF SANITY

As of June 15, the *Chicago Daily Tribune* reported, seven alienists had examined Nathan Leopold and Richard Loeb—three for the prosecution, and four for the defense. The idea that Leopold and Loeb would be declared insane seemed increasingly ludicrous to the press, given the confident and highly articulate manner in which they expressed themselves when interviewed. It appeared that "allegations of sanity which lie in the hands of the state" were likely to prevail.

The June 15 *Chicago Herald and Examiner* sketched for its readers a cameo of Leopold "undergoing the tests in cynical tolerance, maintaining his pose—apparently more dear to him than life itself—of the bored sophisticate, the pessimist, the cynic."

His sanity, it seemed to suggest, might even have been superior to that of his examiners. "He can even be pictured as smiling sardonically, perhaps, at what may seem to him for the moment a bit of ridiculous tomfoolery."

The patient makes no effort to shift the blame for the crime on to his companion [Loeb], although he insists that he did not really desire to commit the crime, and derived no special pleasure from doing it. He does not say this with any appearance of trying to excuse himself or to make himself appear less guilty in the eyes of others, and apparently he is perfectly honest in his statements, and is merely trying to give an accurate account of the whole affair. He feels that his only reason for getting into it, was his pact of friendship with his companion, and his companion's desire to do it. Once started in the plan, he had no feeling of guilt or remorse.

He states that he proposed to his companion that they kidnap his companion's younger brother [Tommy Loeb], and says that he would have been quite willing to go through with this plan if his companion had agreed to it.

They also considered kidnapping their respective fathers, but this idea never got very far, because the immediate objection about securing the money came to their mind. In addition, they felt they would not be free to do as they liked, and would be under a good deal of supervision and observation should they kidnap a member of either of their families.

# 35
# Her absurd taste in dress

## BLAMING THE GOVERNESS

THE HULBERT-BOWMAN REPORT concludes by exonerating Leopold's family from any possible "error or neglect" and assuring them that Leopold's "present condition" is not hereditary—i.e., was not passed down to him by his parents and is not likely to be passed on to subsequent generations. In the psychiatrists' view the only possible explanation for Leopold's behavior rests with the influence of the governess Sweetie, who so thoroughly displaced maternal influence in his childhood that "he even believed that her absurd taste in dress was superior to that of his mother."

The influence of the patient's [Leopold's] governess, "Sweetie", is of great importance in understanding this case. She was a definitely abnormal individual, who, being closely associated with him in the tender and formative years of his development, produced a profound and unwholesome effect. She produced a definite antagonism between the patient and his parents and brothers, which later was developed by the patient as a revolt against all authority. This governess set herself up as being superior to the patient's parents in every way, and the patient accepted this idea. He even believed that her absurd taste in dress was superior to that of his mother. She gave the patient a very abnormal and unhealthy introduction to sex topics, and he has never been able to secure a normal viewpoint on this subject since. Some of the things which she did to him have been forgotten or repressed, but the effects of such treatment still remain and still act as determinants for his behaving and thinking.

The mental condition which the patient manifests is an acquired one, and there is no evidence of any similar disorder in the family, with the possible exception of one incident in the collateral line, namely, a second cousin.

Physically, part of his trouble is hereditary, namely, a predisposition to Bright's disease, and part of his trouble may be associated with his mother's health before he was born, but science has not yet progressed sufficiently to be able to state the exact cause of the rest of his sickness.

However, it may be said that our present degree of knowledge gives us no reason to feel that a mental condition such as the patient's is of a hereditary nature or that it will reappear in future generations.

With the predisposing effect of his physical condition the unfortunate experiences of his early childhood are the most important causes leading to the development of his present condition.

The family have apparently endeavored to do everything possible to bring the patient up in a suitable manner, and there has been no conscious error or neglect on their part. Although he is young, the prognosis is not good.

[dated and signed by hand]

June 30, 1924 Karl M Bowman M.D. Boston

June 30, 1924 HS Hulbert MD Chicago

## A PHRENOLOGIST'S ANALYSIS OF LEOPOLD

The July 28 *Chicago Daily Tribune* accompanied its voluminous, detailed coverage of the psychiatric reports with a sketch by an unnamed phrenologist that purported to illustrate how Nathan Leopold was "mentally inferior" to Richard Loeb and was "acting under the latter's leadership" in committing the murder. Phrenology is a now-discredited nineteenth-century pseudoscience based on the idea that personality characteristics are located in specific areas of the brain and can be deduced from the external features of the head and face. The *Tribune* pictured Leopold's face in profile, with arrows showing readers which of his features betrayed his pertinent character traits. According to the diagram, his forehead showed that he "lacks reason, moral and benevolent power"; his nose shows "aggressiveness" and the spot between his eyebrows "keen perspicacity"; and though his lips are "sensuous," something hidden under the hairline on the back of his head indicates "sex weaker than Loeb."

BRIGHT'S DISEASE: An outdated term denoting various kidney diseases including nephritis, the condition from which Leopold's mother suffered.

The conclusions of the official psychiatric reports on both Leopold and Loeb accomplish several goals that were important to Darrow, and to the families: they absolve the families of any responsibility for having caused the boys' mental disorders—shifting blame vehemently onto the hired governesses to whose care both seem to have been largely abandoned; they offer the families assurance that nothing about the disorders is hereditary; and, while identifying numerous emotional abnormalities, they carefully avoid actually declaring either boy insane, as this would have suggested an insanity defense, which Darrow decided would probably play out badly for them. Here we see the section of the report on Leopold, transcribed on page 123, and on the facing page we see its counterpart from Loeb's section of the report, transcribed on page 144.

(LEOPOLD)

The influence of the patient's governess, "Sweetie", is of great importance in understanding this case. She was a definitely abnormal individual, who, being closely associated with him in the tender and formative years of his development, produced a profound and unwholesome effect. She produced a definite antagonism between the patient and his parents and brothers, which later was developed by the patient as a revolt against all authority. This governess set herself up as being superior to the patient's parents in every way, and the patient accepted this idea. He even believed that her absurd taste in dress was superior to that of his mother. She gave the patient a very abnormal and unhealthy introduction to sex topics, and he has never been able to secure a normal viewpoint on this subject since. Some of the things which she did to him have been forgotten or repressed, but the effects of such treatment still remain and still act as determinants for his behaving and thinking.

-15-                    (LEOPOLD)

(LEOPOLD)

The mental condition which the patient manifests is an acquired one, and there is no evidence of any similar disorder in the family, with the possible exception of one incident in the collateral line, namely, a second cousin.

Physically, part of his trouble is hereditary, namely, a predisposition to Bright's disease, and part of his trouble may be associated with his mother's health before he was born, but science has not yet progressed sufficiently to be able to state the exact cause of the rest of his sickness.

However, it may be said that our present degree of knowledge gives us no reason to feel that a mental condition such as the patient's is of a hereditary nature or that it will reappear in future generations.

With the predisposing effect of his physical condition the unfortunate experiences of his early childhood are the most important causes leading to the development of his present condition.

The family have apparently endeavored to do everything possible to bring the patient up in a suitable manner, and there has been no conscious error or neglect on their part. Although he is young, the prognosis is not good.        June 30, 1924 Karl M Bowman M.D. Boston

-15-            (LEOPOLD), June 30, 1924 HS Hulbert MD Chicago

( LOEB )

For example, he always used a taped
chisel, he always struck from behind;  in several
instances he wanted to leave the signs of a
struggle, and leave a broken watch behind;   in
several instances he thought of kidnapping and
ransom with confederates, in a fantastic way.

There seems to be a poverty of new ideas in the
planning of his various crimes.

- - - - -

There is nothing about the patient's condition to show any evidence of a heridatary nature,
and there is not the slightest reason to suppose
that a condition of this kind will be transmitted
to future generations by any of his siblings or
relatives.  This condition is acquired within
the life history of the individual, and dies out
when he dies

There is nothing elicited, from a most
careful and painstaking history from all possible

139                  (LOEB)

( LOEB )

sources to suggest that the family, either by
omission or commission, contributed towards his
delinquencies in the way they trained this boy.

His early nurse, who early *has* developed an
insane, paranoic state, undoubtedly had a very
serious and deleterious affect on him.

(LOEB)

June 24, 1924  Karl M Bowman M.D. Boston
June 24, 1924  H S Hulbert, M.D, Chicago

140

# I N D E X

## TO COMMENTS OF DOCTOR KARL M. BOWMAN OF BOSTON AND DOCTOR H. S. HULBERT OF CHICAGO, ON THE PRELIMINARY NEURO-PSYCHIATRIC EXAMINATION OF RICHARD LOEB.

Instigation . . . . . . . . . . .P.1
Circumstances surround-
    ing examination. . . .   1
Extent of examination . .   1
Conditions of examination   2

FAMILY HISTORY  . . . . .   3
Paternal side . . . . . .   3
Maternal side . . . . . .   5
Father, Mother, and
    siblings . . . . . . .   6

PERSONAL HISTORY  . . . .   7
Physical history  . . . .   7
Birth . . . . . . . . . .   7
Childhood . . . . . . . .   8
Youth . . . . . . . . . .   9
Endocrine history . . . .  10

GOVERNESS . . . . . . . .  12
Observations  . . . . . .  19
Conclusions . . . . . . .  22

ACADEMIC HISTORY. . . . .  24
Important teachers. . . .  27

CHILDHOOD MEMORIES. . . .  32
Observations on child-
    hood . . . . . . . .  33

THE PATIENT'S ESTIMATE
OF HIMSELF . . . . . . .  36
Love Life . . . . . . . .  44
Sex Life . . . . . . . ...  45

PHYSICAL AND NEUROLOGICAL
EXAMINATION. . . . . . .  47
Basal metabolism  . . . .  52
Blood pressure  . . . . .  52
Blood sugar test  . . . .  53
Wasserman . . . . . . . .  54
Blood Physics . . . . . .  55
Blood Chemistry. . . . .  56
Urine examination. . . .  57
Urine after glucose test  57
X-ray . . . . . . . . . .  59
X-ray head and neck . .  60
X-ray of thorax & wrts   62
Dental X-rays . . . . .  65

CRIMINAL LIFE . . . . . .  66
Reveries or phantasies. . . . .  67
Reading . . . . . . . . .  72
Delinquencies . . . . . .  76
Deceit  . . . . . . . . .  78
Shadowing . . . . . . . .  79
Delinquencies of acquisition. .  81
False telephone messages,
    false alarm, arson . . .  90

THE FRANKS CASE. . . . . .  94

THE KIDNAPPING AND MURDER. . .  107

SUBSEQUENT BEHAVIOR AND
REACTION . . . . . . . .  110
Alibi . . . . . . . . . .  111
Newspapers. . . . . . . .  112
With associate  . . . . .  113
In jail . . . . . . . . .  114

PSYCHIATRIC EXAMINATION . . .  115
Reactions toward the event. .  116
Planning  . . . . . . . . ..  117
Emotion . . . . . . . . .  118
Toward the family . . . .  120
Alternative crimes  . . .  121
Distrust of associate. . .  122
Suicide . . . . . . . . .  124
Depressions . . . . . . .  125
Escape  . . . . . . . . .  126
Morale  . . . . . . . . .  127
Some previous crimes  . . .  129

PSYCHIATRIC OBSERVATIONS . . .  131
Intelligence  . . . . . .  131
Phantasy  . . . . . . . .  131
Inferiority . . . . . . .  132
CRIMINAL PHANTASIES . . .  133
Inadequate emotion  . . .  133
SEX . . . . . . . . . . .  134
Intellectual superiority . . .  134
Compulsion  . . . . . . .  135
Immaturity  . . . . . . .  136
Sense of proportion. . . .  136
Depressions — Insight  . . .  137
Inadequate emotions . . . .  138
Stereotype  . . . . . . .  138
Inheritance or training . . .  139

The index to Loeb's portion of the Hulbert-Bowman Report offers a creepy catalog of where the alienists sought clues and causes for his mental disorders: in his basal metabolism and his urine, as well as in his inadequate emotions, delinquencies, and "some previous crimes." The index to Leopold's part of the report is missing from that document.

Northwestern University Archives

# 36
# The father is fair and just

## LOEB'S FAMILY BACKGROUND

### Daily Highballs

Nathan Leopold recollected much later in his memoir, *Life Plus 99 Years*, that (despite Albert Loeb's disapproval of his son's drinking) Richard Loeb's uncle Jacob's Prohibition-era liquor cellar provided the boys with a nightly cocktail in prison, which *Chicago Daily Tribune* reporter Ty Krum[1] would smuggle through the bars of their cells in exchange for regular exclusive interviews that appeared in the paper. Leopold wrote in his memoir *Life Plus 99 Years* that every afternoon around 5 p.m., "just after we had been locked into our cells, he'd come around on the gallery outside the cell and lean against the bars, talking."

"Somewhere," he continued, "Ty acquired two four-ounce medicine bottles. Nightly he'd fill them with good bonded bourbon from Uncle Jake's [Jacob Loeb's] stock; nightly he'd lean against the bars of my cell, his right arm against the bars. The bottle under his belt, four inches to the right of the buckle and concealed by his coat, was for me; the one four inches to the left was for Dick. During our talk I'd reach through the bars, abstract the bottle. Tom, or Augie, or Johnnie [Leopold's and Loeb's cellmates] would have our two tin drinking cups ready. Into the cups went the whiskey; back in the belt went the bottle. Those daily highballs before supper helped."

LIKE THE REPORT on Leopold, the report on Loeb begins with a family history, based on interviews with members of his family "and others who have been more or less intimately acquainted with him." Of the three wealthy families involved in the crime, the Loebs were the wealthiest and most prominent. Loeb's father, Albert, was at the time vice president of Sears, Roebuck, but his health was already precarious before the crime, and he never appeared at any of the public events surrounding the murder case. The alienists report here that he was even too ill to be "interviewed in relation to the present problem." Albert's younger brother Jacob, an attorney and former president of the Chicago Board of Education, stood in for him, working with Loeb's brother Allan and the Leopold family to manage the legal defense.

### FAMILY HISTORY

The family history was furnished by the Mother, the eldest brother [Allan Loeb], and the uncle, Jacob, on June 15th, 1924.

[Loeb] was born in Chicago, and is nineteen years of age. The Mother is aged fifty, and in good health. She was born in Illinois of German stock. The father, aged fifty-six, was born in Illinois of German-Jewish stock, and for the last year and one-half has been sick with vascular spasm of the heart, a form of angina pectoris. The paternal grandfather died, at fifty-six years of age, of cancer of the rectum. He was a very quick, alert man. He was quite abusive to his children and beat up the boys. The patient's father, Albert H., was particularly the opposite and was, in general, tender to his boys, including Dick, therefore, Dick and his brothers loved and worshiped their father, and did not want to lose their father's love and respect; the father's wish was law; Dick respected it; he was never caught in a lie.

---

1 Ty—Tyrell—was the brother of Morrow Krum, who was also reporting on the case for the *Tribune*.

The paternal Grandmother died, at seventy-three years of age, of hemorrhage of the stomach. She was active and alert; the president of several clubs; interested in social work; associated with Jane Addams; she was very fond of Dick (the patient), of whom she was uncritical and to whom she was devoted; she was interested in all her environment, and she was a healthy woman most of her life.

There were five siblings, four boys and one girl. The girl died at birth. The father of the patient was the third of the four boys. The oldest uncle, Sidney Loeb, aged fifty-nine, recently married, was quite a joker, and the boy enjoyed him greatly. He had asthma, and was not too strong. The second uncle, Julius, age fifty-seven, is a nervous, fidgety, apprehensive and sympathetic man. The third, the father, Albert H., a lawyer, advisor to Sears, Roebuck & Company, and Vice President of Sears, Roebuck & Company. The fourth, uncle Jacob, a public citizen, very active; has been President of the Board of Education of Chicago; interested in welfare movements, broadly; he is a good fellow with his nephews. One notices that he has a private library on crime from a legal viewpoint. None of Dick's cousins were close enough in age to be close playmates. [ . . .]

The father, Albert H. Loeb, is fair and just. He is opposed to the boys' drinking, and often spoke of it. He is not strict, although the boys may have thought he was; he never used corporal punishment. In early childhood he was not a play-fellow with the boys. Mr. Loeb's sickness has prevented him being directly interviewed in relation to the present problem. He has always been somewhat of a worrier, but his wife has been extremely devoted to him.

The mother is a woman in good health, with excellent poise; keen, alert, interested.

Siblings: Allan, now aged twenty-seven; Ernest, aged twenty-four, and Richard, the patient, age nineteen, and Tommy, age ten. Dick wanted to get closer to his older brothers, but as the two older ones were more of an equal age, they naturally associated together. Dick felt that he was unpopular with them at times, and made his associates boys of his own age, or of his own school grade.

# 37
# Her word was law

## LOEB'S GOVERNESS

Loeb's mother, Anna, used her money and leisure to promote social causes as a member of the Chicago Women's Club and a supporter of Jane Addams's Hull House. Like Nathan Leopold, Loeb had been raised by hired help: his baby nurse (identified in the papers as Mrs. Theodore Minaber) and a governess, Miss Emily Struthers. In the view of the alienists, Miss Struthers was as obviously responsible for warping Loeb's childhood as Sweetie had been in ruining Leopold's, but for the opposite reasons. Where Sweetie was vulgar and possibly feebleminded, Miss Struthers was "of attractive appearance, modestly and carefully dressed" but "too anxious to have him become an ideal boy." She did not behave in sexually inappropriate ways, but she had "peculiar sexual ideas probably based on her long celibacy and repression," and was "definitely paranoid towards men in general"—or, in any case, irritable with the alienists.

The outstanding person in [Loeb's] younger days who was not related to him was his Governess, Miss Struthers, now Mrs. Bishop.

His name for her which he got from his younger brother was "Michiumpa". She entered his life when he was four and a half years old. She is a Canadian who had a high school education and she improved her education during the time she was with the Loeb family. She was about twenty-eight years of age when the Loebs first employed her. Her sister died insane.

His earliest recollection of her was when she [first] came (he was in error as this episode occurred about a week after she came)—she went upstairs to unpack or on some such errand and he locked the door as he did not want her to come as his governess.

She had definite ideas of strictness and obedience. She was prompt with her punishments and these punishments were always mild and she never used corporal punishment. He soon developed an affection for her and apparently she loved him. He preferred her company to going with the boys, for example if they were going to the movies of an evening. One way in which she hastened his education was by reading books to him and she standardized his taste for good literature. She read him Ernest Thompson Seton as one of the first things. When he was about ten or eleven she read him Child's histories, "The Rise and Fall of the Dutch Republic", "Quo Vadis", "Ben Hur" and various books of Dickens.

The patient preferred to have her read to him to playing with the other children. She also coached him in his school work, thus enabling him to progress more rapidly than the average school boy and she encouraged him to study history and with the vague idea that some day he might be an ambassador. She accompanied him to and from school daily and kept in contact with his teachers.

With regard to the patient's relationship with his governess he states that she always had a tremendous influence over him. She had charge of disciplining him and was a great believer in law and order. He believes that she was very strict and although she never was brutal or used corporal punishment her punishment was fairly severe and always prompt.

**HE WAS SO SWEET**

According to the June 6 *Chicago Daily Journal*, Richard Loeb's baby nurse, Mrs. Theodore Minaber of Kenosha, Wisconsin, rushed to visit her former charge in jail shortly after he confessed to the murder of Bobby Franks. While talking to him through the screen barrier, she was "overcome by emotion" and fainted, the paper said.

Upon reviving, "she moaned: 'He was so sweet, so sweet when a baby. I can't believe he killed anything. His mother never knew how sweet and good he was, like I did. She never cared for him as I used to when he was a pretty little baby.'"

CHILD'S HISTORIES: Since the psychiatrists specifically mention Dickens in the same breath, this probably references Charles Dickens's three-volume *A Child's History of England*, which, being required reading for English schoolboys well into the twentieth century, would also potentially have been part of a proper American prep school education.

The patient states that he soon discovered that he could escape detection and the punishment by lying to her and he soon started lying to her whenever there was a chance to escape punishment.

The patient states "I always obeyed her to the minute—second. Her word was law. To myself I would think certain things were not as they should be. I would brood some. To 'get by' I formed the habit of lying."

As an example of her strict punishment he states that when he was seven years of age once the nurse failed to meet him to bring him home from school and so he did not wait for her. She put him to bed for the afternoon for doing this.

He states further "As a boy I was kept under and did not do the things other boys did. When she left I sort of broke loose".

The patient was not allowed to walk home from school alone until he was in the fourth or fifth grade. As a small child he did not indulge in athletics to the extent other children did. When he spent his first summer at camp he was very homesick so his governess came up to visit him.

"At ten she treated me as an equal—I think she was so anxious for me to develop into the type of boy she wanted that she overdid it."

The patient feels that her punishment was too severe and that he was too much in her company. "With all her faults I am convinced she loved me intensely and felt she was doing it for my betterment."

The patient feels that his governess was instrumental in having him go through school so rapidly and it was largely due to her urging that he made such rapid progress. He feels that this was a mistake.

As he grew older she was assigned to the care of his younger brother [Tommy Loeb] who was now growing up. She did not like this. There was more or less friction in the family and finally she was "let go". As the rule was in the Loeb household, that all the servants who had been there for any length of time were pensioned when they left, she was pensioned.

Before she left she had encouraged this boy to take her side of the disharmony between herself and Mrs. Loeb and apparently at this time she was becoming very paranoid and suspicious and he uncritically accepted her unusual methods of thinking as normal. However she did try to make him love his parents more than he loved her.

She was not successful at first but later on to her disappointment she was overly successful.

She left the household when Dick was fifteen and since then she has married and has been living in Boston but her married life has not been fruitful nor pleasant. On the other hand she has developed some peculiar sexual ideas probably based on her long celibacy and repression, coupled with her delayed marriage.

Sometime recently she returned to Chicago and made a scene in front of Dick and expressed some sexual delusions of persecution and ideas of reference. She had visited with the patient and they had lunch together at the Drake Hotel. He was obviously interested in her only mildly because she had been his faithful nurse but her reaction was that of a woman spurned and she hoped now that this boy whom she had loved would be a man who had learned to love her.

She returned to Chicago after the arrest of young Richard to help him in any way that she could and through the attorneys, arrangements were made for an interview. She is very reserved, quiet and strict. Her memory is good. She is correctly oriented. She is not frank in her attitude and she has an unusual amount of irritability which is easily aroused and which persists for a long time. It was noticeable that her eyelids were red as though she had been weeping recently. She is a woman of attractive appearance, modestly and carefully dressed. She was under considerable tension. Her mouth was dry; she held her jaw tightly together and talked through her lips. Occasionally she mis-spoke: for example, she said that Dick entered the eighth grade when he was seven years old when she should have said the third grade. She described the same education narrative or school history that had been previously told. She had no criticism of herself. (Her sister died insane). [...]

She visited him in Chicago on a trip west and at Christmas time 1922 and then she noticed a very definite change in him towards her. She did not say that she still loves him and wants him to love her nor that she is jealous of the girls nor jealous of his relations, but it is obvious. She denies totally any naughtiness on his part, or sex impulses in the boy under her care. She denies that he ever questioned her about sex matters and then says that when he did she turned his questions aside in a gentle way.

She denies that he ever had fears or any disorder in his sleep.

She would not say anything which might reflect on the boy even though she was plainly told that a complete understanding of this boy was essential for an accurate diagnosis. Her attitude was definitely paranoid towards men in general. She was very irritable and definitely seclusive and not accessible on complex topics. She denies that she wants money for helping the boy and yet she refuses to tell all that she knew of him.

As unexpectedly as she came to Chicago, so she had departed for Europe.

From her history and observation she gives definitely the impression of a paranoid personality. Her general viewpoint is the conventional one and she shows no real insights into childhood psychology and is quite plainly a person devoid of the understanding necessary to deal properly with children.

Some of the mistakes that she made were that she was too anxious to have him become an ideal boy and would not allow him to mix enough with other boys. She would not overlook some of his faults and was too quick in her punishment and therefore he built up the habit of lying without compunction and with increasing skill. She was quite unaware of the fact that he had become a petty thief and a play detective, but as she was with him so constantly the parents did not scrutinize him particularly.

After she left he reacted like the alleged minister's son and mistook liberty for license.

(LOEB)

their ignorant guesses as to the cause of the fire, offering impossible solutions themselves, and getting a great
feeling of satisfaction from the fact that he knew the
real solution to the mystery, and that nobody else did.

In the matter of arson, the pleasure was not
in the destruction of property, nor in revenge, but was
in both the planning to set fire and escape without identification, and, second, to know more about the affair than
the bystanders who collected, and the experts, such as
the fire attorneys who were called.

He denied being implicated in the so-called
gland robbery of Mr. Ream, and he denied being at Geneva
in the case of the "Ragged Stranger" who was found dead
with his hands cut off and his face mutilated (which crime
is usually attributed to Warren Lincoln), and he denied
having participated in any other delinquencies, but later
referred to four episodes, for which the letters "A.B.C. and
D" were suggested.   It was found, forensically, inadvisable to question him about these.

(LOEB)

93-94

The section
of the original
Hulbert-
Bowman
Report that
mentions
Loeb's alleged
other crimes.
The pencil
markings are
on the original
document.

# 38
# Forensically inadvisable to question him

## THE MYSTERY OF THE "A, B, C, D" CRIMES

THE HULBERT-BOWMAN REPORT says that, when asked directly, Loeb denied involvement in several unsolved crimes in which Chief of Detectives Michael Hughes said Leopold and Loeb were suspected; however, the alienists pointedly refer to "untold stories"—and specifically four particular crimes they label "A, B, C, and D," whose details they felt it would be "forensically inadvisable" to probe with the patients. One involved Charles Ream, a local cabdriver. One night about five months before, Ream had been forced into the back seat of a car by two men who tied him up and chloroformed him. When he regained consciousness the next morning, he found himself, covered with blood, in an industrial lot not far from the culvert where Bobby Franks's body was found. He had been castrated. The newspapers referred to this euphemistically as a "gland robbery." Chief Hughes also believed Leopold and Loeb might have been involved with the murder of University of Chicago student Freeman Tracy the previous November and the April disappearance of Melvin Wolf, a young man who had last been seen alive two blocks away from Leopold's house in the Kenwood neighborhood of Hyde Park, and whose badly decomposed body was found floating in Lake Michigan a month later. Two other cases also sometimes mentioned in connection with the A, B, C, D crimes are the "Ragged Stranger" crime, referenced in this excerpt, and that of a 45-year-old woman named Louise Hohley, who filed suit against Leopold and Loeb in June, accusing them of having kidnapped and raped her the previous February.

## CRIMINAL LIFE

Although this man [Loeb] has indulged in many criminalistic reveries and in more or less criminalistic practices, it was all done without any inkling or knowledge on the part of his parents, brothers, governesses or teachers. It seemed necessary, in his reveries, that he be the "master criminal mind" and have a small group, possibly only one associate, who would look up to him. In his practices this has been carried out, therefore, not even his acquaintances were aware of his tend of thought or his actions, unless they were the one or possibly more boys associated with him in these practices. The possible exception to this, which we have not yet ascertained, is that he may have indulged in boastful reveries in talking with the boy Jack Mengel (Weaver).

It is to be noted that recently he swaggered in front of one of his girls and told her how hard he was, and how he was occupied as a bootlegger, although he had never been bootlegging, so this was purely make-believe.

During the neuro-psychiatrix [should be "neuropsychiatric"] examination, in his recitation of his criminal career he was not altogether frank. Without any indication, facially or otherwise, he would lie or repress certain instances, unless he imagined that the examiner was previously aware of those instances. When questioned about this later he said that he failed to mention certain things because either he thought it advisable not to mention them or because he had been advised

### GLAND THIEVES?

On June 2, as Nathan Leopold and Richard Loeb were returning from the tour they had given detectives of all the sites in the Chicago area where evidence related to the kidnapping and murder of Bobby Franks might be found, they were confronted in the presence of reporters by Charles Ream, "victim of a gland robbery," who had been kidnapped, chloroformed, and castrated by previously unidentified assailants several months before. With the reporters' flashbulbs popping in a corridor of the Criminal Court Building, Ream asserted that he recognized Leopold and Loeb as his assailants.

As reported in the June 3 *Chicago Daily Tribune* by Morrow Krum (brother of Ty Krum, who was smuggling the daily cocktail to Leopold and Loeb

CONTINUED

CONTINUED

in their cells), "The recognition of the confessed slayers by Ream sent an electric thrill through the criminal court building. It was a tense bit of drama, quite as much because of the importance it had in the sensational case as because of the terrifying effect it had upon the accuser."

Krum reported that Ream, who had never fully recovered his health since he was mutilated, was terrified. "He trembled, sobbed, gasped for breath. He could not speak and would have fallen had not a reporter grasped his arm. All because he had looked into and recognized the face of the man who blighted his life in young manhood."

not to mention them. So, obviously, there are gaps in his story of the development of crime. His oldest brother, Allan, does not know of these untold stories, but the patient says he will not tell them unless Allan advises him so to do.

On the other hand, there is a certain legal advantage in minimizing the broadcasting of his episodes, even keeping them secret from his attorneys, examiners or relatives, consequently no great effort should be made to bring forth details which he willfully repressed. [. . .]

He denied being implicated in the so-called gland robbery of Mr. Ream, and he denied being at Geneva in the case of the "Ragged Stranger" who was found dead with his hands cut off and his face mutilated (which crime is usually attributed to Warren Lincoln), and he denied having participated in any other delinquencies, but later referred to four episodes, for which the letters "A.B.C. and D" were suggested. It was found, forensically, inadvisable to question him about these.

# 39
# Criminal "Master Mind"
## LOEB'S FANTASY LIFE

FROM JUNE 13 until June 21, reporters watched a parade of prominent alienists arrive at the jail to examine Leopold and Loeb, but they managed to find out very little about what was actually going on inside the examination room. Their stories are filled with rumor and speculation, and for the most part they continued to regard Leopold as the evil mastermind and Loeb as the friendly, easygoing pal who had somehow been persuaded to join him in his delinquency. Meanwhile, inside the examination room, Loeb was revealing to the alienists that the Bobby Franks crime and its aftermath were the near-perfect culmination of his lifelong fantasies.

### REVERIES OR PHANTASIES

[Loeb's] phantasies usually occurred between the time of retiring and the time sleep came over him. He estimates that this period was, on the average, of half an hour's duration. There were three types to his hypnogognic [should be "hypnagogic"] thoughts. He states that his phantasies first assumed importance at the age of about ten or eleven. Before going to sleep and while lying in bed he would imagine himself living out some scene. He speaks of this as "picturization". There were several phantasies which recurred with great frequency, perhaps the earliest of these was that he would picture himself in jail; he would imagine that he was being stripped of his clothing, being shoved around and being whipped. There was a great feeling of self-pity with this, but no feeling of fear; "I was abused, but it was a very pleasant thought; the punishment inflicted on me in jail was pleasant; I enjoyed being looked at through the bars, because I was a famous criminal". It was not possible to ascertain any connection between his being in jail and his punishment at home for actual things which he had done, but it is noteworthy that at about this time he became proud of his ability as a liar in evading punishments by his governesses. Linked up with the idea of his being in jail was the idea of his being a famous criminal. This phantasy seemed to evolve from the first phantasy of being in jail and came on slightly later. He would particularly imagine himself as the "Master Mind" directing others.

Another phantasy was to think of himself as a frontiersman shooting at others. In this phantasy he would get under the bed clothes which, in his imagination, were impregnable to bullets. He would then live out in his phantasy, various scenes of frontier life. [ . . .]

In his phantasies about crime the patient gradually commenced to imagine himself doing all sorts of crimes; he derived intense pleasure from such phantasy, and particularly felt a feeling of being superior to others in that they did not know he was connected with the crime and he knew the truth about it, while they did not. A number of his actual crimes were the direct result of a great deal of pleasurable phantasy in regard to a particular type of crime.

One particular point connected with all this phantasy was the idea that he was the "Master Mind" who was so clever at planning crimes that he could escape detection from the greatest detectives of the World; thus he would be in truth the "Master Criminal Mind" of the century, and would work out a wonderful plan for a crime which would stir the country and which would never be solved.

HYPNAGOGIC refers to the transitional state between waking and sleeping.

# 40
# In dramatic whispers
## LOEB RECOUNTS THE MURDER AGAIN

L OEB RECOUNTED the details of the murder to the psychiatrists, again, as in the Confessions, agreeing in almost all the essentials with Leopold—except for the question of who had actually committed the murder. He begins with the argument in the car on the way back from the robbery in Ann Arbor, describes the pact he and Leopold established, and details their painstaking preparation for the kidnapping, including "many uncomfortable afternoons going over the Illinois Central tracks looking for suitable locations" where the father of the kidnapped boy might be asked to throw the ransom money off a moving train. He describes how they went about setting up a fake identity as "Mr. Ballard" in order to rent a car because they thought Leopold's own car was too distinctive looking and would be recognized. And at this point, the psychiatrists report, Loeb becomes visibly excited about the story he is telling.

(When the patient [Loeb] came to this point in the narrative he looked decidedly interested, drew up his chair, talked almost in dramatic whispers, with considerable tension, his eyes constantly roaming the room, in fact, he showed intense emotional reaction here in the repetition of that which he said had been very thrilling for him.) [. . .]

The patient and his companion [Leopold] discussed, at considerable length, the choice of a suitable subject for kidnapping. The patient's companion suggested that they get a girl. The patient objected to this, and stated that it would be much more difficult because girls are much more carefully watched than boys, and because, having relations with a kidnapped girl would not necessarily be part of a perfect kidnapping-ransom crime. The patient jokingly also suggested that they kidnap the patient's younger brother [Tommy Loeb], aged ten. The patient did not seriously consider doing this. They then considered half a dozen boys, any one of whom would do, for the following reasons: that they were physically small enough to be easily handled and their parents were extremely wealthy and would have no difficulty or disinclination to pay ransom money. [. . .]

The patient did not anticipate the actual killing with any pleasure, but said that it probably would not have been sickening. The killing apparently has no other significance than being an inevitable part of a perfect crime in covering one possible trace of identification.

They anticipated a few unpleasant minutes in strangling him. (The patient's face registered the expression of disgust), and they planned, for each of them, namely, the patient and his associate, to have ahold of one end of the strangling rope and they would pull at the same time, so that both would be equally guilty of the murder. They did not seem to feel that this would give them a closer tie in their friendship. It was the sharing of culpability. It was not anticipated that the blow on the back of the head with the taped chisel would be fatal.

The patient states that he thinks that during the last week preceding the crime he had less pleasure in his anticipations; he didn't want to back out because of their extensive plans, because of the time spent, because of the trouble they had gone to, and because of his associate being in it with him, and he was afraid of what the associate would think, should he not go ahead. Nevertheless, he states that he had "some relish" for it. [. . .]

They felt perfectly assured that their plans were so perfected that they themselves would never be suspected, and, of course, never be apprehended. They planned to divide the ten thousand dollars ransom money equally, and had made no definite plans as to the expenditure of this money, more than intending to keep it to themselves as security in case their savings and spending money would be insufficient for their respective needs. [. . .]

(At this point he choked up and wiped his nose with his finger.)

"We got him into the car. He was hit over the head with the chisel, dragged him into the back seat from the front seat, gagged, but he was dead when we got to the culvert, and we didn't need to strangle him."

"At the time I got great excitement, great heart-beating, faster, which was pleasant. I was cool and self-possessed. I had quite a time quieting down — (my associate.) I cooled him down in five minutes after we got him into the back seat, thinking him still alive. I got calmer, while quieting my associate. He was hit on the head several times. He bled. My associate said 'this is terrible, this is terrible.' I told him it was all right, and joked and laughed, possibly to calm myself, too." [. . .]

In disposing of the body there was no need to strangle the boy. He was already dead, so he was stripped; hydrochloric acid was poured on the face, some of which ran into the mouth, on the genitals and on the abdomen where there was a surgical scar, in order to prevent or delay identification. No other liberties were taken with the body. The body was put in a funnel-shaped culvert, through which the water was flowing. The water came in through a larger hole, through which the body was placed, and flowed out through a smaller hole, too small to let the body be washed away. Unfortunately, the body was not kicked far enough into this hole and a foot remained protruding, visible to a passer-by.

# 41
# This tickled my sense of humor

## LOEB TAKES STOCK OF HIS FEELINGS

**THE MOTHERS**

Flora Franks's mother was the sister of Albert Loeb's mother, making them first cousins and Richard Loeb and Bobby Franks second cousins. The fact that Bobby had played tennis on the Loeb tennis court a few days before the murder—and that this was one of the first places his father looked for him when he didn't come home for dinner on the night of the murder—suggests that the families had had a close and easy relationship until the murder.

Shortly after the confessions, the August 12 *Chicago Daily News* reported, Anna Loeb "went up the stone steps of the Franks' home on her unhappy mission of expressing her grief and sympathy over the death of the boy her son had killed." Being turned away, she later made a second attempt and was turned away again.

CONTINUED

**T**HE LOEB HOUSE, at 5017 Ellis Avenue, was just down the block and across the street from the Franks house, at 5052 Ellis Avenue, so it was not that surprising that Loeb had been able to watch Bobby's casket being carried from his house to the waiting hearse, as is described in the report below. It would never be possible for anyone from either of the families to leave the house without being plainly in view of the other. As Anna Loeb struggled to reach across the horrifying emotional chasm that now separated her from Flora Franks, her son appears unable to express remorse—except "at his being caught."

### HIS SUBSEQUENT BEHAVIOR AND REACTION

The day after the killing they returned the car at 4:30 to the Renting Agency and went to their homes. The patient [Loeb] discussed the case with his family. At first he stated that he got more of a "kick" in discussing it with his own family, but he later changed his statement and said that he felt he got a little less "kick" because he had "some slight remorse."

His mother said that whoever did it should be tarred and feathered. "This tickled my sense of humor, to think that she was saying this about her own son."

On the other hand, the patient was a little worried by the attitude of his father, who seemed a "little quiet." He wondered whether his father might suspect anything.

The patient witnessed a part of the funeral, in that he passed by the house at the time the coffin was being brought out to the hearse. He stated that he did not purposely pass by at that time to see the funeral, but it should be remembered that he mentioned at one time the idea of kidnapping a close friend in order that he might be one of the pallbearers at the funeral, and hence get an added thrill from it.

The patient states that he experienced no remorse about the crime, except that when he saw the coffin being brought out by the small "bright-faced boys" he felt a little uncomfortable. He denied sending flowers. [. . .]

He expressed remorse at his being caught. When asked if he would go through with this crime again if he felt certain that he would not be discovered, he replied, "I believe I would if I could get the money."

The patient's attention was called to a newspaper account of an interview with Mrs. Franks, the mother of the victim, in which she stated that she had no desire to see the boys hanged, but would like to talk with them to know whether her son suffered and what happened to him in his last moments. The patient was asked whether it would upset him at all to talk with Mrs. Franks and he replied that he thought it would upset him a little and make him feel sad. He said that when he read this interview in the paper "my first feeling was joy, that it might help us, her not feeling vindictive, then a little remorse, not much, perhaps a little bit; but, on the other hand, I forgot it right away in reading another paper. I haven't any distress now in thinking of it. What would make me sad would be to see Mrs. Franks in pain, but it does not make me sad to think about her or anyone being in pain. It is uncomfortable for me to see someone in pain."

The patient stated that although he had no feeling of remorse about the crime he felt "very, very sorry" about it for his family's sake, because it might cause them distress. His manner was not at all convincing as he said this, and he seemed quite unconcerned. "I would be willing to increase the chance of my hanging to save the family from believing that I was 'the arch fiend.' My folks have probably had the blow softened by blaming [Leopold], and his folks by blaming me. But before I decide (to take the responsibility) in order to save my family, I must consult with my older brother [Allan Loeb] first, but it may not reach that importance."

When questioned about his attitude towards his family the questioning was directed toward the possibility of some of them having been considered as the victim for this superior crime, he described having, in a joking way, proposed to his associate that his own younger brother, Tommy, be the victim; and his associate, jokingly, agreed with it, ~~jokingly~~, but they gave up the idea because it was not practicable for this reason: that if Tommy had disappeared, the patient would have to be at the home and with the family during the period of the hunt and could not be foot-loose to carry out the plans of securing the ransom money. "I couldn't have done it because I am tremendously fond of him."

He also contemplated using his older brother, as the victim, but abandoned the idea for the same reason, that it was not practicable, and he, himself, would have to stay at home.

Furthermore, he had contemplated using his own father, Mr. A. H. Loeb, as the victim, but this would not be practicable, because then "who would furnish the money?"

He and his associate had also contemplated using Mr. Nathan Leopold, Senior, as the victim, but the same objection was raised, that it was not practicable, and there would be no one to furnish the money.

He had proposed, and ~~that~~ with his associate had contemplated, using Dick Rubel, a very close friend of the patient and his associate, towards whom neither the patient nor his associate had any ill feeling or grudge, as the victim. The patient stated that he enjoyed this idea immensely, because since he was a close and trusted friend of the family he would undoubtedly be asked to be a pall-bearer at the funeral and "this gave me a tremendous kick."

The plan of kidnapping Dick Rubel was given up because "Dick Rubel's father was so tight we might not get any money from him."

CONTINUED

On her third attempt, she was admitted to the room where Flora was reclining, accompanied by her mother, who had told Flora, "It can do no harm for you to see her."

As the *Daily News* reported the encounter, "Mrs. Loeb entered the room where Mrs. Franks sat—a room whose windows commanded a view of the street. As best she might, Mrs. Loeb fulfilled her almost impossible mission. She falteringly concluded. Mrs. Franks looked at her—a little in surprise—and then her gaze wandered down the street again—toward the Harvard school for boys.

"'But I'm sure Bobby will be coming back pretty soon,' she answered."

Flora Franks sitting outside the courtroom on July 23, the day she briefly testified, between two unidentified men. In the few instances when photographers caught her out in public, her face is always a mask of grief.

## A MOTHER AND HER BOY

On June 28, Anna Loeb saw her son Richard for the first time since he had confessed to the killing. Up till then, she had remained secluded with Richard's father, Albert, whose health was fragile after a series of heart attacks. But finally, according to a dramatic account in the *Washington Post* the next day, "against the warning of physicians, friends and relatives, the mother ventured forth for the first time." Accompanied by her oldest son, Allan, and her brother-in-law Jacob, "She motored to the county jail and walked bravely past the iron doors that keep her son from her side."

When Loeb was told that his mother had arrived, the article said, "He fairly vaulted from his place, pulled a comb from his pocket, passed it quickly through his black hair, and walked with a guard to meet his mother," standing "like a bashful schoolboy expecting a whipping."

Then they fell into one another's arms as she cried "My boy Dickey" over and over, with tears streaming down her face. "In a minute the boy, who calmly planned the death of young Franks 'for excitement,' was sobbing hysterically."

They were given 10 minutes together, which they spent crying and whispering, before Anna gave Loeb a final hug and kiss and "walked bravely from the jail and to her motor."

A prisoner who witnessed this event was quoted as calling it "the best I ever saw. A mother and her boy. But through it all the great heart of the mother refused to do the breaking stunt. She was great."

# 42
# I have always been sort of afraid of him

## LOEB CONTEMPLATED KILLING LEOPOLD

THE QUESTION OF who was the "leader" and who the "follower" in the Leopold-Loeb relationship preoccupied press coverage at the time and has continued to fascinate writers and others dramatizing the case. The relationship was certainly volatile, with strong elements of both attraction and repulsion, and though both claimed to have tried at various times to extricate themselves, they also each seemed to feel that the other's power was overwhelming.

The patient's [Loeb's] attitude towards his associate [Leopold] has been somewhat changeable. He states, "In a way I have always been sort of afraid of him; he intimidated me by threatening to expose me, and I couldn't stand it."

Of late the patient had often thought of the possibility of shooting his associate. "I had always considered him a bad influence upon me." He goes on to explain this by saying that he means that he never could have carried out his crimes alone, but required an associate to be with him, and therefore, his companion, by being his associate, was a bad influence. He was also afraid that his associate might betray him and did not have any confidence in him.

He often contemplated shooting his associate when they were out together and had the associate's revolvers along. He thought of pointing the revolver at his associate and shooting him. He denied ever having thought of hitting him over the head with the chisel. "The idea of murdering a fellow, especially alone, I don't think I could have done it. If I could have snapped my fingers and made him pass away in a heart attack, I would have done it."

One reason why he never murdered his associate was that he felt that he would be suspected, and there was no very safe way of doing it.

In connection with this he had often contemplated murdering his associate and securing a new pal.

# 43
# A pathological minimum of self-criticism

## BLAMING THE GOVERNESS, AGAIN

**A PROMISED TREATISE**

On July 10, the *Chicago Daily Tribune* reported that the alienists' examinations of Nathan Leopold and Richard Loeb were drawing to a close and that they soon would begin "the even more difficult work" of compiling a report that was to aid in supporting an insanity defense.

Not yet knowing what was to be said in the report, it was possible for reporters nevertheless to dramatize its scope and importance. The report would, the *Tribune* said, "be drawn up in similar manner to that of a treatise on biological evolution. . . . The lives of the boys will be opened and laid out much as is the pedigree of animals. The events in their lives which might have had a bearing on their mental condition at 6 o'clock on the evening of May 21, when they lured little Bobby Franks into their automobile and slugged him to death, will be 'ringed' as steps in the process of 'cause and result.'"

Embellishing the degree to which science was expected to illuminate this still-senseless murder, the *Tribune* assured its readers that "The tiny cell in the brains of the boys which reacted in such a way as to emit a stimulus to cause them to commit the act will be sought and the results noted."

AFTER 13 DIFFERENT alienists had poked, prodded, and interviewed Leopold and Loeb, the psychological examinations drew to a close. In Loeb's case, as in Leopold's, the official report claimed that the alienists had found no evidence to support the legal requirements of an insanity defense—or, for that matter, very little explanation for Loeb's "total lack of appropriate emotional response to situations." The Hulbert-Bowman Report does exonerate the prominent, respectable Loeb family in no uncertain terms and assures the family—as it had done in the case of Leopold—that Loeb's condition had not been inherited from them and could not be expected to be passed down to future generations. A gap on the page between the end of the concluding section and one final, tacked-on sentence suggests that the alienists felt they needed to add *some* explanation for Loeb's behavior, and they do just what they had done with Leopold: blame the nanny.

From the earliest age he never seems to have experienced the slightest feeling of remorse or guilt for any misconduct and his only self-reproach has been when he has not been sufficiently clever to escape detection or to lie out of a difficult situation. He has a pathological minimum of critique, or self-criticism. [ . . . ]

The total lack of appropriate emotional response to situations is one of the most striking features of his present condition. This is not carried out in a consistent manner, but is full of contradictions; so that we see the patient refusing to escape from jail because it might hurt the family in some way, and yet contemplating kidnapping and murder of members of his own family without the slightest emotional reaction to it. Although he is quite anxious for his mother to have the minimum amount of suffering, and not wishing to do anything to bother her, he tells how his sense of humor is aroused by his mother's indignation against the kidnappers and murderers of Robert Franks. Another example of this split between his emotions and his ideas is the robbery of his own fraternity house. There are many such instances. [ . . . ]

There is nothing about the patient's condition to show any evidence of a hereditary nature, and there is not the slightest reason to suppose that a condition of this kind will be transmitted to future generations by any of his siblings or relatives. This condition is acquired within the life history of the individual, and dies out when he dies.

There is nothing elicited, from a most careful and painstaking history from all possible sources, to suggest that the family, either by omission or commission, contributed towards his delinquencies in the way they trained this boy.

His early nurse, who ~~early~~ has developed an insane, paranoic state, undoubtedly had a very serious and deleterious effect on him.

[dated and signed by hand]

June 24, 1924 Karl M Bowman M.D. Boston

June 24, 1924 H S Hulbert, M.D., Chicago

# PART IV

# The Court Transcript

IN THE CRIMINAL COURT OF COOK COUNTY.

PEOPLE OF THE STATE OF ILLINOIS

    -VS-

NATHAN F. LEOPOLD, JR. AND

RICHARD LOEB

       BEFORE HONORABLE JOHN R. CAVERLY.

I   N   D   E   X

| WITNESSES | Direct Exam. | Cross Exam. | Re-Direct Exam. | Re-Cross Exam. |
|---|---|---|---|---|
| July 23rd,1924 | | | | |
| Caution by the Court. . | 4 | | | |
| Opening statement by Mr. Crowe. | 16 | | | |
| Opening statement by Mr. Darrow. | 67 | | | |
| Edwin M. Gresham . . . | 73 | | | |
| Jacob Franks . . . . | 76 | | | |
| Joseph Springer . . . | 87 | . 92 | | |
| Axel F. Benson. . . . | 97 | | | |
| Jacob Franks(Recalled) . | 100 | | | |
| Mrs. Flora Franks. . . | 104 | | | |
| J. B. Cravens . . . . | 112 | | | |
| Thomas Taylor . . . . | 120 | | | |
| Charles E. Ward . . . | 124 | .129 | | |
| Arthur Doherty. . . . | 132 | .134 | | |
| Clara Vinnedge. . . . | 135 | | | |
| David L. Barish . . . | 144 | | | |
| Max Tuckerman . . . . | 147 | | | |
| Walter L. Jacobs . . . | 152 | | | |
| William C. Herndon . . | 160 | | | |
| Miss Margaret Fitzpatrick | 167 | | | |
| July 24th,1924 | | | | |
| Andrew Russo . . . . | 174 | | | |
| David Barish . . . . | 179 | | | |
| Frank B. Tuttle . . . | 180 | .182 | | |
| George S. Homer . . . | 185 | | | |
| Emil Deutsch. . . . . | 190 | | | |
| Thomas McWilliams. . . | 194 | | | |
| Elizabeth Sattler. . . | 197 | .204 | | |

(Index continued on next page)

IN THE CRIMINAL COURT OF COOK COUNTY

PEOPLE OF THE STATE OF ILLINOIS

     VS.

NATHAN F.LEOPOLE JR. AND
RICHARD LOEB

                BEFORE HONORABLE JOHN R. CAVERLY.

      I    N    D    E    X  (Continued)

| WITNESSES | Direct Exam. | Cross Exam. | Re-Direct Exam. | Re-Cross Exam. |
|---|---|---|---|---|
| July 24th, 1924 (contd) | | | | |
| Arnold Maremont | 206 | | | |
| Howard Oberndorf | 217 | | | |
| Maurice Shamberg | 221 | | | |
| Lester Abelson | 225 | | | |
| Lucille Smith | 227 | | | |
| Jeannette Smith | 231 | | | |
| Bernard Hunt | 234 | | | |
| Morgan A. Collins | 239 | | | |
| Leon Mandel II | 242 | | | |
| H.C.Stromberg | 250 | | | |
| Albert Hubinger | 255 | | | |
| Aaron Adler | 258 | | | |
| Sven Englund | 261 | 268 | | |
| Mrs.Alma Englund | 270 | | | |
| J.T.Seass | 274 | | | |
| Carl J. Ulvigh | 279 | 282 | 287 | |
| George C. Fry | 291 | | | |
| John F. Ball | 295 | | | |
| Tony Minke | 298 | | | |
| Paul Korff | 305 | | | |
| Anton Shapino | 312 | | | |
| Stanley Olejniczak | 318 | | | |
| John Kaleczka | 322 | | | |
| Dr. Wm. B. McNally | 326 | | | |
| Dr. John A. Wesner | 351 | | | |
| Dr. Ralph W. Webster | 356 | | | |

IN THE CRIMINAL COURT OF COOK COUNTY.

PEOPLE OF THE STATE OF ILLINOIS

    VS.

NATHAN F. LEOPOLD JR. AND
RICHARD LOEB

        BEFORE HONORABLE JOHN R. CAVERLY.

      I  N  D  E  X  (Continued)

---

| WITNESSES | Direct Exam. | Cross Exam. | Re-Direct Exam. | Re-Cross Exam. |
|---|---|---|---|---|
| **July 25th, 1924** | | | | |
| Frank P. Blair | 359 | | | |
| Percy Van De Bogert | 363 | | | |
| James C. Kemp | 365 | | | |
| George Porter Lewis | 367 | | | |
| Thomas C. Wolf | 375 | | | |
| Howard Mayer | 385 | | | |
| Alvin H. Goldstein | 395 | | | |
| James W. Mulroy | 401 | | | |
| Alvin H. Goldstein (Recalled) | 406 | | | |
| Sidney Stein, Jr. | 408 | | | |
| Charles Enos | 411 | | | |
| Frank A. Mulligan | 414 | | | |
| Hugh Byrne | 416 | | | |
| Edward F. Anderson | 419 | | | |
| Joseph Berounsky | 421 | | | |
| Richard St. Germaine | 435 | | | |
| Ernet W. Puttkammer | 439 | | | |
| Max Wester | 446 | | | |
| William Crot | 450 | | | |
| Frank A. Johnson | 467 | | | |
| James J. Gortland | 481 | | | |
| **July 26th, 1924.** | | | | |
| James J. Gortland (Recalled) | 504 | 505 | | |
| Jacob Weinstein | 539 | | | |
| James J. Gortland (Recalled) | ---- | 549 | 553 | 554 |
| William F. Barnes | 557 | | | |
| Edgar R. Yates | 563 | | | |

# 44

# We throw ourselves upon the mercy of this court

## DARROW'S SURPRISE TACTIC

**W**HEN JUDGE CAVERLY convened the case of *People of the State of Illinois v. Nathan Leopold, Jr. and Richard Loeb* on the morning of July 21 and invited any motions from the attorneys, defense attorney Clarence Darrow shocked the courtroom by announcing that the defendants wished to withdraw their former pleas of "not guilty" and instead plead "guilty." They would not dispute the facts of the murder, as set forth in their confessions; they would not attempt to mount an insanity defense; and even their families would not dispute the need to "see that they are safely and permanently excluded from the public." They were simply going to admit guilt, throw themselves "on the mercy of the court," and hope for a "mitigation of the penalties"— in other words, something more merciful than a death sentence.

What this meant, tactically, was sacrificing any miniscule hope the defendants might have had that Darrow could convince a jury to let Leopold and Loeb go free. The far more likely result of a jury trial, Darrow understood, was a conviction and a hanging, given the evidence against them, the public outrage about the crime, and the zeal of the state's attorney to settle for nothing short of the death penalty. On the other hand, admitting guilt outright obviated the need to call a jury at all and thrust the entire burden of the sentencing decision onto one individual judge, whom Darrow was gambling would feel the life-or-death consequences more acutely on his conscience than a jury of Chicago citizens.

State's Attorney Robert Crowe refused to back off from his insistence on staging a prosecution. His goal, as he reiterated in all his public statements, was not to convict the defendants; it was to hang them.

While the statements made by both Darrow and Crowe that day were not included in the bound copy of the sentencing hearing, which began two days later, they were transcribed by reporters and published verbatim in many newspapers.

What follows is Darrow's statement to the court, as reported in the *Chicago Daily News*, and then Crowe's response to the press regarding Darrow's statement, as reported in the same newspaper.

## IN HIS HANDS ALONE

Though generally the most restrained in its tone of all the newspapers covering the case, even the *New York Times* couldn't deny the drama and tension as Judge John Caverly's courtroom filled up with journalists and spectators for the first court appearance by Nathan Leopold and Richard Loeb on the morning of July 21. With the cameras clicking away, Leopold and Loeb, "showing traces of their confinement in their pallor, smiled at their attorneys, Clarence S. Darrow and Benjamin Bachrach." Already present in the courtroom were Nathan Leopold Sr., "his face showing the anguish he was suffering," and Leopold's older brother Foreman ("Mike"). The Loebs were represented by Richard's uncle Jacob and brother Allan; his father, Albert, was too ill to attend and his mother, Anna, was said to be tending to his father.

Then, "With a suddenness and unexpectedness that startled the Court, prosecutors, and spectators, Nathan F. Leopold Jr. and Richard A. Loeb pleaded guilty to kidnapping and slaying Robert Franks when they were arraigned before Chief Justice Caverly of the Criminal Court. In his hands alone, as the result of this plea, instead of in the hands of a jury, will rest the fate of the two prisoners."

## Darrow's Statement

"We know, your honor, the facts in this case are substantially as have been published in the newspapers and what purports to be their confession, and we can see we have no duty to the defendants, or their families, or society, except to see that they are safely and permanently excluded from the public.

"Of course, after that is done, we want to do the best we can for them within those limits.

"After long reflection and thorough discussion, so long as that is the only issue in the case, we have determined to make a motion in this court for each of the defendants in each of the cases to withdraw our plea of not guilty and enter a plea of guilty.

"Your honor, we dislike to throw this burden upon this court or any court. We know its seriousness and its gravity, but a court can no more shirk responsibility than attorneys. While we wish it could be otherwise, we feel that it must be as we have chosen.

"The statute provides that evidence may be offered in mitigation of the punishment, and we shall ask at such time as the court may direct that we may be permitted to offer evidence as to the mental condition of these young men, to show the degree of responsibility they had and also to offer evidence as to the youth of these defendants and the fact of a plea of guilty as further mitigation of the penalties in this case.

"With that we throw ourselves upon the mercy of this court, and this court alone."

## The State's Attorney Fires Back

"The fact that the two murderers have thrown themselves upon the mercy of the court does not in any way alleviate the enormity of the crime they committed," Mr. Crowe said. "As I informed the court this morning, 'the state is going to prove not only that these boys are guilty, but that they are absolutely sane and should be hanged,' such is my present position.

"Every exhibit—the typewriter, chisel, kidnaper's letter to Mr. Franks, the bloody clothing, the automobile they used, Leopold's eye glasses, their confessions—will be laid before Judge Caverly who in this case is the sole judge of the facts as well as the evidence.

"The defense is not permitted to introduce any insanity testimony because the law states that a plea of guilty to a fact automatically presumes the defendant to be sane. An insane man is not allowed to plead guilty to a fact.

"The defense may show certain circumstances which might have been a motive for the murder.

"But for the defense to say they attempt to introduce alienists to testify regarding the mental condition of the two slayers would be going clearly outside the rules of evidence. There can be no insanity for a person who pleads guilty. . . . [T]here is but one punishment which will satisfy the prosecution. All our efforts will tend toward that one goal. They have thrown themselves upon the mercy of the court and we will demand they be hanged."

Defense attorney Clarence Darrow (far left) standing with two unidentified men outside of the criminal court building.

# 45
# I object, if your Honor please

## CROWE AND DARROW SQUARE OFF

**THE PINK TICKET**

Robert Lee, a reporter for the *Chicago Daily Tribune*, described the security procedures designed to limit access to the courtroom on July 23, when the sentencing hearing began. There were policemen standing guard on the streets and sidewalks, allowing entrance only to those with a special pink ticket that had been personally signed by the judge. "The police make you show your pink ticket and you are glad to do it; so many have none; and the hot coppers beam on you with as much graciousness as a hot copper can command on a hot July morning."

When you emerged from the elevator on the fifth floor, he said, there was a double row of police there to greet you, and then, up an-

CONTINUED

AS THE SENTENCING hearing began on the morning of July 23, State's Attorney Robert Crowe reacted officially to the bombshell dropped by Clarence Darrow two days before. He was not about to be cheated out of the opportunity to stage a trial. Despite the fact that the defendants had already pled guilty, Crowe intended to present every sliver of evidence the state had gathered against them, ensuring that Judge John Caverly and the rest of the world would hear every repugnant detail of the crime. In the first hour of his opening argument, Crowe retold the story of the murder, the interrogations, and the confessions in dramatic detail, provoking the first skirmish with Darrow, who here professes to be "outraged" that Crowe would be permitted, by rehashing the evidence, to "stir up anger and hatred in this community that may result in many other crimes, details which have nothing to do with this case upon a plea of guilty and of which the community is already aware." In the transcript of the exchange that follows, Judge Caverly's remarks are attributed to "THE COURT."

**MR. CROWE [winding up his opening statement]:** The State will show to your honor by facts and circumstances, by witnesses, by exhibits, by documents, that these men are guilty of the most cruel, cowardly, dastardly murder ever committed in the annals of American jurisprudence. The State will demonstrate their guilt here so conclusively that there is not an avenue for them to escape, and they make a virtue of necessity, when they have no escape, they throw themselves upon the mercy of this court.

We will prove that these matters happened in Cook County, Illinois, and when the State has concluded, when the defense has concluded, and the final arguments are made, in the name of the People of the State of Illinois, in the name of the womanhood and the fatherhood, and in the name of the children of the State of Illinois, we are going to demand the death penalty for both of these cold blooded, cruel, vicious murderers.

**MR. DARROW:** Your Honor, I want to say a few words at this time. The defendants in this case have entered a plea of guilty. Now, in all cases with any prosecutor, it seems to me, who is interested purely in administering justice, it would not have been possible to go into all the details that have been gone into this morning, and make all the covert threats that have been made. Everybody knows that this was a most unfortunate homicide. That it is the cruelest, the worst, the most atrocious ever committed in the United States is pure imagination without a vestige of truth, and everybody knows that too. Those words are litany of State's Attorney's and that is all.

A death in any situation is horrible, but when it comes to the question of murder it is doubly horrible. But there are degrees perhaps of atrocity, and as I say, instead of this being one of the worst of the atrocious character, it is perhaps one of the least painful and of the smallest inducement. Bad, nevertheless, bad enough of course, but anybody with any experience of criminal trials knows what it is to be branded as it has been repeatedly, as the greatest, most important and atrocious killing that ever happened in the State of Illinois, or in the United States.

**MR. CROWE:** Mr. Darrow, just a minute.

If your Honor please, if the purpose of Mr. Darrow is to make an opening statement as to what they intend to prove, I have no objection, but if his purpose now is merely to make an argument, I object that this isn't the proper time.

**MR. DARROW:** Well, was it the proper time for you to make it?

**MR. CROWE:** If I stepped outside the bounds it was your business to object. I insist that this be conducted like a law suit and not like an experiment.

**MR. DARROW:** Oh, your Honor, he has learned that somewhere in the book. This will be tried like a law suit.

**MR. CROWE:** I object, if your Honor please, to an argument of this sort. I insist that he should confine himself to a statement as to what he expects to prove.

**MR. DARROW:** Your Honor, it comes with poor grace from counsel after for more than an hour he sought to stir up feeling in this community, where he had repeatedly sought to stir it up that justice may be blind in this case.

**MR. CROWE:** I insist on a ruling, your Honor.

**THE COURT:** Well, counsel for the state went further than he should have gone, and if counsel for the defendants had objected of course I would have to sustain it. It is true that this isn't the time for argument. The argument of counsel for either side or both sides will be after all the evidence is introduced.

**MR. DARROW:** Surely, your Honor, but—

**THE COURT:** We will let Mr. Darrow go ahead.

**MR. DARROW:** I wouldn't make an argument.

**THE COURT:** Now, Mr. Darrow, confine it as nearly as you can to that which you expect to prove.

**MR. DARROW:** Very well, your Honor. I am aware at this time it isn't a proper statement, but I felt outraged at the whole statement that has been made in this case. That accounts for it. All this evidence that is sought to be introduced in this case is utterly incompetent; all the statements made in this case are incompetent. All of this is added to the statements already made publicly, and have no bearing on this case whatever, with the plea of guilty in it. No one on the part of the defense claims that there was not a conspiracy, that there was not a murder, that it was not done by these two boys, that it was not done in a way that they have already given to the press for a purpose, rehearsed now, and to be rehearsed later, all of which is incompetent.

We shall insist in this case, your Honor that terrible as this is, that terrible as any killing is, it would be without precedent if two boys of this age should be hanged by the

CONTINUED

other flight where the courtroom was, three more guards to show your pink ticket to. Lee quoted Genevieve Forbes—one of the foremost women reporters on the *Tribune* staff, who was also covering the case for the paper— as saying "it's harder to get through than Ellis island."

"There were some 600 journalists at the Democratic convention in New York," he observed. "It is apparent they all came here. They fill the jury rooms, the jury box, all the space round the rail, and they overflow into the very arena itself, if this battleground of Darrow and Crowe can be so called."

neck until dead, and it would in no way bring back Robert Franks or add to the peace and security of this community. I insist that it would be without precedent, as we learned, if on a plea of guilty this should be done.

We will attempt to inform the court, and inform the court in a way that can leave no chance for reasonable men to doubt, as to the make-up of both these boys, their limited degree of responsibility in this case, and we think all of this is borne out by every fact in this case; no one could imagine that mature people of full responsibility could have done it as it was done in this case.

We think the court should not permit for the pure purpose of rehearsing again to this community, to stir up anger and hatred in this community that may result in many other crimes, details which have nothing to do with this case upon a plea of guilty and of which the community is already aware. We simply ask your Honor to keep this within the legal prescribed grounds of a hearing as this case is presented. Of course I might say to your Honor that we hesitate under our situation in this case where we are asking for the clemency we think we ought to have, and nothing more, we hesitate to be put in the attitude of objecting. We sat and listened to this statement, utterly incompetent and meant only to appeal to the passion of man.

When this case is presented, I know this court will take it, take it calmly and honestly, in consideration of the community and in consideration of the lives of these two boys, and that any echo that may come back from this extravagant and unlawful statement and from the lurid painting in this court room, which was made for nothing excepting that a hoarse cry of angry people may somehow reach these chambers, – we know your Honor would disregard that and do in this case what is just, fair and merciful, and a court must always interpret justice and mercy together.

# 46
# That is what comes from reading detective stories

## LOEB PRETENDS TO GIVE HIS FRIENDS A SCOOP

BECAUSE OF JUDGE John Caverly's liberal attitude toward hearing any and all evidence that might help him weigh the terms of justice in his own mind, the testimony of a large cast of major and minor characters involved in the case has been preserved. Their stories reveal, for instance, that in the week between the murder and their arrest, Leopold and Loeb returned to their normal routines with such insouciance that they even discussed the crime with those around them without anyone ever suspecting their involvement—and that they got an extra thrill out of doing it. Here, for instance, is the account by Loeb's friend Howard Mayer—who also happened to be a reporter for the *Chicago Evening American*—of how, two days after the murder, Loeb actually went out of his way to entice him and two *Chicago Daily News* reporters with the prospect of a big news scoop. Loeb said he would help the reporters hunt for the drugstore where the then-unidentified "George Johnson" had intended for Jacob Franks to await instructions for delivering the ransom money. Mayer also describes Loeb brazenly engaging detectives in conversation about the case and tagging along to the inquest later that afternoon, where Loeb stood next to him while Mayer conversed with Franks.

**[MR. CROWE:] Q** Now, were you assigned by your newspaper to do any work on the Franks case?

**[MR. MAYER:] A** I was told to pick up whatever I could on it.

**Q** When was that?

**A** That was on the morning of May 23rd.

**Q** That is the Friday following the disappearance and murder of the boy?

**A** Yes sir.

**Q** Did you meet Richard Loeb that day?

**A** I did.

**Q** Did you have a talk with him?

**A** I did.

**Q** Who else was present, if anybody?

**A** Well our conversation, when we started our conversation we were alone.

## THE SAME OLD DICKIE

One unique aspect of the press coverage of the Leopold and Loeb case is the fact that several of the reporters had been friends or at least part of the social circle of the murderers. This not only gave them access to Nathan Leopold and Richard Loeb that might otherwise have been more restrained or formal, but also gave the tone of their coverage a more intimate, familial tone.

So, for example, the unbylined reporter of a story in the July 25 *Chicago Daily News* compared the admitted murderer Loeb who appeared in court to the carefree student of whom he seemed to have some personal remembrance, observing "It was the same old Dickie, for all his friends could detect. The boy with murder on his hands was the blythe good fellow of campus days. He discussed the case with his old school mates—three of whom are now newspaper reporters—and even helped them hunt clews to the slayers."

CONTINUED

**Q** Well go ahead and tell it in your own way, where you met him and what followed?

**A** I met him on the campus of the University of Chicago at noon on May 23rd. Our conversation turned to the Franks case, and Loeb suggested that if Mr. Franks were sending ten thousand dollars to a drug store on 63rd Street that he would not be met there by the kidnappers, but that some word would be left at the drugstore directing that the money be sent somewhere else. As I recall his words he said, "you know, these kidnappers would not meet a man on a busy street like that, that is common sense." I agreed with him. He said, "why don't you make the rounds of some of these drug stores on East 63rd Street, and see if you can't find the one at which some word was left for Mr. Franks." I hesitated, I had school work to do that afternoon and I didn't want to go along. About that time Alvin Goldstein and James Mulroy of the [Chicago Daily] News came along. Loeb knew Goldstein and he turned to me and he said, "If you won't take my proposition"—

**MR. CROWE:** Just a moment. Both of these other witnesses are in the room—

**MR. BACHRACH:** No objection.

MR. BACHRACH: The transcript does not specify a first name, but this is most likely Benjamin.

**MR. CROWE:** All right.

**Q** Go ahead.

**[MR. MAYER:] A** He said, "if you won't take my proposition, why I will put it up to them." I told him that I didn't care, and he talked to the other boys and they seemed anxious to go and suggested that as long as I had a car there that I go along with them. It was raining and I was hesitant, but I finally agreed to do that for about an hour. We started out, Goldstein, Mulroy, Loeb and myself, and we drove to 63rd and Stony Island. We started at the drug store on the corner there, and worked our way west on 63rd Street. When we got down as far as Blackstone it was raining pretty hard and Mulroy stayed in the car, Goldstein tried a cigar store across the street, and Loeb and I walked into the drug store of Van de Bogert and Ross and walked up to the colored Porter and asked him if he had been there the day before and he said "Yes". We asked him if any calls had come for Mr. Franks. He said, "Yes," that two calls had been received, but he said the other clerk received the other one, that he is out just now but he will be in in a few minutes.

Loeb turned to me. "You see, I told you we could find it, now you have got a scoop". And suggested that I keep it for myself, and I told him that I couldn't very well, that we had started out with the boys from the News and I suggested that he go over and call them. He did. And by the time the boys from the News came in the other clerk had arrived and we questioned him in detail as to exactly what was said over the phone, and we learned that the boys had called for Mr. Franks and when told that no Mr. Franks was employed there the voice asked the clerk to look about the drug store and see if there was anyone there by that name.

CONTINUED

The story isn't bylined, but two of the three "school mates" and newspaper reporters it refers to would have been James Mulroy and Alvin Goldstein, who both worked for the *Daily News* and were both called as witnesses in the trial for their part in uncovering facts essential to the case. Thus, though they themselves wrote about the case in the papers, they were also a key part of the papers' reports on Leopold and Loeb. The third was probably Howard Mayer, who was also called as a witness.

While we were there—we waited there for some time for the Bureau Squad to come up, after calling our offices, and when the burewe [should be "bureau"] squad came up we talked with, I believe it was Nick Hughes, and Loeb I believe even mentioned that the white clerk had said that he knew more about it than the colored porter. I don't recall the gist of our conversation, that is anything in particular, but I know it all centered about this case, and as we walked out of the drug store Loeb remarked to me "Well, that is what comes from reading detective stories," and I myself honestly believed it.

We then went to the inquest where I spoke to Mr. Franks and Loeb was standing alongside of me. From there we went down to get a newspaper to see if our story had got in and we couldn't get a late edition, but on the way back to Loeb's home, going east on 47th Street, we picked up a police officer who had a late edition of the [Chicago Evening] American and Loeb asked him if he could keep it because it had this story in it. We dropped Loeb off at his home, close to five o'clock.

**Q** Now did you have any conversation with the defendant, Loeb, after that?

**A** I did.

**Q** When was the next conversation?

**A** I don't recall meeting him on campus again, but on the morning, on Decoration Morning I was sent down to the Loeb home about seven o'clock in the morning. I got there about seven fifteen and one of the Bureau Squads came up and Dick stepped out of a Marmon and turned to me, shook hands with me and he says, "You know, Howie, I have always wanted to ride in one of these Marmons, and now I am getting my ride."

DECORATION MORNING: Mayer is probably referring to Decoration Day, another name for Memorial Day, which was Friday, May 30, when he appears to have witnessed Loeb being taken into police custody.

# 47
# I wouldn't put it past that man, Mitchell

## LEOPOLD CASTS ASPERSIONS

ROBERT CROWE called Leopold's University of Chicago criminal law professor Ernst Puttkammer to the stand to recall a conversation he had had with Leopold exactly a week after the murder, before Leopold became a suspect. The conversation is interesting for a variety of reasons: first, because Leopold inquired calmly into the penalties that might face Bobby Franks's murderer, depending on what his intent was; second, because in the list of possible motivations for the murder he included the possibility that the intent was "simply to take improper liberties with this boy"; and third, because he tried to cast suspicion on Harvard School teacher M. Kirk Mitchell. Mitchell had been arrested along with two other Harvard School teachers and brutally interrogated because of the detectives' suspicions about his sexual orientation and his ability to write the kind of highly educated prose used in the ransom note.

**[MR. PUTTKAMMER:] A** Examinations were going on and it is customary for the students to come down and ask questions on points that have troubled them, and he came down on that errand. He asked me relative to the Franks case, what the law would be, that is, he used that, as I understood him, simply as a dramatic state of facts on which to hang his questions. He started out by asking me what the situation would be, that is what crime would be committed if it were supposed that the little boy were taken into the car with the intention of then and there killing him, and I said that it seemed to me that it was perfectly obvious that there the intention would be to take a human life, and human life actually was taken, and so that it would be murder, very clearly.

Then he went on to say, "suppose the intent was simply to kidnap, nothing else apparently", and I said to him, kidnapping itself was a felony, or perhaps I put it in the form of a question and said, "Isn't kidnapping a felony here in Illinois", if I put it in the form of a question I am sure the answer on his part was, immediately, "yes", and I said, "supposing a man causes somebody's death while he is intending to commit a felony, is that murder or manslaughter," I took it for granted that he would be able to answer that question for himself, and apparently he felt satisfied, because he said, "Well now, suppose that that intent were simply to take improper liberties with this boy? I understand"—that was his word—"that this is a misdemeanor here in Illinois." I said, "Well, wholly without regard to that, on your assumed case, you still are talking about someone who had an intent to kidnap at the time, so that it is none the less a case where the intent is to commit a felony, even though other crimes might enter into it which are simply misdemeanors."

**[MR. CROWE:] Q** Now did you have any further discussion with him with reference to the case at law?

**A** I remarked to him that generally I did not take a very deep interest in murder cases, I had enough to do to read them when they appeared in the State Supreme Court reports, but that this case was different because there were a number of elements in it that had justice and personality. That made up all the difference. And I said that the principal one of those was the fact that before going to college I had gone to the

Harvard School, and so I had some sort of personal contact with the surroundings at least, and I believe he said, "You have nothing on me; I went to the School myself."

I said, "Well, then, your interest perhaps is even greater than mine, because you went there so much more recently and must know many more of the people." Perhaps I added then that most of the faculty had changed since then.

**Q** Let me interrupt you just a moment. Do you know whether or not at that time the State's Attorney had in custody a man by the name of Kirk Mitchell, who was a teacher in the Harvard School?

**A** He did, according to the newspaper.

**Q** All right. Now go ahead with the conversation.

**A** We of course immediately drifted onto the question of whether the case would ever be found out, who had done it and so on, and I think that I remember saying that I couldn't imagine Mr. Mitchell's having done it, that I had had a slight acquaintance with Mr. Mitchell for a long time and that he always had impressed me as a very upright, high-grade sort of a man.

Then he answered, "Well, I don't know, I am not so sure about that." And perhaps I looked inquiringly. Anyway, our conversation went on, and he said that he had known of instances in which Mr. Mitchell had solicited boys, presumably boys in the school, to improper sexual relations with him, and I expressed surprise at that. I think I said something about deals like that springing up so easily with Mitchell in custody.

Anyway, he said he had it on very reliable information. And I said, "Are you sure of that?" And he said, "Yes; he made that sort of a proposition to my brother; that is straight enough, isn't it."

Well, of course I couldn't say anything to that, and frankly, I thought to myself—

**MR. BACHRACH:** We object.

**MR. CROWE:** Yes.

**MR. DARROW:** We object to what he thought.

**THE COURT:** Yes.

**MR. CROWE: Q** Now was there any further conversation?

**[MR. PUTTKAMMER:] A** After mentioning this matter in regard to Mr. Mitchell?

**Q** Yes.

**A** Our conversation went on in regard to Mr. Mitchell, but not after we left that subject. He did say "I wouldn't put it past that man, Mitchell; I would like to see them get that fellow," and then he sort of turned on his heel as he went out and he said, "But, I don't say he did it," and he left the sentence up in the air.

Chicago History Museum, DN-0078037

Judge John Caverly, followed by Nathan Leopold (center) and Richard Loeb (right) outside the courtroom on July 26.

# 48
# I will plead guilty before a friendly Judge

## LEOPOLD, CORNERED

IN THE FOLLOWING section of the court transcript, the three police officers—Sergeants William Crot, Frank Johnson, and James Gortland—who had been sent to arrest Leopold on the afternoon of May 29 and were with him throughout much of the interrogation and its aftermath offer some disturbing glimpses of his state of mind in that period. Crot reveals that Leopold had contemplated committing suicide when he realized he was cornered, and that he also considered "tak[ing] a couple of coppers with me," i.e., using the gun he kept in his bedroom to shoot the police who came to arrest him. Comments Leopold had made to the detectives shocked the court-room for their arrogance and lack of remorse—especially the remark Leopold made to Gortland that he might get a reprieve by pleading guilty before a "friendly Judge." This implied that a judge might be made "friendlier" by his family's wealth and influence—a suggestion that deeply offended Judge John Caverly when Robert Crowe hammered it home again during his closing argument (see chapter 65, page 243). We start with Crot, discussing the immediate aftermath of Leopold's confession:

**[MR. CROT:] A** He was given into my custody and we went into one of the small rooms.

**[MR. CROWE:] Q** Small rooms where, in the State's Attorney's office?

**A** In the State's Attorney's office, yes.

**Q** All right. What if anything did he say or did you say?

**A** Well we got talking the case over and that was the first [time] him and I got together since he made the confession, and he stated that he had originally planned—he said, "You or the State's Attorney wouldn't have me," and I said, "How is that?" He said, "Well, I had a plan where I would have twelve headache powders in the box, or some harmless nature and one of them would be strychnine, which would be the same color," and he said, "I expected to be picked up, and if it got to look bad for me I was going to take one of those powders, but," he said, "I thought I was brought in there once and got away," and he said, "I thought I might be able to talk myself away again" and he says, "If I were searched and these were found on me and they were analyzed, it probably would be looked on with suspicion."

Then he got talking about the night we were out to the house looking for the glasses, and he said, "If I knew that Loeb was going to peach I could have killed myself that night," and he said, "While I was doing it I could have taken a couple of coppers with me," and I said, "Why a couple of coppers," and he said, "What was the difference"—

**MR. BACHRACH:** What is that?

**[MR. CROT:] A** He said, "While I was doing it I could have taken a couple of coppers with me," and I said, "Why a couple of coppers," and he said, "What is the difference."

---

"TALK MYSELF AWAY AGAIN": Leopold is referring to having been questioned by police on the Sunday following the murder—when he was not yet actually a suspect—after the detectives learned that his bird-watching expeditions frequently took him to the area where the body was found.

PEACH is 1920s slang for "betray."

**MR. CROWE: Q** Now while he was saying that did he make reference to any weapon?

**A** He was referring to the weapon that was in a drawer in his room.

**Q** What kind of a weapon?

**A** I believe in the upper lefthand drawer, a magazine gun.

**Q** Did you have any further talk with him?

**A** That was about all our conversation. [. . .]

Johnson, who was riding in the car with Leopold in the motorcade to reconstruct the crime on the Saturday after the confessions, recalls two notable moments:

**[MR. JOHNSON:] A** We were in the car, together with [John] Sbarbaro and myself, Sergeant Crot, Dick Loeb and Nathan Leopold, we were riding out toward Cottage Grove Avenue, 47th and Cottage Grove Avenue, and Nathan said to me, "I can't understand why the papers say this is such an atrocious murder," and I said to Nathan "Is it necessary that you had to kill the boy," and he says, "It was," and I said, "Why." Well, [Bobby Franks] knew Dick Loeb and "We couldn't afford to take a chance to have him come back and say it was Dick." I says, "Well, he didn't know you," and he says, "Well, I lived in the neighborhood and it was just a question of time before he would see me."

The second moment came the following day, Sunday, during the second expedition, in which Leopold and Loeb were taken by detectives to show where they had thrown the typewriter off a bridge in Jackson Park, and then down to the area of the culvert, where they had buried Bobby's belt—which was recovered. Johnson recounted an incident that occurred at the restaurant where they stopped for lunch:

**[MR. JOHNSON:] A** There was a lady at the opposite table who said to the gentleman that was with her "There is Nathan Leopold," and Nathan Leopold got up from his chair and he said, "I beg your pardon, Madam, I am not Nathan Leopold. I have been embarrassed several times by being taken for him," and then he sat down and said to me "How would you like to be able to lie like that."

Gortland testifies that when he and Captain William Schoemaker searched Leopold's bedroom at 10:20 a.m. on June 1, in his bureaus they found a .32 caliber Remington automatic and a .38 caliber Remington magazine, both loaded. Gortland also talks about a conversation he had with Leopold in the car on the evening of June 1 as they rode in the crime-reconstruction motorcade:

**[MR. GORTLAND:] A** It was in the early evening. This was after he had made his statement. I asked him how it was that he confessed. He said that it became manifestly impossible to maintain his story. I said, "The people are probably not satisfied with the motive expressed in this case, of adventure, excitement and money," and I says, "Is there any other motive," and he says, "Well, adventure and money," and he says, "But you don't think I am entirely a fool. Don't you think I am entitled to reserve something for my defense."

I said, "Well what do you think your defense will be."

He stated, "Well, that will depend on the wishes of my father and the lawyers. Of course, if they wish me to hang I will plead not guilty and the jury will hang me, or I will plead guilty before a friendly Judge and get life imprisonment." He says, "I have lots of things that I want to work on, and which would be of benefit to the world." He says, "Also there is the insanity plea."

And then I asked him as to whether he was sorry for Robert Franks and he says, "Not at all." I asked him if he was sorry for the Franks people and he said, "I don't give a damn if they would croak this minute."

Then I says, "The people will probably think that this crime was probably due to early religious training," and he says, "No, I went to Sunday school up to the age of eleven," and he says, "To confirmation class, but I was not confirmed on account of being too young." He says, "Up to the age of eight years conscience was drilled into me, but after the age of eight I drilled that conscience out." He says, "Murder, in my code, is not a crime." He says, "My crime was in getting caught."

# 49
# What is the defense trying to do here?

## THE LEGAL QUESTION OF INSANITY

AFTER CALLING 81 witnesses to testify, the state rested its case on the morning of Wednesday, July 30. But the moment defense attorney Walter Bachrach tries to question the first defense witness—alienist William A. White—Crowe goes on the attack, initiating a fierce two-day battle over the role of psychiatric testimony in a case where the defendants had already been established to be legally sane.

**[MR. WALTER BACHRACH:] Q** Will you please state your name?

**[DR. WHITE:] A** Dr. William A. White.

**Q** And your place of residence is?

**A** Washington, D.C.

**Q** What is your profession?

**A** Physician.

**Q** What is your age, Doctor?

**A** Fifty-four.

**Q** Will you please state your professional connections, both present and past.

**MR. CROWE:** Just a moment. I object to that, if your Honor please.

**THE COURT:** Why?

**MR. CROWE:** It is incompetent, irrelevant and immaterial.

**THE COURT:** Why?

**MR. CROWE:** The only purpose of it would be to lay a foundation for him to testify as an expert on the question of the sanity or insanity of the defendants. On a plea of guilty your Honor has no right to go into that question. As soon as it appears in the trial, it is your Honor's duty to call a jury.

**MR. WALTER BACHRACH:** We do not propose, if your Honor please—

**THE COURT:** Overruled, you may proceed.

**MR. CROWE:** I want to be heard on that, your Honor, because if there is any testimony introduced in this trial as to the mental condition of these boys, any act or any order that your Honor enters in the case is a nullity. In other words, if your Honor at the conclusion of this trial, after having gone into the sanity proposition, should sentence these boys to hang, your judgment would not be worth the paper that it was written on, the Supreme Court would set it aside. If you entered a judgment

## THE BATTLE OF THE ALIENISTS

On July 27, the *Chicago Daily Tribune* noted the arrival of Drs. William Healy of Boston, Bernard Glueck of New York, and William A. White of Washington, DC—the alienists for the defense whom State's Attorney Robert Crowe would sarcastically nickname "The Three Wise Men from the East."

Their advent was seen as heralding "the battle of the alienists," which the *Tribune* framed this way:

"If the state's evidence is sustained, Nathan F. Leopold Jr. and Richard Loeb are scheduled to go down in legal history as a pair of the country's most notorious murderers. If the defense has its way they will go down in medical history as two of the world's most remarkable examples of abnormal psychology."

here that is satisfactory to the defendants, they wouldn't have to appeal, and the State has no right to appeal. In other words, the State cannot appeal from any order your Honor enters. The defendants have a right to appeal from all orders. I would have to confess error in the Supreme Court if your Honor hung these men after hearing evidence of insanity. It you gave them life, or if you gave them a term of years that was satisfactory to the defendants and their lawyers, I couldn't appeal, and they wouldn't appeal. I insist that the question of sanity or insanity is a matter, under the law, for a jury. [ . . . ]

Insanity, if your Honor please, is a defense, just the same as an alibi. Would your Honor tolerate or permit these defendants to enter a plea of guilty in this case, and then put witnesses on the stand to show that when the crime was committed they were in California?

Have we got to a point in the law here where we can enter a plea of guilty before the court in order to avoid a jury, and then try that plea as a plea of not guilty and put in a defense?

What is the purpose of entering a plea of guilty and then maintaining that you have a defense and you have a right to hear it, when the law says that that defense has got to be decided by twelve men?

What is the defense trying to do here? Are they attempting to avoid a trial upon a plea of not guilty with the defendants before twelve men that would hang them, and trying to produce a situation where they can get a trial before one man that they think won't hang them? [ . . . ]

**THE COURT:** I have a right to know whether those boys are competent to plead guilty or not guilty. When the defense arrives at such a point that this court, if this court was satisfied that the boys were insane, the court could, and very likely would, direct the plea of guilty to be withdrawn and a plea of not guilty entered and let the defendants plead their insanity as a defense. There are different forms of insanity.

MR. THOMAS ←————— **MR. MARSHALL:** In medicine.
MARSHALL is
an assistant
state's attorney.

**THE COURT:** In medicine, not in law. Is there any mitigation in a murder case at all?

**MR. MARSHALL:** As to insanity, no.

**THE COURT:** We don't talk about insanity.

**MR. MARSHALL:** There is mitigation of course, but insanity is not of a mitigating nature. It is a condition that exists, or it does not exist.

**MR. CROWE:** There are no degrees, if your Honor please, in responsibility.

**THE COURT:** Oh yes there are.

**MR. CROWE:** No, your Honor. We haven't got a statute which says that a man twenty percent normal who commits a certain act will get one punishment, that a man who is thirty percent normal who commits the same act will get another punishment, that another man who is seventy percent normal who commits the same act will be punished more severely, or that a man one hundred percent normal who commits the same act will get a more severe penalty. There is not any such statute here. You are either responsible for your acts under the law, or you are not responsible, and the responsibility is complete. Insanity is a defense just the same as self-defense, just the same as an alibi.

Would your Honor listen to evidence of an alibi in this case?

**THE COURT:** That is not the question.

**MR. CROWE:** If it is a defense, can you listen to any defense on a plea of guilty?

**THE COURT:** The defense hasn't said they are going to put on alienists to show that these men are insane, and I don't think that they are going to attempt to show that they are insane.

**MR. CROWE:** Well then what is the evidence for, what are they going to show?

**THE COURT:** You will have to listen to it. They have said that they are going to put evidence on in mitigation of the crime. Our statute fixes three or four different penalties, one is death, the other is life imprisonment, and the third is penitentiary sentence for a number of years not less than fourteen. Now there certainly must be degrees of murder.

**MR. CROWE:** Yes, your Honor.

**THE COURT:** That is, degrees of punishment, and the punishment that the Court metes out must be guided by the evidence introduced.

**MR. CROWE:** If your Honor please, when a defendant pleads guilty to murder, the only place your Honor can find evidence of mitigation is in the things surrounding the commission of the crime. You do not take the microscope and look into his head to see what state of mind he was in, because if he is insane he is not responsible, and if he is sane he is responsible, then you look, not to his mental condition, but you look to the facts surrounding the case, did he kill the man because the man had debauched his wife? If that is so then there is mitigation here. Did he kill the man because the man had spread slanderous stories about him? Then there is mitigation. Did he kill the man in the heat of passion during a drunken fight? That is mitigation.

But here is a cold-blood murder, without a defense in fact, and they attempt, on a plea of guilty, to introduce an insanity defense before your Honor, and the statute says that is a matter that must be tried by a jury.

**THE COURT:** Has anybody said that they are going to introduce an insanity defense?

**MR. CROWE:** Well, what is the purpose of putting an expert on the stand?

**THE COURT:** They have a right to, in my opinion.

**MR. CROWE:** Aren't they going into his mental condition?

**THE COURT:** Well, suppose they do?

**MR. WALTER BACHRACH:** We have a right to do that, under the authorities.

**THE COURT:** The state of mind of one who is in possession of his ordinary faculties, without any mental disease, I have a right to know that, and that doesn't excuse him from the offense he has committed; but they have a right to show me that was the condition of his mind at that time, and insanity, at law, covers nothing more than the relation of the person to the particular act which is the subject of judicial investigation—the particular act which is the subject of judicial investigation. Now this is the act which is subject to judicial investigation, and I think I have a right to go into it to know the state of one who is in possession of his ordinary faculties and is not affected by any mental disease. Now, if he is affected by mental disease, then he is insane. If that be true, then this Court might, and probably would, insist that the defendants withdraw their plea of guilty and enter a plea of not guilty, and these counsel here have no right to waive the constitutional rights of those men.

If this court at any time is of the opinion they are insane, then he has got his duty to perform; but they have a right, in my opinion, to show the condition of mind of those boys, if they are in possession of their ordinary faculties, and if they are not affected by mental disease, the court has a right to know it.

**MR. WALTER BACHRACH:** May I make this statement, if the court please. We are not interested in this inquiry, in the legal question of insanity. That is a question which relates solely to the knowledge of the accused as to right and wrong and the ability to choose between the two. But what we propose to show here, is a medical condition, a pathological condition, which has absolutely no relation to the legal question presented on an insanity issue, and I have the authorities here.

**THE COURT:** We are not going to try any insanity issue here, gentlemen.

# 50
# What is a mitigating circumstance?

## DARROW URGES OPEN-MINDEDNESS

AFTER ASSISTANT STATE'S ATTORNEY Thomas Marshall cited case after case in support of the prosecution's argument that no psychiatric testimony should be admitted at the hearing, Darrow rose to bring his legendary rhetorical firepower to bear on behalf of the defense. Decades later, his words still ring from the pages of the transcript, a voice unmistakably distinct from all the others: folksy, patient, earthy, but also at times bitingly sarcastic or soaringly eloquent. It was typical of him, also, to build an argument not entirely grounded in law as it was currently accepted, but in law as he thought it ought to be. Arguing that understanding of mental illness had evolved since the time of many of the prosecution's legal precedents, and that an enlightened judgment should not be based on an antiquated understanding of insanity and mental illness, he made a deep impression on all spectators. The August 1 *Chicago Herald and Examiner* reported that "Darrow's speech was pronounced, on all sides, one of the most eloquent forensic efforts ever delivered in a criminal trial here," and added that "even opposing counsel were profoundly impressed."

**MR. DARROW:** If the Court please, I shall not take much time to review this argument, if it was one, and after I get through my associates will probably have something to add.

Now I understand that when everything has been said in this case from the beginning to the end, the position of the State's Attorney is that the universe will crumble unless these two boys are hanged.

I must say that I have never before seen the same passion and enthusiasm for a death penalty as I have in this case, and there have been thousands of killings before this, much more horrible in details, where there was some motive for it. There have been thousands before and there will probably be thousands again, whether these boys are hanged or go to prison.

If I thought hanging them would prevent any future murders I would probably be in favor of doing it. In fact I would consent to have anybody hanged, excepting myself, if I thought it would prevent all future murders. But I have no such feeling. I know the world will go on about the same in the future as it has in the past, at least I think so. My clients are not so important to the economy of things, either in their life or their death, and if this case is like all other cases, it ought to be tried calmly and dispassionately upon the facts in this case.

I think the Court knows, and everyone else who cares to know, that the defense in this case has met these issues perfectly squarely. It has been a distressing case from the beginning, and, as a matter of policy if nothing else, it is our duty to be open handed and state what we expect and what we claim, and we have done it at every stage of these proceedings. We have not invoked any harsh and strained rules of law to save the lives of these defendants, and we protest against any such rules of law being invoked to kill them. Any technicality, any foolish or strained argument is enough that they might accomplish their ends, and their ends are death, that is all. [. . .]

## THE ANGRY LION

Clarence Darrow's words sing on the page, even after all these years, in a way that stands out from the rest of the courtroom dialogue. What Darrow actually sounded like and looked like in the moment was something the newspaper reporters spared no verbal excess trying to convey to their readers. "Into ears hardened to the thunder of the state, callous to detonations of denunciation," wrote Charles V. Slattery in the August 1 *Chicago Herald and Examiner*, "the soft tremolo voice of Clarence S. Darrow yesterday murmured soft and eloquent words of human mercy, carrying shame to those who would hang Nathan Leopold Jr. and Richard A. Loeb."

Slattery contrasted the prosecution's vision of Leopold as the "Slave doing the dirty work of his King" and Loeb as "the King and Master Mind" with Darrow's alternate vision of "two little boys stumbling along in the darkness of immaturity—two boys living in a dream world—two boys to whom nothing is real." He portrayed Darrow as one minute gentle, then shaking with anger and emotion, "with the dramatic quiver of his perorations, and the long gray-black hair whips about his head like the mane of an angry lion."

Our own court has defined insanity; our own courts have defined it. We have had cases from England, a hundred years old, at a time when they could hang a boy of seven. We have progressed; we cannot hang them until they are ten. They could do it at seven.

They have given us the decisions of courts which are absolutely barbarous and come from the middle ages, and which are not the law in the State of Illinois and nothing like it.

A great change has come over the law in reference to insanity within the last twenty-five years; in fact there is a very great change within the last ten years, and even later than that.

My brother [Robert Crowe] used the strongest word he could think of for piling up, and he uses the word mountain. I suppose he means Himalaya. A great mountain of authorities are accumulated, and it makes it hard for courts to keep progress with science. But in this state and in most of the western states we have done something in that direction, we have done a great deal in that direction.

The policy of the law in this state is not the policy of the law in England a hundred years ago, it isn't what the policy was in Pennsylvania fifty years ago or perhaps even today, it isn't what it is in the south, it isn't what it is in many states in the East, especially years ago.

We have learned something from positions and something from imagination. There are very few men nowadays who cannot remember, among his friends or inside of his family or his acquaintances, insane people. There is almost nobody that doesn't know something about mental diseases also. It reaches everywhere, and men of science and learning have been investigating it, and they have been investigating toward humanity.

In the olden days when a man was insane they loaded him with chains and locked him in a dungeon. We have abandoned all that, and we consider that a person who is insane is a human being, entitled to particular treatment.

And we also know that there are many mental conditions and diseases that come far short of a legal defense of insanity; and it would not avail us, for a minute, as a defense in this case.

We know that men and women may be and are very seriously ill mentally; their minds are very seriously affected, and still they may know the difference between right and wrong; they generally do. And still they may, in some instances at least, be able to resist the wrong and do the right, and they are still mentally affected, and courts today take account of that.

Now we have in this State a statute which says that the Court may inquire into any facts mitigating punishment, or aggravating it. My friend puts the aggravation first, and then brings the mitigation; but my remembrance of the statute is that mitigation comes first, and it should, anyhow. With a common feeling of humanity it ought to.

A court before he passes sentence on a human being may inquire as to whether there are any mitigating circumstances.

Now what does that mean? Is there any catalogue of those mitigating circumstances? Is the State's Attorney to tell you what mitigating circumstances are?

There is only one person that can say whether circumstances are mitigating or not, and that is the Court himself, who is charged with the life and the responsibility and the fate of the defendants who are before him. He can tell. Even though he is not sure he must tell, and if a circumstance is mitigating it is for him to say and for no one else.

What is a mitigating circumstance?

Is youth?

If so, why?

Simply because the child has not the judgment of life that a grown person has. A mental condition, nothing else.

Is youth a mitigating circumstance?

Well we have all been young, and we know that phantasies and vagaries haunt the daily life of a child; we know the dream world we live in; we know that nothing is real; we know the lack of appreciation; we know the condition of the mind of a child. And has the Court a right to consider age a mitigating circumstance, and if so, why?

Here are two boys who are minors. The law would forbid them making contracts, forbid them marrying without the consent of their parents, wouldn't permit them to vote. Why? Because they haven't that judgment which only comes with years; because they are not fully responsible.

I am not proposing now to argue to this court whether that would be enough. The court must settle that. I am still saying that it would be a mitigating circumstance which any court would consider for what it is worth. Sometime I may say more upon that subject to this court.

The reason that youth would be a mitigating circumstance is on account of the mind, nothing else, the lack of judgment, the lack of discrimination, nothing else. And with the young that is so strong that they are all wards of the court until they become of age when there is any proceeding necessary to bring them into the court, no matter what it is.

I don't know, I cannot understand the glib, light-hearted carelessness of lawyers who talk of hanging two young boys as if they were talking of a holiday or visiting the races. It seems to me that if I could ever bring my mind to ask for it, I would do it not boastfully or exultingly, or in anger and hate, but do it with the deepest regret that it must be done and with sympathy, even for the ones whose lives they wish to take. That has not been done in this case.

I have never seen a more deliberate effort to turn the human beings of a community into ravening wolves as has been made in this case, and to take advantage of anything that they might get every mind that has to do with it into a state of hatred against these boys.

Now if it be a mitigating circumstance that a boy was young because of his mind, we may say at ten or eleven, or because of his lack of judgment, would it be a mitigating circumstance if, because of mental disease, he had not the full capacity to act, the full judgment that is needed in the manifold situation of life, or who was only partly responsible, but not fully responsible? The Court would have to say that.

And I don't know what there is in Alabama or Pennsylvania or any other state, but I know there is not any court in Illinois that does not consider it, and I know that under our statute they are bound to consider it for what it is worth.

Clarence Darrow, fist raised in the air, addresses Judge Caverly. Two rows behind him is Nathan Leopold, seen in profile, with his chin in his hand.

Charles Deering McCormick Library of Special Collections, Northwestern University Libraries

# 51
# Do not spank these naughty boys

## CROWE DEMANDS THE EXTREME PENALTY

AFTER TWO SOLID DAYS of arguing about precedent and theory (exactly 250 pages of trial transcript), the rhetoric begins to turn personal and snarky. Walter Bachrach continues the defense argument on the morning of August 1 by saying he'd been thinking about the case overnight and he had come to the realization that it was just not the state's attorney's business to recommend punishment to the court. Insinuating that Crowe was trying to manipulate or even bully Judge John Caverly, Bachrach argues that no one should tell the judge what his decision about punishment should be. Crowe's rebuttal drips with sarcasm—but also a level of showmanship that demonstrates what a match he was for Darrow's flamboyant courtroom presence.

**[MR. WALTER BACHRACH:]** As I have listened to the argument of the State's Attorney and pictured the situation presented here before your Honor, with the State's Attorney arguing, on one side, against the admissibility of this evidence, and the defendants' counsel arguing in favor of its admissibility on the other, and your Honor sitting up there on the bench, in the present situation, I find myself wondering, what was the function of each of us in this argument?

I found myself wondering what there was in the office of State's Attorney which made it his duty to determine the punishment in a case like this?

I found myself wondering what there was that gave him a right, as an officer of the law, as a representative of society, to stand before your Honor and demand a certain kind of punishment.

And I found myself also wondering what is the proper function of a judge in a situation like that?

In considering each of the things, I finally concluded, to my own satisfaction, that it was none of the State's Attorney's business, in this proceeding, as to what punishment was to be meted out; that he was an officer of the law whose business it was to see that justice was done, and what form that justice took was none of his business; that having prosecuted the case, having laid the evidence before the Court or before the jury as the case might be, his job was done when the verdict of the jury came in, whether a verdict of acquittal or a verdict of conviction or a plea of guilty, the State's Attorney had one function to serve, and that was to enlighten the court, to enable the court by all the resources at the State's Attorney's command, to come to an enlightened decision and to do justice. Not any particular form of punishment, not to single out and say the State demands hanging. But to lay the evidence before your Honor, before the Judge who is asked to pass upon the punishment and say, here are the facts, your Honor; if I can help you by the citation of authorities, if I can help you by the bringing in of any additional evidence, whether it be against the accused or whether it be in his favor, I shall be glad to respond; that it is as much the duty of the State's Attorney to bring before this court any evidence relating to the mental condition of the defendants as it is of the defendants' counsel, and that a State's Attorney, in the performance of his real duties, would insist that your Honor should hear this evidence and not try to keep it from your Honor. But by resorting to what might be called the "scales of the apothecary" he is asking your Honor to weigh the rights of these defendants and find out, by the use of such a measuring rod, or such an instrument, as to whether or not evidence in mitigation, of a certain kind, which has always been received in this community, shall be received here by your Honor in determining what punishment shall be meted out.

After all, if your Honor please, each one of us, in trying to work out a solution, attempts to identify himself with your Honor. And thus I picture myself sitting in your Honor's place on that bench and trying to solve this question which is now before you, and the first thought which would come to my mind, if I were in a position of that kind, is, I have a tremendous responsibility, I have the question of the punishment of two human beings under my control, and that punishment varies anywhere from fourteen years to death, and I, a human being, am asked to dispose of the lives or liberty of two other human beings, and I have that responsibility on my shoulders, I must uphold that responsibility, I must perform my duty, but how shall I proceed in the performance of that duty so that my conscience will ever remain undisturbed, my conscience must be my guide.

Now with that thought in mind my attitude as a Judge in a situation like this, would be that I would want to know every possible fact that might have a bearing on the question in this case, every possible fact from the point of view of the State's Attorney as well as from the point of view of the defense, so that I might know, weigh, weigh the imponderables as well as the ponderables, so that I might get a feel of the situation, so that I might get an understanding of things, besides the mere things that appear upon the surface, and that I would carry to such an extent that I would lay aside the rules of evidence, they do not matter in a situation like this, and as a matter of fact they do not matter as a matter of law. This is not a trial, this is an investigation which is now being conducted by your Honor to find out every possible fact which will enable your Honor to determine what shall be the punishment which is within your discretion to mete out here, and the rule of law which is applicable. [. . .]

**MR. CROWE:** Are you through, Mr. Bachrach?

**MR. WALTER BACHRACH:** Yes.

**MR. CROWE:** May it please your Honor, I appreciate that your Honor has been very patient in listening to this argument; I appreciate that we have taken up a great deal of time. I am not unmindful of the fact, when I say I appreciate what your Honor has done in that regard, I am not unmindful of the fact that this is a tremendously important case to the People of the State of Illinois.

The issue that is now before your Honor is one of the most important, if not the most vital, issues that will be raised in this case, and for that reason I assume that your Honor has indulged us as long as you have in this argument. I am not going to take up very much of your Honor's time. I think your Honor knows what the situation is, and you have heard it now from both sides.

I would like to, however, before your Honor passes on this important question, reply to one or two of the statements made by Mr. Darrow in his closing argument. As I listened to it I was in doubt as to whether he was before the legislature making a speech advocating them to repeal the death penalty or no. And then, some time, I thought he was making a closing argument to a jury in a guilty case, hoping to save his clients from their just desserts.

I was somewhat surprised at the statements advanced by Mr. Bachrach before he finished, that the State's Attorney had no business in the courtroom after he presents the evidence.

Mr. Darrow told me, when I was presenting the evidence in this case, I had no business to do that, it was all immaterial, they have entered a plea of guilty.

When the jury returns a verdict, Mr. Bachrach says that the State's Attorney ought to leave the court, he ought not to see that judgment is rendered on that verdict and if the verdict is a corrupt verdict he has no business to use the power of his office and the machinery of the law to demonstrate that fact. This ought not to be tried as a lawsuit, according to Mr. Bachrach. We should burn the Criminal Code and destroy the rules of evidence, chase the State's Attorney from the courtroom, and decide it, as what? As an experiment.

Nobody has a right to suggest to your honor what the punishment should be in this case but the defense. The State's Attorney, the sworn officer representing the People of the State of Illinois, has no right to tell your Honor what the facts are, what the law is, and, in his judgment, what the punishment should be. This is not a lawsuit at all. Why, we are roaming around, as Mr. Darrow said yesterday, in Greenland. We are not trying these two defendants for a murder. The State's Attorney is entirely mistaken as to what is going on here. These two men are not men of intellect and men of education, they are not graduates of the universities here that should be held to strict accountability, they are mere infants wandering around in a "boyish dreamland." The State's Attorney ought not to be permitted to discuss the gruesome details of the horrible murder in their presence. A kindly old nurse ought to tell them a bedtime story. They did not commit a murder. They broke a jar of jam in the pantry. That is not blood on their hands, that is jam.

If your Honor please, they are not the cold-blooded murderers, egotistical and secure in their conceit that they are above and beyond the law on account of their wealth and their influence. They have not sat here day after day and mocked the law, and as the details of this murder went in, sneered and smiled and laughed at the representatives of the law. No, they merely committed some little boyish prank, and they are sitting here sobbing for mercy, crying their very heart out.

The State is not asking for the noose here, Mr. Darrow says put away the judicial slaughter and do not spank these naughty boys, but let their nurse take them out to play. They are not the intellectuals who assume a superiority and say there is no God. No; they both believe in Santa Claus yet. Who could be so cruel and vicious, except the State's Attorney, to talk about death in a case of this sort?

Mr. Darrow has chided me because when I occupied the position your Honor now occupies in an attempt to protect the women and the children of this town when a criminal pleaded guilty to the atrocious murder of a little girl I followed the law and sentenced him to death, and was not swayed by all this talk of mercy.

We have a duty to perform. Mr. Darrow would not hang anybody. I have heard him state in the courts of law that he would not convict anybody of any offense. But your Honor and I are not like Mr. Darrow, the paid advocate, who has no oath of office or no duty to the public to perform. We have sworn that we will execute the laws as we find them. The laws in this case demand the extreme penalty, if the facts as presented by the State and uncontroverted by the defense, are true.

Mr. Darrow referred, sneeringly, to a bill I introduced in the legislature three years ago which provided that when mental defectives of criminal tendencies were first discovered, in order to protect the children and the women of this town, that we would not have to wait until somebody laid cold in death in order to prosecute them. Just as soon as it appeared that the person was mentally deranged and had criminal tendencies we could lock them up for the protection of society.

I ask your Honor and I ask Mr. Darrow, assume that I got these two defendants before the day the murder in this case was committed, and the law I introduced had been signed by the Governor instead of vetoed, and I brought them into court, and I said they were mental defectives with criminal tendencies, and unless they were confined they were liable to commit murder, Mr. Darrow would be here, and he would have his array of alienists, and he would say, "Why, two intellectual giants of the Chicago University [should be "University of Chicago"], coming from a cultured, sheltered home, never did a thing in their life that the State's Attorney can point to; if there is any insanity in this case, the insanity is in the State's Attorney."

There is only one issue in this. We have directed our argument to that issue. The purpose of the testimony now sought to be introduced fixes the responsibility of these defendants. I do not care by what name Mr. Darrow and his alienists call it, the legal effect, and the effect it has upon the mind of the layman, is that it is a defense of insanity. Under the law you have no right to hear that defense, any more than you would have a right to hear an alibi. A judgment entered after evidence of insanity is presented to your court is a nullity. The State has no right to appeal from any of your Honor's judgment. That right remains in the defense alone. If the defense is satisfied with your judgment there will be no appeal. If they are not satisfied with your Honor's judgment, then everything that you have done from the point you admit this testimony is a nullity, and the Supreme Court will send it back for another trial.

I insist, under the authorities, under the rules of logic and reason, that this evidence at this time ought to be excluded.

THE ATROCIOUS MURDER OF A LITTLE GIRL: Crowe refers here to the case of Thomas Fitzgerald, which occurred five years previously in 1919, when Crowe had been chief justice of the criminal court. Fitzgerald had pleaded guilty to the murder of 6-year-old Janet Wilkinson, a neighbor in his apartment building whom he had beaten, choked, and possibly also raped, yet who was probably still alive when he buried her with coal in the basement of the building. The killing sparked public outrage in Chicago, and—despite the fact that it had been decades since anyone who pleaded guilty had been given the death penalty—Crowe sentenced Fitzgerald to be hanged.

# 52
# An underdeveloped emotional attitude toward life

## THE PSYCHOLOGICAL DIAGNOSIS

S INCE BEING SWORN IN two days before, William A. White had sat patiently in the courtroom—occasionally appearing to doze—as the war over whether to admit psychiatric testimony was waged. As superintendent of St. Elizabeths Hospital in Washington, DC, and sitting president of the American Psychiatric Association, he was one of the country's leading alienists. On a previous visit, he had interviewed both the defendants personally, but much of his opinion about them was based on his reading of the Hulbert-Bowman Report, which was provided to all the out-of-town experts called by the defense. By the time he finally got up on the stand to testify, the general public was also intimately familiar with a version of the Hulbert-Bowman Report that had somehow found its way into the hands of all the Chicago newspapers the previous weekend, which had devoted pages and pages to such topics as Leopold's king-slave fantasy and Loeb's idea of himself as a "Criminal Master Mind."

Clarence Darrow claimed that a copy of the report had been stolen by one paper, and he had then provided copies to the others to prevent only one of them having a scoop, but others have guessed that he simply leaked the report in the first place as part of his extremely shrewd public relations campaign to reinvent Leopold and Loeb not as sinister thrill-killers but as troubled children. (Throughout their testimony, the defense alienists also used the familiar childhood nicknames "Dickie" and "Babe" to refer to the defendants, whereas the prosecution alienists consistently called them "Mr. Leopold" and "Mr. Loeb.")

The world already knew now about the governesses who had supposedly warped Leopold and Loeb, the string of escalating crimes they had committed together, and the pact they had made in which Leopold owed Loeb his complete obedience. At a time when psychoanalytic jargon had not yet trickled into daily public discourse, the testimony of White and the other alienists that was elicited by Walter Bachrach and Darrow was often designed to educate the judge and the public about the inner conflicts and unseen disturbances that might be at work inside a legally sane but still not wholly "normal" psyche.

**[DR. WHITE:]** Dickie thinks of himself as a master criminal, and he goes through the streets motioning to his subordinates. He plays the part in real life, so far as within him the power lies. He plays out the part of the criminal. When he gets into jail he finds again that he has projected himself into a real situation that comports and measures up and is on all fours, to a certain extent, with his phantasy, so there is a tendency for the phantasy life, an abnormal phantasy life, to realize itself in reality, and in his inability, as I expressed this morning, to distinguish between true and false, the lie and the truth, is basically the inability, which he feels, to distinguish between the real world as it is and the phantasy world which has accomplished such enormous proportions within him.

He has lost the ability to differentiate and to draw clear lines, to tell just where he is.

Now, it is quite proper [for children of] four or five years of age, three and four, especially, to play with their dolls. They give their dolls names. The dolls have personalities. And the onlooker is quite at a loss to know whether the child really

Chicago History Museum, DN-0077510

Jacob Franks (right) in the courtroom, along with Sam Ettelson (left), the family friend and attorney who had come to help look for Bobby on the night he disappeared, and who counseled and supported Franks throughout the proceedings.

believes that doll has a personality which corresponds to the name that the child has given it or not. The distinction is not clear.

Here this lack of reality, this lack of distinction has been carried forward through the years, and his phantasy life, instead of being lived away from, or showing any tendency of development, has been dragged along with him. In other words, he has grown to twenty years of age, but he has carried his infancy within the shape of an underdeveloped emotional attitude toward life.

Now, wherever we have this infantile emotional tendency especially where accompanied by a more or less excessive development upon the intellectual side, we have a tendency gradually increasing as the years go on for the intellect on one side and the emotion on the other to draw further and further apart. In a well rounded, well integrated, well knit personality, emotion and intelligence go hand in hand. People know and feel about what they know at the same level of development. Here they know and feel about what they know on two levels and the two attitudes tend to become further and further separated until we see the marked mental disease. The malignant disease which ultimately lands in many of our institutions. We see a complete estrangement, a complete personality where there is no longer a possibility of bringing the two aspects of personality into sufficient harmonious union. Dickie is in a stage which if it goes on further is capable of developing that kind of very malignant splitting.

**[MR. WALTER BACHRACH:] Q** Doctor, will you now address yourself to Nathan Leopold, Junior, and state what you have obtained as a result of your examination of him.

**[DR. WHITE:] A** Babe, as I will call him, if I may, because that is the nickname by which everybody speaks of him, and I learned to too, –

**MR. CROWE:** Just a moment. I have no objection to your referring to him as Babe if you have no purpose in doing it, but I would like to have him identified as Nathan Leopold, Jr., the defendant in this case. [. . .]

**[DR. WHITE:]** [Leopold] felt that even in his drinking, or anything that he did, he must excel in the doing of. Very early in life he developed a feeling of antagonism toward the tender emotions, of which he was from time to time the host. The tender sentiments and the emotions, the sympathies which ordinarily animate average people, he resented, because they made him suffer. He turned against these tender feelings with the conscious and intentional attitude of destroying them, and he brought into the situation the instrument which already in his early days had been developed to such a marked efficiency, –his intelligence. And he began here to destroy sympathy, emotion, tender feelings, and to develop a philosophy which later on in life has become very much elaborated, which is essentially a hedonistic philosophy, a philosophy wholly of pleasure and pain, a philosophy of complete and absolute selfishness, a philosophy of mechanism in which there is no God, where everything is explained wholly and solely and satisfactorily upon the mechanistic property. He says for example, in relation to this philosophy, to show how far it goes in his thinking and feeling, that murder is a very strong thing to weigh in the balance as against his pleasure. So, in such a philosophy, without any place for emotions or feelings, the intelligence reigns supreme. The only crime that he can commit is a crime of intelligence, a mistake of intelligence, and for that he is fully responsible. He and Dickie he refers to as relative supermen, and despite the fact that he knew that Dickie lied to him about his marks in school, was boastful and untruthful, he nevertheless says that Dickie not only approached perfection, but far surpassed it. And in a scheme of the perfect man which he drew up, he gave Dickie a scoring of ninety, himself a scoring of sixty-three, and various others of their mutual acquaintances various marks ranging from thirty to forty. In discussing later on this appraisal of Dickie as far surpassing perfection, he stated upon one occasion that he had become to have some doubts about it, and upon another occasion he said, very characteristically, I think that he was very skillful in blinding himself to certain facts of reality. He said that about this, and also about some other matters that will appear later. With reference to the idea of supermen, he at one time discussed with the professor, I believe it was one of the professors in the law school, the abstract question of whether supermen should be held responsible or not for their acts,–of course, Babe's view being that they should not. He considers himself, as I have already said, unique; and his differences from others—and by that I refer solely to his mental difference—are all in the direction of superiority. [. . .] It is interesting that in his college course he picked out studies more or less with the conscious intention of emphasizing his uniqueness; that is, setting him apart more completely from others. For example, he picked out such studies as Russian, modern Greek, Sanskrit, and certain Italian dialects which do not exist as languages today at all, but which only exist—and I am giving now the information which he gave me, because I do not know anything about it—in a few inscriptions somewhere. He studied these things because he knew and he felt that his knowledge of these recondite and abstruse subjects that nobody else knew anything about, would set him apart from everybody else as different, unique, intellectually superior.

With regard again to his philosophy—and I must beg pardon if I am a little discreet here, in following my notes—and the fact that there was not any place for God in his philosophy, he disclaims the idea that in his philosophy he is solely interested in over-throwing God, but his interest is more particularly in setting up his own philosophy, which of course repels God. Consistency, as he said, has always been a God with him. This drive for activity took him through many subjects in college, with great activity outside, constant restless activity in all sorts of directions, seeking always for new experiences, new worlds to conquer, if you will, looking forward to new experiences with anticipation. This trial, he said, he looked forward to as being or, as he expected it to be, one of the most keenly interesting, intellectual experiences of his life. Unfortunately he finds it very stupid and boresome.

**[MR. BACHRACH:] Q** Now, will you please—pardon me. Doctor, would you elaborate for us a little bit more the functions of the emotions in relationship with the mind and the necessity in a normal human being for them to function on the same plan [someone has penciled in "e" to correct this to "plane"].

**[DR. WHITE:] A** The old psychologists used to split up the mind into various faculties which they called the will, intellect, and feelings—or emotions. We still use those terms. We differ from the old psychologists because the old psychologists regarded each one of those things as separate entities, as they called them faculties that had separate existence. The will was thought of very much like it was, like a motorman presiding over the activities of an individual. Now, we know that the will and intelligence and feeling are only different aspects of a unity and that they all function together and that the harmonious function of that unity depends upon their relations.

The individual, the moral individual who grows up develops all of these components and parallel experience. An individual has to feel his way into the world in the same sort of a way he has to think his way into the world. The child can not possibly have the feeling or attitude toward responsibilities, for example, as the adult has, and that is generally recognized, and therefore the child is not held to accountability in the same way the adult has, no matter how much he might learn intellectually by rod as to those responsibilities, so that we have to know and we have to feel at the same level and we have to know things and know that we know them by feeling that they are true. And there are two aspects of the same psychological function as it were like the facets of a crystal. You might look at the crystal from one side or the other; if you look at it from one side you see the intellectual aspect in the foreground and if on the other side it is the emotional aspects in the foreground, but the more you tend to separate these two facets the more you permit one to go on developing less—out of relation to the other the more the energies of that individual are poured into one direction and don't get into the picture, and the other direction the more a discrepancy is set up as between what one thinks and what one feels, and that discrepancy gets greater and greater until there is what we call an inner conflict in which we want things but we cannot direct ourselves through our intelligence in a satisfactory way to bring them to pass. And such people spend their lives dreaming dreams to accomplish nothing.

**Q** Now, will you tell us a little more in detail how the defects in the personalities of Richard Loeb and Nathan Leopold, Jr. entered into the commission of a homicide of Robert Franks?

**A** Well, the homicide as I have already stated was to be the perfect crime. That is Dickie's objective. That is Dickie's formulation. Now, because of the affective and emotional relationships between the two boys, because of the identification of Babe with Dickie, because of Babe's desire to play this part with Dickie, that puts him in this double relationship of superior and inferior. He is willing to fall into this plan because of the emotional premium that the relationship offers him. He is willing to do it because it gives him the opportunity for expression along the lines that are essential in his feeling, if he should find the expression.

**Q** Doctor, would the disparity stated in the case of each one of these boys between their emotional development and their intellectual development in any way affect their ability to resist their criminalistic tendencies, if any?

**A** Surely, a wide disparity of that sort throws the whole personality out of balance and therefore destroys or tends to destroy their capacity for social adjustment along generally conceived conventional lines.

**MR. WALTER BACHRACH:** You may cross examine.

# 53
# I don't recall asking the boys that question

## THE DOCTOR DODGES CROWE

IN HIS CROSS-EXAMINATION of White, Robert Crowe first attacked the doctor's credibility by claiming there had been an initial report that White and the other defense alienists produced after their examination of Leopold and Loeb that suggested the boys were, in fact, insane. Crowe claimed that this conclusion was then revised in the final report (the one that was also leaked to the papers) to fit the defense strategy of avoiding a jury trial. White denied possessing a copy of this initial report that he might be able to share with the prosecution. (However, new evidence that emerged during the writing of this book confirms that an initial report diagnosing insanity *did* exist; see page 186.)

Crowe went on to try to undermine his integrity in other ways. Why, he wondered, had White and his associates assumed they could base their assessments of the defendants solely on conversations with them, when both Leopold and Loeb had admitted to long histories of lying freely to their families, their friends, and the police? And, in the following exchange, Crowe pointedly questions White about why he didn't even directly question either Leopold or Loeb about their roles in the crime they were accused of.

**[MR. CROWE:] Q** Now, Doctor, when you were talking to Nathan Leopold did you ask him who actually struck the blows that resulted in the death of Robert Franks?

**[DR. WHITE:] A** No, I don't think I did.

**Q** Did he tell you who actually did?

**A** I don't think he did, no.

**Q** Was there any reason why you did not ask him who the person was who actually struck the blow?

**A** I don't think of any especially, except it had no significance as regards their guilt one way or the other.

**Q** Did you ask him at that time or during any of your subsequent interviews with whom the crime had originated, in whose brain the crime had originated?

**A** I don't know that I did, but my description already indicates what I think about that.

**Q** When you talked to Richard Loeb did you ever ask him with whom the crime had originated?

**A** I don't remember asking such a specific question.

**Q** Or did you ask him who struck the blows which resulted in the death?

**A** I don't think I did.

**Q** Had you read the confessions that appeared in the newspapers purporting to have been made by these two boys?

**A** I had read Dick's confession. I don't think I had read Babe's.

**Q** Well, you knew in a general way each boy blamed the other for having originated the crime?

**A** Yes, I read that.

**Q** And each blamed the other for having committed the actual killing?

**A** Yes.

**Q** And that was of no moment or consequence to you in forming your opinion in this case?

**A** Well, I don't recall my mental state regarding that particular thing. I don't recall asking the boys that question.

**Q** Did you ask Richard Loeb to detail the manner in which the crime was committed?

**A** I don't think I did. I knew that pretty generally.

**Q** Well, did he tell you the details of the crime?

**A** I did not go all over the details of the crime with the boys, no.

**Q** Well, did he tell you any of the details of the crime?

**A** I asked some questions about matters that I thought were pertinent, about the chisel, about the acid, and about things of that sort.

**Q** Did you ask Richard Loeb or Nathan Leopold, Jr. to give you the details of the crime?

**A** No.

**Q** Now for how long a time did you question both of these boys while they were in each other's company?

**A** Oh, practically not at all.

**Q** Well, they were in each other's company occasionally?

**A** Well, I think the only time I questioned them at all when they were in each other's company was particularly this week, when I questioned them perhaps half an hour, each separately, when they were in the same room, and occasionally they were together for a few minutes when they were shifting from one to the other, but practically the entire examination was conducted separately.

**Q** Would it make any difference in your opinion, Doctor, if the facts were both of these boys while in the custody of the authorities, each insisted that the crime had originated in the brain of the other and each strenuously [insisted] that the actual killing was done by the other, and they showed so much heat that for hours they would not talk to one another and had threatened personal violence to one another for being blamed for the crime.

**A** No, I practically know that. Not all of it, but I knew in a general way that attitude of the boys.

**Q** Well, would that indicate to you that situation that one was a slave and the other the king?

**A** I don't think that would have any bearing on the discussion as I have developed it.

**Q** Have you any opinion as to who actually committed this murder, which one of the two?

**A** Which one did the actual—

**Q** Yes.

**A** I think so.

**Q** Which one, in your judgment.

**A** I think it was Dickie.

**Q** Do you know of any reason why he should not have admitted that to the authorities when he was detailing all the other facts and circumstances in reference to the crime?

**A** Well, I presume he wanted to avoid the final issue, to lessen the offense.

**Q** He wanted to lessen his responsibility?

**A** Sure.

# Were Leopold and Loeb insane?

The versions of the Hulbert-Bowman Report that remained in the historical record—the versions that were leaked to the newspapers, were read into the record of the court proceedings, and were donated by Dr. Hulbert himself to Northwestern—do not at any point declare Leopold and Loeb to be insane. Robert Crowe's contention that an earlier report by Darrow's alienists *had* found the defendants insane—a diagnosis which would have required a jury to determine their fate, rather than a single judge—has only recently been confirmed by archival evidence. In July of 2017, the Charles Deering McCormick Library of Special Collections at Northwestern acquired from a reputable dealer a document that had been in private hands, apparently, since the time of the trial. This was a bound collection of carbon copies of a series of reports on Leopold and Loeb composed by Harold Hulbert, followed by analyses and diagnoses provided by Doctors Bernard Glueck, William A. White, and William Healy—the three primary defense alienists who testified at the hearing and to whom Crowe liked to refer sarcastically as "The Three Wise Men from the East." Contrary to the position they took in court, in this document, the doctors quite unequivocally pronounce Leopold and Loeb to be legally insane.

It's not clear how this newly discovered document got into the hands of its apparent owner for the intervening decades. The name scrawled on its cover is that of Ira A. Darling, a psychiatrist who at the time was on staff at the State Hospital for the Insane in Warren, Pennsylvania. Darling had published articles on the medical problems of the insane, but he doesn't seem to have ever been publicly associated with the case and was not one of the defense experts. The document appears to have been in his possession and that of his descendants until it re-emerged at Northwestern.

It does, however, confirm the extent to which Darrow was willing to manipulate the definition of legal insanity in the service of his clients—and how the hired alienists were willing to manipulate their own professional diagnoses to suit the terms of their employment.

> In conclusion, this man is insane, in my opinion, based on detailed study and realizing the diagnostic, and also the prognostic importance of many characteristics which, at the present time, of

HULBERT'S REMARKS about Richard Loeb, from the newly discovered report.

> themselves, are small.
>
> This opinion is subject to modification by further study and by further data or corrections becoming available.

DEMENTIA PRAECOX is an outdated diagnostic term for what we would be more likely to call schizophrenia.

> This type of insanity, according to the 1920 scheme of classification used in the United States is, of course, Dementia Praecox, or Pre-dementia Praecox. However, this classification may be misleading, because the boy's life has not been typical of Praecox, in that he has had more educational advantages and has had more social contacts than the average Praecox has, consequently his ultimate dementia will not be typical of the average case of dementia Praecox.

When he is forced to realize that he cannot plan his own life, and the things he desires are impossible of attainment, he will probably seek solace, more and more, in Dementia Praecox autistic thinking, and will believe his phantasies much more firmly, with a consequent disbelief in painful realities. However, the evolution of his disease will not be normal, because of two reasons; first, because of his peculiar physical constitution, and, second, because he will not have his liberty and ordinary social contacts. The Prognosis is not good, medically. He will always be a typical form of Dementia Praecox. His knowledge of right and wrong in relation to his acts is academic entirely and he is unable to apply this knowledge to modify his conduct. His crimes are due to his insane extreme suggestibility from one who fits in with his insane delusion of "King and Slave". His Kings suggestions are irresistible impulses to him and he complys inevitably and uncritically.

HULBERT'S REPORT on Leopold also originally diagnoses him with "Dementia Praecox" and seems targeted toward a formulation of legal insanity, i.e., suggesting that while Leopold intellectually knew the difference between right and wrong, he was "unable to apply this knowledge to modify his conduct."

, it would seem obvious that under the ordinary conceptions of right and wrong tests he is insane within the meaning of the law. He acted under the influence of motives which estranged him entirely from reality, which made it impossible for him to see right and wrong in any sense comparable to the sense in which it is conceived that the average man sees it. He has no conception of his relation to society, and not a vestige of any feeling of duty or responsibility to others than himself. He has none of the inner standards which are supposed to control the conduct of the average individual.

WILLIAM WHITE'S ANALYSIS of Leopold claims that it was "impossible for him to see right and wrong in any sense comparable to the sense in which it is conceived that the average man sees it."

-12-

CONCLUSION.

On account of all the above, I am forced to conclude that in Loeb we have an individual with a pathological mental life; he is a case of abnormal split personality with an obsessive thought life that has such compulsive force that his acts can be seen to be directly dependent on the diseased elements of his mental life.

HEALY'S CONCLUSIONS about Loeb and Leopold don't specifically use the word insane but do refer to Loeb's "pathological mental life" and his "abnormal split personality," and Leopold's "psychosis."

CONCLUSIONS:

On account of all these, I see no other conclusion possible but that Leopold is a thoroughly unbalanced individual in his mental life, really mentally diseased, of the paranoiac or monomaniac type, which has produced so many criminals. He is a socially dangerous person, suffering from a psychosis. As is not uncommon in this type,

Darrow, facing the
camera. To the left is
Benjamin Bachrach,
and to the right,
slightly out of focus,
Nathan Leopold.

Charles Deering McCormick Library of Special Collections, Northwestern University Libraries

# 54
# Unfit for publication
### THE FATAL PACT, PART II

## FOLIE A DEUX

Deemed unsuitable
to be heard by the
ladies present in
the courtroom or for
publication in the
newspapers, William
Healy's testimony about
the sexual relation-
ship between Nathan
Leopold and Richard
Loeb, and the terms of
their "compact," was
therefore conducted in
whispers only the judge
and the attorneys could
hear. Though most of
the papers published
extensive transcriptions
of the daily court pro-
ceedings, this verbatim
conversation is omitted
and only obliquely
referred to, as when
Genevieve Forbes of the
*Chicago Daily Tribune*
alluded on August 5
to "testimony heard
only in chambers" in
which Healy described
"an incredibly childish
compact."

CONTINUED

**O**N MONDAY, AUGUST 4, William Healy was the next of the defense alienists to take the stand. He was at the time the director of the Judge Baker Foundation in Boston, which was devoted to the study of juvenile crime, and from 1909 to 1917 he had headed the Juvenile Psychopathic Institute of the Juvenile Court in Chicago. He lectured at Harvard, Columbia, and Boston University and had written several books on delinquency and mental illness. One of the most sensational revelations in his testimony never appeared in the press coverage; it concerns the exact terms of the pact made by Leopold and Loeb on their way home from the fraternity house robbery in Ann Arbor (see chapter 32, page 114).

**[DR. HEALY:]** In the matter of the association, I have the boys' story told separately about an incredibly absurd childish compact that bound them, which bears out in Leopold's case particularly the thread and idea of his fantasy life. For Loeb, he says, the association gave him the opportunity of getting someone to carry out his criminalistic imaginings and conscious ideas. In the case of Leopold, the direct cause of his entering into criminalist acts was this particularly childish compact.

**MR. CROWE:** You are talking about a compact that you characterize as childish. Kindly tell us what that compact was.

**[DR. HEALY:]** I am perfectly willing to tell it in chambers, but it is not a matter that I think should be told here.

**MR. CROWE:** I insist that we know what that compact is, so that we can form some opinion about it.

**MR. DARROW:** I suggest it be in chambers.

**THE COURT:** All right.

**MR. CROWE:** Tell it in court. The trial must be public, your Honor. I am not insisting that he talk loud enough for everybody to hear, but it ought to be told in the same way that we put the other evidence in.

**THE COURT:** It would be public, if there was only one outside in here. If it is something that is unfit for publication—

**MR. CROWE:** There is no desire on my part to bring out something unfit for publication—

**MR. [WALTER] BACHRACH:** It ought not to be given to the newspapers by this reporter, your Honor.

**THE COURT:** Oh no. This is not for the papers at all. This will not be given to the newspaper, Mr. Reporter.

The witness then made the following statement to court, counsel and court reporters:

**[Dr. HEALY:]** This compact, as was told to me separately by each of the boys on different occasions, and verified over and over, consisted in an agreement between them that Leopold, who has very definite homosexual tendencies, which have been a part of his makeup for many years, was to have the privilege of—do you want me to be very specific?

**MR. CROWE:** Absolutely, because this is important.

**[DR. HEALY:]** (Continuing)—was to have the privilege of inserting his penis between Loeb's legs at special rates; at one time it was to be three times in two months, if they continued their criminalistic activities together, and then they had some of their quarrels, and then it was once for each criminalistic deed. Now, their other so-called perverse tendencies seemed to amount to very little. They only engaged in anything else, so far as I can ascertain, very seldom, but this particular thing was very definite and explicit.

**MR. [WALTER] BACHRACH:** So that it need not be repeated, make it clear what the compact was.

**MR. DARROW:** I do not suppose this should be taken in the presence of newspapermen, your Honor.

**THE COURT:** Gentlemen, will you go and sit down, you newspapermen. Take your seats. This should not be published.

**MR. CROWE: Q** What other acts, if any, did they tell you about? You say that there are other acts that they did rarely or seldom?

**[DR. HEALY:] A** Oh, they were just experimenting once or twice with each other.

**Q** Tell what it was.

**A** They experimented with mouth perversions, but they did not keep it up at all. They did not get anything out of it.

**Q** And Leopold was—

**A** Leopold has had many years—shall I get into this whole subject while we are here now?

**THE COURT:** Yes.

**[DR. HEALY:]** Leopold has had for many years a great deal of phantasy life surrounding sex activity. That is part of the whole story and has been for many years. He has phantasies of being with a man, and usually with Loeb himself, even when he has connection with girls and the whole thing is an absurd situation because there is nothing but just putting his penis between this fellow's legs and getting that sort of a thrill. He says he gets a thrill out of anticipating it. Loeb would pretend to be

CONTINUED

"By the terms of this agreement," Forbes wrote, "Richard Loeb was enabled . . . to have power over an associate who would carry out his [Loeb's] criminal-istic imaginings and conscious ideas. And, by the same arrangement, Leopold won a personal premium on every crim-inal act he did for and with Richard Loeb."

Forbes reported that, after reading the terms of the compact into the record "for the judge's ear alone," Healy went on in his public testimony to link it to "the curious dovetailing of the two personalities," which she also described as a "folie a deux."

drunk, then this fellow would undress him and then he would almost rape him and would be furiously passionate at the time, whereas with women he does not get that same thrill and passion.

**MR. CROWE: Q** That is what he tells you?

**A** Surely.

**MR. DARROW:** That is all I believe of that.

**[DR. HEALY:]** That is what he tells me. And of the other part, of course, Loeb tells me himself. That is exactly what they did, and how he feigns sometimes to be drunk, in order that he should have his aid in carrying out his criminalistic ideas. That is what Leopold gets out of it, and that is what Loeb gets out of it.

**MR. [WALTER] BACHRACH: Q** When in connection with the compact in point of time did they start, with reference to the compact?

**A** Their criminalistic ideas began on the same day, when they began cheating at bridge. It was on the day when they first made it out. It was the first time in a berth, and it was when Leopold had this first experience with his penis between Loeb's legs, and then he found it gave him more pleasure than anything else he had ever done. To go on further with this, even in jail here, a look at Loeb's body or his touch upon his shoulder thrills him so, he says, immeasurably.

Is that enough?

**MR. CROWE:** I think that is all.

The next day, Crowe cross-examines Healy about the exact nature of the "perversion" involved in the pact:

**[MR. CROWE:] Q** Doctor, you talk about a childish pact, that is the pact that you related to the court yesterday so the audience generally could not hear it. In that pact these boys agreed to practice forms of perversion, didn't they?

**[DR. HEALY:] A** A childish form, yes, but not what as generally the public would understand, I think by that.

**Q** Doctor, do you know any children who make those agreements and enter into those pacts that are not criminals and perverts?

**A** Yes, I have known of them.

**Q** You have?

**A** Yes.

**Q** So you regard perversion not as a crime, but as a childish act?

**A** This is not, you know—as I said, it is a childish form of perversion. There are different kinds of perversion. But, as far as that goes, there are many children, very innocent children of fine people who get into many things of that sort.

**Q** Now, doctor, wait a minute.

**MR. DARROW:** I insist on letting him finish his answers.

**MR. CROWE:** All right.

**MR. DARROW:** Go ahead and finish your answer, doctor.

**[DR. HEALY:] A** Many children who have been very nice children and grown up in very nice ways have at one time done things like that.

**MR. CROWE: Q** How many different forms of perversion did you state yesterday that Leopold practiced on Loeb?

**MR. [WALTER] BACHRACH:** If the Court please, if there is any purpose in having the thing done quietly in the court room, the effect is altogether lost if the prosecutor can cross examine openly about that thing and give those things to the public.

**MR. CROWE:** Oh no. No, your Honor. I have no desire to bring this out and give it to the public, but when a doctor says that boys who agree to practice forms of perversion are merely doing childish things, I disagree with him.

**MR. DARROW:** Well, he spoke about different forms of perversion, as you know.

**THE COURT:** The cross examination of this doctor along that line will take the same form as his direct [examination]. It will be done quietly and without any heralding to the world.

**MR. CROWE:** All right.

**THE COURT:** No good can come from it.

(Whereupon the following examination was continued out of the hearing of the public generally):

**MR. CROWE: Q** Didn't you testify yesterday that Leopold—I don't know the exact expression you used—but indulged in some form of cunnilingualism?

**[DR. HEALY:] A** No, that is not the term at all. You have got the wrong term. Did you mean malpractice?

**Q** Malpractice?

**A** I said that according to both of their stories they experimented with it, but did not practice it. They gave it up after once experimenting with it, once or twice.

**Q** Didn't you testify yesterday that on several occasions at least Leopold—and when you say "malpractice" you mean that Leopold had Loeb's penis in his mouth, and after once or twice he did not find the same satisfaction in that as he did in the other forms of perversion?

**A** Yes.

**Q** And you think that that is a childish pact?

**A** No, no, hundreds of children, sir, have done it.

**Q** Aren't you ashamed of yourself, doctor, to testify on that matter?

**A** No, I should say not. I have known of very nice children of very nice families who have gotten through with things of that sort.

Crowe then switches topics, and the cross-examination continues in open court.

# 55
# No remorse, no regret, no compassion

### LOEB STRUCK THE BLOW

**NATIONAL HEADLINES**

Bernard Glueck's admission that Richard Loeb had told him he was the one who had actually killed Bobby Franks made headlines across the country. "SAYS LOEB ADMITTED KILLING" screamed the banner across the full front page of the August 6 *Boston Globe*, followed in smaller headline type by "First Time the Actual Slayer of Franks Boy Has Been Named."

According to the story, Loeb "remained impassive" as he listened to this part of Glueck's testimony. On the other hand, "Leopold leaned forward, a grimace on his face, smiled slowly and talked with counsel."

WILLIAM A. WHITE and William Healy both claimed that they hadn't thought to ask either Leopold or Loeb to talk directly about the crime they had committed but had relied on the Hulbert-Bowman Report and the confessions as they read them in the newspapers for information about the murder. But in his testimony on Wednesday, August 6, Bernard Glueck, a privately practicing psychiatrist who had formerly supervised the criminal ward at the Government Hospital for the Insane (now St. Elizabeths) in Washington, DC, as well as the psychiatric clinic at Sing Sing Prison in New York, said he *had* asked who killed Bobby, and that Loeb had confessed to the crime. As you'll see in following section of the transcript, a few days later, when Harold Hulbert, coauthor of the Hulbert-Bowman Report, takes the stand (described as "The Witness" here), he confirms that Loeb had told him the same thing, though he had not included this information in his report and it has never been considered part of the official record of the case.

**MR. BENJAMIN BACHRACH: Q** When court adjourned you were relating what you learned in your interview with Richard Loeb. Continue and tell further what he told you, his reactions, etc.?

**[THE WITNESS:] A** I then took up with Loeb the Franks crime, and asked him to tell me about it. He recited to me in a most matter of fact way all of the gruesome details of the planning and execution of this crime, of the disfiguring and the disposal of the body; how he and Leopold stopped with the body in the car to get something to eat on the way. He spoke to me in a most matter of fact way about his doings and movements immediately following this act. As his recital proceeded, I was amazed at the absolute absence of any signs of normal feeling, such as one would expect under the circumstances. He showed no remorse, no regret, no compassion for the people involved in this situation, and as he kept on talking it became very evident to me that there was a profound disparity between the things that he was talking about, the things that he was thinking about, and the things that he claimed he had carried out, and there became evident the absolute lack of normal human emotional response that would fit these situations, and the whole thing became incomprehensible to me except on the basis of a disordered personality.

I tried to visualize my own past experience in talking with a great many criminals of all sorts, probably about two thousand of them, and never before have I seen such disparity between one's ideation and talking and emotional response to it, except in cases of disordered personality.

In the course of my conversation with him, he told me how his little brother, of whom he said he was most fond of any member of the family, how this boy passed in review before him as a possible victim of the kidnaping and killing. Even in connection with this statement, he showed the same lack of adequate emotional response to the situation.

I asked him to tell me how he accounted for this attitude of matter of factness to all these things, and he mentioned to me the same thing that he mentioned to one of the other examiners, that it struck him as unusual when he sat in the court room listening to the testimony of Mrs. Franks and that he came to explain it to himself as having nothing within him that might call forth a response to the situation.

**MR. BENJAMIN BACHRACH:** Can't you keep your voice up? We have difficulty in hearing.

**THE WITNESS:** I then took up the discussion with him of his stay in jail, having in mind the background—the social and cultural background into which this boy was born and in which he was reared.

**MR. BENJAMIN BACHRACH:** Let me interrupt you, doctor, before you leave the other subject.

In the conversation with Richard Loeb, did he say anything about who it was that struck the blow to the head of Robert Franks with the chisel?

**THE WITNESS:** He told me all the details of the crime, including the fact that he struck the blow.

**Q** Now come back to the conversation in the jail.

**A** He also referred to the situation which came out here yesterday, this peculiar compact between him and Leopold.

**Q** Now get to the jail proposition.

**A** I then took up the question of this stay in jail and the manner in which he was adapting himself to that situation, and as I say, in view, keeping in mind the background from which he came, the fact that he had been used all his life to luxury and refinement in all his contacts, that again strengthened my belief in the peculiar disparity, the peculiar disorder of this boy's personality.

He seemed to be perfectly satisfied with the jail. He told me the whole thing seemed natural to him. He mentioned the fact that he was given a fairly good looking coat and he preferred a ragged coat.

I have observed his coming to the examinations, the various interviews I had with him, and considered it as one of the important points that would lead me to my conclusion about him, the manner in which he entered the room, the levity, the perfect matter of factness, the childish playfulness that was evident, as though he did not at all take in the seriousness of the situation in which he found himself. Even if I had not talked with him any great length of time the whole impression he made upon me as I compare it with my experiences of disordered people was obviously that of a person who was in a disordered state of some sort.

I have been sitting here in the courtroom watching the two boys, keeping in mind the fact that they have listened to the State's Attorney's very effective delineation of their depravity, of their ruthlessness and cruelty; that they have listened to the doctors reveal their innermost thoughts, their innermost secrets, details of their intimate life; they have seen and listened to the witnesses in this gruesome tragedy, and as I watched them it seemed to me that they absolutely did not take in emotionally the meaning of this whole situation.

Once or twice as I see them coming in and going from the courtroom, as I see them sitting there in a seat, it impresses me as though he were attending a college play of some sort. And it is extremely significant in formulating my opinion about these boys, that in the midst of this acute situation they fail so consistently to show the kind of emotional response that you would expect of any normal human being.

**Q** Did Loeb tell you anything else, doctor?

**A** In the course of my conversation with him, while I was trying to formulate my opinion as to his emotional makeup, I discussed the possible outcome of this whole situation. We spoke of the possibility of terminating his life by hanging and he said in a most matter of fact way, "Well, it's too bad a fellow won't be able to read about it in the newspapers".

We talked about what would happen if after having spent a lifetime in prison he should come out. He wanted to know whether at that time he could get a complete file of the newspapers of this period."

# 56
# I did not have time

## WHY IT WAS FORENSICALLY INADVISABLE TO QUESTION LOEB ABOUT HIS PAST CRIMES

HAROLD HULBERT, coauthor of the Hulbert-Bowman Report, was called by the defense to testify primarily about the medical examinations he had made of both defendants. He and Karl Bowman—a renowned expert on "the influence of the ductless glands upon human behavior"—had put Leopold and Loeb through a battery of X-rays and endocrinological tests to try to identify a biochemical explanation for their apparently diseased mental conditions. Robert Crowe was highly skeptical that what Hulbert described as Leopold's prematurely calcified pineal gland accounted for his role in murdering Bobby Franks. And he was equally skeptical about any claim to scientific objectivity and neutrality being made by Hulbert and Bowman. He found it very suspicious, for example, that the doctors explicitly acknowledged in their report—which they had expected would be kept confidential and shared only with other defense psychiatrists and the defense team—that they had decided not to question Loeb about the mysterious "A, B, C, and D" crimes, calling an examination of the crimes "forensically inadvisable" (see chapter 38, page 134). In this segment of his cross-examination on August 11, Crowe makes it clear that he thinks the doctors were colluding with the defense in suppressing information about the severity of Loeb's previous criminal behavior.

**[CROWE:] Q** There are things [Loeb] has not told you up to date?

**[DR. HULBERT:] A** Yes.

**Q** And he might have been advised not to tell you those things?

**A** He might have.

**Q** Then don't you go on [in the Hulbert-Bowman Report], "His oldest brother, Allan [Loeb], does not know of these untold stories, but the patient says he will not tell them unless Allan advises him to do so."

**A** Yes that is just what I wrote.

**Q** And that is true?

**A** Yes.

**Q** So just how important those matters are that he had been advised not to tell you, you don't know?

**A** No, I don't know.

**Q** And you don't know what effect they would have upon your conclusions if you did know them?

**A** I don't know.

**Q** Then you go on and say, "On the other hand, there is a certain legal advantage in minimizing the broadcasting of his episodes".

When you use the expression "There is a certain legal advantage", you are thinking about his defense, are you not?

**A** Yes.

## PINEALS AND PITUITARIES

Like State's Attorney Robert Crowe, the press also appeared skeptical that Harold Hulbert's extensive discussion of the results of the various physical tests and measurements of the defendants was shedding any light on why Nathan Leopold and Richard Loeb had committed the murder. Certainly, tension in the courtroom, which had remained high as one sensational revelation followed another, took a precipitous dip, with even the dogged reporters starting to lose interest as Hulbert droned on the first day about Loeb's blood pressure, his blood sugar, and the percentage of carbon dioxide in his blood. The *Chicago Daily Tribune*'s Genevieve Forbes observed on August 9 that "The more technical the phrases grew, the less noisy the typewriters which had been clicking

CONTINUED

Harold Hulbert, holding up
a skull X-ray at the Leopold
and Loeb hearing.

**Q** In other words, importing matters of mitigation to Judge Caverly here, it is to the advantage of the defendants to have withheld certain information from you so that the conclusion you now have arrived at won't be disturbed, is that true?

**A** I was interested in this crime, the Franks crime.

**Q** And don't you further state, "Even keeping them secret from his attorney, examiners or relatives, consequently no great effort should be made to bring forth details which he willfully repressed."

**A** That is the way I felt about it.

**Q** Now, doctor, do you think an opinion based upon a partial statement of the fact when that opinion might be changed by your knowing all the facts, don't you think that is a might unsafe guide for the court to go on?

**A** No, I think the essential facts in relation to this particular crime are brought out.

**Q** You say you don't know what the facts are that he withheld or how important they might be?

**A** No.

**Q** And they might be important enough to lead you to a different conclusion?

**A** They might.

**Q** Now, doctor, Dr. [William] Healy, Dr. [William A.] White and Dr. [Bernard] Glueck testified that in making up their minds in this matter they had taken into consideration your report—answer that.

**[A]** What is the question?

**Q** Do you know that Dr. Healy, Dr. White and Dr. Glueck testified that in coming to their conclusion they had considered your report?

**A** Yes, they told me so.

**Q** Now, you say [Loeb] denied being implicated in the so-called gland robbery of Mr. [Charles] Ream, denied having been in Geneva in the case of the ragged stranger who was found with his hands and face mutilated, which crime is usually attributed to Warren Lincoln, and he denied having participated in any other delinquency but later referred to four episodes where the letters A, B, C and D were suggested. Have you anything else in your report about these A, B, C and D episodes?

**A** No.

**Q** Well, that would not be very illuminating to the other doctors to read about withholding information and later telling you about four episodes which you refer to as A, B, C and D, would it?

**A** Not very illuminating.

**Q** Then you said, "It was found forensically inadvisable to question him about these." Now, by "forensically", you mean, what, legally, don't you?

**A** Just a pressure of time. We were concentrating on this case to get our report in before these doctors came from the East.

**Q** What does "forensic" mean?

**A** From the forum.

CONTINUED

along so busily. Presently there was but one caligraph (it was run by a studious looking man from New York) trying to follow the report."

The next day, Forbes described Hulbert holding up "a sinister enough picture of [Leopold's] skull," at which point Judge John Caverly got up from his seat and came over to look at the X-ray as Hulbert held it up to the light.

"The pineal gland shows a shadow," Hulbert announced. "This indicates the gland calcified early, before 19, and the normal time for such calcification is 30."

Forbes added drily, "Then the courtroom fans, doubtless for the first time in their lives, concentrated their attention on the pituitary gland, situated somewhere in that skull."

**Q** It means legal?

**A** Yes, legal or pulpit.

**Q** So this might have read, "It was found legal" and the only thing the lawyers are thinking about is the trial of this case in this connection?

**A** Yes.

**Q** It was found legal or in reference to this particular trial inadvisable to question him about these?

**A** Yes, we had so much to get out in relation to this trial we did not go into anything else.

**Q** Oh, no, you didn't say you didn't have time. Just get this; it was found forensically—

**A** Yes, that was the reason.

**Q** Not that you didn't have time, but forensically it was found?

**A** That is the forensic reason.

**Q** And legally it was found?

**A** That is the forensic reason.

**Q** Yes, but legally it was found inadvisable to question him about these. Now, just what did you mean by that that it would not help his case any if you went into it?

**A** No, to get the report through by the 21st if we could possibly do it.

**Q** And you want us to understand that that is the meaning of those words, that you did not have time to go into these matters?

**A** I did not have time.

**Q** Why didn't you say that? As to these matters, didn't have time to develop them; why didn't you say that?

**A** That is the way I felt about it.

**Q** You thought it would sound nicer to say it was found legally inadvisable to question him about them?

**MR. WALTER BACHRACH:** I object to the form of the question.

**THE COURT:** Let him answer.

**MR. CROWE: Q** Is that true?

**[DR. HULBERT:] A** Oh, approximately.

**Q** And you thought the court and the rest of us would understand that by that sentence you mean you did not have time to go into these matters?

**A** Absolutely not, for this reason; this report was not prepared for you, it was prepared for other physicians who were coming on from the East. I had no idea this report would be submitted to the public or to you. It is a medical report.

# 57
# Just from the waist down

## WHY WAS THE CORPSE UNDRESSED IN TWO STAGES?

O N TUESDAY, AUGUST 12, after the defense had rested its case, the prosecution be-gan calling its own alienists in rebuttal of the defense alienists. Hugh T. Patrick, Archibald Church, and William O. Krohn had been present in the state's attorney's office on June 1, the day following the confessions, as the defendants were offered the chance to comment on each other's accounts of the murder. Robert Crowe at that point had been actively holding Walter Bachrach and Clarence Darrow at bay outside the office, hoping to have his alienists establish conclusively that Leopold and Loeb were sane before defense attorneys could call in their own psychiatrists.

One ambiguous topic that arises in the court testimony of both Church and Krohn—but, like other testimony involving the sexual relationship of the defendants and any possibly sexual aspect of the crime, was not reported in the newspapers—was that they both saw something suspicious in Leopold's and Loeb's accounts of having initially undressed Bobby's corpse in two separate stages. According to Loeb (see chapter 16, page 69), "We stopped the car, got out, removed young Franks' shoes, hid them in some bushes and removed his pants and stockings, placing them in the car." Loeb explained that "We did this in order that we might be saved the trou-ble of too much undressing him later on." They then got back in the car with the half-undressed body, drove around waiting for it to get dark, stopped for a snack of hotdogs and root beer, stopped again so Leopold could call his girlfriend, and finally parked near the culvert, where they dragged the body out of the car and finished undressing it.

None of the defense alienists reported having found this narrative suspicious, but Church and Krohn both bring it up. As was true throughout the trial, the moment the subject of "aberrant sexual relations" comes up, testimony is given in whispers only the judge, attorneys, and court reporter could hear, in order to prevent the public and the press from being exposed to any "inde-cencies." Both testimonies are quoted here, though they were given four days apart.

Here, Church is being questioned by Darrow:

**[MR. DARROW:] Q** What other topics did anybody discuss with either Leopold or Loeb?

**[DR. CHURCH:] A** Other than the crime?

**Q** Than the crime, and this that you have already stated?

**A** The question came up as to aberrant sexual relations between them.

**Q** Now, just a moment. The court has directed that you do that quietly, doctor.

(Whereupon the following examination was carried on out of the hearing of the public).

**A** Well, they intimated they had been accused of such practices, and that for a long period of time they took precautions not to be seen together.

**Q** A little lower, doctor.

**A** In order that no gossip might be favored by such apparent society. They denied them, they denied having done such things. One of them said that they did not want to be seen together, but they were like the young ladies that needed a chaperon, for the good of the public.

## FLORA WAS FRAGILE

While the men repre-senting the Leopold, Loeb, and Franks fam-ilies were a constant, relatively stoical pres-ence in the court, Anna Loeb remained secluded with her ailing husband at the Loebs' palatial estate in Charlevoix, Michigan, and Flora Franks—who did make a brief court appear-ance at the beginning of the hearing—was rarely seen. Papers such as the August 14 *Los Angeles Times* reported that the Frankses would be soon moving from their home due to an unbearable flood of macabre tour-ism that engulfed the house daily. Tour buses were said to be pulling up a dozen times a day, with conductors shout-ing into their mega-phones—fully audible inside the house—that this was the home of little Bobby Franks who had been killed by Nathan Leopold and Richard Loeb.

CONTINUED

CONTINUED

On August 15, a small item in the *New York Herald Tribune* reported that Flora "was in a state of collapse, the result of a forbidden visit to the grave of her son." Despite the pleas of family members, she had slipped away to visit her son's grave while her husband was in court, and, according to the paper, "was found semi-conscious, lying across the grave." In fact, Bobby had been interred inside the family's mausoleum, so some degree of poetic license may have been at work. Nevertheless, her psychological state was obviously fragile and physicians were said to be in constant attendance.

**Q** Did you ask anything about that?

**A** Well, I asked them if anything of that sort had happened.

**Q** Why did you ask that?

**A** Sir?

**Q** Why did you ask that?

**A** Because the subject had been broached.

**Q** How is that?

**A** Because the subject had been broached.

**Q** Is that all?

**A** And because, of course, I wanted to know.

**Q** Why did you want to know?

**A** Because those practices are not so very uncommon among people who are closely associated in companionship.

**Q** That would not be a reason, would it?

**A** Yes.

**Q** Was that the reason you wanted to know?

**A** I wanted to know if there was anything of that sort in the case.

**Q** Why?

**A** I think I had seen in the paper some intimation that they had taken sexual liberties with the body of the boy.

**Q** I see.

**A** And I wanted to know if they had this aberrant sexual trend.

**Q** Did you ask them whether there had been sexual relations between themselves?

**A** Yes.

**Q** Why did you ask them that?

**A** For the same reason. I wanted to know if they had a tendency to those things, whether it was a sexual crime or not.

**Q** Does that fact ever have a bearing on mental condition?

**A** Oh, I think it does.

**Q** Yes. That is why you asked, was it not?

**A** Yes.

**Q** All right. That is what I was getting at. And you assumed, didn't you, that there was no such thing?

**A** That was their statement.

**Q** I say you assumed—you did not come to an opinion, did you?

**A** I was not sure that the statement on their part was entirely dependable.

**MR. DARROW:** Will you repeat that.

(Whereupon the answer was here read by the Court Reporter).

**MR. DARROW: Q** Did you assume either way, come to any opinion?

**A** No. There was something else on that subject. Oh, yes. They said that the gossip had been set afloat by a young boy who had a week-end party at some country place, had accused one of them of getting into the hammock or bed with the other, and that that was the reason this story got about, and the reason they had to avoid any appearance of great personal intimacy.

**Q** Now, you don't know whether after you asked that question you assumed they had or had not?

**A** No, I did not assume anything.

**Q** But you do know that it is one of those things that a physician inquiries into in considering mental condition, don't you?

**A** Oh, yes.

**Q** Doctor, may I ask, if this matter comes up again, we have an understanding—

**A** Pardon me.

**Q** I say, if this matter comes up again we have an understanding that it should be private?

**A** I see.

**Q** So if you will let us know.

**A** Yes.

At this point, the public proceedings resumed. Later, Krohn, being questioned by Assistant State's Attorney John Sbarbaro during the afternoon session on Monday, August 18, says he was also suspicious because Leopold and Loeb had undressed the corpse "from the waist down." He recounts the story as he heard Loeb telling it on June 1 in the state's attorney's office, after Krohn got there around 3 in the afternoon:

**[DR. KROHN:]** He remembers later of driving on Indianapolis Avenue, outside of South Chicago, and finally in a winding road, Calumet Drive, and another winding road, until they got to a blind road near a Russian Orthodox cemetery; that there they stripped the body from the waist down; took off the little panties, shoes and stockings, the belt and the buckle; that they buried certain metal portions that they knew would not burn when they tried to dispose of the other clothing. Now, there is a little matter here that I would like to speak of just before you and the attorneys, if I may, Judge, and then I can be through with that phase of it.

(The witness then stated the following to court, counsel and court reporters.)

**[DR. KROHN:]** It was because of this circumstance of undressing the boy just from the waist down that caused me to ask a good many questions about a certain letter that Leopold wrote to Loeb, in which it seemed to imply that there were certain homo-sexual practices. The natural thing, I thought, or the natural way to undress the boy is to strip his clothes off, taking his waist and other things off, but they only took the clothes off from the waist down. This letter was explained as a letter that was written out of—or as the result of a certain fellow with whom they were angry, Buckley, who had written to their fraternity over at Ann Arbor that they had taken two cocksuckers into their fraternity, and was based on an incident that had happened at Loeb's house at Charlevoix, when all three of them were drunk one night, and one of them—Loeb coming back from the toilet had gotten into bed with Leopold; that Buckley had drawn certain conclusions, and had written to Leopold's brother, or called his attention to it, and also had written a letter to the fraternity after they had joined over in Michigan.

That was the occasion of my asking a great many questions along the line of sexual perversion and homo-sexual practices. I didn't want to refer to it any further here, and I simply wanted to get rid of that phase of it.

**THE COURT:** All right.

(The witness then continued his statement in the usual way.)

Darrow, leaning forward to address Judge Caverly. Robert Crowe can be seen seated behind Darrow (second from right), in a photo that dramatizes how closely packed the courtroom was, with the fan on the judge's desk providing only slight relief from the high summer temperatures.

## THE TECHNICAL STAR

The August 19 *Chicago Daily News* reported that as the "technical star" of the state's attorney's staff, it was Thomas Marshall's job to give the court "a cold, unemotional statement of the prosecutor's interpretation of the law."

Compared to the speeches of the two flamboyant rhetorical stylists, Clarence Darrow and Robert Crowe, Marshall's statement comes across as dull and utilitarian, and the newspaper suggested that his delivery matched that style. He had written out his speech "and had rehearsed it too, apparently," reciting to the judge the logical reasons why the defendants should be executed.

"Marshall's high-pitched voice began almost a scream whenever his argument brought him back to the phrase he used at every opportunity—'the extreme penalty, death,'" the paper said. "Loeb and Leopold weren't four feet behind him, but the phrase didn't even make them wince. They listened with as little interest as if they were casual spectators. Leopold leaned over Darrow's shoulder at one point to read a letter the lawyer had drawn from his pocket. He laughed easily and naturally at its contents."

# 58
# Responsibility, mitigation, turpitude

## THE PROSECUTION DEFINES ITS TERMS

WHEN CLOSING ARGUMENTS begin on Tuesday, August 19, at 10:30 a.m., Assistant State's Attorney Thomas Marshall begins by laying out the exact legal framework according to which the prosecution believed the judge should weigh his decision.

**[MR. MARSHALL:]** I am dividing then the discussion on the legal side to these three phases, responsibility, mitigation, and turpitude.

In a former discussion a large number of cases on this question of responsibility were read to the court. I shall only cite and read a very short extract from any of the cases that have been referred to before, because I feel your Honor has the substance of that discussion before you now, but it is necessary to refer in passing to some of them.

Responsibility then is a condition, a status. There are no grades or degrees. One is either responsible or is not responsible. And in this case the responsibility is admitted by the pleas of guilty. It is proved by the confessions and by the evidence in the case and it is repeatedly insisted upon by the assertions and arguments of their counsel.

The responsibility being fixed, anything in mitigation, as well as evidence of aggravation, that is, of depravity, showing the turpitude is to be considered by the court in the matter of arriving at the punishment in the case.

Now, on this question of responsibility, keep this in mind: If Loeb and Leopold are responsible enough to receive a sentence to the penitentiary, they are by that same responsibility responsible enough for the extreme penalty. There is no distinction there in the matter of responsibility. The measure of responsibility is the same in either case. There is nothing to mitigate as to responsibility. Mitigation goes only to the fixing of the punishment. They cannot be sent to the penitentiary unless they are legally responsible, and if they are legally responsible their fate is determined not by weak mind or phantasy, delusions, or mental disease, but by the turpitude of their crime.

When he continues his argument on Wednesday, August 20, Marshall cites the basic statute for the punishment of murder:

"Whoever is guilty of murder shall suffer the punishment of death, or imprisonment in the penitentiary for his natural life, or for a term not less than fourteen years. If the accused is found guilty by a jury, they shall fix the punishment by their verdict; upon a plea of guilty, the punishment shall be fixed by the court." [Smith & Hurd Statutes, Chapter 38, Par. 360. (Murder - punishment) (Sec.142.) 1923]

Previously in his argument, Marshall has defined TURPITUDE by quoting *Holloway v. Holloway*, 126 Georgia, 459:

"Turpitude in its ordinary sense involves the idea of inherent baseness or vileness, shameless wickedness, depravity (Webster's International Dictionary). In its legal sense it includes everything done contrary to justice, honesty, modesty, or good morals. (Black's Law Dictionary, and Bouvier.)

"The word 'moral' which so often precedes the word 'turpitude' does not seem to add anything to the meaning of the term, other than that emphasis which often results from a tautological expression. All crimes embraced within the Roman conception involve turpitude, but it is not safe to declare that such crimes only involve turpitude. Murder involves vileness and depravity, or it is the result of an abandoned and malignant heart.

"Wherever one intentionally and wrongfully takes human life he does an act which is base, vile and depraved, and contrary to good morals."

Marshall then asserts that neither their mental state nor their ages should disqualify Leopold and Loeb from the maximum penalty:

"A person shall be considered of sound mind who is neither an idiot nor lunatic, nor affected with insanity, and who hath arrived at the age of fourteen years, or before that age if such person know the distinction between good and evil." [Par. 590 from the Smith & Hurd Statutes] [. . .]

PRIMA FACIE DOLI
INCAPAX: In other
words, that between the
ages of 7 and 14, the law
would presume that the
child was incapable of evil
intent, unless contrary
evidence proved that this
child had intentionally
done something that was
clearly especially evil and
malicious.

Between the ages of seven and fourteen years, an infant is deemed prima facie doli incapax; but in this case the maxim applies, malitia supplet aetatem—malice, which is here used in its legal sense and means the doing of a wrongful act intentionally without just cause or excuse, supplies the want of mature years. Accordingly, at the age above mentioned, the ordinary legal presumption may be rebutted by strong pregnant evidence of mischievous discretion; for the capacity of doing ill or contradicting guilt is not so much measured by years and days as by the strength of the delinquent's understanding and judgment.

Then Marshall moves on to the matter of how to "correctly determine here whether the turpitude in this case, the depravity and viciousness of this crime, are of the kind, of the type that requires the extreme penalty":

I have searched them out and ascertained the facts, and your Honor will conclude, I believe, after a recital of the facts in these various cases, that nowhere in the whole history of murder in Illinois is there a crime so cruel, so brutal, so vicious, as this crime at bar.

COWARDLY MURDER:
Marshall refers to a
case—State v. Junkins,
147 Iowa, 588, decided in
1910—in which mitigation
for the death penalty was
sought but denied for a
defendant convicted of
murdering Clara Rosen,
"a reputable young lady
residing in the City of
Ottumwa," who left her
house to call on her sister
a few blocks away but
never arrived. A few hours
later her body was found
in a vacant lot near her
sister's house. Her skull
had been crushed, her
valuables stolen, "her
clothes were torn and
when found her limbs were
exposed. Whether the
attack on her had been
made for the purpose of
sexual crime is a matter
of perhaps not conclusive
inference."

Marshall recites the facts of a number of cases in the state of Illinois where men received the death penalty for murder, including the shooting of a police officer during a robbery, the shooting of a man believed by the shooter to be having an affair with his wife, the shooting of a man who had walked into a bar and was shot by another man for no apparent reason at all, the shooting of a man who was eating in a Chinese restaurant and noticed two men trying to steal his car outside and went to confront them, and the shooting of a man who confronted a burglar in his house. Finally, Marshall concludes his legal argument:

In conclusion, then, if your honor please I want to call your attention particularly to the language of the Iowa court where it characterized that murder as a cowardly murder and ask this court to contemplate the record here before you with that thought in mind.

Could anything be more cowardly, more terribly cowardly than the crime that was committed here? A fourteen year old helpless school boy lured by deceit into the automobile, by two stout robust young men, bent upon murder, bent upon kidnaping for ransom, for Ten Thousand Dollars in old bills; lured into that car, seated in the front seat to talk about a tennis racket with his friend, whom he had known for a long time; and while he is facing forward in that car, and talking about a tennis racket, he is beaten upon the head with a steel chisel, and his life crushed out at the hands of two strong young men, –a helpless boy. Cowardly? There is nothing in Illinois jurisprudence that compares with it. It cannot be found on the books. If the killing of the young woman in Ottumwa was cowardly, this is a dastardly cowardly crime.

And so upon the whole of the record, compare all of the Illinois cases I have cited from the beginning down to this moment, and nowhere in any of them will you find the premeditation, the deliberate malice, the cunning plans, the months of preparation, the thought, the science, the ability.

None of these things are to be found in the books in connection with the crime of murder, and here we have it in connection with two of the three highest crimes in the statute, the only two crimes in the state that are provided by the law with the death penalty. The statutes of the state say that the penalty shall be death. Here the murder and the kidnaping statutes each prescribe death. That is the law of the land. It still exists.

The authorities construing those statutes, our Supreme Court opinions say that the punishment under those statutes shall be proportionate to the turpitude of the offense. All three elements are here, responsibility, aggravation beyond anything in the books anywhere, and no mitigation.

No case compares with it for atrocity and depravity. Then the court being bound by the law to follow the law and the law being clear and plain, it only remains for the court to say that this is a case indeed where the turpitude of the crime fixes the punishment that is so richly merited here, the only punishment that fits the crime, the extreme punishment provided by the law.

There is only one sentence that can be imposed upon these vile culprits that fits the act they committed, yea, the acts they committed.

Twice over the law requires their lives upon their admissions of record in this court, and any lesser penalty than the extreme penalty of the law under such circumstances and upon the record in this case, would make a mockery of the law itself.

I thank your Honor for the patience you have shown me.

# 59
# What mercy did they give that little tot?

## THE PROSECUTION'S CASE FOR THE EXTREME PENALTY

**TEARS WERE FLOWING**

The tone of the courtroom drama changed abruptly on the afternoon of August 20, when Assistant State's Attorney Joseph P. Savage took up his part in the closing argument. The next day's *Chicago Daily Tribune* sharply rendered the contrast between Thomas Marshall and Savage: Marshall droned like an accountant through his list of precedents "in a high-pitched, sing-song" voice that was "somehow not so convincing." At points in his argument, even Richard Loeb, who had been taking a keen interest in the details of the grislier cases Marshall was citing, seemed to glaze over.

But "Now comes Savage, the orator, Savage of the booming voice that can be toned so easily down to the vibrant inflection, that thrills and makes lumps rise in throats and tears well up in the eyes."

CONTINUED

**THE MOTHER WHO STILL BELIEVES:** Savage may have read this in a newspaper—specifically the account in the August 12 *Chicago Daily News* of the conversation between Anna Loeb and Flora Franks (see chapter 41, pages 138–139).

O**N THE AFTERNOON** of Wednesday, August 20, after Marshall had carefully laid out the prosecution's legal argument for the harshest possible sentencing, Savage followed him with a highly emotional appeal, retelling the entire story of the murder and suggesting that if the judge failed to hang Leopold and Loeb, it would be a total miscarriage of justice.

**[MR. SAVAGE:]** In conclusion, your Honor has never had a case before you with such evidence presented for mitigation, as you have had in this case.

Why, your Honor, at the outset of this case, Mr. Darrow walks in before the court, and makes a virtue out of a necessity.

He pleads both defendants guilty before your honor to murder, and to kidnaping for ransom.

Why?

Why, your honor well knows that if the State's case was not ironclad and bound Darrow would have tried his case before a jury.

If there was any way out from this mass of facts that were presented to your Honor, Darrow would have taken his chance with a jury.

But, he knows from his long experience that he would not find twelve men, your honor, not only in this county but any county, that would not have arrived at the one conclusion—guilty.

So he comes before your Honor and he pleads for mercy.

He asks your Honor for mercy, and he tells your Honor they are both youths, boys.

What mercy did they give that little tot?

And, your Honor, the families, the Loeb family, highly respected citizens in this community, each and every one of them, and the Leopold family, highly respected citizens of this community . . . both highly respected families in this community, and your Honor feels sorry for them and so do I, and you feel sorry for every family, because they are the ones who always suffer; and you feel sorry for the Franks family, and you feel sorry for the mother who still believes that her little boy will return, who still cherishes that hope that she will have her little boy back again.

**MR. DARROW:** Where is the evidence on that, Mr. Savage?

**MR. SAVAGE:** It is a fair inference.

**MR. DARROW:** Oh!

**MR. SAVAGE:** That is fair to infer, your Honor, that that mother who cherished the boy is still waiting for his return from school; and then they ask your Honor for mercy, for mercy, two cold-blooded murderers.

Why, your Honor, the law is made for all people, rich and poor, Jew or Gentile, black or white. The law applies to all the same.

And these two murderers sitting before your honor are not immune to that law. Justice sits by, and the world looks on, and this community. And when I say this community, your honor, every mother and father should get down on their knees and pray to Almighty God their thanks that their daughter was not the victim of this fiendish conspiracy, as Leopold planned. I wonder how many think today how fortunate they have been that they are not missing their little daughter.

Why, judge, if ever there was a case in history that deserves the most severe punishment, this is the case. And I want to say, your honor, that it is a fair inference, if your honor does not hang both of these murderers, it will be a long time in Cook County before we ever hang another murderer.

I want to say, your honor, that if we do not hang these two most brutal murderers, we might just as well abolish capital punishment, because it will mean nothing in our law.

And I want to say to your honor that the men who have reached the gallows prior to this time have been unjustly treated, if these two do not follow. And I know your honor will live up to his full responsibility; and that you will enforce the law as you see it should be enforced. The people of this great community are looking to your honor to mete out justice, that justice that the murderers in this case so richly deserve.

And when your honor metes out that justice we will have no more supermen; we will have no more men with phantasies whose desires are to ravish young children and then murder them. We will send out a warning that the people of this community will not stand to have their children's lives in danger.

And, your honor, when you undertake the extreme penalty in this case, the only penalty that should be meted out under the facts and circumstances as presented here, you will have told the world that Cook County is a safe place for one's children to be raised in and that the people will have no fear; that they will have no fear for their children's lives when they are returning home from school.

And you will have set, your honor, you will have set that confidence, that stability in our laws and in our justice that will waiver if we fail to see that the defendants here are properly punished.

You will stabilize the laws of this community so that everyone, rich and poor, will realize that the law applies to them no matter what their station in life may be.

And without going into it, your honor, your Honor well knows what juries have said in your court room, in other court rooms since your honor has been the chief justice of this court, that murder must stop, and the only way you will stop murder is by hanging the murderers; and if your honor hangs these two murderers, it will set an example to the others, if we have any of them among us, that justice is swift, and that justice is sure, and that if they fail to live up to the letter of the law they will receive the extreme penalty of the law.

CONTINUED

As Savage dramatically reprised the story of Bobby Franks's murder from beginning to end—telling what these "cold-blooded fiends" had done to the boy seated so innocently in the car "as he thought with friends," the whole courtroom went into emotional meltdown.

"The tears of mothers and sisters of other little boys like Bobby Franks were flowing." Leopold and Loeb, who had alternately smirked or spaced out during other graphic testimony, "stared soberly at the floor with studied efforts not to meet eyes that sought them out." As Savage described the mutilation of Bobby's body, Jacob Franks, unable to bear any more, got up and "stumbled out."

After a month of testimony about the murder—with days spent contemplating the psyches and pituitaries and nannies of Leopold and Loeb—"It was the first time that eyes have been moist with sympathy for the victim."

# 60
# You stand in a relationship of father to these defendants

## THE DEFENSE URGES WISDOM AND UNDERSTANDING

WALTER BACHRACH BEGAN the defense's closing argument by suggesting that the prosecution had misrepresented the defense's effort to present evidence of mental disease: the intent had not been to lessen the responsibility or guilt for the crime, which was fully admitted, but only to help guide Judge John Caverly as he weighed what punishment should be applied, since he had such wide discretion to apply anything ranging from death to life imprisonment, with a minimum of 14 years in prison. The most eloquent section of Bachrach's plea urges Caverly to see himself in a fatherly role—reinforcing the defense tactic of reminding the court and the media at every opportunity that while "Dickie" and "Babe" might have killed a child, they were still virtually—and certainly emotionally—children themselves.

**[MR. WALTER BACHRACH:]** The State's Attorneys who preceded me have laid much stress upon the proposition that your Honor ought to follow the law—that your Honor ought to follow the law, and that they have great confidence and great faith that your Honor will do what he thinks is right under all the circumstances.

That your Honor will do what he thinks is right under all the circumstances, there is no question in my mind. What the law is that your Honor shall follow is another question, and an attempt has been made to give the impression that there is some sort of a legal precedent somewhere which requires your Honor to impose a death penalty rather than some other minor penalty in this case.

The legislature has given to your Honor the discretion, in cases where pleas of guilty are entered, to fix a penalty anywhere between a minimum and a maximum terms of years, or at death. Your Honor is given a latitude, your Honor is given a discretion, and there is no precedent in any decision that tells your Honor how your Honor should exercise that discretion which the Legislature has given to you.

Your Honor sits here very much in the position of a father whose child or children have committed some wrong, and the legislature has given your Honor something of the same discretion that every father exercises or has with respect to the correction of his children; and your Honor has the same necessity for the exercise of wisdom and understanding that every father must exercise in correcting his child.

Now, there are some fathers, I will grant, who if a child should commit a misdeed, would inflict the extreme penalty on the child that did the deed. They would be in favor of very severe punishment.

There are some fathers who before they inflict the punishment would try to find out why the child did it; what was the matter with the child at the time the child did it; did the child do it because it was sick; did the child do it because it was suffering from a disease; did the child do it when he was in a fever; did the child do it when he was mentally diseased?

And, if he found that the child did it because he was mentally diseased, he would not punish it to the severest extent that he could.

He might separate that child for the time being, and prevent it from committing the wrong deed it had already committed, again. He would not permit it to cause further injury, but what would he do? He would call in a specialist, he would call in a doctor who would try to understand the child. He would try to find out what it was that made that child what it was; and try to bring about a situation which would be less brutal than the wrong which the child itself had committed.

Now, here you stand in the relationship of a father to these defendants. Every Judge does. Every man in his heart knows that the judge on the bench is his father; his punisher when he is wrong; that he must come before him and receive his punishment, his chastisement.

But, when he comes before his legal father on a plea of guilty, that father is faced with the necessity which every father has of desiring understanding of the wrongdoer, of trying to understand what it was that brought about the situation, before the punishment is inflicted.

It is so easy to hang; the important problem is put out of sight.

It requires more understanding, it requires more intelligence to investigate.

And as I listened to Mr. Savage and heard his easy disposition of the evidence in this case with respect to the mental condition of these boys, I could not believe my ears.

Was it because he did not understand?

Was it because we were not able to make him understand?

Was it because he did not want your honor to understand?

I do not know.

But whatever it was it sounded to me like quite a distortion of the facts in this case with reference to the identical issue that your honor has to pass upon here.

Walter Bachrach then argues that claims by the state's alienists that they had not observed any signs of mental disease during their cursory examination of the defendants could no more prove the absence of such disease than an examination of someone's left hand by a physician could prove that he did not have a wound on his right hand. He characterizes the diseases from which Leopold and Loeb are respectively suffering with diagnoses from a book by prosecution alienists William O. Krohn and Harold Singer[1]—though of course Krohn and Singer had not themselves made such diagnoses about Leopold and Loeb. Bachrach identifies Leopold as having a paranoiac psychosis, illustrated by his superman delusion, and Loeb as having schizophrenic psychosis, or "splitting of the mind," illustrated by his fantasies of being a great criminal. Finally he concludes that Leopold had an abnormally premature calcification of the pineal gland, which, according to a book by one Walter Timme, a New York neurologist (who did not examine the defendants or testify at the hearing), would give him a diagnosis of "precocious pineal involution," said to cause all kinds of disturbances of the blood gasses and sugars and therefore having a "direct effect upon the functioning of the mind" (though Bachrach does not specify what exact effect this was).

---

1 Harold Singer, then chair of the psychiatry department at the University of Illinois, had also testified for the prosecution, arguing that based on the Hulbert-Bowman Report, as well as on his own brief discussions with Leopold and Loeb, and the other alienists' testimony, there was no evidence of mental disease.

# 61
# If these boys hang, you must do it

## CAVERLY'S LONELY DECISION

**T**HE COURT RECESSED for lunch after Walter Bachrach had finished his closing argument, and by the time it resumed in the afternoon, word had gotten around that Darrow was about to start his speech, triggering a violent stampede of would-be spectators. The court transcript conveys how chaotic and noisy the scene was—such that Caverly interrupts Darrow and orders the police to clear the crowds out of the hallways because their noise is drowning out the proceedings. The following text is the only part of Darrow's closing argument that appears in the original court transcript. His argument continued for two more days after this, but a note at the beginning of Volume VII of the transcript declares that he borrowed the rest of his own argument from the court records, apparently to edit and polish the text for a version that was later published in a stand-alone pamphlet, and presumably never returned it. However, since the text that does survive in the transcript matches word for word the transcripts that appeared in several Chicago newspapers, it's reasonable to surmise that reporters were all working from the official court transcript—and that therefore newspaper text for the days that are missing from the transcript is a reliable record of Darrow's original speech.

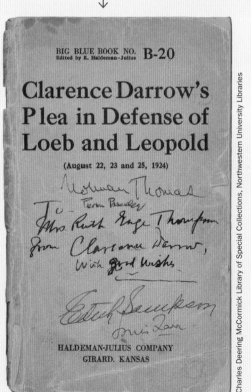

BIG BLUE BOOK NO. **B-20**
Edited by E. Haldeman-Julius

# Clarence Darrow's Plea in Defense of Loeb and Leopold

(August 22, 23 and 25, 1924)

HALDEMAN-JULIUS COMPANY
GIRARD. KANSAS

**THE COURT:** Keep that door closed. If they persist in coming in bring somebody up here and I will send them over to jail.

Keep the doors closed.

Do not let anybody else in. Those who did not come until this hour are late, I do not care where they belong, keep them out. Now find seats, you that are in.

No more crowding in back there.

Keep quiet; keep back out of the way.

Mr. Bailiffs, do not let anybody in, it does not make any difference who.

All right Mr. Darrow.

(Whereupon Mr. Clarence Darrow began his closing argument on behalf of the defendants as follows):

**MR. DARROW:** It has been almost three months since I first assumed the great responsibility that has devolved upon me and my associates in this case; and I am willing to confess that it has been three months of perplexity and great anxiety. A trouble which I would have gladly been spared excepting for my feelings of affection toward some of the members of one of these families.

It is a responsibility that is almost too great for any one to assume that has devolved upon me. But we lawyers can no more choose than the court can choose.

**THE COURT:** Pardon me just one moment. Sergeant, I want the whole building cleared out.

**MR. DARROW:** My worry over this case—your Honor, I think you had better wait, if you don't mind.

**MR. CROWE:** We had better wait, hadn't we, Judge, until they clean out the corridor, so there will be no interruptions.

(The court here took a short recess).

**MR. DARROW:** I don't know what we can do, your honor, unless the inside is cleared out.

**THE COURT:** The police will be here in a minute.

**MR. DARROW:** I think I had better wait, your Honor.

**THE COURT:** All right.

**MR. DARROW:** Are you going to get somebody there pretty quick?

**THE COURT:** Oh, yes. Is that hall filled outside there? Is that hall still packed?

**A BAILIFF:** I beg your pardon?

**THE COURT:** Is that hall still packed?

**THE BAILIFF:** Yes. There are four of your friends out here.

**THE COURT:** Let them stay there.

(After a further wait the Court said, addressing the bailiff at the door):

**THE COURT:** Go downstairs and see if the police have arrived yet.

**THE BAILIFF:** They have. They are out there.

**THE COURT:** Well, I want that hall cleared. You might as well have twenty wooden policemen out there if they don't do what they are told.

**THE BAILIFF:** The press don't want to get out.

**THE COURT:** I don't care about that. Everybody out of there.

(At this time the police officers sent for by the Judge arrived.)

**THE COURT:** Officers, clean out the hall, please, and if you have not got enough men, get fifty more. Put everybody out of the building except those in the room now.

**THE SERGEANT:** They are all out now but the press.

## A TIDAL WAVE OF MEN AND WOMEN

On the day that Clarence Darrow was scheduled to begin his segment of the closing argument, the drama building around the case supported his contention that the court was the only thing standing between the defendants and a blood-thirsty mob.

"Police reserves couldn't hold the frenzied crowd," the August 22 *Chicago Daily News* reported. "Word that Darrow was about to make his speech had brought to the old courthouse hundreds more than all the court-rooms in the building could have seated."

"The tidal wave of men and women swept over and flattened a skirmish line of bailiffs at the main entrance and poured up the stairs and the elevators, sweeping all obstacles away." A bailiff broke his arm trying to hold the mob back.

Judge John Caverly himself had to "fight his way" into the court-room, as did Nathan Leopold's father and brother. And, as always seemed to happen at moments of extreme drama throughout this case, "a woman fainted."

**THE COURT:** All but what?

**THE SERGEANT:** All but the press. I can't make them understand that you want them out of the hall.

**THE COURT:** Have they got press tickets?

**THE SERGEANT:** Some of them have, but there is a runner out here who has not.

**THE COURT:** Let the press in. They are entitled to come in and out.

(The door was opened to admit one copy boy).

**THE COURT:** Clean out that hall, and clean out the fifth floor after that, and then put everybody outside of the building who has no business here.

**THE BAILIFF:** The hall is clear, your Honor.

**A BAILIFF:** Yes, your Honor.

**THE COURT:** All right, Mr. Darrow:

(Whereupon Mr. Darrow here resumed his closing argument on behalf of the Defendants as follows):

**MR. DARROW:** Your Honor, our anxiety over this case has not been due to the facts that are connected with this most unfortunate affair, but to the almost unheard of publicity; to the fact that newspapers all over this country have been giving it space such as they have almost never given to a case before. The fact that day after day the people of Chicago have been regaled with stories of all sorts about it, until almost every person has formed an opinion.

And when the public are interested and want a punishment, no matter what the offense is, great or small, they only think of one punishment, and that is death.

It may not be a question that involves the taking of human life; it may be a question of pure prejudice alone, but when the public speaks as one man they only think of killing someone.

We have been in the presence of this stress and strain for three months. We did what we could and all we could to gain the confidence of the public, who in the end really control [the outcome], whether wisely or unwisely.

It was announced that there were millions of dollars to be spent on this case. Wild and extravagant stories were freely published as if they were facts. Here was to be an effort to save the lives of two boys, that should not have required an effort even, but to save their lives by the use of money, in fabulous amounts, such as these families never had nor could have.

We announced to the public that no excessive use of money would be made in this case, neither for lawyers, for psychiatrists or in any other way.

We have faithfully kept that promise which we made to the public.

The psychiatrists, as has been shown by the evidence in this case, are receiving a per diem, and only a per diem, which is the same as is paid by the State.

The attorneys of their own motion, at their own request, have agreed to take such amount as the officers of the Chicago Bar Association may think is proper in this case.

If we fail in this defense it will not be for lack of money. It will be on account of money. Money has been the most serious handicap that we have met.

There are times when poverty is fortunate, and this is one of those times.

I insist, your honor, that had this been the case of two boys of this age, unconnected with families who are supposed to have great wealth, that there is not a State's Attorney in Illinois who would not at once have consented to a plea of guilty and a punishment in the penitentiary for life. Not one.

No lawyer could have justified it.

No prosecution could have justified it.

We could have come into this court without evidence, without argument, with nothing, and this court would have given to us what every judge in the City of Chicago has given to every boy in the City of Chicago since the first capital case was tried. And we would have had no contest.

We are here with the lives of two boys imperiled, with the public aroused.

For what?

Because, unfortunately, their parents have money. Nothing else.

I told your honor in the beginning that never had there been a case in Chicago, where on a plea of guilty, a boy under twenty-one had been sentenced to death. I will raise that age and say, never has there been a case where a human being under the age of twenty-eight or thirty has been sentenced to death. And, I think I am safe in saying, although I have not examined all the records and could not—but I think I am safe in saying that never has there been such a case in the State of Illinois. [. . .]

It was not correct that we would have defended these boys and asked for a verdict of not guilty if we thought we could win. We would not. We believe we have been fair to this court; we believe we have been fair to the public. Anyhow we have tried, and we have tried under terribly hard conditions.

We have said to the public and to this court that neither the parents, nor the friends, nor the attorneys would want these boys released. That they are as they are. Unfortunate though it be, it is true and those the closest to them know perfectly well that they should not be released, and that they should be permanently isolated from society. We have said that; and we mean it. We are asking this court to save their lives, which is the least and the most that a judge can do.

We did plead guilty before your Honor because we were afraid to submit our cause to a jury. I would not for a moment deny to this court or to this community a realization of the serious danger we were in and how perplexed we were before we took this most unusual step.

I can tell your Honor why.

I have found that years and experience with life tempers one's emotions and makes him more understanding of his fellow men.

When my friend [Joseph P.] Savage is my age, or even of yours, he will read his address to this court with horror.

I am aware that as one grows older he is less critical. He is not so sure. He is inclined to make some allowance for his fellow man.

I am aware that a court has more experience, more judgment and more kindliness than a jury.

And then, your honor, it may not be hardly fair to the court, because I am aware that I have helped to place a serious burden upon your shoulders. And at that, I have always meant to be your friend. But this was not an act of friendship.

I know perfectly well that where responsibility is divided by twelve, it is easy to say:

"Away with him".

But, your Honor, if these boys hang, you must do it. There can be no division of responsibility here. You must do it. You can never explain that the rest overpowered you. It must be by your deliberate, cool, premeditated act, without a chance to shift responsibility.

We did it, your Honor.

It was not a kindness to you. We placed this responsibility on your shoulders because we were mindful of the rights of our clients, and we were mindful of the unhappy families who have done no wrong.

Darrow offers the following statistics: in the whole history of Chicago, 90 people have been hanged; of those, only three had been hanged on a plea of guilty.

**[MR. DARROW:]** I heard them talk of mothers.

Mr. Savage is doing this for the mothers, and Mr. [Robert] Crowe is thinking of the mothers, and I am thinking of the mothers. Mr. Savage, with the immaturity of youth and inexperience, says if we hang them there will be no more killing.

My God! This world has been one long slaughter house from the beginning until today, and killing goes on and on and on, and will forever.

Why not read something, why not study something, why not think instead of blindly calling for death?

Kill them.

Will that prevent other senseless boys or other vicious men or vicious women?

No.

It would simply call upon every weak minded person to do as they have done. I know how easy it is to talk about mothers when you want to do something cruel, as some men talk about patriotism when they want to get something. I know all about it. But I am thinking of the mothers, too. I know that any mother might be the mother of a little Bobby Franks, who left his home and went to his school, and whose life was taken, and who never came back. I know that any mother might be the mother of Richard Loeb and Nathan Leopold, just the same. The trouble is this, that if she is the mother of a Nathan Leopold or of a Richard Loeb, she has to ask herself the question,

"How came my children to be what they are? From what ancestry did they get this strain? How far removed was the poison that destroyed their lives? Was I the bearer of the seed that brings them to death?"

Any mother might be the mother of any of them. But these two are the victims. I remember a little poem that seems to me to illustrate the soliloquy of a boy about to be hanged, a soliloquy such as these boys might make. He says:

"The night my father got me
    His mind was not on me.
He did not plague his fancy
    To muse if I should be the son you see.


The day my mother bore me
    She was a fool, and glad
For all the pain I caused her,
    Because she bore the lad which borne she had.


My father and my mother
    Out of the light they lie.
The warrant could not find them,
    So here am only I, must hang so high.


O let not man remember
    The soul that God forgot.
But fetch the county sheriff,
    And noose me in a knot, and I will rot.


And so the game is ended,
    That should not have begun.
My father and my mother
    They had a likely son, but I have none."


No one knows what will be the fate of the child they get or the child they bear, and the fate of the child is the last thing they think of. This weary old world goes on, begetting, with birth and with living and with death; and all of it is blind from the beginning to the end. I do not know what it was made these boys do this mad act, but I do know there is a reason for it. I know they did not beget themselves. I know that any one of an infinite number of causes reaching back to the beginning might be working out in these boys' minds, whom you are asked to hang in malice and in hatred and injustice, because someone in the past has sinned against them.

I am sorry for the fathers as well as the mothers, for the fathers who give their strength and their lives toward educating and protecting and creating a fortune for the boys that they love, for the mothers who go down into the shadow of death for their children, who nourish them and care for them, who risk their lives for them, who watch them with tenderness and fondness and longing, and who go down into honor and disgrace for the children they love.

They are helpless. We are all helpless. But when you are pitying the father and the mother of poor Bobby Franks, what about the fathers and mothers of these two unfortunate boys, and what about the unfortunate boys themselves, and what about all the fathers and all the others and all the boys and all the girls who tread a dangerous maze in darkness from the cradle to the grave?

And do you think you can cure it by hanging these two? Do you think you can cure the hatreds and the mal-adjustments of the world by hanging them? You simply show your ignorance and your hate when you say it. You may here and there cure hatred with love and understanding, but you can only add fuel to the flames by hating in return.

What is my friend's idea of justice? He says to this court, whom he says he respects—and I believe he does—your honor, who sits here patiently, holding the lives of these two boys in your hands:

"Give them the same mercy that they gave to Bobby Franks."

Is that the law? Is that justice? Is this what a court should do? Is this what a State's Attorney should do? For God's sake, if the state in which I live is not kinder, more human, more considerate, more intelligent than the mad act of these two mad boys, I am sorry I have lived so long. I am sorry for these fathers and these mothers. The mother who looks into the blue eyes of her little babe cannot help wonder what will be the end of this child, whether it will be crowned with the greatest promises which her mind can imagine or whether he may meet death from the gallows. All she can do is to raise him with care, to watch over him tenderly, to meet life with hope and trust and confidence, and to leave the rest with fate.

# 62
# Giving the people blood is like giving them their dinner

## DARROW'S APPEAL FOR JUDICIAL PROGRESSIVENESS

THE SATURDAY SESSION was only two hours long, and Clarence Darrow filled all of it with masterful rhetoric, respinning the entire case so that it became not about the evil act of the two murderers, but instead about the opportunity offered to the judge, to the spectators, and to the world to throw off the lingering traces of barbarism in civilization and become more human(e).

**[MR. DARROW:]** Your honor, we do not need to believe in miracles; we need not resort to that in order to get blood. If it were any other case, there could not be a moment's hesitancy. I repeat, you may search the annals of crime, and you can find no parallel. It is utterly at variance with every motive and every act and every part of conduct that influences normal people in the commission of crime.

There is not a sane thing in all of this from the beginning to the end. There was not a normal act in any of it, from its inception in a diseased brain, until today, when they sit here awaiting their doom. But, they say, they planned. Well, what does that mean?

A maniac plans, an idiot plans; an animal plans; any brain that functions may plan, but their plans were the diseased plans of a diseased mind of boys.

Do I need to argue it? Does anybody need to more than glance at it? Is there any man with a fair intellect and a decent regard for human life, and slightest bit of heart that does not understand this situation?

And still, your honor, on account of its weirdness and its strangeness, and its advertising, we are forced to fight. For what?

Forced to plead to this court that two boys, one 18 and the other 19, may be permitted to live in silence and solitude and disgrace and spend all their days in the penitentiary. Asking this court and that state's attorney to be merciful enough to let these two boys be locked up in a prison until they die.

I sometimes wonder if I am dreaming. If in the first quarter of the twentieth century there have come back into the hearts of man the hate and the feeling and the lust for blood which possesses the primitive savage of primitive lands.

What do they want? Tell me, is a life time for the young spent behind prison bars, is that not enough for this mad act? And is there any reason why this great public should be regaled by a hanging?

I can't understand it, your honor. It would be past belief, excepting that to the four corners of the earth the news of this weird thing has been carried, and men have been stirred, and the primitive has come back, and the intellect has been destroyed, and men have been controlled by feelings and passions and hatred which should have been dead centuries ago.

## PERFORMING A MIRACLE

Clarence Darrow's court performance delivered everything the crowd of spectators had expected based on his reputation as a consummate orator and brilliant tactician. The *Chicago Daily Tribune*'s Orville Dwyer depicted him as mythic in the paper's August 24 edition, comparing him to the legendary Greek hero Theseus in that he had "wandered in a labyrinth of laws" and "slain a dragon—man's inhumanity to man." Although Dwyer had his mythology a little jumbled—Theseus had slain the Minotaur, not a dragon—he effectively dramatized how Darrow characteristically relied less on the letter of the law to score points than on his righteous sense of what the law *ought* to say, and on an emotional appeal to the human hearts of his audience.

As tears welled up in the eyes of everyone listening, Dwyer reported, Darrow "performed a miracle," so that spectators who had come to court convinced that only the hangman could expiate the cruel murder of Bobby Franks "have wavered and changed their minds, and come to believe that, after all, Nathan Leopold Jr. and Richard Loeb must not be sent to the gallows."

Clarence Darrow (right)
consulting with Loeb (center),
Leopold (partially obscured),
and Benjamin Bachrach (left)
during the hearing.

My friend [Joseph P.] Savage pictured to you the putting of this dead boy in this culvert. Well, no one can minutely describe any killing and not make it shocking. It is shocking.

It is shocking because we love life and because we instinctively draw back from death. It is shocking if death comes into a home, if it comes to a hospital. It is shocking, wherever it is, and however it is, and perhaps always is almost equally shocking.

But here is the picture of a dead boy, past pain, when no harm can come to him, put in a culvert, after taking off his clothes so that the evidence would be destroyed; and that is pictured to this court as a reason for hanging.

Well, your honor, that does not appeal to me as strongly as the hitting over the head of little Robert Franks with a chisel. The boy was dead.

I could say something about the death that, for some mysterious reason, the state wants in this case. Why do they want it? I don't know. To vindicate the law? Oh, no.

The law can be vindicated without killing any one else. It might shock the fine sensibilities of the state's counsel that this boy was put into a culvert and left after he was dead, but, your Honor, I can think of a scene that makes this pale into insignificance.

I can think, and only think, your Honor, of taking two boys, one 18 and the other 19, irresponsible, weak, diseased, penning them in a cell, checking off the days and the hours and the minutes, until they will be taken out and hanged.

I can picture them, wakened in the gray light of morning, furnished a suit of clothes by the state, led to the scaffold, their feet tied, a black cap drawn over their heads, placed on a trap door, and somebody pressing a spring, so that it falls under them, and they are only stopped by the rope around their necks.

It would surely expiate the placing of young Franks, after he was dead, in the culvert. That would bring immense satisfaction to some people.

It brings a greater satisfaction because it is done in the name of justice. I am always suspicious of righteous indignation.

Nothing is more cruel than righteous indignation. To hear young men talk glibly of justice, well, it would make me smile if it did not make me so sad. Who knows what it is?

Does Mr. Savage know? Does Mr. [Robert] Crowe know? Do I know? Does your Honor know? Is there any human machinery for finding it? Is there any man can weight me and say what I deserve? Can your Honor? Let us be honest. Can your Honor express yourself and say what I deserve? Can your Honor appraise these two young men and say what they deserve?

It may take account of infinite circumstances which a human being may not understand.

If there is such a thing as justice it could only be administered by one who knew the inmost thoughts of the man to whom he was meting it out.

Aye, who knew the father and mother and the grandparents of every soul that went into their body, who could understand their structure and how it acted.

Who could tell how the emotions that sway the human being affected that particular frail piece of clay. It means more than that.

It means that you must appraise every influence that moves them, the civilization where they live, their living, their society, all society which enters into the making of a child.

If your honor can do it—if you can do it you are wise, and with wisdom goes mercy. [. . .]

Now, your honor, let me go a little further with this. I have gone over some of the high spots in this tragedy. This tragedy has not claimed all the attention it has had on account of its atrocity. There is nothing to that. Why is it?

There are two reasons, and only two, that I can see. First is the extreme wealth, reputed at least, of these families; not only the Loeb and Leopold families, but the Franks family, and of course it is unusual.

And the next is the fact that it is weird and uncanny and motiveless. That is what attracted the attention of the world.

They may say now, many of them, they want to hang them. I may be a poor prophet, but giving the people blood is something like giving them their dinner. When they get it they go to sleep.

They may for the time being have an emotion, but they will bitterly regret it. And I undertake to say that if these two boys are sentenced to death, and are hanged, on that day there will be a pall settle over the people of this land that will be dark and deep, and at least cover every humane and intelligent person in the land.

I wonder if it will do good. I wonder if it will help the children, and there is an infinite number like these. [. . .]

Mr. Savage is an optimist. He says if they are hanged there will be no more boys like these.

I could give him a sketch of punishment beginning with the brute, which hurt something because something hurt it; the punishment of the savage; if a person's injured in the tribe, they must injure somebody in the other tribe; it makes no difference who it is, but somebody, if one is killed they must kill somebody else. You can trace it all down through the history of man.

You can trace the burnings, the boilings, the drawings and quarterings, the hanging of people in England at the crossroads, carving them up and hanging them as examples for all to see.

We can come down to the last century, when nearly 200 crimes were punishable by death, and by death in every form; not only hanging—that was too humane—but burning, boiling, cutting into pieces, torturing.

You can read the stories of the hangings on a high hill, and the populace for miles around coming out to the scene, that everybody might be awed into goodness.

Hanging for picking pockets—and more pockets were picked in the crowd that went to the hanging than had been known for years.

Hangings for murder—and men were murdered on the way there and on the way home.

Hangings for poaching, hangings for everything, and hangings in public, not shut up cruelly and brutally in a jail, out of the light of day, wakened in the night time and led forth and killed, but taken to the shire town on a high hill, in the presence of a multitude, so that they might know that the wages of sin were death.

What happened? I have read the life of Lord Shaftsbury [should be "Shaftesbury"], a great nobleman of England, who gave his life and his labors toward modifying the penal code.

I have read of the slow, painful efforts through all the ages for more humanity of man to his fellow man.

I know what the history says, I know what it means, and I know what flows from it, so far as we can tell, which is not definitely.

I know that every step has been met and opposed by prosecutors, many times by courts. I know that when poaching and petty larceny was punishable by death in England, juries refused to convict.

They were too humane to obey the law, and judges refused.

I know when the delusion of witchcraft was spreading over Europe, claiming its victims by the millions, many a judge so shaped his cases that no crime of witchcraft could be punished in his court. I know that it was stopped in America because juries would no longer convict.

I know that every step in the progress of the world in reference to crime has come from the human feelings of man.

It has come from that deep well of sympathy, that in spite of all our training and all our conventions and all our teaching, still flows forth in the human breast. Without it there would be no life on this weary old planet.

And gradually the laws have been changed and been modified, and men look back with horror at the hangings and the deaths of the past.

Darrow and
Caverly, facing
toward the
witness box.

# 63
# The death of poor little Bobby Franks should not be in vain

## DARROW CONCLUDES HIS ARGUMENT

Darrow's closing argument built to a crescendo on its third day, which was Monday, August 25. Despite sweltering heat in the crowded courtroom, his listeners sat transfixed. Darrow, who was 67 and had been struggling with his health in recent years, had announced that he would be retiring after this case. (In fact, two of his most legendary cases—the Scopes trial and the Ossian Sweet trial—still lay ahead.) Many were aware of the irony that a man whose fame rested mainly on his defense of the poor and disenfranchised was closing his legal career by not only defending such rich and well-connected clients, but by aggressively asserting that their wealth and privilege had actually been one of their greatest curses. But his rhetoric soars to its most compelling as he builds a case that the death of Bobby Franks could only be redeemed and made meaningful by a courageous decision to show mercy to his killers.

**[MR. DARROW:]** I have tried to study these two lives, the lives of these two most unfortunate boys. Three months ago, if their friends and the friends of the family had been asked to pick out the most promising boys of their acquaintance they probably would have picked these. With every opportunity, with every advantage, with a good intellectual equipment, with plenty of wealth, they would have said that these two would succeed.

In a day, by an act of madness, all this is destroyed, until the best they can hope for now is a life of silence and pain, judging from their years.

How did it happen?

Let us take Dickie Loeb first. I do not claim to know how it happened; I have sought to find out. I know that something, or some combination of things, is responsible for his mad act. I know there are no accidents in nature. I know that effect follows cause. I know, if I were wise enough, and knew enough about this case, I could lay my finger on it. I will do the best I can, but it is largely speculation.

The child, of course, is born without knowledge. Impressions are made upon its mind as it goes along. Dickie Loeb was a child of wealth and opportunity. Over and over in this court your honor has been asked and other courts have been asked, to consider boys who have no chance; they have been asked to consider the poor whose home had been the street, with no education and no chance; and they have done it, and done it rightfully.

But, your honor, it is just as often a great misfortune to be the child of the rich as it is the child of the poor. Wealth has its misfortunes. Too much, too great opportunity and advantage given to a child has its misfortunes, and I am asking your honor to consider the rich as well as the poor, and nothing else. Can I find what was wrong? I think I can.

Here was a boy at a tender age placed in the hands of a governess [Miss Emily Struthers], intellectual, vigorous, devoted, with strong ambition for the welfare of this boy. He was made to study books as plants are grown in hothouses. He had no pleasures, such as a boy should have except in what was gained by lying and cheating.

Now, I am not criticizing the nurse. I suggest some day your honor look at her picture. It explains her fully. Forceful, brooking no interference, she loved this boy, and her ambition was that he should reach the highest possible [left incomplete in original transcript].

He early developed the tendency to mix with crime, to be a detective; as a little boy shadowing people on the street; as a little child going out with his fantasy of being the head of a band of criminals and directing them on the street. [. . .]

The books he read by day were not the books he read by night. We are all molded somewhat by the influences around us and of those to people who read, perhaps books are the most and the strongest.

He was not his own father; he was not his own mother; he was not his own grandparents. All this was handed to him.

He did not surround himself with governesses and wealth. He did not make himself. And yet he is to be made to pay.

Do you mean to tell me that Dickie Loeb had any more to do with his making than any other product of heredity that is born upon the earth?

Both of these boys in the adolescent age, both these boys when every alienist in this case on both sides tells you it is the most trying period of the life of a child, both these boys when the call of sex is new and strange, both these boys at a time seeking to adjust their young lives to the world, moved by the strongest feelings and passions that have ever moved men, both these boys at the time boys grow insane, at the time crimes are committed, all this added to all the rest of the vagaries—do you charge them with the responsibility that we may have a hanging, that we may deck Chicago in a holiday garb and let the people have their fill of blood, that you may put stains upon the heart of every man, woman and child on that day and that the dead walls of Chicago will tell the story of blood? [. . .]

I know that one of two things happened to this boy; that this terrible crime was inherent in his organism, and came from some ancestor, or that it came through his education and his training after he was born.

I do not know what remote ancestors may have sent down the seed that corrupted him, and I do not know through how many ancestors it may have passed until it reached Dickie Loeb.

All I know is, it is true, and there is not a biologist in the world who will not say I am right. If it did not come that way, then I know that if he was normal, if he had been understood, if he had been trained as he should have been, it would not have happened.

I know that if this boy had been understood and properly trained, for him, and the training he got might have been the very best for some one else, but if it had been the proper training for him, he would not have been in this courtroom today with the noose above his head.

If there is responsibility anywhere, it is back of him, somewhere in the infinite number of his ancestors, or in his surroundings, or in both.

And I submit, your honor, that under every principle of natural justice, under every principle of conscience, of right and of law, he should not be made responsible for the acts of somebody else, whether wise or unwise.

And I say this again, let me repeat without finding fault with his parents, for whom I have the highest regard, and who doubtless did the best they could. They might have done better if they had not had any money. I do not know. Great wealth curses everybody it touches.

This boy was sent to school. His mind worked; his emotions were dead. He could learn books, but he read detective stories. There never was a time since he was old enough to move back and forth according to what seemed to be his volition, when he was not haunted with these fantasies. Never once.

It is when these conditions of boyhood, these fantasies of youth still stay, and the growing boy is still a child in emotion, a child in feeling, a child in hallucination, that you can say that it is the dreams and the hallucinations of childhood which are responsible for his conduct.

I say, your honor, it would be the height of cruelty, of injustice, of wrong and barbarism to visit the penalty upon this poor boy.

Your honor, again I want to say that all parents can be criticized, grandparents and teachers. Science is not so much interested in criticism as in finding out the causes.

This boy needed more home, needed more love, more affection, more directions, directing. He needed to have his emotions awakened. He needed to have guiding hands along the serious road that youth must travel.

Had these been given him, he would not be here today.

Now, your honor, I want to speak of the other lad, Babe. Babe is somewhat older than Dick, and is a boy of remarkable mind, everybody concedes that, away beyond his years.

He is a sort of freak in this direction, as in others, a boy without emotions, a boy obsessed of philosophy, a boy obsessed of learning, busy every minute of his life.

He went through school quickly, he went to college young; he could learn faster than almost everybody else.

His emotional life was lacking, as every alienist witness in this case, excepting Dr. [William] Krohn has told you.

He was just a half boy, an intellect, an intellectual machine going without balance and without a governor, seeking to find out everything there was in life intellectually, seeking to solve every philosophy, but using his intellect only.

Of course his family did not understand him; few people would. His mother died when he was young; he had plenty of money; everything given that he wanted and too much given.

Both these boys with unlimited money; both these boys with automobiles; both of these boys with every luxury around them and in front of them. They grew up in that environment.

He grew up in this way. He became enamored of the philosophy of Nietzsche.

Your Honor, I have read almost everything that Nietzsche ever wrote. A man of a wonderful intellect; the most original philosopher of the last century.

Nathan Leopold is not the only boy who has read Nietzsche. He may be the only one who was influenced in the way he was influenced, and even that is not true, most likely. [...]

I might say further about Nathan Leopold, where did he get his philosophy, at college? He did not make it, your honor. He did not write books, and I will venture to say there are at least 50,000 books on Nietzsche and his philosophy.

The universities perhaps do not all teach it, for perhaps some teach nothing in philosophy; but they give the boys the books of the master and tell them what they think about it, and discuss it. There is not a university in the world of any high standing where the professors do not tell you about Nietzsche.

Your honor, it is hardly fair to hang a 19-year-old boy for the philosophy that was taught him at the university. It does not meet my ideas of justice and fairness to visit upon his head the philosophy that has been taught by university men for twenty-five years. Now, I do not want to be dishonest, and tell this. Even for the sake of saving the lives of my clients, I do not want to be dishonest, and tell the court something that I do not honestly think in this case.

I do not think that the universities are to blame. I do not think they should be held responsible. I do think, however, that they are too large, and that they should keep a closer watch, if possible, upon the individual.

So, your honor, I do not mean to unload this on that man or this man, or this organization or that organization. I am trying to trace causes. I am trying to trace them honestly, I am trying to trace them with the light I have. I am trying to say to this court that these boys are not responsible for this, and that their act was due to this and this, and this and this, and asking this court not to visit the judgment of its wrath upon them for things for which they are not to blame.

There is something else in this case, your honor, that is stronger still. There is a large element of chance in life. I know I will die. I don't know how; I don't know where; and I don't want to know. I know it will come. I know that it depends on infinite chances. Do I live to myself? Did I make myself? And control my fate? Can I fix my death unless I commit suicide, and I cannot do that because the will to live is too strong. I know it depends on infinite chances.

How did these boys happen to do this?

These boys, neither one of them could possibly have committed this act excepting by joining. It was not the act of one; it was the act of two. It was the act of their planning, their conniving, their believing in each other; their thinking themselves supermen. Without it they could not have done it. It would not have happened.

They happened to meet; some sort of chemical alchemy operated so that they cared for each other, and poor Bobby Franks' dead body was found in the culvert. [...]

Your honor, I am sorry for poor Bobby Franks, and I think anybody who knows me knows that I am not saying it simply to speak. I am sorry for the bereaved father and the bereaved mother, and I would like to know what they would do with these poor unfortunate lads who are here in this court today. I know something of them, of their lives, of their charity, of their ideas, and nobody here sympathizes with them more than I.

I know it came through the mad act of mad boys. Mr. [Joseph P.] Savage told us that Franks, if he had lived, would have been a great man and accomplished much. I want to leave this thought with your honor. I do not know what Bobby Franks would have been had he grown to be a man. I do not know the laws that control one's growth.

Sometimes, your honor, a boy of great promise is cut off in his early youth. Sometimes a boy of great promise stands on a trap door and is hanged by the neck until dead. Sometimes he dies of diphtheria.

Perhaps, somewhere in fate and chance, it might be that he lived as long as he should.

And I want to say this, that the death of poor little Bobby Franks should not be in vain.

Would it mean anything if on account of that death, those two boys were taken out and a rope tied around their necks, and they died felons, and left a blot upon the names of their families? Would that show that Bobby Franks had a purpose in his life and a purpose in his death?

No, I say this, your honor, that the unfortunate and tragic death of this weak young lad should mean something.

It should mean an appeal to the fathers and mothers, an appeal to the teachers, to the religious guides, to society at large. It should mean an appeal to all of them to appraise their children, to understand the emotions that control them, to understand the ideas that possess them, to teach them to dodge the pitfalls of life. It should be, to the millions of mothers who have read of this case, and the millions of fathers who have read of it, that the death of Bobby Franks will teach them to examine their own children, their own families, their own brothers, their own sisters, to see what there is in them or what may be in them, or what may be avoided to prevent future tragedies like this. And society, too should take its share of this case, and make not two more tragedies, but use it as best it can to make life safer, to make childhood easier and safer, to do something to cure the cruelty, the hatred, the chance, and the willfulness of life.

Now, your honor, I suppose I would never close if I did not see that I should.

Has the court any right to consider anything but these two boys?

Yes.

The state says that your honor has a right to consider the welfare of the community, as you have.

If the welfare of the community would be benefited by taking these lives, well and good. I think it would work evil that no one could measure. Has your honor a right to consider the families of these two defendants?

I have been sorry, and I am sorry for the bereavement of Mr. and Mrs. Franks, and the little sister, for those broken ties that cannot be mended. All I can hope and wish is that some good may come from it. But as compared with the families of Leopold and Loeb, they are to be envied. They are to be envied, and every one knows it.

I do not know how much salvage there is in these two boys. I have to say it in their presence, but what is there to look forward to? I do not know but what your honor would be merciful if you tied a rope around the necks and let them die; merciful to them, but not merciful to civilization, and not merciful to those who would be left behind. I do not know; to spend the balance of their days in prison is mighty little to look forward to, if anything. Is it anything?

They may have the hope as the years roll around they might be released. I do not know. I don't know. I will be honest with this court. I have tried to be from the beginning.

I know that these boys are not fit to be at large.

I believe they will not be until they pass through the next stage of life, at 45 or 50. Whether they will be then, I cannot know. I am sure of this: that I won't be here to help them. So, so far as I am concerned, it is over.

I would not tell this court that I would not hope that some time, when life and age has changed their bodies, as it does, and has changed their emotions, as it does, I would not say that they would not be safe. I would be the last person on earth to close the door of hope to any human being that lives, and least of all my clients.

But what have they to look forward to? Nothing. And I here think of the stanzas of [A.E.] Housman:


Now, hollow fires burn out tonight

And lights are guttering low;

Square your shoulders and lift your pack

And leave your friends and go.

Don't ever fear, lads, naught's to dread;

Look not left nor right.

In all the endless road you tread

There is nothing but the night.


I don't care, your honor, whether the march begins at the gallows or when the gates of Joliet close upon them, there is nothing but the night, and that is enough for any human being to ask.

But there are others. Here are these two families, who have led an honest life, who will bear the name that they bear, and future generations will bear the name that they bear.

Here is Leopold's father—and this boy was the pride of his life. He watched him, he cared for him, he worked for him, he was brilliant and accomplished, he educated him, and he thought fame and position awaited him, as it should have. It is a hard thing for a father to see his life's hopes crumbling into the dust.

Should he be considered? Should his brothers be considered? Is it going to do society any good or make your life safe or any human being's life safer that it should be handed down from generation to generation that this boy, their kin, died upon the scaffold?

And Loeb's, the same. The faithful uncle and brother, who have watched here day by day, while his father and his mother are too ill to stand this terrific strain, waiting for a message which means more to them than it seems to mean to you or me.

Have they got any rights? Is there any reason, your honor, why their proud name and all the future generations that bear it shall have this bar sinister attached to it? How many boys and girls, how many unborn children will feel it? It is bad enough as it is, God knows. It is bad enough, however it is. But it's not death by the scaffold. It's not that. And I ask, your honor, in addition to all I have said, to save two honorable families from a disgrace that never ends, and which could be of no avail to any human being that lives.

Now, I must say a word more and then I will leave this with you where I should have left it long ago.

None of us are unmindful of the public; courts are not, and juries are not. We placed this in the hands of a trained court, thinking that he would be less mindful than a jury. I cannot say how people feel. I have stood here for three months as somebody might stand at the seacoast trying to sweep back the tide. I hope the seas are subsiding and the wind is falling and I believe they are, but I wish to make no false pretense to this court.

The easy thing and the popular thing to do is to hang my clients. I know it. Men and women who do not think will applaud. The cruel and the thoughtless will approve. It will be easy today, but in Chicago and reaching out over the length and breadth of the land more and more are fathers and mothers, the humane, the kind and the hopeful, who are gaining an understanding and asking questions not only about these boys but about their own.

These will join in no acclaim at the death of these boys. These would ask that the shedding of blood be stopped, and that the normal feelings of man resume their sway. And as the days and the months and the years go on, they will ask it more and more. But, your honor, what they ask cannot count. I know the easy way.

I know your honor stands between the future and the past. I know the future is with me, and what I stand for here; not merely for the lives of these two unfortunate lads, but for all boys and all girls; all of the young, and as far as possible, for all of the old. I am pleading for life, understanding, charity and kindness, and the infinite mercy that forgives all. I am pleading that we overcome cruelty with kindness and hatred with love. I know the future is on my side. Your honor stands between the past and the future. You may hang these boys; you may hang them by the neck till they are dead. But in doing it you will turn your face toward the past. In doing it you are making it harder for every other boy.

In doing it you are making it harder for unborn children. You may save them and it makes it easier for every child that some time may sit where these boys sit. It makes it easier for every human being with an aspiration and a vision and a hope and a fate.

I am pleading for the future; I am pleading for a time when hatred and cruelty will not control the hearts of men. When we can learn by reason and judgment and understanding and faith that all life is worth saving, and that mercy is the highest attribute of man.

I feel that I ought to apologize for the length of time I have taken. This may not be as important as I think it is, and I am sure I do not need to tell this court, or to tell my friend Mr. Crowe, that I would fight just as hard for the poor as for the rich.

If I should succeed in saving these boys' lives and do nothing for the progress of the law, I should feel sad, indeed. If I can succeed, my greatest award and my greatest hope and my greatest compensation will be that I have done something for the tens of thousands of other boys, for the other unfortunates who must tread the same way that these poor youths have trod, that I have done something to help human understanding, to temper justice with mercy, to overcome hate with love.

I was reading last night of the aspiration of the old Persian poet, Omar Khayyam. It appealed to me as the highest that I can envision. I wish it was in my heart, and I wish it was in the heart of all, and I can do no better than to quote what he said:

So I be written in the Book of Love,
I do not care about that Book above.

Erase my name or write it as you will,
So I be written in the Book of Love.

# 64
# How do you undress a child?
## CROWE DROPS HIS BOMBSHELL

Right: Little Dickie Loeb dressed up as a cowboy and holding a toy pistol.

CROWE'S FINAL CLOSING argument methodically attacks Darrow's, with special ridicule reserved for the defense alienists William A. White, William Healy, and Bernard Glueck, to whom Crowe referred sarcastically as "The Three Wise Men from the East." The newspapers depicted Crowe and Darrow as perfectly matched opponents, both strategically and rhetorically, and they were. Darrow had opened the trial with the tactical bombshell of changing his clients' plea to guilty, and Crowe closes with one of his own: an assertion that the crime had been motivated by and had included a sexual assault on Bobby or his corpse. The court transcript includes an outburst by Caverly at the women in the audience who refuse to leave the courtroom so that the graphic details in the coroner's report can be read into the record.

**[MR. CROWE:]** There is something in the nature of the crime itself that arrests the attention of every person in the land. A child is stolen.

The heart of every father, the heart of every mother, the heart of every man who has a heart, goes out to the parents of the child.

Bobby Franks was kidnaped, and when we had not the slightest notion of who was guilty of the dastardly crime, the papers were full of it.

It was the only topic of conversation.

It remained the only topic of conversation for a week before the State's Attorney of this County called in Nathan Leopold, Jr.

Their wealth in my judgment has not anything to do with this, except it permits a defense here seldom given to men in the criminal court.

Take away the millions of the Loebs and the Leopolds, and Clarence Darrow's tongue is as silent as the tomb of Julius Caesar.

Take away their millions, and the "Wise men from the East" would not be here, to tell you about phantasies, and teddy bears and bold, bad boys who have their pictures taken in cowboy uniforms.

Take away their money, and what happens?

The same thing that has happened to all the other men who have been tried in this building, who had no money.

Chicago History Museum, DN-0077990

A plea of guilty, a police officer sworn, a coroner's physician sworn, the parents of the murdered boy sworn, and a sentence. [. . .]

Clarence Darrow once said that a poor man on trial here was disposed of in fifteen minutes, but if he was rich and committed the same crime and he got a good lawyer, his trial would last twenty-one days.

Well, they got three lawyers and it has lasted just a little bit longer, in addition to the three wise men from the east. [. . .]

They had the power of choice, and they deliberately chose to adopt the wrong philosophy, and to make their conduct correspond with it.

Way last November, after these two defendants had had a quarrel and made it up—and I will not go into the nature of that quarrel, there is a lot of evidence in this case that has not come out, and I do not intend to repeat it, to shock any person who may be listening.

These two defendants were perverts, Loeb the victim and Leopold the aggressor, and they quarreled.

Then they entered into a childish compact, –a childish compact, Dr. Healy says; a compact between these two so that these unnatural crimes might continue.

Dr. Healy says that that is a childish compact.

I say if Dr. Healy is not ashamed of himself, he ought to be.

My God, I was a grown man before I knew of such depravity. They talk about what lawyers will do for money, but my God, I am glad that I do not know of any lawyer who would get on the witness stand and under oath characterize an unnatural agreement between these two perverts as a childish compact. Darrow and Bachrach that is an evidence of insanity.

The statutes of Illinois say that crimes against nature are crimes punishable by imprisonment in the penitentiary.

It is not a defense to a murder charge.

Mitigation! Mitigation!

I have heard so many big words and foreign words in this case that I sometimes thought that perhaps we were letting error creep into the record, so many strange, foreign words were being used here, and the constitution provides that these trials must be conducted in the English language; I do not know; maybe I have got aggravation and mitigation mixed up.

It is a mitigating circumstance, if your honor please, that Leopold when they were outlining the plan of this conspiracy and murder, wanted to take a little girl, a daughter of the rich, and first rape her and then murder her and then collect the ransom.

If that evidence had been put in by the state I would have thought it was an aggravation. These three wise men, with their distorted theories, hired by the

MADE IT UP: Crowe is referring to the letter from Leopold to Loeb that detectives had found in their search of Leopold's house, before the confession (see chapter 12, page 39).

another deserted road leading west.    We stopped

the car, got out, removed young Franks' shoes, hid

them in some bushes and removed his pants and stock-

ings, placing them in the car.    We did this in order

that we might be saved the trouble of too much un-

dressing him later on.        We also left his belt

buckle and belt with the shoes, not in the same place, but

very near there.

        We then proceeded to drive around back and

forth and back and forth.

    Q    Waiting for it to get dark?

    A    Waiting for it to get dark.  We stopped at a

little sandwich shop on the road, and Leopold got

out and purchased a couple of redhot sandwiches and

two bottles of root beer.      We then kept driving more

and more, untillit was fairly dusk.

Loeb's description of how they partly undressed Bobby Franks, in his original confession. This section of the original confession is transcribed on page 69 in chapter 16.

defense, they put that evidence in, and Clarence Darrow calls it a mitigating circumstance.

Why, when they murder a boy they ought to be treated with kindness and consideration. If they had taken a little tot, a little girl, debauched and raped her, I suppose we ought to have given each a medal and told them to go their way. My god, what are we coming to in this community?

I want to tell your honor, bearing in mind the testimony that was whispered into your ear, one of the motives in this case was desire to satisfy unnatural lust. They first wanted a little girl so that Leopold could rape her and then they decided on a little boy. What happened? Immediately upon killing him they took his trousers off. How do you undress a child? First the little coat, the collar, the tie, the shirt, and the last thing is their trousers. Yet, immediately after killing this poor little boy, his trousers alone came off, and for three hours that little dead boy, without his trousers but with all his other clothes on him, remained in that car, and they did not take the balance of the clothes off until they pushed the body into the culvert.

You have before you the coroner's report, and the coroner's physician says that when little Robert Franks was examined, his rectum was distended that much, indicating almost the size of a half-dollar.

**MR. DARROW:** Well, now—

**MR. BENJAMIN BACHRACH:** If the court please, I take exception to that statement. The coroner's report said there was no sign of recent dilation.

**MR. CROWE:** Your honor has the report.

**MR. BENJAMIN BACHRACH:** Your honor will look at the report.

**MR. CROWE:** He says there was no sign beyond a distended rectum.

**MR. DARROW:** No, that isn't what he said at all.

**MR. CROWE:** And I want to call your Honor's attention to the fact that this little naked body lay in the water all night long with running water going over it, and that is why there wasn't any other evidence.

Crowe goes on to talk about other things but later Darrow and Benjamin Bachrach return to the subject:

**MR. BENJAMIN BACHRACH:** The suggestion I have to make to Mr. Crowe about this matter is that this is the first time it has been charged in this case that the committing of a sexual act was the purpose of this crime upon the part of this boy. Now if that is not cleared up at this time, if it goes out to the newspapers it will do us no good unless it is cleared up at this time, and it is not a fair inference from that report.

**MR. CROWE:** I think I know what the evidence was in this case and I think all my arguments are based on facts and not on dreams or phantasies.

**MR. DARROW:** We know exactly what the coroner's report shows.

**THE COURT:** Look it over and I will stop the argument when you get to it.

At this point, Joseph P. Savage is sent to fetch a copy of the report, and when he returns with it, Caverly asks to have it read into the record. "But first," he adds, "I would ask the ladies, if there are any here who do not want to hear testimony that might be embarrassing to them, to kindly step out." He seems to think all ladies would automatically recoil at the thought of hearing such testimony, but when a large number remain in the room despite the recess called to allow them to leave, he demands that they go.

(During the recess, the following occurred):

**MR. CROWE:** The Coroner's report says that he had a distended rectum, and from that fact, and the fact that the pants were taken off, and the fact that they are perverts, I have a right to argue that they committed an act of perversion.

That is the extent of my argument. I do not contend that the coroner's report states that an act of perversion was committed. It merely says that the rectum was distended.

There was no evidence of semen, but it was washed away, I contend.

**THE COURT:** I have asked the ladies to leave the room. Now, I want you to leave. If you do not, I will have the bailiffs escort you into the hallways. There is nothing left here now but a lot of stuff that is not fit for you to hear. There will be nothing else but that to be read. Why do you persist to listening to such rot. Step out into the hallway.

———

(An elderly woman came to the bench and started to ask the Court a question:

"Does that mean that even us—"

When the Court interrupted her with–

"It means that all of you ought to go. You men in the corner here go back and sit down over there. If those men standing don't take seats I wish the bailiffs would escort them to the hall.

"Now don't tell them again.

"Just take them out.

"Find seats, please, or do you want me to put you out?")

———

**THE COURT:** Now then, you might read it, Mr. Darrow, Mr. [Walter] Bachrach, Mr. Crowe or Mr. Savage. I don't care which.

**MR. CROWE:** I would rather have young Mr. [Walter] Bachrach read this because it contains a number of these strange, foreign words.

**THE COURT:** Go ahead.

Will you read it into the record so we will have the record straight?

I don't know myself what it contains because I haven't read it yet.

It will be part of my duty after this case is over, to read all this, some twelve hundred pages of stuff. I don't know who is right in the matter. We will have it read into the record, and be sure about it.

**MR. DARROW:** You read it, Walter.

(Whereupon the record referred to was here read into the record by Mr. Walter Bachrach, in the words and figures, as follows):

**MR. WALTER BACHRACH (Reading):** The statement of Coroner's Physician A. F. Benson on the 22nd day of May: "I made a post mortem on the body of Robert A. Franks at 13300 Houston Avenue, the body being identified by Edwin M. Gresham. Upon general inspection the body measured five feet in length, and one hundred pounds in weight.

"There was evidence of exposure to sand and water. The body was nude. Upon examination I found two cuts in the forehead inside the hairy margin, two inches above the left and right eyebrow, the left cut one and a half inches in length and the right three quarters inches, both with dull edges, and ante-mortem. There were numerous scratches about the left side of the forehead, also, which were ante-mortem. The face presented a peculiar appearance, with a marked outline around the nose and mouth and part of the chin, the color of the skin in this area being pale, the rest of the face presented a flushed and streaked appearance such as would result from acid fumes. There were a number of scratches on the back over the left shoulder and the right buttock, all of which were ante-mortem. There was one superficial sharp edged cut off the spine one inch to the left of the median line and just above the buttock. This was post mortem.

"I found cutis anserine of the hands and only the scrotum showed evidence of having been submerged in the water. The genitals were intact, and the rectum was dilated, would easily admit one finger. There was no evidence of a recent forcible dilation."

**MR. WALTER BACHRACH:** Now, I think that is all that is necessary.

**MR. CROWE:** It is a matter of argument.

**MR. DARROW:** I don't think that is a matter of argument.

**MR. CROWE:** I don't think you and I are going to agree. You have your theory, and I have mine.

**MR. DARROW:** The coroner's physician says there is no evidence of it.

**MR. CROWE:** I understand. My contention is that any evidence has been washed away by the water.

**MR. DARROW:** That isn't what [the coroner's physician] says.

**MR. CROWE:** You have your contention, and I have mine.

**MR. BENJAMIN BACHRACH:** The unfairness of it, if your honor please, is that the charge comes in the closing argument. There was no hint at all that such a claim would be made, and now all our opportunity to reply is gone.

**MR. CROWE:** Oh, no. You have made three speeches. Mr. Darrow has just finished his talk, Mr. Walter Bachrach made his argument and you have made your argument. You have had three opportunities to answer it.

**MR. DARROW:** You had two speeches in opening.

**THE COURT:** Is there anything further in the report other than that?

**MR. SAVAGE:** The testimony of Dr. [Joseph] Springer [also a coroner's physician, who examined the body and who testified during the hearing] here is substantially to the same effect, that the rectum was dilated.

**MR. CROWE:** I am not making any contention that there was anything further than that.

**THE COURT:** The doctor says in this report that the genitals were intact and the rectum was dilated and would admit, easily, one finger: that there was no evidence of a recent forcible dilation. Now, that is the testimony, gentlemen, and that is as far, I think, as you want to go.

**MR. CROWE:** I had finished my argument on that a long time ago.

**THE COURT:** All right. Is there anything further that you want on the matter?

**MR. WALTER BACHRACH:** No. But there is just one thing that I would like to say in addition to what has already been said here, and that is, before the State's

---

CUTIS ANSERINE: Medical term for "goose bumps," which can be caused postmortem by cold exposure and are often found in drowning victims.

Both SPRINGER and A.F. Benson, whose report was being read, were coroner's physicians who had participated in the autopsy.

Attorney would be entitled to draw any inference that there was any evidence of mistreatment of the body in the sexual way, there would have to be some evidence upon which he could base such an argument or from which he could draw such an inference, and I say that it is a question of law for the court to say whether or not this statement here—

**MR. CROWE:** Oh, no, there is no other evidence.

**MR. WALTER BACHRACH:** Pardon me—

**MR. CROWE:** The evidence is that these two defendants are perverts, and when they took the body of the boy in, the first thing they took off was his trousers.

**MR. WALTER BACHRACH:** Irrespective of what the evidence shows concerning the two boys, if your honor please, there is no evidence to show that this body was mistreated in a sexual way.

**THE COURT:** This is the evidence of the coroner and certainly conclusive, and we will let it rest with what the coroner says.

# 65
# This court will not be intimidated by anybody

## CAVERLY REBUKES CROWE

**CROWE STAMMERS**

Judge John Caverly's outrage at Robert Crowe's "cowardly and dastardly assault on the integrity" of the court was visible to all. The August 28 *Chicago Daily News* reported that his eyes were "blazing" as he rebuked Crowe, who was staggered by the judge's reaction and thrown completely off balance.

Apparently, Crowe's "tongue had run away with him. He stammered huskily, then closed his argument and sat down."

CROWE HAD DONE a thorough and effective job of rebutting the defense and was approaching the intended climax of his closing argument when one of his tactics backfired badly. Intending to counter Clarence Darrow's rather implausible claim that the defendants' great wealth had been a handicap to them in this case, Crowe tries to remind Caverly of Nathan Leopold's assertion just after he confessed that his family could probably use its resources to find a "friendly" judge who wouldn't invoke the ultimate penalty for his crime (see chapter 48, page 164). Caverly reacts angrily to what he interprets as a direct assault on his integrity, and Crowe, recognizing his miscalculation, sputters through his conclusion, bringing the 32nd and final day of the hearing to an anticlimactic end.

**[MR. CROWE:]** Mr. Darrow has preached in this case that one of the handicaps the defendants are under is that they are rich, the sons of multi-millionaires. I have already stated to your honor that if it was not for their wealth Darrow would not be here and the Bachrachs would not be here.

If it was not for their wealth we would not have been regaled by all this tommy-rot by the three wise men from the east.

I don't want to refer to this any more than Mr. Darrow did, but he referred to it and it is in evidence, and he tried to make your honor believe that somebody lied, that Gortland lied when he talked about a friendly judge. —

On June 10th, 1924, in the Chicago Herald-Examiner—that was before this case had been assigned to anybody; that was when Darrow was announcing and he did announce in this same article, that they were going to plead not guilty—there was an article written by Mr. Slattery, sitting back there, on June 10th: —

"The friendly judge resort suggested for the defense will be of no avail. It was mentioned as a possibility that a plea of guilty might be entered on the understanding it would result in life sentence. If this becomes an absolute probability, Crowe announced that he will nolle prose the case and reindict the slayers." —

Did Gortland lie?

He gave the name of witness after witness that he told the same story to, as he told it to Slattery, before the case was even assigned.

He says that was told to him by Leopold. I don't know whether your honor—

**MR. DARROW:** Are you quoting from his testimony?

**MR. CROWE:** I am talking about his testimony.

He said it was told to him by Leopold. I don't know whether your honor believes that officer or not, but I want to tell you, if you have observed these two defendants during the trial, if you have observed the conduct of their attorneys and their families

**JAMES GORTLAND** was one of the arresting officers. He had previously testified about Leopold's statement that he would use his family's influence to get a "friendly" judge (see chapter 48, page 164).

**CHARLES V. SLATTERY** was a reporter for the *Chicago Herald and Examiner*.

**NOLLE PROSE:** In other words, that he would drop the case and enter a new indictment.

with one honorable exception, and that is the old man who sits in sackcloth and ashes and who is entitled to the sympathy of everybody, old Mr. [Nathan] Leopold, with that one honorable exception everybody connected with the case have laughed and sneered and jeered and if the defendant, Leopold, did not say that he would plead guilty before a friendly judge, his actions demonstrated that he thinks he has got one.

**MR. DARROW:** I want to take exception to this statement. It has not any place in a court of justice—

**MR. CROWE:** You brought it up and argued on it, and I am replying to it.

**MR. DARROW:** Oh, no.

**MR. CROWE:** But now, if your honor please, you have listened—

**THE COURT:** Let the reporter write up that statement, have that statement written up.

**MR. CROWE:** You have listened with a great deal of patience and kindness and consideration to the state and the defense. I am not going to unduly trespass upon your honor's time, and I am going to close for the State.

I believe that the facts and circumstances proven in this case demonstrate that a crime has been committed by these two defendants and that no other punishment except the extreme penalty of the law will fit, and I leave the case with you on behalf of the State of Illinois, and I ask your honor in the language of Holy Writ to "Execute justice and righteousness in the land."

(State's Attorney Crowe concluded his final argument to the Court).

At this point, the kidnapping case is tried separately as a formality by having Jacob Franks testify that his son had been kidnapped and murdered, having the ransom note read into the record, and having Captain William Schoemaker testify that Leopold had told him that he and Loeb had kidnapped and killed Bobby Franks. The defense presents no argument, and the state again rests. Then Caverly comes back to the "friendly judge" issue, which had clearly continued to bother him:

**THE COURT:** Before the State rests in the other case, the court will order stricken from the record the closing remarks of the State's Attorney as being a cowardly and dastardly assault upon the integrity of this court.

**MR. CROWE:** It was not so intended, your honor.

**THE COURT:** And it could not be used for any other purpose except to incite a mob and to try and intimidate this court. It will be stricken from the record.

**MR. CROWE:** If your honor please, the State's Attorney had no such intention.

**THE COURT:** We will go on—

**MR. CROWE:** I merely want to put my personal feelings plainly before the court. It was not the intention of the State's Attorney.

**THE COURT:** The State's Attorney knew that would be heralded all through this country and all over this world, and he knows the court hasn't an opportunity except to do what he did. It was not the proper thing to do.

**MR. CROWE:** It was not the intention.

**THE COURT:** This court will not be intimidated by anybody at any time or place as long as he occupies this position. [ . . . ]

I have nineteen hundred and fifty odd pages, practically two thousand pages of exhibits. When I say exhibits, it is part of the testimony; it is the Hulbert-Bowman report; parts of the confession; some of testimony that was read in secret that contained matter that was not fit for publication and should not be heard in the courtroom, and it will take me some little time to do that, and to prepare to decide this matter and render judgment in this case.

I think I ought to have ten days or so, and I will fix the day at September 10th.

I will fix the day as September the 10th, at 9:30 o'clock, and I will say to those people who are here now that there will be nobody admitted in this room on that day, except members of the press and members of the family and sheriffs and the State's Attorney's staff.

If anything occurs whereby I could not be in a position or cannot be in a position to render it on that day, I will notify the press and the authorities at least three days in advance. But there will nothing deter me from rendering judgment on that day, gentlemen, unless it is illness.

We will continue this case now until September the 10th at nine thirty o'clock.

# 66
# Grief, worry, broken heart

## THE WAIT

The national press—and much of the press abroad—held its collective breath for Judge John Caverly's decision. The September 8 *Chicago Daily Tribune* reported that the opinion the judge spent most of September 7 drafting "with the aid of an ordinary lead pencil" would "go down as one of the important decisions of modern criminal jurisprudence."

That sentiment was echoed by the United States's newspaper of record, the *New York Times*, which featured a very long op-ed on September 7 by George W. Kirchwey, dean of the Columbia Law School and later warden of Sing Sing Prison (the notorious maximum-security prison in upstate New York). He praised Caverly's "far-sighted and courageous" decision to admit psychiatric evidence about Nathan Leopold and Richard Loeb to the court proceedings and predicted that the implications of that decision "for the future of legal procedure in this country [were] far more important than his legal decision of life or death for the individual defendants at the bar."

THE DAY AFTER the sentencing hearing ended, Judge Caverly spent his afternoon at the Hawthorne Race Course, where he bet on a horse called Bad Luck. After 32 days of confinement in a sweltering, confrontational courtroom, he was reaching for the bits of normal life he could grab as he took two weeks to ponder the life-or-death decision that was being tensely awaited around the world. But emotional relief was elusive. There were death threats from crackpots on both sides of the case, and, according to the *Chicago Daily Tribune*, on September 2, as Caverly attended the funeral of an old friend, his wife received a phone call informing her that her husband had been shot dead and was lying at the entrance to Calvary Cemetery. Along with the detective assigned to guard their apartment, she jumped into a taxi and raced to the cemetery, where she emerged from the vehicle in hysterics only to find her husband calmly talking to some other mourners. Her nerves were so shattered that he abandoned his plan to spend a few days' retreat in the northern woods, where he had hoped to contemplate his decision.

The nerves of the affected families were also shattering. The *Chicago Daily News* reported that at the Loebs' summer estate in Charlevoix, Michigan, Loeb's already-frail father had suffered a new heart attack on August 30. Albert Loeb had not been seen in public since news of the confessions broke, retreating with his wife to Charlevoix before the start of the trial while his brother Jacob and eldest son, Allan, kept an eye on the courtroom drama. A Chicago doctor called to the home was quoted in the *Chicago Daily News* as saying, "When people die of a broken heart, as the phrase goes, it is this muscular inflammation that causes death, largely brought on by grief and worry." The doctor, who had requested anonymity, added that "Mr. Loeb is a very brilliant and fine man and a philosopher as well—almost a stoic. He has prepared himself for either verdict, and I believe he will be able to stand the shock. But he will be physically unable to come to Chicago, had it ever been his intention to come."

And even before the verdict, Jacob Franks and his wife had decided to escape the home and the neighborhood which had once seemed so safe and where now they were trapped in an ongoing horror show. "During the last months their home has been a sort of mecca for the cranks and the terrorists and curiosity's thousand eyes," observed the August 31 *Tribune*. "Automobiles slow to a walk as they pass the slain boy's dwellings. Pedestrians linger to stare at it, at the lilac bushes which fringe the southern sidewalk, at the drawn blinds that hide the sorrowing family from morbid watchers." Along with the sympathy mail, hate mail poured in daily, as did death and kidnap threats involving Bobby Franks's two surviving siblings, Jack and Josephine. Right down the block was the Loeb mansion, a looming, unavoidable monument to their tragedy, where their dead son's bloody clothes had been burned in the basement furnace by a murderer who had been a trusted member of their family circle; it must have seemed unimaginable that, whatever the outcome of the court case, the Frankses might have to encounter the Loebs on the street at any time. Fifteen years before,

Jacob Franks had bought his property from Albert Loeb—who shared a grandmother with his wife, Flora. On August 31, the *Tribune* reported that Franks had just sold the house to "cinema magnate" Joseph Trinz for $60,000 and would soon be moving his family to the Drake Hotel.

The only place any of the protagonists seemed to be enjoying themselves, as the clock ticked down to the scheduled verdict on September 10, was the county jail. When sometime-girlfriend Germaine K. ("Patches") Reinhard arrived for a visit with Loeb on the day after the sentencing hearing ended, the *Chicago Herald and Examiner* reported that Loeb "fairly enchanted the eye in his new pea-green tweeds, tailored along the latest collegian lines." Sporting a "gold button with the letter 'M' in blue enamel in his coat lapel, the student emblem of the University of Michigan," he evinced no self-consciousness about his own suitability as a collegiate poster boy for the institution whose fraternity he had burglarized—armed with a loaded revolver—on the night he and Leopold said they began to form the murder plan.

Leopold's sweetheart Susan Lurie was present only in the form of a soulful photograph with "large, innocent eyes" and a "sweet smile," according to the *Chicago Herald and Examiner*, which hung on his cell wall "at such an angle that it involuntarily smiles 'Good Night' and 'Good Morning' at Nathan when he climbs onto his hay mattress at night or arises from it in the morning." Lurie herself had wisely evaded a state's attorney's subpoena, either to avoid appearing on the stand for the prosecution, as the newspaper suggested, or simply to avoid any further actual contact with Leopold or his sordid situation.

But the boys were international celebrities now and enjoyed a constant stream of visitors, including six members of the Chicago Cubs who showed up to tour the prison and "see the young murderers." As the inmates took part in one of their regular prison baseball games, the *Chicago Herald and Examiner* reported that Leo "Gabby" Hartnett, "one of the Cubs' chief sluggers, showed Leopold how to do some lusty straight-arm batting." Leopold and Loeb avidly monitored their own coverage in the Chicago papers—at one point announcing that they would no longer speak to out-of-town reporters because they had no way of checking what those writers were saying about them—and professed no regret and no concern about their possible execution. Loeb declared to the *Herald and Examiner* that he was glad the trial was finally over because it would give him "more time to make a name for myself in the jail baseball league," while Leopold said he was planning the farewell speech he would make if he was hanged, and hoped the event would include a jazz band and "plenty of hard punch."

> The boys were international celebrities now and enjoyed a constant stream of visitors, including six members of the Chicago Cubs who showed up to tour the prison and "see the young murderers."

# 67
# The dictates of
# enlightened humanity

### CAVERLY'S VERDICT

**EXTRA, EXTRA!**

The press braced for news of the decision. *Chicago Daily Tribune* readers who couldn't wait for that paper's extra editions could tune their radios to its recently launched station WGN, headquartered at the Drake Hotel, which "will be in direct communication with Judge Caverly's court room and the radio listeners will learn of the verdict almost simultaneously with the persons in the courtroom."

A correspondent for the *Chicago Daily News* foreign service reported that London newspapers were planning to issue extra editions the moment news was cabled across the Atlantic. "Anything short of the death penalty," he wrote, "is bound to create in the

CONTINUED

O N SEPTEMBER 10, the day the verdict was to be announced, public suspense had reached a fever pitch. Getting into the actual courtroom was impossible unless you were a family member, one of their attorneys, or a designated member of the press. Judge Caverly had ordered that no one else would be allowed within a block of the court building until the verdict had been announced and the defendants had been safely returned to the jail. Even so, the *Chicago Daily News* estimated, the crowd in the streets around the building that morning swelled to 5,000, as Caverly arrived with an entourage of 12 bodyguards assigned to protect him from potential bombers, assassins, and cranks. The verdict is not included in the bound edition of the transcript of the sentencing hearing, and may no longer exist in an original document, but the court stenographer's transcript of the proceedings was provided to newspaper reporters and was printed verbatim in many papers, as it appears below. The court stenographer reported that he entered the courtroom promptly at 9:30 a.m. and recorded the proceedings as follows:

**THE BAILIFF:** Hear ye, hear ye, this honorable court is now in session pursuant to adjournment.

**[THE COURT:]** Everybody must be seated. If you cannot find seats leave the room. Find seats or leave the room, everybody. If they cannot find seats, put them out, officers.

**THE CLERK:** Nathan F. Leopold Jr. and Richard Loeb.

The defendants then entered the courtroom and took their seats and Judge Caverly began reading his decision, as follows:

**THE COURT:** Have the two defendants anything to say in either case?

**MR. BENJAMIN BACHRACH:** No, your honor.

**THE COURT:** In view of the profound and unusual interest that this case has aroused not only in this community but in the entire country and even beyond its boundaries, the court feels it his duty to state the reasons which have led him to the determination he has reached.

It is not an uncommon thing that pleas of guilty are entered in criminal cases, but almost without exception in the past such pleas have been the result of a virtual agreement between the defendant and the state's attorney whereby, in consideration of the plea, the state's attorney consents to recommend to the court a sentence deemed appropriate by him, and, in the absence of special reasons to the contrary, it is the practice of the court to follow such recommendations.

In the present case the situation is a different one. A plea of guilty has been entered by the defense without a previous understanding with the prosecution and without any knowledge whatever on its part. Moreover, the plea of guilty did not in this particular case, as it usually does, render the task of the prosecution easier by substituting admission of guilt for a possibly difficult and uncertain chain of proof. Here the state was in possession not only of the essential, substantiating facts but also of voluntary confessions on the part of the defendants. The plea of guilty, therefore, does not make a special case in favor of the defendants.

Since both of the cases: that, namely of murder and that of kidnaping for ransom, were of a character which invested the court with discretion as to the extent of the punishment, it became his duty under the statute to examine witnesses as to the aggravation and mitigation of the offense. This duty has been fully met. By consent of counsel for the state and for the defendants, the testimony in the murder case has been accepted as equally applicable to the case of kidnaping for ransom. In addition, a prima facie case was made out for the kidnaping case as well.

The testimony introduced, both by the prosecution and the defense, has been as detailed and elaborate as though the case had been tried before a jury. It has been given the widest publicity, and the public is so fully familiar with all its phases that it would serve no useful purpose to restate or analyze the evidence.

By pleading guilty, the defendants have admitted legal responsibility for their acts; the testimony has satisfied the court that the case is not one in which it would have been possible to set up successfully the defense of insanity, as insanity is defined and understood by the established law of this state for the purpose of the administration of criminal justice.

The court, however, feels impelled to dwell briefly on the mass of data produced as to the physical, mental, and moral condition of the two defendants. They have been shown in essential respects to be abnormal; had they been normal they would not have committed the crime. It is beyond the province of this court, as it is beyond the capacity of human science in its present state of development, to predicate ultimate responsibility for human acts.

At the same time, the court is willing to recognize that the careful analysis made of the life history of the defendants and of their present mental, emotional, and ethical condition has been of extreme interest and is a valuable contribution to criminology. And yet the court feels strongly that similar analyses made of other persons accused of crime would probably reveal similar or different abnormalities. The value of such tests seems to lie in their applicability to crime and criminals in general. Since they concern the broad questions of human responsibility and legal punishment, and are in no wise peculiar to these individual defendants, they may be deserving of legislative but not of judicial consideration. For this reason the court is satisfied that his judgment in the present case cannot be affected thereby.

The testimony in this case reveals a crime of singular atrocity. It is, in a sense, inexplicable; but it is not thereby rendered less inhuman or repulsive. It was deliberately planned and prepared for during a considerable period of time. It was executed with every feature of callousness and cruelty.

And here the court will say, not for the purpose of extenuating guilt, but merely with the object of dispelling a misapprehension that appears to have found lodgment

CONTINUED

European press a storm of criticism of American court procedure as well as ironic comments on the influence of wealth in such cases."

The *Chicago Daily News* reported that as Judge John Caverly took his seat in the courtroom, fixed his glasses down toward the end of his nose, and began to read calmly, "the clicking of a battery of cameras interrupted him, but left him unruffled."

"The white faces of the boys, sitting directly under the judge's eyes, grew whiter. Nathan Leopold, Sr., seated back of his son, gripped the arm of his bench, and looked down at the floor. Jacob Loeb, Dick's uncle, and young Allan Loeb, the brother, leaned forward."

in the public mind, that he is convinced by conclusive evidence that there was no abuse offered to the body of the victim. But it did not need that element to make the crime abhorrent to every instinct of humanity, and the court is satisfied that neither in the act itself, nor in its motive or lack of motive, nor in the antecedents of the offenders, can he find any mitigating circumstances.

For both the crime of murder and kidnaping for ransom, the law prescribes different punishments in the alternative.

For the crime of murder, the statute declares:

"Whoever is guilty of murder shall suffer the punishment of death, or imprisonment in the penitentiary for his natural life, or for a term not less than fourteen years. If the accused is found guilty by a jury, they shall fix the punishment by their verdict; upon a plea of guilty, the punishment shall be fixed by the court."

For the crime of kidnaping for ransom, the statute reads:

"Whoever is guilty of kidnaping for ransom shall suffer death, or be punished by imprisonment in the penitentiary for life, or any terms not less than five years."

Under the plea of guilty, the duty of determining the punishment devolves upon the court, and the law indicates no rule or policy for the guidance of his discretion. In reaching his decision the court would have welcomed the counsel and support of others. In some states the legislature in its wisdom has provided for a bench of three judges to determine the penalty in cases such as this. Nevertheless, the court is willing to meet his responsibilities. It would have been the path of least resistance to impose the extreme penalty of the law. In choosing imprisonment instead of death the court is moved chiefly by the consideration of the age of the defendants, boys of 18 and 19 years. It is not for the court to say that he will not in any case enforce capital punishment as an alternative, but the court believes that it is within his province to decline to impose the sentence of death on persons who are not of full age.

This determination appears to be in accordance with the progress of criminal law all over the world and with the dictates of enlightened humanity. More than that, it seems to be in accordance with the precedents hitherto observed in this state.

The records of Illinois show only two cases of minors who were put to death by legal process—to which number the court does not feel inclined to make an addition.

Life imprisonment may not, at the moment, strike the public imagination as forcibly as would death by hanging; but to the offenders, particularly of the type they are, the prolonged suffering of years of confinement may well be the severer form of retribution and expiation.

The court feels it proper to add a final word concerning the effect of the parole law upon the punishment of these defendants. In the case of such atrocious crimes it is entirely within the discretion of the department of public welfare never to admit these defendants to parole. To such a policy the court urges them strictly to adhere. If this course is persevered in the punishment of these defendants will both satisfy the ends of justice and safeguard the interests of society.

At this point the sentences formally were passed, as follows:

"In No. 33623, indictment for murder, the sentence of the court is that you, Nathan F. Leopold Jr., be confined in the penitentiary at Joliet for the term of your natural life. The court finds that your age is 19.

"In No. 33623, indictment for murder, the sentence of the court is that you, Richard Loeb, be confined in the penitentiary at Joliet for the term of your natural life. The court finds that your age is 18.

"In 33,624, kidnaping for ransom, it is the sentence of the court that you, Nathan F. Leopold Jr., be confined in the penitentiary at Joliet for the term of 99 years. The court finds your age 19.

"In 33,624, kidnaping for ransom, it is the sentence of the court that you, Richard Loeb, be confined in the penitentiary at Joliet for the term of 99 years.

"The clerk will distribute to the newspaper men copies of the opinion, to those who want them. The sheriff may retire with the prisoners."

At 9:40 a.m. Judge Caverly left the bench and the hearing was concluded.

# 68
# What have they to look forward to?

## REACTIONS TO THE DECISION

## Robert Crowe
### STATE'S ATTORNEY

"When the state's attorney arrested the defendants, solved what was then a mystery and by the thoroughness of his preparation compelled the defendants to plead guilty, presented a mountain of evidence to the court and made his argument, his duty was fully performed.

"He is in no measure responsible for the decision of the court. The responsibility for that decision rests with the judge alone. Like all other law abiding citizens, when the court pronounces his decision, I must be content with it, because his decision in the case is final.

"While I do not intend and have no desire to criticize the decision of the court, I still believe that the death penalty is the only penalty feared by murderers.

"Fathers and mothers in Cook county may rest assured as long as I remain state's attorney I will always do everything within my power to enforce the law honestly, fearlessly and vigorously, without regard to the status of the criminal."

—as reported in the *Chicago Daily News*, September 10, 1924

> "While I do not intend and have no desire to criticize the decision of the court, I still believe that the death penalty is the only penalty feared by murderers."

## Clarence Darrow
### DEFENSE ATTORNEY

"I have always hated capital punishment. This decision at once caps my career as a criminal lawyer and starts my path in another direction. This verdict so encourages me that I shall begin now to plan a definite campaign against capital punishment in Illinois. Perhaps I may be able to take up the matter with the legislature immediately."

—as reported in the *Chicago Daily News*, September 10, 1924

> "I have always hated capital punishment."

## Harold Hulbert
### PSYCHIATRIST AND COAUTHOR OF THE HULBERT—BOWMAN REPORT

Hulbert asked for and received police protection at his home in Aurora, Illinois. "He said he had received many threatening letters, saying he would be killed if Leopold and Loeb were not hanged."

—as reported in the *Chicago Daily Tribune*, September 11, 1924

## Sam Ettelson
### FRANKS FAMILY FRIEND AND ATTORNEY

Sam Ettelson was "disappointed" that the death penalty had not been imposed. "He declared, however, he was expressing his personal feeling and did not speak for Mr. Franks."

—as reported in the *Chicago Daily Tribune*, September 11, 1924

## Jacob and Flora Franks

Flora Franks was at her new home in the Drake Hotel when the news came, and she said that it was exactly what she had expected. "She told those who were near and dear to her that it was what she wanted."

"'They did such earnest work, and all did their duty,' she told them, 'but Bobby didn't believe in capital punishment. He wrote about it and read his article at school, and he told me it was wrong, and somehow, after that—how could I ask it? I didn't want to do or say anything to interfere with the prosecution, of course, but—I didn't want them to hang. I have felt for the past three weeks that they wouldn't hang.'"

Strangely, Jacob Franks was neither in court at 9:30 a.m. when the verdict was announced, nor home with his wife Flora. He was reached around 3 p.m. at the Edgewater Beach Hotel on Chicago's North Side, where he was said to be visiting a sick friend, and he said he didn't know whether his wife had yet heard the news.

"I am glad it is over," he said, "because this means the end. There can be no hearing in regard to their sanity, there can be no appeal, there can be no more torture by seeing this thing spread over the front pages of the newspapers. It will be easier for Mrs. Franks and for me to be relieved of the terrible strain of all this publicity. It has kept the picture before us constantly."

—as reported in the *Chicago Herald and Examiner*, September 11, 1924

## "I am glad it is over, because this means the end."

## Jacob Loeb
### ON BEHALF OF THE LEOPOLD AND LOEB FAMILIES

"There is little to say. We have been spared the death penalty; but what have these families to look forward to?

"Mr. Leopold Sr. is 64 years old. He has lived in Chicago practically his entire life, and he has been an exemplary citizen. His youngest son was his special pride. He justly believed his boy was a genius, a most brilliant student, and a loving son. He hoped this boy would make his mark in the world and become the solace and comfort of his old age.

"Now Mr. Leopold, in his declining years, is crushed in spirit.

"Albert H. Loeb, my brother, has spent his entire life in this city. He is 56 years old. He came from the ranks, worked his way through college, and made himself a lawyer of repute. Then he became a great business man.

"I repeat, here are two families whose names have stood for everything that was good and reputable in the community. Now what have they to look forward to?

"Their unfortunate boys, aged 19 years, must spend the rest of their lives in prison.

"What is there in the future but grief and sorrow, darkness and despair?"

—as reported in the *Chicago Daily Tribune*, September 11, 1924

## "What is there in the future but grief and sorrow, darkness and despair?"

## Nathan Leopold Jr. and Richard Loeb

"'Go out,' said young Mr. Leopold, 'and order us a big meal. Get us two steaks—that thick!' and he measured off a liberal three inches with thumb and forefinger.

"'Yes,' said young Mr. Loeb, 'and be sure they are smothered in onions. And bring every side dish that you can find. This may be our last good meal.'

"'And,' added Mr. Leopold, 'bring chocolate eclairs for dessert.'"

—as reported in the *Chicago Daily Tribune*, September 11, 1924

# 69
# Lifers

## COLLATERAL DAMAGE

A S SENSATIONAL AS it had been, the case faded quickly from the newspapers soon after Leopold and Loeb were sent off to Joliet (and later, to Stateville) to embark on their sentences of "life plus 99 years." Periodically, there were glimpses in the press of the collapse all three families continued to experience.

## The Franks family

On September 22, 10 days after Leopold and Loeb entered Joliet prison, the former home of Bobby Franks at 5052 Ellis Avenue was opened to the public for an auction of all the family's personal belongings, which they had decided not to take with them as they tried to start a new life for themselves in an apartment at the Drake Hotel. Twelve hundred people crowded into the house, fighting "to get into the rooms where Robert Franks had slept before he was made the victim of Richard Loeb's and Nathan Leopold Jr.'s experiment," a September 23 edition of the *Chicago Daily Tribune* wrote. "The Franks furniture was not of an exceptional type," according to the *Tribune*. "There were one or two oriental rugs—the rest of domestic make. There were no antiques to be obtained 'as prizes.'"

There were still games and a radio set in Bobby's room, but these had been reserved for the family, as was a stained-glass window on the first-floor landing that depicted Bobby, his sister, Josephine, and his brother, Jack. The Frankses were planning to have that removed.

A few weeks later, Jacob Franks gave a reporter this glimpse of what life was like for him and his wife at the Drake:

"Sometimes I think she is recovering," he said, "and then she and I go through a night of horror. Last night she cried the whole night through and never went to sleep.

"School has started again, and when she sees the children coming and going, she bursts into tears. She goes to the box where we have kept Bobby's essays and looks at them until she comes to the one that tells what our son thought about capital punishment. He thought it was wrong to put people to death and that comforts his mother a little, because she knows that Robert would be satisfied because his slayers were not put to death."

The paper says Franks went to work every day, supposedly to run his real estate business, but he had gotten very little work of any kind done since Bobby's murder. Instead, "he spends most of his time going over dozens of letters that pour into him from all parts of the world, most of them tendering him sympathy."

When Jacob Franks died four years later, in the apartment at the Drake Hotel, newspapers all across the country—from the *New York Times* to the *Los Angeles Times*—ran the AP story that said, "Despite the fact that the Franks family had moved from a mansion-like home on the south side to the hotel to get away from tragic surroundings of their son's death, the father never was able to recover from his grief and today, surrounded by his wife and two other children, Jack and Josephine, he gave up the struggle."

## The Loeb family

After months of confinement at the family estate in Charlevoix, Michigan, where he was said to be too ill to attend his son's sentencing hearing, Albert Loeb finally returned in October to his mansion down the street from the Franks house. He died there two weeks later, on October 28—barely two months after Richard had been sent to prison. His struggle with heart disease predated his son's troubles, but no one doubted that it was the murder that had been the fatal blow. He was 56.

Anna Loeb inherited an estate valued at $3 million, including the Charlevoix and Chicago mansions. Richard engulfed the family in scandal for a second time when he was murdered at Stateville Correctional Center 11 years later—slashed more than 50 times with a razor by a fellow inmate, James Day, who claimed to have been defending himself from Loeb's homosexual advances. Many—including Leopold, who rushed to Loeb's side in the prison infirmary and was with him as he bled to death—were skeptical of Day's story, though a jury exonerated him of guilt.

The killing generated yet another legend about the case, gleefully repeated in journalism circles: that possibly the cleverest newspaper lead ever written ran in Edwin A. Lahey's story on Loeb's murder for the *Chicago Daily News*. Harking back to the reputation both Leopold and Loeb had had as boy geniuses, the lead is supposed to have read (though the wording varies slightly from account to account): "Despite his erudition, Richard Loeb today ended his sentence with a proposition." Researchers who have tried to verify that legend in recent years have been disappointed. The surviving microfilmed editions of the *Daily News* include an unbylined story in the late edition on the day of the murder, January 28, which reads, "Richard Loeb, one of the slayers of 14-year-old Bobby Franks nearly 12 years ago, was slashed to death this afternoon by another convict in a fight at Statesville prison."

Two different editions on the following day, January 29, preserve a bylined story by Lahey that is almost as irreverent but not nearly as clever as the legendary one: "James Day, 23-year-old Chicago thief, who is otherwise normal, told today how and why he cut Richard Loeb, brilliant young moral anarchist, to a fringe in the Stateville penitentiary yesterday."

## The Leopold family

Like both of the other families, the remaining Leopolds found it impossible to remain in the Kenwood neighborhood. By the end of November, the *Washington Post* reported that Nathan Leopold Sr. and his son Foreman ("Mike") had filed a petition with the city to tear down their mansion at 4754 Greenwood Avenue.

Three years after the murder, Nathan Leopold Sr. married Mrs. Daisy K. Hahn of Los Angeles. In 1929, after the couple returned to Chicago from a winter in California, Leopold was operated on for an ailment "similar to gallstones" at Michael Reese Hospital, where he died 10 days later, on April 4. The *Tribune*'s article notes that although he had been "a respected and well liked business man," his life "was saddened in 1925 [should be "1924"] in the discovery that his son, Nathan F. Leopold Jr., had killed little Bobbie Franks."

Both of his other sons, Foreman and Sam, remained in Chicago, but they changed their last name in order to spare themselves and their families the stigma that had become associated with the name Leopold.

# PART V

# The Gertz Papers: Leopold's Later Years

# 70
# Elmer Gertz

ELMER GERTZ had been 17 years old in the summer of 1924, when the murder of Bobby Franks brought sudden notoriety to the wealthy Kenwood section of Hyde Park, Chicago. Born into a family of far more modest means than the Leopolds, the Loebs, and the Frankses, Gertz lived on what he recalled as the "shabby genteel periphery" of that neighborhood—about a mile and a half north on Ellis Avenue. Gertz and his younger brother Bob spent many evenings "walking up and down the tree-lined streets that had been trod by Nathan Leopold and Richard Loeb, and by the victim of their crime, Bobby Franks," talking about the crime to anyone who would listen. Gertz's older brother Edward had worked as a chauffeur to millionaire Julius Rosenwald, Albert Loeb's boss at Sears, Roebuck—whose grandson Armand Deutsch was one of the boys Leopold and Loeb considered kidnapping before they chose Bobby. But that—and the fact that he worshipped Clarence Darrow—was for the next 30 years the extent of Gertz's relationship to the Leopold and Loeb case.

Then, as an attorney in the early 1950s, Gertz found himself drawn into a Chicago literary circle that included a rare-book dealer named Ralph Newman and a wealthy friend of his called Mike. As they got to know each other better, Mike eventually revealed himself to be Nathan Leopold's older brother Foreman—the brother who had sat through the sentencing hearing in 1924, day after day, supporting their devastated father. Writing about him later in his memoir *A Handful of Clients*, Gertz was careful never to mention Mike's last name—the name that both Mike and Nathan's other brother, Sam, had changed to try to escape the family's disgrace.

By then Loeb had been dead for nearly 20 years, but Leopold, through the years, had assembled an impressive track record of credentials suggesting his rehabilitation in prison: he had helped run a school for fellow prisoners, worked as an X-ray technician in the prison hospital, and volunteered himself as a guinea pig to test antimalarial drugs, an experience that left him with symptoms of kidney disease and diabetes. In 1949, Illinois governor Adlai Stevenson commuted his sentence to 85 years, making him eligible for parole in January 1953.

Newman and Leopold's brother Mike were actively campaigning for Leopold's parole, soliciting testimonials on his behalf from family friends, people who had worked with Leopold in prison, and celebrities. Newman was also acting as the literary agent for Leopold's memoir, titled *Life Plus 99 Years*, which Leopold hoped would make the case to the general public that he had fully atoned for his crime. Newman asked Gertz to serve as Leopold's attorney for the book deal—thus kindling a relationship between Gertz and Leopold that would last for the rest of Leopold's life and represent one of his most profound friendships.

Gertz's papers, now in the Charles Deering McCormick Library of Special Collections at Northwestern University, include the transcript of the sentencing hearing, which had once been Darrow's personal copy; it had passed after his death to the Leopold family and was turned over to Gertz for the work he would eventually do on Leopold's parole. They also include 53 archival boxes of letters, court documents, newspaper clippings, manuscripts, and other materials, on which the final chapters of this book are based, that trace the arc of Leopold's life as he began to believe in the possibility of a life beyond prison—and eventually, to lead one.

Right: Leopold holding his memoir, *Life Plus 99 Years*.

# 71
# How bitterly I regret the past

## THE 1953 PAROLE BID

A S PART OF his 1953 parole bid, Leopold made two follow-up statements to the parole board suggesting he realized that he had failed to address two of the mysteries that, perhaps more than anything else, haunted everyone who knew the details of his crime. First: *who had actually struck the blow that killed Bobby Franks?* And second—the question that had never been satisfactorily answered by any of the reams of coverage and interpretation devoted to the case: *why had they done it?*

Jan. 14, 1953

Board of Pardon and Parole
Armory Building
Springfield, Ill.

Gentlemen:

Since my hearing before the Parole Board, January 8, I have read the argument of State's Attorney [John] Gutknecht, as published in the press.

In his fourth paragraph, Judge Gutknecht says:

"You notice that I do not mention even Loeb in the same class and all students of this case will know why I classify the dupe Loeb below these two in the enormity of their crimes and the degree of their responsibility."

Like Robert Crowe, GUTKNECHT had served as a judge before becoming state's attorney.

Again in his seventh paragraph, Judge Gutknecht speaks of Loeb as my "dupe." I was not asked at the hearing nor did it occur to me to speak of the individual degree of responsibility for the crime of my co-defendant Richard Loeb and myself for two reasons: first, I feel that, regardless which of us may have been the prime mover and regardless of which of us may have struck the actual blow, we are both equally guilty; and second, Richard Loeb is dead and so is unable to speak in his own defense. Further, I am very acutely conscious that it might well be presumed that whichever of us survived would attempt to shift the major portion of the blame to his dead companion. I realize, therefore, that any statement I might make would not carry much conviction.

Since, however, Judge Gutknecht has chosen, in direct contradiction to the facts, to impute the major responsibility to me, I hope you will consider it permissible for me to call your attention to the testimony on this point of the late Clarence Darrow, our lawyer at the trial.

In 1932, four years before Loeb's death, Mr. Darrow published a book entitled "The Story of My Life." When the book was published, Mr. Darrow could have had no idea whether Loeb or I would survive the other and could, therefore, have had no motive in helping the survivor.

On page 228, last paragraph, Mr. Darrow writes:

"It seemed that Loeb had gotten it into his head that he could commit a perfect crime, which should involve kidnapping, murder, and ransom. He unfolded his scheme to Leopold because he needed some one to help him plan and carry it out. For this plot Leopold had no liking whatever, but he had an exalted opinion of Loeb. Leopold was rather undersized; he could not excel in sports and games. Loeb was strong and athletic. [ . . .]

"Several times there was trouble between the boys about going on with their plan. At one time their correspondence, offered in evidence, and published by the press, revealed that they nearly reached the point of open breach, and extreme violence."

Page 229, next to last paragraph:

"One after another was surveyed by the boys in the car until poor Robert Franks came along. He was invited into the car for a ride; he got into the front seat with Leopold, who was driving; and within ten minutes he was hit on the head by a chisel in the hands of Loeb, was stunned by the blow, and soon bled to death."

Page 231, next to last paragraph:

"Leopold had not the slightest instinct toward what we are pleased to call crime. He had, and has, the most brilliant intellect I ever met in a boy. At eighteen he had acquired nine or ten languages; he was an advanced botanist; he was an authority on birds; he enjoyed good books. He was often invited to lecture before clubs and other assemblages; he was genial, kindly, and likable. His father was wealthy, and this son was his great pride. Every one prophesied an uncommon career for this gifted lad. He is now in prison for life and for the most foolish, most motiveless act that was ever conceived in a diseased brain by his boon companion.

"Leopold had scarcely seen Robert Franks before the fatal day. Loeb had played tennis with him and they were good friends."

Page 239, second paragraph:

"These boys, especially Loeb, had carried the phantasies usual in children into later youth. Loeb had read and studied detective stories since he was very young and had experimented a great deal as an amateur detective since childhood. The detective was always the hero of the stories that he read, and he conceived the idea that a perfect crime could be accomplished that would baffle for all time the real detectives and police. He had lived this dream for years."

Aside from myself—and my testimony would properly be suspected of bias—Mr. Darrow, as our lawyer, to whom both Loeb and I told our whole story, would be the best witness to the actual facts. In 1932, when Richard Loeb was still alive, Mr. Darrow could not be suspected of attempting to help the survivor. I trust you will weigh his testimony in this matter and, above all, I hope you will consider it justifiable on my part to call it to your attention.

Respectfully,
N. L. [hand-initialed]

## A BRILLIANT PRISONER

A rare public glimpse of Nathan Leopold at the age of 48, upon the denial of his parole bid in May 1953, conveyed mixed messages about how nearly three decades in prison might have changed him. He was still said to be an overachieving intellectual, with the May 15 *Chicago Daily Tribune* calling him a "brilliant prisoner" with a "working knowledge of more than a score of languages" and "an intelligence quotient, according to records, of 208—well above the genius level."

Nevertheless, psychiatrists and social workers were said to be "divided" on the question of whether he was fit for parole, and, in announcing the parole board's decision to deny him, the chairman said it was "debatable" whether he had been rehabilitated and that the board didn't think him "the right type of man to go back into society."

At Stateville Correctional Center, Leopold was said to have received the news unemotionally, saying, "I am naturally somewhat disappointed. I had hoped the board would see fit to parole me, but since it hasn't, I can accept its decision as gracefully as possible and hope that some time a board will feel my debt is paid."

And, in a second follow-up letter, Leopold addressed the question of "why?"

PAROLE AND PARDON BOARD
ARMORY BUILDING
SPRINGFIELD, ILL. May 8, 53

Gentlemen:

There are two reasons for my taking the liberty of addressing this letter to you. First, I want to thank you for granting me the privilege of appearing before you personally. That you should spare the time to give me the opportunity of adding to my testimony at the January hearing is an act of kindness which I appreciate deeply.

Second, after very long and careful reflection, I feel that I did not answer as adequately as I might have the question asked me by one of the Members—Mr. Buchwalter I believe. He asked whether, after the opportunity for reflection offered by my 29 years in prison, I could now explain what caused me to commit the crime. I answered that, although I had spent long hours in thinking about this question, I was still unable to advance any explanation that makes sense: that my crime was a completely motiveless, senseless, stupid act.

And that, gentlemen, is the sober truth. After all these years of thinking about it, I cannot assign a single motive or reason for what I did that makes sense even to me. There was just no reason. Mr. Darrow, in his closing argument, stressed the utter absence of motive, the utter senselessness of the act as giving evidence of my emotional immaturity. This is what I meant when, at my hearing in January, I testified that my crime was the senseless, brainless, damn fool act of an irresponsible and immature kid.

But this is very far, gentlemen, from saying that I am not bitterly sorry for the horrible thing that I did and for the enormous damage, grief and sorrow I caused. I have been, through all these years, and I am today bitterly regretful for what I did. I have repented earnestly and sincerely. Since about 1929, the day has not passed that I have not prayed for the repose of Bobby Franks' soul and, during their lifetime, for the lightening of the grief of his parents. The thought that I had cut off an innocent young life and the knowledge of the grief I had caused both his family and mine has been present in my consciousness every day of every year for the past quarter century. It is not, gentlemen, an easy thought to live with. At any time in the past 25 years, I would have welcomed joyously the chance to take Bobby Franks' place—to lay down my life if it would restore his.

But that, of course, is impossible; I cannot undo what I did. What little I have had the opportunity of doing by way of atonement and expiation I have, within my limitations, attempted to do. I have tried to conduct myself properly and to do what little I could to be helpful to others. It is pitifully little, of course, in comparison with the awful wrong I did; still, it represents all I could do and it has, at least, lightened a trifle the burden of my own conscience.

MR. BUCHWALTER: He means John M. Bookwalter, an attorney from Danville, Illinois, who was a member of the parole board. Leopold, who learned German at home as a child, is intuitively using the German spelling for "book."

I have hesitated, gentlemen, to speak of my repentance for what I have done; I can only hope and pray that you will not interpret this expression as a maudlin bid for sympathy—or worse, a calculated and motivated piece of special pleading. I stand before you in what is probably the most crucial moment of my life; you have the power and the obligation to decide whether to grant me the right to live out what remains of my life in the free world or to condemn me to drag out the remainder of my existence in prison. Do you wonder that I have hesitated long to mention how sorry I am for what I did, for fear that you might think that it is merely talk? By the very nature of the matter, my repentance and my desire to atone are not susceptible of proof. You have only my word for how bitterly sorry I am for what I have done. And how can I hope that you will believe my word when there is such tremendous motivation involved? It is so easy to <u>say</u> these things; everyone who appears before you must say that he is sorry—whether it is true or not. I can only hope that a careful consideration of my behavior over a period of 25 years and the opinions of those who have known me best during that time will give some support to my own word.

It is this fear, gentlemen—the fear that you might think, "Of course he'd say that," which has prevented me from speaking of my repentance before. But I feel that I cannot answer Mr. Buchwalter's [Bookwalter's] question properly without telling you how bitterly I regret the past. I still cannot give a single sensible reason for what I did; it still remains for me the completely motiveless act of a socially and emotionally immature boy; but I can assure you that remorse has been the daily companion of the man who grew out of that boy. It is my firm resolve, gentlemen, to devote the remainder of my life to atoning in some small measure for my terrible wrong. I pray God that you may find it in your hearts to make it possible for me to make what expiation I can in the world of free men.

# 72
# Nothing monstrous in his current bearing

## GERTZ MEETS LEOPOLD

Letter of Introduction ─────────────────────────────

May 13, 1957
Mr. Nathan F. Leopold, Jr.
9306 – D
1900 Collins Avenue
Joliet, Illinois

Dear Mr. Leopold:

Our mutual friend, Ralph Newman, has spoken to me about the various matters that you want me to handle for you, and I have several thoughts of my own that I want to take up with you.
    I am planning to visit with you this Thursday as early in the day as possible.
    For the moment there is no point in saying any more except to add that I knew and treasured your older brother, and I would regard it as a privilege to do anything of which he would approve.

Sincerely yours,
Elmer Gertz

NATHAN LEOPOLD'S BROTHER Mike (Foreman) died in November of 1953, six months after the parole attempt failed. The obituaries that appeared in the Chicago papers suggest he had succeeded, to some extent, in escaping the notoriety of his family. He was not identified in any way with the Leopold family or the notorious Nathan—only as a business executive and prominent "collector of Lincolniana." Still, there were those, including his good friend Elmer Gertz, who believed that all those years later, he was yet another collateral casualty of the events of 1924. "His heart impaired for years, he seemed to have been kept alive by the hope of seeing his brother out of prison," Gertz wrote in his memoir *A Handful of Clients*. "When that hope was thwarted, he died." According to Gertz, it was Ralph Newman, the bookdealer, who continued to press for Leopold's release and looked after his other interests, especially managing the publication of the memoir Leopold had been writing in prison.

    In the spring of 1957, Doubleday expressed interest in publishing the book, and Newman and Leopold decided they needed an attorney to consult on legal aspects of the book and several other matters about which Leopold was concerned. Gertz's notes on his first impressions of Leopold survive in his files as he first scrawled them on legal paper just after the meeting, and as they were neatly typed up by his secretary shortly afterwards. He used them nearly verbatim in the account he later published in *A Handful of Clients*—though the slight changes he made are microstories in themselves.

Notes on First Meeting with N.F.L., Jr.

Thursday, May 16, 1957 - from about 10:50 A.M. to 1:30 P.M.

From the first moment to last, we spoke with complete freedom. The only time a guard came near us was when I forgot the regulation and placed my hand and a paper too close to the glass partition.

He said that he wanted to see me because of what Ralph Newman said of me (that he would be "charmed" by me, that I would help, etc.) and because he knew how close I had been to his brother "Mike" and that he knew from various sources that I had a very great reputation, etc. He saw me on the Camera Two Darrow program quite accidentally. We talked about his brothers Mike and Sam, about "Bal," Ralph, Henry Steele (who has never communicated with him in any way although Steele had lived in his home), Arnold Maremont (his class-mate, who is still friendly), Bill Friedman (Do.), Abe Brown (about whose kindness he spoke with real feeling), Leigh and Jos. Block (his cousins), the Bachrachs ("whose sole qualifications as criminal lawyers is that they belonged to the Standard Club with my father"), Robert Hicks (who is a nut and is causing him a lot of embarrassment), Dickie Loeb ("the other fellow"), [Carl] Sandburg, Billy Graham, Lohman, [Adlai] Stevenson, the south side Jewish community generally, Warden [Joseph] Ragen, and many other persons and subjects. We had a long discussion of Darrow in which he confirmed that Darrow came into the case after the confession. He told a priceless story about Darrow's last visit with him. ("Is he still good?") We talked about his book and writing in general, religion, prison regulations, the parole situation, Meyer Levin and "Compulsion," the different matters he wanted me to look into, etc.

(This is only the barest account of all that was said by both of us. He had a little blue card on which he had typed some notes and I had one sheet of notes—hereto attached. He said that without seeing his card, I was actually discussing everything that he had in mind. He checked off each item and pressed me to make notes from time to time. I made more notes than I normally would, since I usually depend too much on memory.)

He was soft-spoken, highly articulate, polite, friendly, humorous and smiled most of the time. Occasionally, I had a feeling of posturing on his part, but only occasionally. He had more poise than I would have anticipated. Even in discussing the Bobby Franks kidnapping and murder, he was unself-conscious. He said, "The kidnapping and murder were a terrible crime and inexcusable. I won't try to defend them, because they are indefensible, but I will say nothing of them in my book. I am inflexible on that point." In referring to Loeb, he sometimes called him "the other fellow." I had the feeling that he had distasteful recollections of Loeb, although he did not say so. I also had the feeling that he thought Loeb more responsible for the crime, although he did not say so. Throughout the meeting and when I left, I could not get myself to believe that he was the monster who had murdered a youngster; for there was nothing monstrous in his present bearing.

STEVENSON: In 1949, during his term as governor of Illinois, Adlai Stevenson II had commuted Leopold's prison sentence, reducing it from "99 plus life" to 85 years, thus making him eligible for parole as of January 1953.

WARDEN [JOSEPH] RAGEN: The warden at Stateville Correctional Center, where Leopold had been incarcerated since being transferred from Joliet prison in 1925.

"BAL": A cousin who had grown up in the Leopold household and was considered by Leopold to be virtually another brother.

HENRY STEELE: Another cousin, though in 1962, when Leopold reviewed Gertz's manuscript for *A Handful of Clients* before its publication, he said Steele had not actually grown up in his house. The name was omitted in the published version.

ARNOLD MAREMONT: Maremont had been one of the law students in Leopold's study group who was rounded up by the police before Leopold confessed in order to confront him with the fact that the "dope sheets" had been typed up on an Underwood portable typewriter that Leopold professed not to own.

BILL FRIEDMAN: The attorney who had handled the first parole attempt.

ABE BROWN: Abel Brown, the friend with whom Leopold had planned to sail to Europe in the summer of 1924.

BACHRACHS: The Bachrach brothers, Walter and Benjamin, had represented him and Loeb along with Clarence Darrow at the sentencing hearing— apparently not very impressively, in his opinion; in the published book they were referred to only as "certain persons," not by name.

ROBERT HICKS: An attorney who had once been a law clerk for Darrow. Hicks had made an unsolicited and, Leopold felt, damaging appearance at the 1953 parole hearing.

Through Newman, the poet Carl Sandburg (standing) had become very interested in Leopold's parole case and contributed a testimonial to the parole effort saying he felt Leopold should be freed. Elmer Gertz is seated at center, seen in profile.

After a discussion of the details of the book deal he wanted to negotiate, with Newman as his agent, the talk turns to the subject of *Compulsion*, the novel Meyer Levin had published the previous year, which was closely based on the Leopold and Loeb case. Leopold knew Levin, who had been a University of Chicago student with him; in fact, when word had gotten out that Levin wanted to write about Leopold and Loeb, Newman had suggested that he work with Leopold on a nonfiction account of the case, but after driving out to prison to discuss the project with Leopold, Levin was disappointed that he refused to consider writing about the actual murder in his book. (As a sidenote, author Hal Higdon, who later interviewed Levin for his book *Leopold and Loeb: The Crime of the Century*, reports that Levin later found out that the Leopold family chauffeur who had driven him out to Stateville for this visit was Sven Englund—the same man whose testimony had blown Leopold's alibi to bits in 1924 and forced him to confess to the murder; the family was still employing him 20 years later.) Leopold, in turn, decided to cooperate with the *Saturday Evening Post* on an exclusive nonfiction account of his life in prison, and Levin decided to go ahead with his own book, which became an instant best seller. He was at the time at work on a theatrical and a film version, and Leopold was afraid that Levin's various portrayals of him and the story would doom any chance he still had at gaining parole.

Compulsion. He is not supposed to have read the book, but actually he read it <u>four</u> times. I am to get permission officially to send him a copy, so that we can discuss it openly. He says the trial itself is handled accurately, but he has distaste, bitterness and resentment about the rest. He says that Levin invents things, charging him with other crimes that he did not actually commit. He resents the references to homosexuality. He would like if possible to get an injunction against the book, play, movie, TV, damages, special concessions as to contents of movie, drama, TV, so that no harm will be done him. He thinks that Levin wrote the Coronet article urging parole out of a guilty feeling. Compulsion has harmed him. I am to study the situation and advise him.

Handling of money. N.F.L. wants something set up which will give him the indicia and general feeling of controlling his money that may come in. He thinks that there should be an account in his name, with Ralph or I or both of us having the power of attorney for withdrawals, subject to revocation. He is skeptical about a trust or any complicated arrangement. He recognizes that it is best not to have the account with the penitentiary, because of prying eyes, etc. I am to work out something and let him know.

Parole. He does not entertain much hope for the present application which comes up in July. Attorney Varian B. Adams (30 No. LaSalle) is handling it. If it fails, as he anticipates, then he will want me to take care of all future efforts. He wants me to remind Ralph to get letter from [Carl] Sandburg to [Illinois Governor William] Stratton. He wants me to write letter to Stratton care of Adams. He also wants me to get Rabbi Isserman to write. He says that it will take something truly dramatic, imaginative, and resourceful, nothing routine, to get him out. In this connection he read a proposed letter to Billy Graham, which I am to discuss further.

Fees. To avoid trouble later, he wants clear understanding as to fees. This visit, I told him, was just a friendly get-together. By next time I can be more definite. Fees are to be considered (a) for his book alone, (b) for his book and Compulsion, and (c) for his book, Compulsion and Parole.

This is the barest outline of our conversation.

COMPULSION: Gertz wrote in his memoir *A Handful of Clients* that it was against prison regulations for Leopold to obtain the book.

In the published version, RESENTS was changed to "was hurt by."

This proposed LETTER TO BILLY GRAHAM was never sent.

# 73

# The correction of the century

## THE 1957 CLEMENCY HEARING

AS ELMER GERTZ mentioned in his notes about meeting Leopold in May of 1957 (see chapter 72, page 267), an attorney named Varian B. Adams was already handling Leopold's attempt to get released from prison, which was an application for clemency.[1] With the hearing scheduled for July 9, time was too short for Gertz to get deeply involved in the logistics, but he did appear at the hearing along with Adams and was listed on the official roster as "Attorney's Friend." Though this appeal was, as Leopold expected, also unsuccessful, his supporters were exhilarated afterwards, feeling that momentum was building in his favor. Some of the most powerful statements at the hearing came from Leopold's old friend Abel Brown and from Meyer Levin, who appeared (over Gertz's objections) in order to insist that nothing about his book *Compulsion* suggested that Leopold should not be released. Their testimony illustrates how the narrative of Leopold was being reshaped: to separate him from his conjoined status with Richard Loeb in the popular imagination, and to transform him—as Levin put it—from a symbol of "the crime of the century" into a symbol of "the correction of the century." Here is Abel Brown's testimony:

**MR. GERTZ:** [Abel Brown] has been in the real estate business in downtown Chicago for thirty-two years, except for two and a half years when he was an instructor in the Air Force Officers Candidate School. He was a classmate of Leopold and kept in touch with him throughout the years and he has a story to tell you. Mr. Brown:

**MR. BROWN:** I have come here, gentlemen, to help my friend, Nathan Leopold if I can. I have come here because I feel his record in prison merits all the help any one of his friends can give him. I have come here as well because I feel I can be helpful to you in putting the life of Nathan Leopold into focus so that you can determine whether or not it is safe to recommend commutation to the Governor.

There has been a great misconception about Leopold and Loeb in the minds of the public, in the minds of a good many people they have been thought of as one individual. That is not true. They were totally different as youngsters. Their life patterns have been totally different. Loeb was a leader, aggressive, crafty, smart. Leopold was definitely a follower. Loeb induced Leopold to make the tragic mistake of his life. He misled him into committing the dreadful crime that has ruined his life. That single misstep—the single misstep in his entire lifetime—a lifetime that has been a good one other than for that great and dreadful error, was made because as a youngster he was a lonely kid. His mother had died. He sought friendship from whoever he could get it from. That misstep has caused Leopold to fall into a pit. A pit that is as black as life can make it—a lifetime in prison. He is crying out now at the

---

1 Under his original sentence, Leopold was not eligible for parole, but in 1949 Governor Adlai Stevenson had commuted the original sentence to 85 years, making him eligible for parole in 1953. Having been denied at his first parole bid, and then further denied in his request for another hearing two years after that, Leopold was now requesting clemency a second time, either in the form of immediate release or a further reduction in his sentence to 64 years, improving his chances of an imminent parole.

end of his life for help. If you gentlemen and the Governor don't give it to him now you will cut the heart out of him and he will rot and die in prison.

I knew both boys well. Loeb was a fraternity brother of mine [at the University of Chicago]. I had lunch with him every day and many evenings. He was a very handsome boy, athletic and a ladies man, but beneath that handsome exterior there was an arrogance, a sadistic streak. There was an interest in crime and crime stories, the only subject he wanted to read and discuss with anyone he could get hold of, there was a sick mind. I felt and others who knew him felt he was a bad apple.

How about Leopold? He was a quiet, studious, serious, very gentle boy. He was very anxious for friendship. His brothers and his father were interested in business and much older than himself. I know he sought my friendship. We were going to Europe together as a matter of fact.

Jack Long and Leopold and I, a few fellows, had a small discussion group. We met on Sunday evenings. There was David Shipman, a Chicago Attorney, Jack Long, Leopold and myself. We got to know him awfully well. I can assure you that a nicer kid has never lived than Nathan Leopold. All of us have maintained our friendship with him through out the years because we knew when the crime was committed that Leopold and Loeb were not one. They were totally different individuals and their record in prison has borne that out.

I mean no disrespect for the dead when I told you that Loeb died as he lived, a violent death. Leopold has matured intellectually. The dreadful crime he was led into committing was not conceived by him. It was not committed by him. Loeb needed him because he needed a car and he needed a driver and he sensed that this kid was so fascinated by him that he could be intimidated into going along on the dreadful adventure that ended in the death of a little boy.

The State of Illinois believes, I am sure, that rehabilitation as well as punishment is an important part of the State's penal system. The State of Illinois penal system, its correspondence school, has been copied and has served as a model for nineteen other State Prisons. That correspondence school was founded and developed and built by Nathan Leopold.

The Malaria Experiment we all know about was initiated at Stateville to serve an extremely important purpose. Our troops in the South Seas were dying of malaria. There was no known cure that could reach them and help them. The doctors took what they believed might be a cure to Stateville. It had never been tried on a human and Leopold was one of the first to bare his arms to the Anopheles mosquito, and thereafter he served as technician on the project and as a devoted nurse to help bring through some of those men who didn't have the will to live when they got that fever of 107 and 108. They would call Leopold and he would stay with them as long as 48 hours if necessary to bring them through. No lives were lost in that experiment.

I have a letter here from Professor William F. Byron, who is Professor of Sociology at Northwestern University. He tells me that this Board, in its compassion for prisoners who have observed the rules, who have been good inmates, that this Board has seen fit in its consideration for them, has seen fit to parole within a three year period, 133 men convicted of murder.

My question is this: were these men younger or older than Leopold? He was 19. He had never committed a crime before. This crime was a single aberration. Were any of these men better prisoners than Leopold? Were they more helpful in furthering the cause of other prisoners? Did they serve a longer time than Leopold? If that is not true, if the answer to those questions is no, then I feel that in simple justice, Nathan Leopold's sentence should be commuted now. It is not fair to cause him to remain in prison any longer. He has been punished. What can he do? What is it possible for him to do to indicate that he has wanted to make amends for his crime? He has lived a lifetime as a prisoner.

No man in the penal system of the United States has done more for other prisoners. Leopold asked for mercy. As a citizen of this State I ask for justice and I think your recommendation, without question, to the Governor, should be that he give serious consideration to commutation.

JOSEPH CARPENTIER was a member of the parole board who ask questions in this section, along with John Bookwalter, J.F. Novotny, R.J. Branson, and Parole Board Chairman Franklin Stransky.

**MR. CARPENTIER:** Mr. Brown, you describe Loeb as a sadistic, reckless sort of person. At what point in your association with him did you discover that?

**MR. BROWN:** I can answer that. In college fraternities there is a practice known as "Hell Week". It is a kids practice, but the practice has been continued because it is a lot of fun and it is done in fun, but not with Loeb. When Loeb paddled a freshman he would force him to the opposite wall with the blows he would hit.

If you want another story, these are kids stories. I don't know how important they are. One winter evening about two o'clock in the morning, I was awakened by a commotion, in my bedroom, and the sound of running water, and there was Loeb dead drunk. I saw there was a freshman and he was running a tub of water in the bathroom. I said to Loeb, "what's this all about?" Loeb said, "Well, this blankety-blank freshman forgot to say sir to me and I am having him run a tub of ice water so it will never happen again." I told him if he didn't get out in a hurry and get his clothes on in a hurry he would be the guy in the tub. He left.

All fraternity groups have a bad apple. Unfortunately the worm crawled over to Leopold and he made the only mistake in his life going along with Loeb, as Loeb needed a driver and needed a car, and this impressionable boy was talked into going along with him.

**MR. CARPENTIER:** You feel then, that this crime would have been perpetrated if Leopold had never existed?

**MR. BROWN:** I feel he would have secured someone else. Loeb was a pathological liar. He had every bad quality that a kid can exhibit and I knew him well for over a year.

**MR. CARPENTIER:** Was Loeb a member of the discussion group you had?

**MR. BROWN:** No. His only interest was his preoccupation with crime stories and crime mechanisms. He read them constantly and the only discussion he was interested in having with you was working out a criminal plot and trying to determine what to do to fool the authorities.

**MR. CARPENTIER:** Now in your discussion group, what were the theories on the part of Leopold?

**MR. BROWN:** Like all youngsters, we discussed the group discussions of the times—war, freedom, liberty.

**MR. CARPENTIER:** Did he talk about crime?

**MR. BROWN:** No, Leopold's reactions to the philosophies we discussed were very much along the lines as ours. There was no aberration on his part to indicate he believed he was a superman. On the contrary, he was a quiet kid. His interest was in birds. He was regarded as a very fine ornithologist.

**MR. CARPENTIER:** To you did he exhibit any tendencies toward Nietzscheism?

**MR. BROWN:** That was strictly a figment of a reporter's mind, because it seemed to strike the public in a very interesting fashion. "Here is a fellow that regards himself as a superman". That is not true at all regarding Leopold.

**MR. CARPENTIER:** In your association with Loeb, did he ever express anything along that line?

**MR. BROWN:** Loeb was only interested in crime. I was never able to determine any other interest in that kid's mind. If you were willing to sit down with him and discuss a crime situation he was delighted. I figured he was a sham. His handsome exterior, his good appearance, belied his inner-self.

**MR. CARPENTIER:** It is difficult for me to understand—you said you had lunch with him every day?

**MR. BROWN:** As fraternity members it was required that we eat meals together. I knew both of them well, and I can assure you that the same thing could happen to one of my youngsters, and perhaps to one of your youngsters, if that youngster was impressionable, to be misled by a kid he regards as being pretty good.

**MR. BOOKWALTER:** How long did these two boys know each other?

**MR. BROWN:** I don't think they had much contact with each other before the death of Mrs. Leopold. I think after that Leopold was very lonely and needed friendship.

**MR. BOOKWALTER:** How long would you say they knew each other? Four - five - six - seven years?

**MR. BROWN:** No, I'd say three or four years.

**MR. BOOKWALTER:** Now, you deducted this Loeb, as you describe him, to be a bad apple?

**MR. BROWN:** Without question.

**MR. BOOKWALTER:** Didn't you think Leopold had the same opportunity of discovering that fact?

**MR. BROWN:** He once told me he was an evil influence, that he had the wrong ideas, but I think he was fascinated by him because Leopold was a homely kid and Loeb was tall and handsome. He had flash, style and glamour, and I think that Leopold was flattered right off his feet by the fact that Loeb was willing to go out with him and give him attention, because Leopold was a homely little kid and very quiet, very reserved, very shy.

**MR. BOOKWALTER:** What about the fact they hadn't been in any trouble? There was some trouble before, wasn't there?

**MR. BROWN:** I think the record indicates Loeb had been in trouble but not with Leopold. I think if you will read a transcript of their interviews with doctors, you will find that, in the doctors' opinions, Leopold had gone along on this single adventure and was not involved in other crimes either that they believed that Loeb might have been. One doctor points out that in his opinion, that the crime was conceived, planned, and carried out and the actual killing was on the part of Loeb.

**MR. BOOKWALTER:** Was Leopold a fraternity man?

**MR. BROWN:** No, he was not. There was no fraternity hostility, he was just a shy kid.

**MR. BOOKWALTER:** Did he come over to the house and eat lunch?

**MR. BROWN:** On several occasions, yes.

**MR. BOOKWALTER:** Did Loeb bring him there?

**MR. BROWN:** No, he was there as my guest. As a matter of fact, Loeb objected to my bringing him. It was my home at the time and I told him it was my privilege to bring a guest, but he did object.

**MR. BRANSON:** Are you acquainted with the records in this case, the previous statement of facts?

**MR. BROWN:** Yes, sir.

**MR. BRANSON:** The trial?

**MR. BROWN:** Yes, sir, I have read it. I have read the transcript of the records and I have read Leopold's petition for clemency.

**MR. BRANSON:** Don't you think it is fair to the public that your statement you made here this morning does not agree with the facts in this case?

**MR. BROWN:** To what extent?

**MR. BRANSON:** To a great extent.

**MR. BROWN:** Could you be more specific?

**MR. BRANSON:** Yes. According to the facts in this case Leopold was just as aggressive as Loeb.

**MR. BROWN:** I would dispute that, and if you read Mr. Darrow's book you will find that is not so.

**MR. BRANSON:** We only have the record to go by.

**MR. BROWN:** I think if you will go over the medical history, medical testimony, you will find that that is not true. In the very nature of the two people, because I knew them as well as the inside of my hand, that one was the leader and the other was the follower, and I think that was indicated. I think Leopold was intimidated. I think that Loeb actually intimidated him into going along. Thank you.

ON THE PART OF LOEB: Brown is wrong here. The Hulbert-Bowman Report in fact said that Leopold had participated with Loeb in a whole series of escalating crimes, that in fact they began to plan the kidnap/murder scheme on the night they were driving home to Chicago together from burglarizing Loeb's former fraternity in Ann Arbor. It is true, however, that two of the three psychiatrists who testified for the defense at the sentencing hearing said Loeb had told them he had wielded the chisel, and the third one guessed that he had (see chapter 55, page 195).

Here is Meyer Levin's testimony:

**MR. GERTZ:** The Board may have seen in the May issue of Coronet Magazine an article entitled "Leopold Should Be Freed!" by Meyer Levin. I would like to offer that in evidence, that issue of the magazine, and we are proud to have here today the author of that article. He is also the author of the best selling book, "Compulsion", based on the crime of Leopold and Loeb. I think what he has to say is of peculiar interest to this Board and to the public.

**MR. LEVIN:** Gentlemen: I was attracted to the story of this subject after all these years because I felt that, not only my point of view might have matured, but the whole way of thinking of the public in our time, the greater spirit of forgiveness, would indicate new values to be read into the crime, and if studied in the light of today instead of that time of hysteria, our thinking might be changed, so I undertook that study.

I wrote "Compulsion" as a close parallel to the Leopold and Loeb case. I didn't write it as a crusade to Leopold. I wrote it as a study.

I was interested after it was published to receive the many letters in which people asked me which side I took, which side I was standing on. I was glad to see that my objective stand had been realized.

After so many of these questions I decided that I would state my views in Coronet. After Leopold had said in his article in Life Magazine that my book had injured his chances for parole, I particularly felt that my personal views should be stated, hence, the article in Coronet.

In connection with this novel I have, since the publication, had the opportunity to amass a body of efforts that I think is unique with me, that is, reactions to the novel. I have been astonished at the letters that have come to me, letters as the result of the publication of the novel, the article in Coronet, and my lectures all over the country. They have exhibited first—intelligent interest in this crime, sincere interest. I have repeatedly stated that Leopold was the victim of public opinion and to release him would be to release a flood of public protest. I believe public opinion has changed. I have lectured before mother's groups, ladies' groups, church groups, small towns, big cities. I have lectured in Chicago, Philadelphia, Cincinnati, and Cleveland, all over, and I have found an almost uniform reaction. After my lecture, people begin discussions of crime and parole. I would say ninety percent of them are in favor of parole or commutation on an intelligent basis. They say that if this was the crime of the century let us say, this would be an example of correction of the century. This man who became the symbol of crime can be the symbol of correction.

I was particularly astonished when mothers would rise in his defense. They would study the psychiatric views and they would say, now, we know some of the signs and if this case would occur today, we could detect it in our own children and prevent such a thing, and if signs of loneliness could have been detected in this small boy in time, and he had been given therapy in his case, if not Loeb's, he might have been rehabilitated.

This article was the kind of article which stimulates argument. I expected a flood of letters saying no, don't release him. On the contrary, again the same as in my lectures, over ninety percent were favorable to parole. In many cases they were deep and passionate letters, and these are all voluntary letters.

I have felt that a new chance for this man would be a great symbol of the advance in public thinking. The very fact it is a case that has attracted great public attention and will continue to attract attention, should serve for his release as the advance that has been made during this thirty-years in our thinking.

I know that while you are experts, it is always interesting to know the feeling of the public. When I called that the "crime of our century" in this book, I didn't say the "crime of the century". I said "our century". It is a crime that exemplified the spirit that led to the second World War. They were factors of the general thinking of that time. I believe that Leopold has shown that he has gone far beyond that thinking and has great humanity. Thank you.

**MR. CARPENTIER:** When you completed your novel "Compulsion", at that time did you have a fixed opinion of this case?

**MR. LEVIN:** I didn't make this a crusade, a novel for his release. I made it an objective study and withheld my opinion, and people couldn't tell from the book how I felt about his release. That was my plan, and apparently I attained it for I received a flood of letters from people all over the country asking my opinion of the case.

**MR. CARPENTIER:** I had read your book and thought maybe I had missed the point. At that time you had no opinion?

**MR. LEVIN:** No, I had the opinion that I felt the reader should make up his own mind. As an example, in Highland Park [Illinois] I was giving a lecture and in the audience was a young niece of the Franks family. After the lecture she came to me and she said "In our family we have always hated these boys. After I read your book, I felt also that this man should be paroled."

I would like to refer to a statement of Mr. Brown that even today after this length of time, the two men are always associated together. Perhaps it has to do with the alliteration in names—Leopold and Loeb. Very often today we stumble and say "Leopold" when we mean "Loeb". It makes it very difficult. They were completely different personalities. I can confirm what Mr. Brown said, that Loeb was aggressive. The word he used was criminalistic, and Leopold was not criminalistic, Leopold could never have become a criminal but for the influence of Loeb.

**MR. CARPENTIER:** Wasn't your book "Compulsion" actually on the basis that it took two people to commit this crime? Singly it could never have been committed?

**MR. LEVIN:** Singly, no. If he hadn't found Leopold, he would have found somebody else, but Leopold wasn't looking for someone with whom he could commit a crime. I don't think his participation could be called on the aggressive side.

# 74
# I have gotten over being nineteen

## THE 1958 PAROLE BID

ONCE THE CLEMENCY bid failed, Gertz promptly followed Governor William Stratton's advice that Leopold apply for a parole rehearing, and the Illinois parole board granted this request. At this point, Gertz was fully in charge of Leopold's legal interests, and he threw himself wholeheartedly into the preparation of the case, sparing no time or effort to solicit testimonials from celebrities (Carl Sandburg, the poet, and Erle Stanley Gardner, the writer who created the character Perry Mason, were staunch champions), former University of Chicago Law School classmates of Leopold's, religious officials, psychiatric and social-work professionals—and, cunningly, veterans of the original prosecution in the case.

Gertz's chance encounter one day during a routine court matter with John Sbarbaro—at the time of the encounter, a judge, but who in 1924 had been an assistant state's attorney for Robert Crowe, and who had obtained the confession from Richard Loeb—led to Sbarbaro's offer to testify on Leopold's behalf. Gertz also pursued evidence that a nun who had cared for Judge John Caverly during an illness in his old age said he had told her that he had always considered Loeb to be the guiltier of the two boys. But some of the most interesting testimony generated by this hearing were the statements by Leopold himself. By 1958 he had been sensationalized, analyzed, and fictionalized many times over in the public imagination—which included, of course, the officers of the parole board.

The famous Alfred Hitchcock film *Rope*, released in 1948, had begun life as a stage production in London in 1929; then in 1956 came the novel *Compulsion* by Meyer Levin—a University of Chicago contemporary of Leopold and Loeb's—which was produced in 1957 as a play and, at the time of the parole hearing, was also in development as a film. Though Levin had gone out of his way to testify for Leopold at his recent clemency hearing, Leopold would later sue him for character defamation. It was clear to Gertz that in order to make this effort successful, the "real" Leopold needed to speak forcefully on his own behalf.

Ironically, the several surviving drafts of Leopold's formal statement show how heavily Gertz coached him to hit the proper notes in articulating his motive for the crime and expressing his remorse. Both the formal and informal remarks Leopold makes to the board on February 5, 1958, offer insight into what he was like as, in his own self-description, "a fat, middle-aged man." After all these years, he could distance himself from Nietzsche, but he could still not—quite—distance himself from Loeb.

Unlike the previous attempts, this parole bid proved successful: On February 20, 1958, the five-man parole board ordered that Nathan Leopold be "immediately" paroled. The board issued no statement about its reasoning, but it appeared that, just as Clarence Darrow's intervention in the original case had saved Leopold and Loeb from hanging, the intervention of another superbly talented attorney had finally won his freedom. Through his clever coaching, sage advising, and canny instinct for public relations, Gertz had reshaped the narrative about Leopold in the public mind, as one of the great penal rehabilitation stories of the twentieth century.

Here is Leopold's statement to the parole board:

## SOCIETY CANNOT AND SHOULD NOT DEAL LENIENTLY

At the parole hearing in February of 1958, along with the parade of friendly witnesses attesting to Nathan Leopold's rehabilitation under the coaching of attorney Elmer Gertz, there was to be one more confrontation with a state's attorney who continued to see Leopold as a menace to society.

Shortly before Leopold himself entered the packed room, State's Attorney Benjamin S. Adamowski read a statement opposing freedom for Leopold—*ever*.

"It is my honest conviction," said Adamowski, according to the February 6 *Chicago Daily Tribune*, "that as to crimes as senseless and heinous as this—murder, if you please—society cannot and should not deal leniently with the perpetrators. Particularly must society deal harshly where the crime is as calculated and as cold-bloodedly executed as was this one."

Gertz then challenged Adamowski, asking if he thought that Leopold's "33 years of good works in prison" should be ignored. Adamowski said that Leopold's celebrity, and the huge amount of attention paid to the case over the years, was a significant factor in the way the case had played out.

"If it had not been for the fact of all this attention, you might get an entirely different concept," Adamowski said.

Gentlemen:

It isn't possible to compress into a few minutes the thoughts and feelings of 33 years and some months. Especially if those years have been spent in prison. For here we have long hours to think—to think painfully, to regret bitterly, and to repent fervently.

I have given a lot of those hours to trying to understand how I could have taken part in the horrible crime of which Richard Loeb and I were guilty. I can't explain it to my own satisfaction; perhaps it can't be explained fully to anyone's satisfaction. But I can give you the few facts and impressions that have come out of my thinking. Believe me, I have been trying desperately to fathom the situation. I shall never give up the effort.

I admired Richard Loeb extravagantly—beyond all bounds. I literally lived and died on his approval or disapproval. I would have done anything he wanted—even when I knew he was wrong; even when I was revolted by what he suggested. And he wanted very badly to commit this crime. Why, I can't be sure. Surely it was mad, irrational. It may have been some kind of juvenile protest, an overwhelming desire to show that he could do it—and get away with it. I am afraid that young people don't always act sanely. Certainly we didn't. He had spent years reading detective stories, and acting the parts of both detective and criminal. He admitted to a number of delinquencies.

I had no wish to do this dreadful thing. Quite the opposite; it was repugnant to me. For weeks and weeks—until only a day or two before the crime—I was sure we would never go through with it. That it was something we would talk about and plan, but never actually carry through. Loeb made certain that we would commit this mad act. I didn't, couldn't stop him.

And then it was too late. I couldn't back out of the plan without being a quitter. And without losing Loeb's friendship. Hard as it is for me now to understand it, these seemed more important to me at that time than a young boy's life. True, Loeb did the actual killing, but that does not exonerate me.

Where were my defenses? Where was my moral strength, my conscience? This is the point I wish I could explain, even to myself. The only thing that bears on it that long thinking has produced is that my growth and development were unnatural. I was bright, and yet undeveloped. I thought like a grown-up person, and felt like an undeveloped infant.

At school I had no trouble at all; I learned easily. I was several years ahead of the kids my age: I entered college at 15. The result was that I was always with boys three or four years older than I. What a difference three or four years can make at that age.

With school studies—with what you learn from books—I had no trouble. But what you learn from people—from your friends—I missed entirely. My emotional development was at least five years behind. In some respects, I hadn't then developed at all emotionally. I was like an intelligent savage, knowing no restraints, no law except my own elementary desires. You might say that I skipped entirely the early 'teens. And with that skip I lost the growth of personality and character that go with it. My emotions—the feeling side of me didn't catch up with the thinking side of me until I had been in prison five years, and I was shocked by the fact that I hadn't felt things deeply earlier. From that time on, I began to live for others as well as myself.

This doesn't explain much; I wish to God I could explain more. But it is all that has come from years of thinking about it. I shall never cease thinking about it, never cease trying to explain. On the one hand I was overwhelmingly attracted to Loeb—with the violence and lopsidedness that only extreme youth can know. On the other,

I had missed entirely the character growth that normally takes place in the early teens; I did not have the moral strength or understanding to resist.

When my emotions did mature, when I was about 25, remorse for what I had done set in. Maybe the more strongly because it was late in developing. It has never left me since—not for a single day. It is with me constantly.

How can I hope to describe that remorse to you. To understand it, a man would have to have experienced it—to have done something as horrible as I did and to have repented. You can't possibly picture it! I can't describe it.

Certainly it is the strongest emotion I have ever had. It is with me constantly. Sometimes it is in the front of my mind so that I can think of nothing else. But even when my mind is occupied with other problems, it is always there, in a corner of my mind. It tinges my thinking all day, every day.

If you've stolen something, you can return it or work to pay its owner back. Even if you have injured someone physically, you can try to make it up to him. But if, like me, you have participated in the taking of a human life, what is there you can do to atone? You cannot bring the victim back to life. It is not easy to live with murder on your conscience! The fact that you didn't do the actual killing yourself does not make it any easier.

The final sentence of this paragraph was actually contributed by Gertz, clearly scrawled in his handwriting on the draft he reviewed, among his many other suggestions.

The only thing I have found in all these years that helps at all is to try to be useful to others. There aren't many opportunities here in prison to help others. What few I have been able to find, I have tried my best to employ: the correspondence school, for instance, and the malaria project. To them I have given my best effort. For it is when I have been able to be useful in a minor way that I have been happiest—or, at least, least unhappy. It is chiefly because I hope that in the free world I can be of some use to other people that I pray that you will see your way clear to giving me that opportunity.

One suggestion has been made that horrifies me. It is that if you order my release I spend my time in lecturing—on juvenile delinquency, or the causes of crime. Gentlemen, I shudder at the thought. I am not an expert on anything. I will be very fortunate to be able to make my own way. I certainly am not capable of lecturing to others.

And I wince at the thought of trading on my notoriety. If I am so supremely fortunate as to be given my liberty, I want only to find a modest niche where I can attain anonymity, where I can sink from sight and live humbly and modestly. Above all, where I can be useful. I am fortunate in having offers of jobs which will give me just that chance.

All I want is to get away from the spotlight, to live honorably and modestly, to do what I can to atone for my crime by usefulness to others.

Gentlemen, you see before you not the arrogant, conceited, smart-alecky boy of 19 who came to prison. I am a broken old man, who humbly begs for your compassion. Christianity can, I think, be called the religion of the second chance. It teaches repentance, atonement, and forgiveness. How I hope that you can find it in your hearts to give me that second chance.

What I want most in life is the opportunity to prove to you and to the people of Illinois and of America what I know in my own heart to be true: that I can and will become a decent, self-respecting, law-abiding citizen. To have the chance to find redemption by usefulness to others.

It is for that chance that I humbly beg.

After Leopold delivers his prepared statement, members of the board begin questioning him about what, specifically, he planned to do if paroled, and about other topics of interest to them. Here are his remarks to the parole board:

**Q** What about your religious beliefs today?

**[MR. LEOPOLD:] A** I am a practicing, believing Jew.

**Q** In other words you have given up this philosophy of Nietzsche?

**A** I never had the philosophy of Nietzsche.

**Q** There have been some statements about that. What is your philosophy today, tell me about your religion, what do you believe in?

**A** I believe in the existence of one God, the Creator of the World. I believe He has given us the laws and Commandments through Moses on Mt. Sinai. I believe the essential part of the moral law is summed up in the Ten Commandments. I believe in the trials and laws of my religion, faith, Judaism. I studied art in this prison, learned Hebrew.

Are there any specific questions I can answer?

**Q** That answers the question pretty well. You have gotten over this super–

**A** I have gotten over being nineteen.

**Q** Super ego that prevailed in you.

**A** Many years ago.

**MR. CARPENTIER:** Actually didn't you have some discussions with Father Weir concerning the philosophy of Nietzsche; didn't you argue that with him in your early incarceration?

**A** I don't remember, I have had a number of philosophical discussions with Father Weir in the 20's, I don't remember discussing Nietzsche with him.

Actually I don't know much about Nietzsche. I know in general I have read the history of philosophy in which the subject is outlined, but I am not a follower.

**Q** You had the study of Nietzsche previous to your incarceration, while going to school?

**A** I took a course or two in general philosophy and he must have been mentioned. I know of the theory but never read a book by him. [. . .]

**MR. BOOKWALTER: Q** One question: When was Dick Loeb, when did he die here?

**[MR. LEOPOLD:] A** January 28, 1936.

**Q** And in these articles in the [Chicago] Daily News I think you said on that day when he died you lost the greatest pal you had ever known.

**A** And also the worst enemy.

**Q** What is your feeling on that today? Here is a fellow takes you down and some years later, twelve years later, you still have the same feeling; is that true or not?

**A** Mr. Bookwalter, my feeling is very amphibolant [should be "ambivalent"] about the thing. I would not repudiate that now. Dick Loeb was a living contradiction. In many ways he was not only a charm person, but had great character traits, in spite of everything. It is unbelievable almost to me. I don't see how you could understand it, not having known the man, but Dick had a lot of good in him. Certainly he was the

FATHER ELIGIUS WEIR was the chaplain at Joliet when Leopold first arrived. Leopold developed a genuinely close relationship with him.

cause of my downfall. Certainly he was the worst enemy I ever had. He lost me my life, still he was the best pal I ever had. Is that understandable?

**Q** I can't understand how he would be the best pal you ever had.

**A** I mean here in prison he was, for instance, he showed his devotion to the school. He was not all bad. Perhaps nobody is all bad. His loyalty, I think he would have been loyal to the end. How can I repudiate him otherwise now the man is dead.

**MR. BRANSON:** One other question. He went to his death claiming you struck the final blow [that] killed Franks, and you say the contrary; how do you reconcile that?

**A** You say [Loeb] went to his death claiming I struck the final blow. Certainly that is the last remark he made, but that was made in 1924, twelve years earlier. The question had not arisen in the last twelve years of his life. There is no question about it now. There is the testimony of Dr. Glick [should be "Dr. Glueck"] the psychiatrist, who examined both of us. Loeb told him he struck the blow and Dr. Glick, under oath testified that he told him. There is Mr. Darrow's full story of my life published in 1932, ⟶ four years before Loeb's death, when Mr. Darrow wrote it he could not have known who would be the survivor. He says unequivocally that Loeb struck the blow. My word would amount to little but it is all in supporting evidence.

MR. DARROW'S FULL STORY: Clarence Darrow's book entitled *The Story of My Life*, not Darrow's account of Leopold's life.

**Q** How would he know?

**A** How would Darrow know?

**Q** No, the doctor.

**A** Because Dick told him, that is what he testified to.

**MR. BOOKWALTER:** You have no idea of publishing anything in the book, have you?

**A** No, sir.

**MR. CARPENTIER:** In your opening remarks you said you did not think this crime would be accomplished two days before it was?

**A** That's right.

**Q** And you made some statements you tried to dissuade Loeb from going through with it, tell us about that.

**A** I delayed the thing. I was to leave for Europe a little over a week after the crime actually took place. I had been trying to put off the date of the commission for several months by interposing objections, by suggesting this was not well enough worked out, we ought to try this. I had an idea, terribly heroic, the thing would never come to a head. It was one of those things [that] was a thing to talk about, to plan a thing, to be serious about it but it would not actually happen. Apparently that was not Loeb's idea.

When we were in a couple of days of the crime, I again suggested putting it off and he was firm about it, this was it.

**MR. CARPENTIER:** Actually this crime would have been perpetrated if up to Loeb alone but you were putting him off?

**A** Yes, sir.

**Q** And you claim the attraction you had for Loeb got you into this thing?

**A** Yes, sir.

**MR. CARPENTIER:** That is all.

# 75
# Say what you damn please

## THE PAROLE YEARS IN PUERTO RICO, 1958–1963

### From Leopold to Gertz

Castaner, P.R.
Sunday
Mar. 16, 1958

Dear Elmer,

It's all more wonderful even than we had imagined—the people, the gorgeous country—everything.
How I wish you were here to share this unimaginable new world with me.
But I guess we can't have everything—at least all at the same time. And it isn't too awfully long till April.

   As you can see this is being finished on a borrowed typewriter. Since we arrived San Juan on a Saturday afternoon, I wasn't able to buy one but we're going back in to S.J. tomorrow and I surely hope to pick one up then.

   It is ten-thirty at night and I can hardly keep my eyes open. Give my love to Ceretta and to Ted and Midge [Gertz's wife, son, and daughter]. It wasn't enough to be hopelessly in your debt—now I'm that way to the whole Gertz family. What wonderful people you all are.

   I hope to write a more coherent letter, Elmer, if I ever get settled and simmer down a bit (which appears doubtful at this point) but just now I'll have to quit or fall asleep right here at the machine.

Bestest,
Babe

---

AFTER HIS RELEASE from prison on March 13, 1958, Nathan Leopold went to Puerto Rico, where he had been offered a job as an X-ray technician by the Brethren Service Commission of the Church of the Brethren, headquartered in suburban Chicago. Both he and the parole board had been concerned that attempting to lead any kind of normal life in Chicago, where he still had friends and family, would be impossible because of his notoriety, and Leopold was vehement in his insistence that what he most craved for his remaining years was the chance to become a "nobody." His conditions of service in Puerto Rico would be "identical with arrangements for hundreds of other Brethren Service volunteers who are serving in the United States and abroad in various social welfare projects," according to the public statement made by the Brethren. Leopold would receive transportation to work, a single room to live in, meals, and a $10-per-month cash allowance. Elmer Gertz continued to serve as his attorney, adviser, confidant, and friend, and as the years passed the milestones and achievements in both their lives were documented by a generally cordial and sometimes quite affectionate correspondence. Gertz became increasingly prominent as an attorney, securing an important victory for author Henry Miller in the obscenity case over his novel *Tropic of Cancer* (a copy of which he smuggled to Leopold in Puerto Rico—though Leopold didn't find it anywhere near as titillating as it was made out to be, and in fact was never able to get through it) and defending Jack Ruby, killer of Lee Harvey Oswald, from the death penalty. Leopold, for his part, tried hard to avoid publicity—which had been made a legal condition of his parole. He studied social work at the University of Puerto Rico, where he earned a master's degree in 1961, and he was appointed to the faculty to teach mathematics. Also in 1961, he married a widow named Trudi Feldman, who had been running a flower shop since the death of her first husband. For the most part he appeared to be as much the model parolee as he had been the model prisoner, but a letter he wrote to Gertz in the late winter of

Elmer Gertz (left, in hat and glasses) with Nathan Leopold on the day of Leopold's release from Stateville, the Illinois state penitentiary. Leopold made a speech to the 100 or so reporters who covered the event, saying that he looked forward to "a gift almost as precious as freedom itself—a gift without which freedom ceases to have much value—the gift of privacy."

1962 provides a rare convincing glimpse into the unabridged psyche of the later Leopold—much more than his self-aggrandizing memoir, his public statements, or his other generally much more guarded correspondence does. Admittedly furious and possibly intoxicated, Leopold displays his infamous contempt for rules, regulations, and morality to which he doesn't believe he ought to be subjected, and he reveals that he's been flouting many of his parole conditions regularly. His anger was triggered by a letter Gertz had written him after a former cellmate of Leopold's named Paul Henry had just been granted parole. Leopold was hoping that Henry, too, would be allowed to come to Puerto Rico, and he had expressed excitement about meeting Henry's plane at the airport and mentoring him in his new freedom. But Gertz and Harold Row, who was sponsoring Leopold's parole work with the Brethren, feared the publicity that might ensue could cause Leopold to have his own parole revoked, and Gertz had written Leopold a letter of caution whose tone Leopold found patronizing.

PRIVATE AND CONFIDENTIAL

March 4, 1962

Dear Elmer,

I've labeled this letter "Private and Confidential" for the sole reason of keeping it from [Gertz's secretary's] eyes and thus sparing her what might be a harrowing experience. For I suspect that, before I finish, I may be writing pretty much in the style of Henry Miller. It is even possible that you may learn an epithet or two which even he didn't know.

I'm doing this, Elmer, let me assure you solemnly, not for the purpose of showing off my lexicon of obscenity, but rather, because I feel that perhaps some of the subjects on which I will have to touch are expressed most naturally and most forcefully in gutter-snipe argot. Certainly, when I think of some of the subjects, as I have been doing pretty much of late, I find that I think of them most easily and naturally in these terms. Nor should this occasion too much astonishment. For language is a pretty immediate habit, and one picked up, as every tyro knows, from one's in-group environment. Since many of these concepts developed during my 33 years at Stateville, where the People of Illinois, in their wisdom, had sent me (for the good of my soul?), it is only natural, I suppose, that I express them as my "comates in exile" were wont to phrase them.

The probabilities are greatly in favor of your never laying eye on this missive. I'll most likely write it and then mail it via the toilet. But write it, apparently, I must—or take a chance on a cerebrovascular accident because of the elevated state of my blood pressure.

One other specific consideration, beside the polity of doing so, militates, against my ever actually sending you this letter. It is the enormous probability—indeed, the near certainty—that you will interpret it as caused by, and in protest against your letter of February 28—the one that deals with . . . the pro's and con's of Paul Henry's coming to Puerto Rico, being allowed to talk to me, being met at the airport, etc. [. . .]

For four—nearly five years, Elmer, you have been, and still are, one of the two people in the world whom I regard most highly, think most of, cherish most deeply. Or, perhaps, it's one of the three latterly, for Harold Row has been steadily closing the gap that separates him from you two lead horses. Of this you cannot fail to be aware.

And it has two consequences. Consequences diametrically opposed. On the one hand, it causes a guy to say, "There is nothing in the world that Elmer could conceivably do, which I would let offend me or fail to forgive him. If, occasionally, he slops over a trifle and shows a speck of his clay feet, I am so deeply in his debt that behooves me to say nothing, to try to put the incident out of my mind completely— certainly to hold my tongue and not let him see that I am disappointed or hurt." This I've been doing to the best of my frail ability.

In the first of your two letters of February 14, you write:

"The tables are now reversed. I am wondering about your long silence. It seems to me that I have not heard from you in many days, despite the several communications that I have sent to you. Is there anything wrong?"

Yes, Elmer, there was something wrong. I deliberately withheld my answer to your letter of February 1 until I felt I had mastered my emotions to the extent that I could reply without bitterness or vitriol. Your letter arrived on Feb. 5; I was scheduled to leave the morning of the 9th for Castaner [Puerto Rico]. I deliberately and purposely, and after consultation with Trudi, deferred answering your letter until after my return from Castaner, the 12th, because I did not trust myself to do so earlier.

What's all the fireworks about? Why your discussion of the Holman incident. After telling me of his request and your answer, you wrote:

"You will not see the gentleman or anyone else."

Now this is the way I speak to an idiot, a child, a servant, or a dog.

I know you didn't mean it that way, Elmer; that attitude is just not part of your personality. But in your frayed state of nerves in your "out of sorts" attitude, you SAID it.

Of course I'm hypersensitive to this type of thing—precisely because I had to put up with 33 years of it, not only from ignorant, bigoted, sadistic motherfuckers in the employ of the State, but also from my own brother. Like you, he always patronized me only out of the purest motives—for my own good. (And that's the worst kind). He was perfectly honest; he acted, I am sure, always for the right, as God gave him to see the right. That's one reason that your advent and that of Ralph [Newman] on the scene was a God-given breath of fresh air in a stagnant dungeon. Here were two guys, not my social or intellectual inferiors, not yet people who were trying to get something out of me, who appeared perfectly willing to treat me as an adult and not as a Mongoloid idiot, who didn't know how to wipe his own ass or blow his own nose. What a shot in the arm that was for my psyche (to mix metaphors a bit.)

Don't, for Christ's sake, become a Sam [Leopold's older brother], even when you're out of sorts!

The opposite consideration operates on this wise. It causes a fellow to say to himself:

"Elmer's friendship is one of the things I hold most dear in life. I cannot and must not allow it to fritter away; I must do anything to preserve it. But if, occasionally, he does something or says something that hurts me, and if I allow it to pass without challenge, it is only too likely to fester in my consciousness. After all, altho it hurts like hell to lance a boil, that's certainly the medical treatment of choice. You don't just let it sit, perhaps spread into a generalized furunculosis and even kill the patient with septicemia. So better take a chance on alienating him and almost certainly hurt him temporarily rather than to let the thing fester and grow and become infected."

After all, Buster, if our relationship isn't completely open and above-board, completely honest, it isn't after all very valuable.

So let's have at it, and let the chips fall where they may.

You're one of the grandest guys I've ever had the rare good fortune to meet in a long, and not uncheckered, career. Which doesn't mean you're perfect. You're not God; you're just a damn fine, damn intelligent, generally honest, generally broad-minded man, who, by an almost incredible stroke of good fortune, happens to like me. You've done more for me than anyone, with the possible exception of Ralph and of Harold; you've shown a thousand times, and in a thousand ways, that you are completely and absolutely in my corner.

OK. Want to know some of the negative points? You and I, I think, are the two vainest, most conceited humans I've ever met in that same career. Like me, you tend to arrogate unto yourself all the credit for anything good that happens and to disclaim responsibility for anything that blows up in our face. I understand this so well because it is so characteristic of me.

You, again like me, lap up praise and adulation and publicity, even when your good sense tells you it's bologna. It's awfully hard to disbelieve anything really fine someone else says of you, even in the face of superior knowledge.

And of course you, again like me, rationalize like a sonofabitch. Everything either of us does is always done, of course, for the very noblest motives. Unfortunately, we've both got brains enough generally to be able to put up a pretty convincing story.

And you're not very consistent. Because the pull on you of expediency is very strong, you're not above changing ground in midstream if it suits your purpose. A sweet, simple guy like Harold doesn't do that; apparently Principle (with a capital P) means so much to him, and expediency, so little, that he hews straight to the line, no matter what. You and I aren't that simple—that uncomplicated—that good. [. . .]

Nor have you—or you and Harold—invariably given me sound advice. Sometimes you've given me bum advice.

Remember your first trip down here, in June 1958. At your very urgent suggestion, I refrained from drinking (while I was in your company.) To refresh your memory, in the dining room at the Villa Parguera, you ordered a bottle of native beer and suggested that I have orange juice. After you'd had your beer you remarked that had you known how good it was, you would have assented to my having a bottle too. Now, almost from day one, I have not abided by the parole regulation against drinking. I've made no secret of this; you've known it from the very beginning. I have drunk in the presence of Harold, . . . of Governor [Luis] Munoz, and, just recently, of Ramon Perez, my parole supervisor. So far, I have not been caught and so had no reason to regret it. Certainly, it would be SAFER not to drink. It would also be safer to spend my life in bed, where there is less chance of stumbling over something and breaking your neck.

I might add, parenthetically, tho it doesn't fit logically here, that I have also failed to observe the parole rules against (1) staying out after 10:00 PM (sometimes in your company); (2) communicating with other prisoners or ex-prisoners. Harry Golden, who did a bit in New York for embezzlement, is to be the guest of honor in my home a week from Monday; (3) going to places of questionable reputation. I have visited most of the better whore-houses, cheap bars, and gambling casinos in Greater San Juan and like 'em fine. (4) possession of weapons of any kind. I have, briefly, had possession of a shot gun and a rifle, when my ornithological activities required it, and am about to order an air rifle for permanent possession. I also have in my home, as an ornament, a machete, whose primary use is chopping sugar cane, etc., but which is also frequently used for chopping your wife's head off; (5) I have associated with people with a police record. My thesis was written on the basis of interviews obtained with inmates of the Commonwealth Penitentiary and I have known others, beside Harry Golden and John Forbes, who did two years and a half at Springfield, Missouri; (6) I frequently leave the County (Municipio) of San Juan without first obtaining permission; (7) I have usually changed address and employment first and then notified my agent later.

But that ain't all, Butch. I intend to continue violating these provisions whenever the occasion arises. [. . .]

In general, about the advice, Elmer, I don't know of anyone's I value more—except that again I'd be hard put to it to assess yours in comparison with Ralph's and Harold's, and both men are much better diplomats than you. But, once more, you are not H. Sebastian Godd; you have been wrong sometimes. And my idea of the function of advice, given between equals and friends, is that it is something to be considered carefully by the person who must make the ultimate decision, but not necessarily followed blindly. Any other relation deprives one party of his adulthood and independence. So I shall, with your permission, continue to follow, or not to follow your advice, as I see fit. After all, you do the same. You don't, for instance, always take a vacation when, in my opinion, you need one badly.

MY THESIS: ← Leopold earned a master's degree in social medicine at the University of Puerto Rico, graduating first in his class.

And Elmer, while I repeat that you're one of the grandest guys I know and I value your opinion very highly—else I wouldn't seek it so often—I must also add that sometimes you remind me of nothing so much as a broody mother hen. You cluck and summon your chicks to such an extent that I'm constantly waiting for you to produce an egg.

As a liberal (at least most of the time), Elmer, I wonder if you don't agree that some laws—and this includes rules and regulations of administrative boards—are morally wrong and SHOULD be disobeyed. I'd gamble that you do it sometimes in practice. Didn't you ever buy or transport liquor during prohibition; don't you ever exceed the speed limit in your car, or park in a no-parking zone? [. . .]

I have looked forward for years to just this consummation. During the past weeks or months my sense of anticipation has heightened. Since news of Paul's parole to Puerto Rico, it has reached a fever heat. I'm not going to be deprived of one of the most exquisite pleasures in my life. . . . If they are so concerned about Paul's and my seeing each other, they'd better deprive him of his chance and parole him to Sioux City Iowa, where he can learn to make rattan furniture, or put me under house arrest. Because, unless they do something of that nature, I am going to see Paul whenever I think I can safely do so, and they can pound their "ground rules" up their ass sideways.

Sorry, Elmer, and perhaps you'll never see this screed. At least Freud is right about the value of catharsis. Having got all this crap and poison out of my system— even if no farther than ten blank sheets of paper, I feel better.

I hope I haven't lost your friendship. And I don't think I have. But I'd rather do even that than keep it under false colors. If you can't stand me as I really am, I guess we'll have to call it quits. And if I can't say how I really feel without offending you mortally on such occasions as my pressure gets to the point of threatening the integrity of my vascular system, I suppose loss of you is slightly the less undesirable alternative.

If you are still "rapping" to me, and if you find the time to read this volume, I shall, of course, be interested in your reactions.

Bestest,
Babe


Leopold had not lost Gertz's friendship. In fact, Gertz's reply stands as a testament to how strong that friendship had become and to the unconditional compassion Gertz seemed to feel for Leopold as a human being.

AIR MAIL

March 8, 1962

Dear Babe,

I was tired, peevish, utterly out of sorts and worried, for a variety of known and unknown reasons, when your letter of March 4 arrived. I am still not myself, but I have the feeling that I have read a masterpiece—not of literature, but, as Henry Miller would say—of life. Don't be concerned for one moment about my being angry at anything said by you, even when I am the victim. I agree wholeheartedly with you. All I can plead by way of defense is that I am so deeply concerned with your welfare that I do act like a hen clucking about her chicks. In the past, particularly, and even today, I sometimes wake up in a sweat after having a nightmarish dream about the authorities doing something to interfere with your freedom. This has been so hard-won a gift from God that I cannot imagine anything causing me more grief than if anything should go wrong. You must remember that I have had several tragic experiences in my own life. I have also had the experience of being patronized, sometimes by my peers, but more often by those who are not fit to be in my company. Don't worry, I repeat; say what you please and I will understand it. I shall try to make every effort hereafter not to give directives, not to state anything in a peremptory tone, not to treat you like a child, not to act as if your rights and dignity are any less than mine. I think I usually write as man to man, because that is how I feel towards you. It seldom occurs to me that there was ever anything in your life history that makes you different from me. I think that I know almost everything there is to know about you, insofar as it is given to another person to know such things, and I know no reason why you and I should not be considered as equals.

What happens to prompt silly language, or conduct, or attitudes on my part, or, for that matter, on the part of anyone else, is that we are constantly under stress and strain, sometimes connected with you and sometimes unconnected with you. At the moment, for example, I have a sort of emotional and physical crisis, although I have won some of the most striking victories of my professional career and seem on the verge of others. It sometimes takes real effort for me to talk or write to anyone, even those I love. Nine-tenths of the time, for example, Mamie [Gertz's wife] understands it, but every once in a while even she is hurt by what seems to be my self-centeredness. Since you are a human being, you have been hurt also. . . . We always expect much more of those for whom we care than from others. I can take insolence, ignorance, anything from those for whom I have contempt, but not those for whom I have admiration and affection, like yourself.

I hope that it won't be necessary again for you to speak out. I am very happy that, instead of throwing away the letter as you wanted to, you sent it on to me. No, it does not have Henry Miller's so-called obscenity as you feared, but, now and then, it comes pretty close to it. [ . . . ]

Our love to Trudi, and say what you damn please at any time. We will think more, rather than less, of you, if you have sufficient faith in us to be honest.

Always yours,
Elmer Gertz

MAMIE was Gertz's second wife, whom he married after the death of his first wife, Ceretta.

# 76
# Happiness is a perfume
# (reprise)

### THE FINAL YEARS, 1963-1971

O F THE PAROLE restrictions Leopold had not been able to find a way to circumvent, the one that seemed to chafe at him most was a prohibition on traveling. Two months after his release from parole, he and his wife, Trudi, left for a trip to Europe and the Mediterranean whose ambitious itinerary included Paris, Lucerne, Lausanne, Grenoble, Nice, Rome, Florence, Venice, Innsbruck, Salzburg, Amsterdam, London, Athens, Cairo, and Tel Aviv. They were winding up the trip in October when Leopold wrote Gertz a letter from Portugal, in which, exhilarated by his travel experiences, he told Gertz that for most of his adult life he had felt deeply ambivalent about not committing suicide in prison when chances had presented themselves, "Until now! For the first time I can say definitely and without reservation that I'm glad I did not do away with myself."

On the way home to Puerto Rico, he stopped in Chicago, where he visited with Gertz and some of his other friends, and, for the first time in his life, was able to visit the graves of his father and brother Mike at Rosehill Cemetery, then buried there in the family plot along with his beloved mother. Though at the time free to give interviews to the press, he had continued, on the advice of Gertz, Ralph Newman, and others, to avoid the media—refusing hefty offers for exclusive interviews, though he felt pressed for money. So he was shocked to discover, after his return to Puerto Rico, that the *Chicago Tribune* had published a front-page story headlined "Leopold Tells Views on Life After Prison," extensively quoting remarks he had made at what he had assumed was a private, off-the-record gathering with staff of the Church of the Brethren—the group that had sponsored his parole job in Puerto Rico.

Though apparently taken from a transcript leaked by a staff member to the paper, his remarks were framed as an exclusive interview, "the only open interview he gave during his visit to Chicago last week," the story claimed. Leopold was quoted as saying that his main value in the fight against capital punishment was probably "as an object at which to point rather than as a person to get up and talk. I mean, for those against abolition of capital punishment, it is natural to say: 'Well, of course, he's against it; they almost hanged him.'" There were flashes of humor, as when someone asked him about his "personal disciplines," and he replied, "Well, I never drink when I can't get it. I never overeat if I don't like the food that's being served. I never smoke after I run out of cigarets. What else—well, I go to bed when it's convenient." That he was very accurately quoted is suggested by his reply to the question, "What lies behind your own zeal for Humanitarian service?"

First, he joked, "I didn't know I had any."

The newspaper then reported, "Then he said, 'Well, I like people. I feel I have a debt to repay and this is perhaps one way to start doing it. Besides, I am utterly selfish and believe in my mother's motto: "Happiness is a perfume you cannot sprinkle upon others without getting a few drops on yourself." I am avid for the drops.'"

These were the exact words Harold Hulbert and Karl Bowman had quoted him using to describe his late mother's spirit in their infamous psychiatric report in 1924.

Typically, Gertz attempted to soften the blow of the unauthorized publication in a letter to Leopold assuring him that, besides the fact the whole thing had been done without Leopold's knowledge and consent, the article itself wasn't a bad one.

But Leopold was furious, as he makes clear in his reply, excerpted below—which he wrote while drunk and which contains an extremely rare reference to "the murder of 1924," and to the role his mother's early death might have played in it.

### GRATITUDE

In March of 1963, nearly 40 years after the murder of Bobby Franks, Nathan Leopold Jr. regained his full freedom when the parole and pardon board of the state of Illinois approved his discharge from parole after the maximum parole period of five years.

Through his attorney, Elmer Gertz, Leopold released a statement for the public, published in the March 13 *Chicago American*, about how he felt at that moment:

"My first emotion is gratitude.

"Gratitude to the many persons, organizations, and agencies which have made successful completion of my parole possible.

"My other emotion is a determination to prove that the kindness, friendship, and opportunities lavished on me have not been bestowed in error."

Gertz told the press that Leopold hoped to take his wife to Europe in the summer and that he "would like to complete his studies in sociology and acquire a doctorate."

Following his trip to Europe, Gertz said, Leopold was planning to come to Chicago to visit the graves of his family and friends and would then return to Puerto Rico to live.

November 18, 1963

Dear Elmer,

I'm marking this letter "Private, Confidential, etc., etc." because I don't want Gladys [Gertz's secretary] to open it. Not that there is any substantive material in it which she is not welcome to read, but because I suspect that before I get thru I'll be using some homely four letter Anglo-Saxon words. Now, either she's heard them before or she hasn't. If she has, she'd think less of me for using them; if she hasn't, I don't want to be the one to teach 'em to her. Please apologize to her for me. You might read her this paragraph. TO HERE!

Thanks for your good wishes for my birthday. Personally, I can't see that it is the subject for felicitations—I myself, wish I hadn't been born.

I had a swell talk with the Padre, but I'm certainly in no mood to tell you the details tonight. I'm drunk—have been drunk for 24 hours and expect to stay drunk indefinitely. And when I'm drunk my muscular fine movements aren't so good—I have trouble typing. You may have trouble reading this. Frankly, I couldn't care less. Pitch it in the wastepaper basket if it doesn't seem worth the trouble of reading. It's written mostly for catharsis anyhow. [. . .]

I certainly do know about the "long article about my talk in Elgin [Illinois] that appeared in the Chicago Tribune Sunday." That's why I am drunk. What I'd like to write him, but don't want to–, so will use you as a captive audience to get it off my chest is this. Prices have gone up in 1930 years. Judas Iscariot got only "30 pieces of silver" for his snitch-pigeoning; I could have got between $2,000 and $5,000 (for Castaner Hospital) for this precise article, given as an exclusive interview to the Trib. I hope this Mother-fucker Howard Royer, who "was intimidated by the religion editor of the Chicago Tribune" held out for more than that.

In general, what other people do doesn't affect me too deeply, and I couldn't care less what this son-of-a-bitch did. What does affect me is two things: the proof positive that I am still a chump, still a babe in arms and the collateral, tangential harm resulting from the bastard's action. I've been proved a chump, lost from 2 to 5 G I could have got, had I been willing to sell the article to the Trib and $50,000 in futures that Sam [his brother] had in a trust fund for me. I hope the Momser-ben-anidah (and you might ask Rabbi [Louis] Binstock what that means if your Hebrew isn't up to it. On second thought, I'd better tell you—it might make his other eye cock.) It means a bastard conceived while his mother was flagging. [. . .]

The last time someone destroyed my "simple, child-like faith," when I was 17 and my mother died. I decided that (a) either there was no God or, if there was, I didn't want anything further to do with the son-of-a-bitch. I think the murder of 1924 was not too indirectly connected.

But Joe Mother-fucker at Stateville and his minions have done an A-number 1 job of rehabilitating me—that is a word Sam loves so Pfui on it! I probably won't kill a single solitary soul this time. Just write you this nasty letter because you're the handiest (tho surely the most innocent whipping boy!) and maybe, if I don't cook down before the cacoethes scribendi leaves me—a similar one to Royer. Meantime I'm having fun kicking over waste-baskets and being mean to Trudi and Susie [the dog]. I'm a whole hearted believer in guilt by association and they're (or at least Trudi is) a member of the human race. As for Susie, I haven't had a dog yet that did me a really dirty trick—maybe they haven't got sense enough to. [. . .]

Give my love to Mamie [Gertz's wife] and TEAR UP THIS LETTER!

BABE

Leopold (left) with Elmer Gertz at a dinner party at Gertz's house on June 16, 1964, during Leopold's visit to Chicago.

# Epilogue

He Was a Puzzle ───────────────────────────────────────────────

In his memoir *To Life*, Elmer Gertz recalled that Nathan Leopold's health was bad from around April of 1971 until the end of his life, that he was in and out of the hospital and had to carry around heart medication and keep oxygen on hand. But if he knew he was dying, Gertz says, "he gave few objective signs of it."

Summing up what insight he had gained over their years of friendship, Gertz wrote that Leopold "never ceased to be on trial. At times the world expected too much of him, and some were too critical. He expected too much of himself, but was not always self-critical enough. His life will be studied for what it can teach us about the good and bad possibilities of human beings. He was a puzzle even to those like me who knew him best."

LEOPOLD MADE HIS last visit to Chicago in the summer of 1971. He was hospitalized twice during the visit; Gertz, who drove him to an emergency room the second time, recalled that during the ride, "I had a sense of impending disaster. I thought that the chances were great that we would arrive at the hospital with a corpse." The final letter from Leopold that is preserved in Gertz's files at Northwestern—written to his friend Abel Brown on August 15, after Leopold had returned home to Puerto Rico—recounts a few of his final activities during the Chicago trip, including a visit with some friends who took him to see "where I used to go birding in the Calumet Swamp district (that was)—108th and Avenue F. It's all built up now; I would never have recognized it." This happened also to be the exact location from which, he had said in his murder confession 47 years before, he and Loeb had proceeded with Bobby Franks's corpse down the path leading toward Hegewisch, Indiana, "to the prearranged spot for the disposal of the body" (see chapter 15, page 62).

The day before he left Chicago, the same friends drove him to Rosehill Cemetery to visit the family plot, where his father and his brother lay, along with his beloved mother. Unless they went out of their way not to take the most direct route from the main entrance, Leopold and his friends would have passed directly by the small marble mausoleum where, by that time, Bobby Franks lay in the company of both of his parents as well as his older brother, Jack. Though in life the three families and their descendants had long since scattered, in death they came back to eternal rest at Rosehill in plots that eerily mimic the proximity of their houses to one another in Kenwood at the time of the murder, with the Loebs about half a city block from the Frankses, and the Leopolds a short distance farther down the path.

There the families remain linked forever by ties that are invisible to the casual observer but that continue to fascinate anyone who knows their story. All of the family members except the protagonists, that is. The site of Richard Loeb's burial after his murder at Stateville on January 26, 1936, is unknown. And after Leopold's death on August 29, 1971, in Puerto Rico, an ophthalmologist came to remove his corneas, which were given to two separate strangers, and his body was donated to science.

# Acknowledgments

M Y HEARTFELT THANKS go to all the people who've helped and supported me on this book's very eventful journey from concept to publication, over the course of nearly a decade:

- Mike Levine, who thought this would make a great book, and got me started on it.
- The diligent and cheerful staff at the Northwestern University Archives and the Charles Deering McCormick Library of Special Collections, who patiently provided access to most of the critical documentation and in some cases performed additional research: Kevin Leonard, Janet Olson, Scott Krafft, Jason Nargis, Nick Munagian, and Sigrid Perry.
- Northwestern's Alice Kaplan Institute for the Humanities, where as a fellow I treasured both the quiet space to write and the intellectual companionship of other fellows.
- The Archivist of the United States, David Ferriero, who took an interest in this project from the very beginning and kindly provided the images from Nathan Leopold's passport application.
- Postal historian Leonard Piszkiewicz, who analyzed the markings on the ransom note for me.
- John Russick of the Chicago History Museum, who by sharing the labels from his own exhibit about Leopold and Loeb, provided me with an influential lesson in how artifacts can tell a story; and the staff of the Museum's Research Center, who helped me with the photo research and permissions for the book.
- My colleagues on the Clarence Darrow Memorial Committee, which faithfully summons the spirit of Darrow every year on March 13, the anniversary of his death, as he requested: Anita Weinberg, Tracy Baim, and Nina Helstein.
- Attorney Charles Valente, the Clarence Darrow who championed me when I needed it.
- Literary Agent Extraordinaire, Anne Edelstein.
- Graphic designer Amanda Good, who helped me visualize the way the story would unfold across the pages.
- Doug Seibold, founder and publisher at Agate Publishing, and the team who transformed this project from a manuscript into exactly the kind of book I had envisioned: Jessica Easto, Morgan Krehbiel, and Helena Hunt.
- The family of Elmer Gertz, which granted me permission to use Gertz's correspondence with Leopold and other documents.
- Those who provided copyright advice and permissions assistance along the way, including Geoffrey Jennings, William T. McGrath, Stephen Lubet, and Adele Hutchinson.
- And to my Number One Head Cheerleader and Favorite Personal Services Librarian, Jeffrey Garrett.

# Resources

To LEARN MORE about the Leopold and Loeb case, I suggest the following other reading—all of which was helpful to me in researching *The Leopold and Loeb Files*:

*Attorney for the Damned: Clarence Darrow in the Courtroom*, ed. by Arthur Weinberg, University of Chicago Press, 1989 (originally published in 1957)
A curated collection of Darrow's most important courtroom speeches, including his closing argument in the Leopold and Loeb case.

*Clarence Darrow for the Defense*, Irving Stone, Doubleday, 1989 (originally published in 1941)
Though fictionalized, this engrossing telling of Darrow's life and career stays very close to the facts.

*Compulsion: A Novel*, Meyer Levin, Fig Tree Books, 2015 (originally published in 1956)
Nathan Leopold sued Meyer Levin over this fictionalized telling of the Leopold and Loeb case, but reviewers said it offered more insight into the minds of the killers than Leopold's own memoir, *Life Plus 99 Years*.

*Crimes of the Century*, Gilbert Geis and Leigh B. Bienen, Northeastern University Press, 1998
The authors analyze the legal implications of this and several other sensational murder cases, including the Lindbergh kidnapping and the O.J. Simpson case.

*Evil Summer: Babe Leopold, Dickie Loeb, and the Kidnap-Murder of Bobby Franks*, John Theodore, Southern Illinois University Press, 2007
An engrossing retelling of the events of the summer of 1924.

*For the Thrill of It: Leopold, Loeb, and the Murder That Shocked Chicago*, Simon Baatz, Harper, 2008
Baatz's telling offers in-depth context about 1920s Chicago and the historical and political context in which the crime and the sentencing hearing took place.

*A Handful of Clients*, Elmer Gertz, Follett, 1965
One of Gertz's memoirs, which includes his account of his developing relationship with Leopold and how he helped Leopold win release from prison.

*Leopold & Loeb: The Crime of the Century*, Hal Higdon, University of Illinois Press, 1999 (originally published in 1975)
Higdon's highly readable journalistic account of the crime and its aftermath is rich with detail based on interviews he did with many of the original participants in the drama, who were still alive when he was researching the book.

*Life Plus 99 Years*, Nathan Leopold, Doubleday, 1958
Leopold declined to discuss the murder itself in his memoir, which was written while he was still in prison and seems crafted to convince the public of his rehabilitation.

"Making and Remaking an Event: The Leopold and Loeb Case in American Culture," Paula S. Fass, *The Journal of American History*, Volume 80, Issue 3, Dec. 1993, 919–951
A pioneer in the field of children's history, Fass has done some of the most important and incisive scholarly writing about this case.

*To Life: The Story of a Chicago Lawyer*, Elmer Gertz, McGraw-Hill, 1974
In another installment of his memoirs, written after the death of Leopold, Gertz looks back on their relationship in the years after Leopold's release from prison.

# Index

Note: page numbers in *italics* include photos and photo captions

## A

A, B, C, D crimes, 133–134, 197, 199–200. *See also* crimes committed by Leopold and Loeb
Abelson, Lester, 48, 50–51, *147*
Adamowski, Benjamin S., 275
Adams, Varian B., 267, 268
alibis, 15, 18, 36–37, 55–57, 76–78, 267
alienists, 96, 122, 229: defense, 3, 90, 95, 97, 100, 114, *126*, 127, 129, 133, 135, 136, 144, 150, 165, 167, 177, 178, 183, 186, 190, 197, 201, 236, 272; prosecution, 81, 84, 85, 95, 178, 201, 213. *See also individual alienists*
Allen, E.M., 22, 55, 59, 73
Aretino, Pietro, 31–35, 54

## B

Bachrach, Benjamin, 97, 149, *188*, *222*, 243, 265: court speeches and questioning, 156–157, 159, 162, 194–196, 239, 241, 248
Bachrach, Walter, 97, 100, 176, 178, 201, 214, 237, 243, 265: court speeches and questioning, 165, 167–168, 174–175, 180–182, 190–193, 200, 212–213, 240–242
Ballard, Morton (pseudonym of Loeb), 65, *66–67*, 136
Ballenberger, Adolph, 59, 265
Benson, A.F., *146*, 240–241. *See also* coroner's report
bird-watching. *See under* Leopold, Nathan ("Babe")
Bookwalter, John M., 262–263, 270–272, 278–279
Bowman, Karl, 96, 97, 103, 106, 108, 123, 144, 197, 287. *See also* Hulbert-Bowman Report
Branson, R.J., 270, 272, 279
Brethren Service Commission of the Church of the Brethren, 280, 281, 287
Brown, Abel, 114, 265, 268, 274, 290: parole testimony, 268–272

## C

Carpentier, Joseph, 270–271, 274, 278–279
Caverly, John, 3, 6, 149–150, 152, 155, *160*, 162, *172*, 174, 178, 199, *204*, 212, *226*, 236, 239, 243–245, 246–247, 275: court questioning, 153, 159, 165–168, 190–191, 193, 200, 203, 215–216, 239–241, 244–245, 248; sentencing by, 248–251
Charles Deering McCormick Library of Special Collections at Northwestern University, 3, 186, 258, 291
Charlevoix, Michigan, 201, 203, 246, 255
Church, Archibald, 81, 201–203
confessions, 2–3, 59–92, 94, 149, 164, 194, 203, 207, 249, 275: "Confessions and Other Statements of Leopold and Loeb," 2, 3–4, 19–92, *21*, *58*, *74–75*, 136, *238*
coroner's report, 8, 18, 31, 62, 236, 239–242
crimes committed by Leopold and Loeb, 6, 113–115, *132*, 133–134, 136, 143, 178, 190–193, 199–200, 272. *See also* A, B, C, D crimes
Criminal "Master Mind," 108, 133, 135, 169, 178, 213
Crot, William, *148*, 162–163
Crowe, Robert, 3, 6, 59, 62, 69, *71*, 79, 94, *106*, *146*, 149, 162–163, 165, 169, 174, 177, 186, 196, 201, *205*, 206, 218, 223, 252, 254, 275: court speeches and questioning, 150, 152–167, 175–177, 180, 183–185, 190–193, 197–200, 236–245; questioning by, 15, 20, 22–57, 73, 77–78, 81, 84–85, 88–90

## D

Darrow, Clarence, 2, 3, 94–95, 97, 100, 108, 124, 149, *151*, 163, 169–170, *173*, 174, 176, 178, 186, *189*, *205*, 206, *222*, *226*, 236–238, 252, 258, 260–261, 265, 275, 291: court speeches and questioning, 150, 152–154, 159, 169–171, 190–193, 201–203, 210, 214–235, 239–241, 243–244; The Story of My Life, 260–261, 272, 279
death penalty, 3, 81, 94–95, 136, 138, 149–150, 152–154, 163, 165–171, 174–177, 206–209, 211, 212, 216–235, 243, 248–251, 252–253, 254, 287
detectives, 8–11, 12, 15, 18, 36, 39–40, 46, 56, 76, 79, 89, 94, 133, 155, 157, 162–164. *See also individual detectives*
*Detective Story Magazine,* 9, 10, 18, 89. *See also* ransom note
Drake Hotel, 31, 40, 130, 247, 248, 253, 254

## E

Englund, Sven, 55–57, 59, 63, 76, *147*, 267
Ettelson, Sam, 6, 8, 15, 18, 20, 46, 53–54, 73, 91–92, *179*, 252
evidence, 20, 77, 94, 150, 152–153, 207: horn-rimmed glasses, 8, 12–13, 15, 20, 27–30, *28*, 38, 62, 77, 98, 150, 162; ransom note, 1, *2*, 3, 8–11, 15, *10–11*, 20, 23, 38, 46, 54, 60–61, 65, 71, 89–90, 113, 150, 158, 244, 291; rental car, 56, 63, 65, *66–67*, 73, 79, 136, 138; typewriter, 8, *9*, 11, 46, 48–54, 65, *71*, 72, 79, 90, 113, 150, 163, 265

## F

Fass, Paula, 2, 97, 103, 292
Feldman, Trudi, 280, 283, 286, 287, 288
Fitzgerald, Thomas, 177
Forbes, Genevieve, 153, 174, 190–191, 197, 199
For the Thrill of It (Baatz), 2, 292

Franks, Bobby (Robert), 6, 7, 16, 23–24, 69, 82, 89, 103, 138, 211, 232, 253, 254, 290: discovery of, 8, 12, 23, 27, 46, 47, 61, 63, 92, 133; funeral, 16, 18, 22, 106, 138; murder, 1, 3, 6, 18, 59–80, 97, 120, 136–137, 158–159, 163, 184, 194, 209, 240–242, 249–251, 261, 265 (*see also* murder, Franks); undressing of, 59, 62, 69, 201, 203, 223, *238*, 242

Franks, Flora, 6, 8, 16, 62, 79, 80, 82, 92, 138–139, *141*, *146*, 195, 201–202, 210, 246–247, 253, 254–255, 290

Franks, Jack, 79, 246, 254–255, 290

Franks, Jacob, 1, 6, 8, 15, 16, 18, 62–63, 71, 82, 91–92, *146*, 155–157, 174, 178, *179*, 211, 244, 246–247, 253, 254–255, 290: home of, 24, 80, 82, 138, 201–202, 246–247, 254–255

Franks, Josephine, 16, 246, 254–255

## G

Gertz, Elmer, 3, 258, 264–268, *266*, 275, 280–290, *281*, 287, *289*, 292: *A Handful of Clients*, 258, 264, 265, 267, 292; letters with Leopold, 3, 264, 280, 282–286, 288; parole testimony, 268, 273; *To Life*, 290, 292

Giessler, Marie, 100

glasses, horn-rimmed. *See under* evidence

Glueck, Bernard, 165, 186, 194, 199, 236, 279

Goldstein, Alvin, 46, *47*, *148*, 156

Gortland, James, *148*, 162–164, 243

governesses, 178: Leopold's, 100–102, 103, 123, 124; Loeb's, 90, 129–131, 135, 144, 228–229. *See also individual governesses*

Graham, Billy, 265, 267

Gresham, Ed, 8, 92, *146*, 240

guilty plea, 149–150, 152, 162, 164, 165–167, 176–177, 207, 210, 212, 217–218, 236, 243–244, 248–250, 252

Gutknecht, John, 260

## H

Harvard Law School, 12, 121

Harvard School, 4, 8, 12, 15, 16, 18, 22–24, 59, 65, 68, 111, 139, 158–159

Healy, William, 114, 165, 186, *186–187*, 190–193, 194, 199, 236, 237

Henry, Paul, 281–282, 285

Hicks, Robert, 265

Hohley, Louise, 133

Housman, A.E., 233

Hughes, Michael, 22, 55, 59, 73, 81, 133

Hulbert-Bowman Report, 3, 93–144, *99*, *105*, *109*, *120*, *124–126*, *132*, 178, 186–187, 197, 213, 245, 272: leak, 97, 108, 112, 178, 194, 287

Hulbert, Harold, 3, 96, 97, 103, 106, 108, 123, 144, 186, *186–187*, 194–200, *198*, 252, 287. *See also* Hulbert-Bowman Report

Hyde Park, 6, 10, 12, 106, 133, 258

Hyde Park State Bank, 65, *66*

## I

insanity: defense, 3, 81, 85, 95, 97, 124, 144, 149–150, 164–171, 177, 249; legal definition, 85, 95, 208; of Leopold and Loeb, 97, 121–122, 124, 144, 183, 186–187, 213, 221, 249

investigation, 8–15, 18, 20–92, 94, 162–164: field trips, 3, 79–80, 89, 94, 133, 163; questioning, 2–3, 12–13, 15, 18, 19–92, 162; suspects, 9, 12, 15, 20, 22–23, 36, 158–159

## J

Johnson, Frank, *148*, 162–163

Johnson, George (pseudonym of Leopold), 6, 8, 11, 15, 47, 62, 80, 91–92, 155

Judaism, 16, 94, 98–99, 278

## K

Kenwood neighborhood, 6, 133, 255, 258, 290

Khayyam, Omar, 235

kidnapping. *See under* murder, Franks

king-slave fantasy, 109–111, *109*, 169, 178, 182, 185

Krohn, William O., 81, 136, 201, 203, 213, 230: questioning by, 86, 90

Krum, Morrow, 89, 91–92, 127, 133–134

Krum, Ty, 127, 133

## L

LaSalle Hotel, 15, 36

lawyers: defense, 3, 20, 59, 79, 81, 84, 85, 94–95, 97, 134, 149, 164, 177, 201, 216–217, 236–237, 252; prosecution, 15, 79, 81, 94, 95, 150, 171, 174–177, 206, 212, 252. *See also individual lawyers*

Leonard, Kevin, 1, 291

*Leopold and Loeb: The Crime of the Century* (Higdon), 2, 108, 267, 292

Leopold, Florence, 38, 98, 100–105, 230, 268, 271, 287, 288, 290

Leopold, Foreman ("Mike"), 15, 59, 103, 108, 149, 178, 255, 258, 264–265, 287

Leopold, Nathan ("Babe"), 1–2, 6, 12–15, *14*, *82*, *118*, *161*, 162–164, *173*, 183, *189*, *222*, 243–244, 247, 253, *259*, 265, *281*, *289*: alibi, 15, 18, 36–37, 55, 76–78, 267; bird-watching, 6, 12, 26, 27, 29, 37, 39, 76, 101, 162, 271, 284, 290; childhood, 98–104, *105*, *99*, 108, 110, 112, 123; confession, 2–3, *58*, 59–64, 73, *74*, 78, 79–80, *87*, 165; death, 290; intelligence, 3, 12, 20, 25–26, 38, 39, 53, 98, 180–181, 230–231, 261, 275; medical examination, 3, 97, 196; passport, *116–118*, 291; prison years, 103, 127, 258, 269; psychiatric evaluations, 3, 81, 83, 84, *87*, 88, 94, 97–124, *99*, *105*, *109*, *120*, *124–125*, 135, 144, 180–187, *186–187*, 190–193, 201–203, 249 (*see also* king-slave fantasy); questioning, 2–3, 12–13, 15, 18, 22–54, 59–64, 73, *74*, 78, 79, 88–92, 162; religion, 38, 94, 98–99, *99*, 100, 104, 164, 180–181, 277–278, 288; remorse, *87*, 121, 162–164, 262–263, 277; sentencing, 3, 248–251; sexuality, 3, 31–35, 39–45, 57, 101, 106–107, 113, 119, 190–193, 201–203, 237–242, 267

Leopold, Nathan F., Sr., 12, 20, 22, 25, 59, 81, *83*, 84, 95, 116, 139, 149, 165, 178, 233, 243–244, 253, 254, 255, 261, 287, 290: home, *12*, 255

Leopold, Samuel, 59, 101, 103, 255, 258, 265, 283, 288

letters: between Gertz and Leopold, 3, 264, 280, 282–286, 288; between Leopold and Loeb, 15, 18, 39–45, 55, 57, 203, 237; to parole board, 3, 260–263

Levin, Meyer, 99, 265, 267, 268, 275: *Compulsion*, 2, 20, 99, 108, 265, 267, 268, 273–274, 275, 292; *In Search*, 99; parole testimony, 273–274

Levinson, John, 68

*Life Plus 99 Years* (Leopold), 2, 3, 76, 106, 127, 258, *259*, 264, 292

Lincoln, Warren, *132*, 133–134, 199

Loeb, Albert, 16, 65, 138–139, 142, 149, 246–247, 253, 255, 258: homes, 4, *16*, 65, 81, 127–128, 138, 201, 246, 255; sickness, 85, 127–128, 142, 149, 246, 255

Loeb, Allan, 127–128, 134, 139, 142, 149, 197, 246, 249

Loeb, Anna, 16, 18, 20, 65, 127–128, 129–130, 138–139, 142, 144, 149, 201, 210, 246, 255

Loeb, Ernest, 128

Loeb, Jacob, 16, *82*, 95, 127–128, 142, 149, 246, 249, 253

Loeb, Richard ("Dick"), 1–2, 6, 16–18, *17*, *83*, *161*, *222*, *236*, 247, 253, 265, 268–269: alibi, 55–57, 76–78; childhood, 90, 112, 127–131, 228–230; confession, 2–3, 59, 65–73, *75*, 76–78, 80, *87*, 194, 203, *238*, 275; crime obsession, 18, 89–90, 131, 133–135, 178, 182, 190, 229, 261, 269–271, 276; death, 255, 278, 290; medical examination, 3, 196; psychiatric evaluations, 3, 81, *83*, 85–88, *87*, 94, *124–126*, 127–144, *132*, 178, 180, 180, 182–187, *186–187*, 190–193, 194–196, 201–203, 249 (*see also* Criminal "Master Mind"); questioning, 2–3, 55–57; 65–72, *75*, 76–78, 80, 85–88, 89–90; remorse, 85–88, *87*, 138–139, 144, 194; sentencing, 248–251; sexuality, 35, 39–45, 57, 113, 131, 190–193, 201–203, 237–242, 255

Loeb, Tommy, 16, 68, 90, 122, 128, 129–130, 136, 139, 194

Lurie, Susan, 6, 15, 69, 91–92, 106, *106*, 247

## M

Mandel, Leon, 32, 33, 54, *147*

Maremont, Arnold, 48, 50–51, *147*, 265

Marshall, Thomas, 169, 206, 210: court speeches, 207–209

Mauretania, 114–115

Mayer, Howard, *148*, 154–157

McMillan, Robert, 46, 73

Miller, Henry, 280, 282, 285, 286

Minaber, Mrs. Theodore, 129

Mitchell, Mott Kirk, 22–24, 158–159

mitigation, 149–150, 166–168, 170–171, 175, 178, 199, 207–209, 210, 212, 237–238, 249

motives. *See under* murder, Franks

Mulroy, James, 46, *47*, *148*, 156

murder, Franks, 1, 3, 6, 10, 18, 59–80, 97, 120, 136–137, 158–159, 163, 184, 194, 240–242, 249–251, 261, 265: identity of murderer, 3, 62–64, 69, 73, *74*, *75*, 76–77, 108, 122, 136, 139, 183–185, 194–195, 209, 260–261, 269, 272, 275, 279; kidnapping, 6, 23, 47, 62, 79, 80, 136, 158, 244, 249–251; motives, 8, 88, 94, 96, 142, 164, 260, 262; plan, 18, 60, 65, 68, 70, 73, 76, 114–115, 119–120, 136–137; sexual aspects, 8, 15, 23, 31, 39, 62, 69, 119, 136–137, 158–159, 190–193, 201–203, 236–242, 249–250

*Murder That Wouldn't Die: Leopold and Loeb in Artifact, Fact, and Fiction, The*, 3–4

## N, O

*Never the Sinner* (Logan), 4

Newman, Ralph, 258, 264–265, 267, 283, 284, 287

Nietzsche, Friedrich, 112, 119, 231, 271, 275, 278

Northwestern University: Archives, 1–4, 97, 291; Charles Deering McCormick Library of Special Collections, 3, 186, 258, 291; Gertz papers, 3–4, 258, 290; Harold S. Hulbert Papers, 3, 97, 186; law school, 1; library, 1, 3

Novotny, J.F., 270

Obendorf, Howard, 45, 50–51, *147*

## P, Q

pact between Leopold and Loeb, 114–115, 122, 136, 178, 190–193, 195, 237

parole, Leopold's, 3, 251, 258, 267–290

Patrick, Hugh T., 81, 201: questioning by, 81, 86, 88

*psychiatric evaluations. See under* Leopold, Nathan ("Babe") and Loeb, Richard ("Dick")

Puerto Rico, 280–282, 285, 287, 290

Pulitzer Prize, 46, 47

Puttkammer, Ernst, *148*, 158–159

questioning, 2–3, 12–13, 19–92, 162. *See also* confessions

## R

Ragen, Joseph, 265, 288

"Ragged Stranger," *132*, 133–134, 199

ransom note, 1, *2*, 3, 8–11, *10–11*, 15, 20, 23, 46, 54, 60–61, 65, 71, 89–90, 113, 150, 158, 244, 291: ransom scheme, 18, 36, 60, *61*, 62–64, 79–80, 91–92, 136–137, 139, 155–157. *See also* typewriter, Underwood

Ream, Charles, *132*, 133–134, 199

Reinhard, Germaine K. ("Patches"), 11, 247

Rent-A-Car, *66–67*, 73, 79, 139

Rope, 20: movie (Hitchcock), 2, 119, 275; play, 4, 275

Rosehill Cemetery, 16, 18, 106, 287, 290

Rosen, Clara, 208–209

Rosenwald, Julius, 16, 59, 258

Row, Harold, 281–283

Royer, Howard, 288

Rubel, Dick (Richard), 31, 39–40, 42, 139

## S

Sandburg, Carl, 265, *266*, 267, 275

Sattler, Elizabeth, 51–54, *146*

Savage, Joseph P., 22, 46, 55, 77, 81, 88, 212, 213, 217, 218, 223–224, 232, 239–240: court speeches, 210–211; questioning by, 48–53, 59–60, 62–64, 73, 78, 85–86

Sbarbaro, John, 73, 81, 203, 163, 275: questioning by, 65, 68–72, 79–80

Schoemaker, William, 46, 65, 72, 73, 81, 163, 244: questioning by, 49–53, 70

Schwab, Birdie, 102, 103

Sears, Roebuck, 16, 127, 128, 258

Seass, James, 65, 68, *147*

sentencing, 3, 248–251

sex, 31–35, 119–120: assault on Bobby Franks, 8, 15, 23, 31, 39, 62, 137, 158, 201–203, 236–242, 249–250; relationship between Leopold and Loeb, 3, 18, 35, 39–45, 57, 113, 114, 190–193, 201–203, 237

Shanberg, Maurice, 46, 48–49, 51, *147*

Singer, Harold, 213

Slattery, Charles V., 163, 169, 243

Smith, Milton D., 22, 81

Springer, Joseph, *146*, 241

Stateville Correctional Center, 254, 255, 261, 265, 267, 268, 269, 281, 282, 290

Stevenson, Adlai, II, 258, 265, 268

Stransky, Franklin, 270

Stratton, William, 267, 275

Struthers, Emily, 90, 129, 228–229

suspects. *See under* investigation

**T**

"The Three Wise Men from the East," 165, 186, 236–238, 243. *See also* alienists

Thrill Me (Dolginoff), 2

Timme, Walter, 213

Tracy, Freeman, 133

trial, 3, 20, 145–251: coroner's report, 236, 239–242; death penalty, 3, 81, 94–95, 136, 138, 149–150, 152–154, 163, 165–171, 174–177, 206–209, 211, 212, 216–235, 243, 248–251, 252–253, 254, 287; guilty plea, 149–150, 152, 162, 164, 165–167, 176–177, 207, 210, 212, 217–218, 236, 243–244, 248–250, 252; insanity defense, 3, 81, 85, 95, 97, 124, 144, 149–150, 164–171, 177, 249

turpitude, moral, 207–209

typewriter, Underwood, 8, 11, 46, 48–54, 65, *71*, 72, 79, 90, 113, 150, 163, 265

**U, V**

University of Chicago, 12, 16, 25, 33, 36, 38, 46, 57, 59, 91, 94, 133, 156, 267, 269: law school, 1, 12, 48, 59, 158–159

University of Michigan, 16, 59, 65, 113, 203, 247: fraternity-house burglary, 113–114, 136, 144, 190, 272

Van den Bosch, Pauline, 100–101

**W**

Wantz, Mathilda ("Sweetie"), 100–102, 123, 129

Watkins, Maurine, 16, 22, 65, 89, 119

Weir, Eligius, 278

White, William A., 165, 178–187, *187*, 194, 199, 236

Wilkinson, Janet, 177

Williams, Richard P., 22–23

Willys-Knight automobiles, 36, 55, 59, 65, *66*

Wilson, Walter, 22–23

Wolf, Melvin, 133

Statement of          Page

Nathan F. Leopold, JR.    1

Richard Albert Loeb    44

"    "    "    76

Nathan F. Leopold, Jr.    111

Loeb, Leopold    154 )

    )

H. C. Stranberg    156 )

Leopold & Loeb    166

"    "    287

"    "    290

Leopold, Loeb & othe

Sam Barish

Max Tockerman

ear Sir:

Proceed immediate
latform of the train. Wat
f the track. Have your pa
r the first LARGE, RED,
ated immediately adjoining
ast. On top of this facto
atertower with the word CH
. Wait until you have COM
uth end of the factory -
ly and then IMMEDIATELY t
r east as you can.

Remember that this
ance to recover your son.

Yours tru

GEORGE JO